Just One SIMAIR Story

Just One SIMAIR Story

RICH SCHAFFER

iUniverse, Inc.
Bloomington

Just One SIMAIR Story

iUniverse books may be ordered through booksellers or by contacting:

iUniverse
1663 Liberty Drive
Bloomington, IN 47403
www.iuniverse.com
1-800-Authors (1-800-288-4677)

ISBN: 978-1-4759-4348-1 (sc)
ISBN: 978-1-4759-5528-6 (ebk)

Library of Congress Control Number: 2012919249

Printed in the United States of America

iUniverse rev. date: 01/22/2013

CONTENTS

This book is dedicated to all the missionaries and nationals who flew on SIMAIR over the years, may it take you down memory lane as you read this story. We lifted you off the hot dusty roads in the dry season, or allowed you to skip that quagmire of mud in the rainy season . . . it was our humble privilege to serve you while you were in His service. It is also a 'how to' book to young people who may be called to follow in our steps.

This book is especially dedicated to . . . Bill Tuck . . . the best aircraft mechanic there ever was . . .

So why write this book? Hopefully to bring glory to God . . . hopefully that it might be a blessing to you who read it.

And it's a story for my kids; Mark, Jim, and John, who were born out there in Nigeria, West Africa. Many a time I remember them climbing into our bed and snuggling down comfy-like with the words, "Daddy, tell us a story about when you were a kid!" And I would spin out a tale about some exciting moment in time . . . in my life . . . that with the telling also became a part of them. And then later my wonderful Marg became part of my life and so this also became her story.

Yes, we all have a story to tell . . . "so this is my story, this is my song . . . praising my Savior all the day long!"

Pencil drawings were done by Don Quarles who was a bush missionary out near the Yankari Game Reserve.

I have also added a lot of pictures relating to the chapter.

Rich Schaffer served the Lord for 20 years with SIM in Nigeria, West Africa as a missionary pilot.

Here are some "blurbs" written by Harold Fuller who has read the book which I sent to him for his critique . . .

"Great stuff, Rich. You have a very interesting writing style . . . reconstructing conversation, describing vividly, building suspense. We're enjoying the chapters as you send them. I knew you were an accomplished pilot, but had no idea of your writing skills. Glad you are now using them!"

"Flying with Rich at the controls was always okay. Although my heart at times pounded as the tiny Cessna faced a threatening tropical storm, I knew this matter-of-fact guy of few words had the courage and professional experience to find a hole through or around the thunderheads and bring us out safely on the other side. And Rich always acknowledged that the Lord had given him the qualities that made him a top-rate pilot for Africa's uncertain weather and questionable landing strips."

"In this story of SIMAIR, Rich takes the reader through many an adventure that showed God's hand to be on the mission aircraft and its occupants. With vivid description and homey dialogue, Rich weaves an honest account of how God took a little boy from a tarpaper shack in America's Midwest and made him part of a team that brought the Gospel to the neglected interior of West Africa . . . fulfilling his boyhood dream of flying. Down-to earth humor, growing pains, high adventure, finding God in dry season and rainy-season tempest . . . Rich holds the reader's attention from page one to the story's end."

W. Harold Fuller, Lit. D.

(SIM Nigeria Director for several years of the Schaffer's ministry)

CHAPTER 1
How Can I Reach Them?

Come with me . . . I will fly you in any direction that you choose, and I will show you a hundred villages . . . villages where no white man has ever set his foot. 16 March, 1960.

"There's another one!"

A slight dip of the wing and we're headed for a small cluster of grass huts.

"Okay . . . drop'em!"

And down fluttered the little red booklets, "Hanyar Cheto". "The Way of Salvation" literally, the message of God falling from heaven itself.

On to the next village, we barely skimmed the tree tops, following the gentle contour of the rolling land. The people hear a snarling roar. Goats, sheep, and chickens dive for shelter. A great "bird" flashes across the open patch of sky. Suddenly, silence reigns once more.

From petrified immobility, the natives make a wild dash to capture the falling "feathers" from the bird. Shrieks and laughter become a free for all.

"The end of the world has come!"

"Allah save us!"

"No, we are still alive!"

"Catch the feathers!"

"What strange looking feathers!"

The swift joyfully display their rewards for swiftness. The slow snatch them by cunning for examination.

The wise one proclaims, "This not feathers . . . this talking words!" And an awed silence steals over the village as the wise one slowly begins to read the message from the sky . . . "A chikin farko Allah ya halitta sama da kassa!" . . . ("In the beginning God created the heaven and the earth . . . !")

And the raptured silence is not broken until the whole of God's message of love and salvation for man has been spoken. A shout of joy rings forth . . . "Great and mighty things have visited us this day!"

I used to do a lot of this Gospel "bombing" way out in the remote areas. On some of my journeys, I would be forced to fly low because of the heavy clouds or strong headwinds at the higher altitudes. I could look down . . . little clusters of habitation everywhere in the endless jungles and bushlands. For certain, no white man had ever set his foot in these hard to reach places. For certain, the good news of Jesus Christ had never been there. I could pass within a few hundred feet, and yet I could not reach them.

The reactions of the people were varied. Some would simply stare. Others would wave their hands and jump about. Sometimes they would pick up stones or spears to throw at me. I have seen them kneel and pray to the great bird as if it were a god. How I longed to lift them from their fear and tell them about the real God. How could I do it? Thus began my "bombing" missions. I developed a low tree-skimming attack . . . mainly because it never gave the villagers enough time to panic. Often I would be over and gone before they could lift their heads to wonder what all the noise was about. Also, no sense in getting hit by some lucky rock slinger!

I was doing a lot of concentrated bombing down in the SUM (Sudan United Mission) country, where they liberally supplied me with gospel tracts in the Tiv language, which also had an invitation to visit the new mission hospital opening in Takum. Each time, I tried to take a little different route so as to cover as many villages as possible.

I was heading home to Jos one day, and I still had a bunch of tracts left. As I passed over the large town of Wukari, I looked down. It was Friday, and the open marketplace was literally teeming with humanity! I spiraled down, zoomed low, and let them have the whole works!

Now that was one sad mistake! The result was that I was reported to the Nigerian government which severely reprimanded me . . . "For indiscriminately forcing your religion on the masses without their consent . . . any further occurrences of such procedures will result in severe action being taken!"

Thus my gospel bombing came to a screeching halt, lest I endanger the good position of the whole Mission. I limited my gospel distribution to Sunday morning runs on the bush trails around Jos with my motorcycle.

What an opportunity lost. With the rising nationalism that was sweeping across the land, everyone was learning to read and write. They will read anything they can put their eyes on . . . and what they read they believe. As one man said to me one day, "It must be true if it was important enough to be printed!"

Maybe someday, in heaven, I will meet someone who came to know Jesus Christ by reading "the feathers" that fell from the great bird that one day swooped low over their tiny secluded village!

CHAPTER 2
THUNDERSTORMS AND THE JOS PLATEAU

One of those unusually beautiful days . . . visibility unlimited . . . you could see sixty miles in every direction. We slipped over the south edge of the Jos Plateau, heading for Gboko, 175 miles away. A thousand shades of lush green below . . . "Thank you Lord, for the rainy season!"

My passengers were three missionary kids—two Pooles and one Terpstra; going home to visit their moms and dads who hadn't seen them since Christmas.

As we passed over the Benue River, we saw several hippos in the swampy pool on the south side of the river. I buzzed down to a few feet above the water and shot them with my camera.

Twenty-five more miles, I flew over the Gboko station, and made an extra wide swing so the parents would be at the airstrip when we landed. Those kids could hardly sit still. They began squealing and jumping around when they spotted their folks standing beside the fuel shed. To watch that joyful reunion was my pay for the day.

I unloaded the plane . . . kids' baggage, mail, medicine, and fresh vegetables from the plateau. Then I opened the petrol shed to take on a bit more fuel. Lizards, hiding there, scurried everywhere. I checked for snakes, and then rolled a fifty gallon drum of aviation-gas out the door. The funnel and leather chamois filter were stored under a five gallon kerosene tin . . . mice love to chew holes in the filter.

The refueling ritual out in the bush goes like this: You shake out the filter and hold it toward the sun to check for holes. Check the neck of the funnel for spiders or dirt. Open the bung of the barrel, and roll it to the side. Catch the fuel in the kerosene tin as it comes splashing out. The fuel has the right color and smell for av-gas. Step on the tire, then up to the wing strut, open the tank, and set up the funnel. You do the balancing act as someone hands you up a tin of fuel. Pour it carefully. The chamois filter catches any water, dirt, and rust that may be in the fuel. Dip the tanks with the fuel stick and calculate . . . "we have four hours of fuel." You put everything carefully away, and lock the door . . . no need really . . . not once in twenty years has any gas ever been stolen from our fuel sheds out in the bush!

Paul Rogalsky refueling Cessna 170

Next stop is Takum, seventy miles to the east. My passenger is Anne Browneye . . . dark tan, and the darkest brown eyes you will ever see . . . they sure named her right!

We take off, stay low, and swing a few miles south to parallel the regular course so we can "bomb" any villages that we might see enroute. (This was before the bombing ban.) I lined up village after village, and Mrs. Browneye would drop the tracts out the window when I gave her the word. "Hey, this is the greatest!".. her brown eyes were sparkling with delight.

We buzzed over Lupwe, and swung four miles to the north to land at the little airstrip near Takum. Shortly, Ray Browneye rolled up in his pickup truck. I had to smile. Browneye was a handsome fellah . . . blonde hair and blue eyes . . . and with a grin a mile wide.

Ray said, "You're not in a hurry, are you? Why not come to the station for lunch?"

I hesitated . . . looking toward Jos. "Okay, I shouldn't have any trouble getting back home today . . . the visibility is fantastic . . . why, I could see Wase rock eighty miles away!"

We tied the plane down, jumped into the pickup, and started down the two-track, winding our way through the tall grass and sparse trees. Suddenly, Ray slammed on the brakes just as a native girl stepped out from a hidden path. She jumped back in fright, almost losing the water pot she had balanced on her head. "Wow! . . . sure a good thing I saw that pot moving along above the grass," Ray exclaimed, "You really gotta watch'em!"

"Yeah, I've had them walk right across the runway, just as I'm about to land . . . and those crazy goats will do it to you, too! I like to give the strips a real buzz job to let them know that I'm around."

Buzzing the airstrip before landing

As we pulled into the Lupwe compound, the sun shining on the white walls made my eyes squint. We stopped in front of the Browneyes' house. It was simply beautiful . . . glistening white walls, grass-thatched roof, large shaded porch where the scarlet bougainvillea climbed onto the roof. Orange, lemon, tangerine, and grapefruit trees mingled with the flowering frangi-pangi . . . papaya trees everywhere. Marigolds bordered the pathway, and the edge of the house.

"Hey, this is really nice!", I marveled.

"Welcome to our humble home.", Anne smiled with just a hint of pride.

"Someone around here has a green thumb."

"We both work at it", Ray exclaimed, "and it sure takes a lot of that . . . every tree and plant has its special bugs and fungus . . . except the marigolds . . . nothing will touch them!"

"I'll have something to eat in a few minutes", Anne tossed over her shoulder, "you guys can unload the truck."

Ray and I lugged in a large heavy bag of flour, and dropped it into a fifty gallon drum in the storeroom. I immediately sensed the coolness inside the house, as I wiped the sweat from my brow. Ray voiced my thoughts, "It's the thatched roof . . . lots better than those tin roofs you have in Jos."

"Really nice."

"Rich, I'll get the rest of the stuff . . . you can wash up . . . the bathroom is the first door on the left."

In a few minutes, we were seated at the dining-room table munching on lettuce and tomato sandwiches made with homemade mayonnaise and warm homemade bread, carrot sticks, and ice-cold tea with fresh lemon.

"You bush missionaries really suffer!", I joked.

"It's not too bad with those fresh vegetables that you bring from the plateau . . . by the way, thanks a lot . . . you fly-boys can spoil us any time you want." Ray laughed.

"And this fresh bread . . . you didn't have time to make that."

"Oh, Ali, our house boy, makes that.", Anne beamed.

As we were eating I glanced around the room. The furnishings were the usual, made by the local craftsmen, except everything had a deep, glowing, glasslike shine to the wood. The curtains at the windows were a cool bright green with large white flowers. By the window was a desk with a short wave radio.

Ray read my thoughts, "It's the one I got from Heber Richins. I got it hooked up just like he said, but I can't get the crazy thing working. I've been trying for a couple of weeks. Everything seems to work, but I can't raise a soul."

We were finished eating, so I went over to the radio for a closer look. It was a DX-40, made from a Heathkit. "This looks just like one I put together for Heber. It's really a simple rig, fun to build, and they usually work quite well. When Heber was testing the one I built, a fellow in Bakersfield, California, who was calling CQ, came booming in. Heber replied, and we about fell off our chairs when he answered us. Just forty watts, and we were talking to this guy over 7000 miles away!"

"Well", Ray said disgustingly, "all I want to do is reach Jos headquarters and the other stations around here when they get set up."

I looked out the window. "Let's see . . . yeah . . . you have the antenna set in the right direction for Jos."

The antenna tuner was mounted on the wall. As I turned the knob, Ray said, "Now, that is one thing I don't know where to set."

I scratched my head, "About a month ago I stopped at the radio room when I was picking up the mail at the BD. (Business Department) One of our stations was having trouble hearing Jos, and I watched Heber put a loop of wire with a flashlight bulb in the tuner coil.. here . . . then he turned the knob, and the bulb would glow when he got to a certain point. He turned the knob back and forth, and then left it where the bulb glowed the brightest. Then, when Heber talked to that station, they could hear him okay!"

"Hey, I'll have to try that . . . what did that coil look like?"

"It was just a loop of plastic-covered wire the same size as the turns in the tuner coil . . . I guess one end of the wire would be soldered to the tip of the bulb, and the other end to the metal side."

"Okay", Ray smiled, "that sounds simple enough . . . I'll give it a try."

Ray took me back to the airstrip. The sun was really getting hot. I almost burned my arm on the window ledge of the truck. As we rattled along, I learned that Ray had come out as a builder, and was presently building the new hospital at Takum. He just loved to hunt and fish. We had a lot of things in common. He was also a pilot with about fifty hours of flying time.

He expressed his frustrations about waiting for the ferry at the Katsina Allah river, and had high hopes . . . that just maybe . . . the SUM would someday have their own airplane.

I replied, "Maybe they can buy one of ours. Johnny Clay is home on furlough, and he is looking for a replacement for our Cessna 170's."

Ray untied the plane while I did the preflight inspection. As I climbed into the plane, I said, "Someday, you will be sitting here!"

Ray shook his head, "I'll believe that when I see it!"

We bowed our heads, and Ray committed the flight to the Lord.

"Thanks, Ray . . . see you again . . . I appreciated the break, and it sure was nice to see your place, and man, you really have quite a gal there . . . wish I had someone like that!"

"With all those single girls in the SIM, you shouldn't have any problem.", he grinned.

I laughed, "Yeah, man . . . one at every airstrip."

I cranked up the engine, did the pre-takeoff check, and was soon rumbling down the laterite strip. The Cessna leaped lightly into the air, did a right bank, and I was homeward bound for Jos. I quickly climbed up to 2500 feet. The air was still bumpy there, so I eased her up to 4500 feet where it was smooth and cool. My sweat-soaked T-shirt acted like an air-conditioner as the breeze came in from the air vents.

"Wow! . . . just look at the visibility . . . wish it was like this every day." I could see the Benue river forty miles away, meandering off to the east. "I'll bet I can see a hundred miles!"

A hundred miles out of Jos I could see those glistening white thunderheads building up over the plateau. What a fantastically, beautiful sight, but experience gives you that feeling in the gut that works its way to the backbone, and then up, until it's crawling the back of your scalp. You get kicked around a few times by a thunderstorm, and you will know the feeling. You would really like to head another direction, but the Jos Plateau is where you live. That's home . . . so you go for it.

That ol' weather factory is just doing its thing. During the rainy season, the warm, moist marine air is pushed inland at the ground level. The hot tropical sun causes the clouds to rise as the day progresses. Four hundred and fifty miles inland, that warm air hits the edge of the Jos Plateau. Up she goes, like an elevator, sometimes to thirty or forty thousand feet. Thus spawns some of the most beautifully awesome thunderstorms in the world.

"What's that Bible verse? . . . Hezekiah 14:11? . . . If you get lost, head for the biggest thunderstorm you can see . . . that's home . . . that is the Jos plateau!"

Fifty miles out of Jos, I eased over the edge of the plateau and began cutting a bit east of course, hoping to get on the backside of the storm.

Forty miles out, I called Jos on the radio . . . "Jos tower, Jos tower . . . this is Victor Romeo November Charlie Golf."

(VR-NCG was the registration of the plane I was flying that day. On the radio you give the registration in a phonetic alphabet . . . A is Alpha, B is Bravo, C is Charlie, etc. The word, Roger, is airplane lingo for: 'I heard your last transmission, understood what you said, and will comply with your instructions.')

"Victor Romeo November Charlie Golf . . . this is Jos tower . . . go ahead!"

"Roger, Jos . . . Charlie Golf at your boundary . . . inbound from Takum . . . flight level four five . . . estimating Jos at three two . . . requesting your latest weather."

"Roger, Charlie Golf . . . the winds are zero eight zero at fifteen knots . . . QNH is 29.81 inches . . . heavy rain, thunder, and lightning to the west of station!"

"Thank you, Jos . . . Charlie Golf will call you field in sight."

"Roger, Charlie Golf . . . be advised there's a large amount of water on the runway . . . light rain still falling at the station."

"Roger, Jos . . . call you field in sight."

Good . . . the storm had just passed over the airport . . . and I could see that. By the time I get there it would be pretty well over.

"Jos tower . . . Charlie Golf two zero miles out . . . have your field in sight."

"Roger, Charlie Golf . . . the winds are now zero nine zero at twelve knots . . . QNH is 29.81 inches."

"Roger, Jos . . . call you right base for runway one zero."

"Roger, Charlie Golf."

Looking down at the farmers' fields, I could see that the ditches between the row crops were brim full . . . all the little streams were gushing with red brown water . . . everything green had a new washed glow. The air was cool, moist, and fresh. I took big gulps of it. "Thank you, Lord, for the rainy season!"

I positioned myself for a right base leg, slowed the plane down, put down one notch of flaps, and began my descent.

"Jos tower . . . Charlie Golf turning right base for one zero."

"Roger, Charlie Golf cleared to final, winds are zero nine zero at ten knots."

"Call you final."

I turned on to final, eased the flaps full down, and kept my descent for the end of the runway.

Landing on the blacktop runway 10-28 is a little like landing on a roller coaster. The first five hundred feet is uphill. Over the crest is a slight dip, and that is where all the water flows across the runway. The remainder of the runway continues at a slight rise toward the east, with the end being almost flat . . . the whole thing sort of tilts north to south.

"Jos tower . . . Charlie Golf on final!"

"Roger, Charlie Golf cleared to land . . . wind zero nine zero . . . ten knots."

"Roger, Charlie Gulf . . . cleared to land."

I set the Cessna down, and stopped before the top of the rise, turned around, and taxied back toward the SIMAIR hangar.

"Charlie Golf . . . your landing time was three two."

"Thank you, Jos . . . see you tomorrow."

"Roger."

As I shut down the engine, I glanced out the window at the new washed earth, and simply bowed my head . . . "Thank you Lord, for this beautiful day . . . give those kids a good vacation with their parents . . . bless those people in those villages we bombed today . . . bless Ray and Anne there at Lupwe . . . help Ray to get that radio working . . ."

Little did I realize how crucial that radio would be in a few days.

Musa, our hangar boy, was waiting with the baggage cart when I jumped out of the airplane. He unloaded the mail from Gboko and Lupwe . . . and the bags of citrus fruits that Ray sent to be distributed among the missionaries in Jos. Fruit on the plateau ripens a couple of months later.

I filled in the day's flight in the airplane journey log, my pilot log, and the passenger charge slips. Looking at the flight schedule, I saw that I would be going from Jos to Kaduna to Oyi to Ilorin, night stopping Ilorin, and then returning the next day via Oyi to Minna to Jos.

"Musa, let's top up the tanks for tomorrow, okay?"

"Yes sir."

Refueling the planes at Jos is a bit more modern than at the bush strips. We use a barrel pump with a hose and nozzle, and a nice stand which eliminates the balancing act on the wing strut. One person holds the nozzle while the other turns the pump handle. The tricky part is to turn the handle at just the right speed to keep the fuel from running

9

over the top of the filter. Then you need to stop pumping at just the right moment, so the last drop of fuel drains from the filter and the tank is completely full, or however much fuel you want for the next flight.

We pushed the plane into the open hangar, loaded the freight into the rickety Ford station-wagon, and I was on my way into Jos.

CHAPTER 3
THE STUKEY BERGSMA STORY

A few days later, I found myself stopping over at Ilorin again. I flew down some administrators for the board meeting at the seminary at Igbaja, which is twenty-five airmiles east of Ilorin, but you have to go forty miles over a terrible road.

For some reason, I elected to stay at Ilorin rather than spend the night at Igbaja. Maybe it was the stomach cramps I was having, or maybe it was that washed out feeling from flying a heavy schedule. Anyway, I was looking forward to having a good rest hour, which rarely happened with all the flying.

Ilorin is a large, bustling Yoruba city, and the SIM has a small BD there to accommodate the needs of the missionaries located at the various bush stations in the area. Clarence and Martha Giesbrecht, from Dalmeny, Saskatchewan, maintained the small store, mission post office, and the guest house. They kept their eyes and ears tuned to the market, buying quantity supplies of sugar, flour, etc, when things became available at a good price. Missionaries could send in an order for supplies via a friendly truck driver. Clarence would fill that order and send it out by the same driver . . . also their mail, medicine from the Jos pharmacy, and even forward any money needed from their personal accounts.

When the missionary came to the city, they could stay at the comfortable guesthouse for as long as needed. There are no Hiltons or Motel 6's . . . no McDonalds or Wendys, so the guesthouse became a fair haven for many a weary traveler.

So after lunch, I was having my rest hour in one of the guest rooms . . . on the bed, shoes off, reading a months-old Time magazine, when Clarence came pounding excitedly on my door.

"Rich, come quick . . . Jos is on the phone!"

"Jos? . . . you mean, long distance?"

"Yeah . . . you better hurry!"

I jumped into my shoes, and ran to the main house. I picked up the phone, "Hello, this is Rich Schaffer!"

All I could hear was a sizzling, crackling, static sound.

"Hello . . . hello!," I shouted.

When Clarence came in, I gave him a hopeless look. "It's dead . . . wonder what they wanted?"

"They said something about a medical emergency at . . . at Lupwe?"

"Lupwe?" . . . My mind flashed to that tiny mission station nestled at the edge of the Cameroon mountains . . . "The Ray Browneyes?"

I looked at my watch, "Fourteen twenty . . . man, Lupwe is four hundred miles from here . . . if we hurry, maybe I can get there before dark!"

I ran to the room for my bag, and Clarence went for his car.

Soon we were across the bridge, bouncing down the muddy bypass, allowing us to skirt around the southeast side of the city with its narrow, winding streets crowded with people, bicycles, carts, trucks, and animals.

Clarence smiled, "You know, that is absolutely fantastic."

"What's that?"

"A phone call, clear from Jos . . . a couple of weeks ago, I had to call Lagos about a passport. It took me three days to get through . . . never had a call from Jos before!"

"I know what you mean. The phones in Jos are no better. Just to make a call from the hangar into town is something when you actually get through. The first big storm that came through Jos bent some of those metal telephone poles right down to the ground! That put the phone service out for over a month! So to get a call from Jos to here has to be a real miracle, for sure."

Ilorin airport is about three miles from the guesthouse. Even with the shortcut, it took a good ten minutes to get there, because of the thick traffic, and all the huge potholes.

As we rolled up to the plane, I jumped out. "Clarence, open up the gas shed . . . I'll have to take on some fuel."

"Got you."

I untied the plane, and taxied over to the shed. Refueling the plane takes forever when you're in a hurry. The leather filter will take the gas only so fast.

I did a quick preflight of the plane as Clarence took a turn at pouring the fuel into the funnel. He almost fell when he stepped down from the wing strut . . . "You've gotta be a genuine monkey to do that job!"

"Yeah, that's for sure, it would be nice to have a stand like we have in Jos."

"Why not give me a drawing sometime, and I'll have one made?"

"Hey, I'll do that."

The airport manager had sauntered over from the terminal with the airport log. I signed out, which was the equivalent to making out a flight plan . . . date, aircraft registration, flying from Ilorin to Takum, departure time, estimated time of arrival, alternate airport, endurance, number of people on board, and my signature. I politely thanked him as I handed him the ledger.

We pushed the plane away from the fuel shed. Clarence committed the flight to the Lord as I fastened the safety belt, and did the startup check.

"Thanks for all your help . . . I imagine Jos will send another plane down for the guys tomorrow."

"Okay, you take care, and have a good flight!"

I did the takeoff check on my way out to the broad 3000 foot grass runway, did a downwind takeoff, a right turn out, and quickly established a heading of 100 degrees. Takeoff time: 1504. The cloud coverage was about three-eights, and I studied the shadows they made on the ground. They were sailing along at quite a fast clip toward the northeast. I made a correction for the wind, and leveled off 500 feet below the clouds. That course took me just north of Igbaja in ten and a half minutes, giving me a ground speed of 143 miles per hour. Twenty-one minutes later I passed a couple miles south of Oyi where the SIM has a leprosarium. I rechecked my ground speed at 144 mph. Nice tailwind. Therefore, I should cross the Niger river at 1554, and arrive at Takum at 1750 . . . just ten minutes before dark!

To make this more interesting for you, just pretend that you are my passenger. You notice my deep interest in the cloud drift . . . my constant use of the calculator, confirming my ground speed. We stay below the clouds in the hot, bumpy air.

"Why not go above the clouds where it's smooth and cool?"

"Headwind up there. Let me give you an idea what we're up against. We are flying to Takum, 400 miles away . . . with full tanks, we have a range of 450 miles . . . if we have a headwind, we will not make it! The chance of thunderstorms at this time of year is 100%. We'll get there just ten minutes before dark . . . and that's with the tailwind we've got! No runway lights at Takum. There are no navigational aids, and this plane has no navigational radios, even if there were. We need to get there, because there's a medical emergency . . . someone's life may be in danger. Oh yes, the last 265 miles will be flown without a chart for this area! . . . dum-dum neglected to bring one, because this trip was only going to be a routine Jos-Ilorin-Jos flight."

You get that panic feeling. "You're crazy . . . how will you find your way? Experience, that's it . . . you've flown this route before?"

"Yeah . . . once!"

I leave you in suspense until we cross the mighty Niger river, right on schedule. "Good, our ground speed is still 144 mph."

Then I point over the nose. Straight ahead you see another river, just as big as the Niger, winding its way eastward, as far as the eye can see. "That's the Benue River . . . all we have to do is follow that river to Makurdi, head southeast to hit the Gboko-Takum road, and follow it to Takum . . . see . . . nothing to it."

You breathe a little easier.

"But we really need to get past Makurdi, for that's our alternate. If thunderstorms, or a line squall cuts us off from there, we don't have an alternate airport except way back here at Lakoja!"

But I try to make you feel better by telling you . . . "We could probably get down in one piece on one of those sandbars on the river. I have a survival kit, so we can catch fish. Even have a mosquito net, so we won't be eaten alive at night. Not so sure about the big crocodiles, though!"

Then I get a smug smile on my face . . . "One day I landed on a sandbar because of engine trouble. I fixed the problem with the engine okay, but then, the sand was too soft . . . I couldn't get up enough speed for takeoff. So there I sat for three whole days until air search found me. I fished to my heart's content . . . Nile Perch . . . this big!" I stretch out my hands about three feet.

"The net kept the mosquitoes off, but one morning I woke up to find this huge crocodile, twelve feet long, sleeping right beside my net! Thought he was sleeping anyway, so I quietly slipped out the other side of the net. Suddenly, this guy starts after me! I barely escaped by jumping inside the plane . . . SNAP!"

"There I sat . . . in that hot ol' airplane. There he lay with those mean, yellow eyes and long, sharp teeth. Boy, the cabin of that plane was really getting hot! That ol' croc just lay there, licking his chops, waiting for broiled Rich Schaffer to step outside."

"Then I got an idea. I started the engine, and revved it up, blowing sand in his eyes! Guess he didn't like the noise, either, because he slithered off into the river, and never came back."

"Well, anyway, air search finally found me. I got on the radio, and told them my problem . . . 'got the engine fixed, but the sand is too soft . . . can't take off!'

"They circled around for awhile. Then, Bill Tuck, our smart mechanic, came up with an idea. Says he, 'We'll fly you down some sacks of cement, and you can build yourself a hardtop runway!'

"Great! . . . And sure enough, the next morning at the crack of dawn, here they come, bombing me with sacks of cement . . . four fifty-pound bags a trip, which they picked up at Makurdi. They also dropped me a shovel, and a bucket."

"They had lots of fun, and I had lots of work. Using a stick, I laid out two narrow tracks, just the width of the main wheels. I scooped out just enough sand, so when I mixed the cement with the sand, the two tracks were level with the surrounding sand again. I carried water from the river, poured it on the tracks, mixed it all up, and smoothed it out again to dry. It was a back-breaking, sweat-in-your-eyes kind of job."

"Well, a couple of fishermen came along in a canoe . . . eyes as big as dollars. To see that metal bird sittin' there on the sand . . . Wow! They joined in the fun, and in three days, the Benue River had its first two-track concrete airstrip!"

"For their labors, I gave one fellow my shoes, the other, my shirt. Actually, the new runway was not all that long. I needed to get rid of some excess weight. So I drained out the gas from the wing tanks, leaving just enough fuel to get me to Makurdi. I also gave the fellows the emergency water canteens, the tie down ropes, the shovel, and bucket . . . even the coffee cans that we used for air sickness! Boy, they thought it must be Christmas. The only thing I kept was a sack of mail, after all, the mail must go through."

"The next morning, the air was cool, and there was a slight breeze blowing up the river. This would be it. I set the brakes, and revved up the engine full-bore, did my check, and let her go. She started slow at first. When I got up enough speed to lift the tailwheel off the sand, she really began picking up speed. But I was running out of runway fast! Just as she reached the waters edge, I popped the flaps . . . and . . . and . . . I woke up!"

"You woke up! What do ya mean . . . you woke up?"

"Yeah", I laughed, "this was just a dream!"

"A dream?," you say, as you are getting ready to toss me from the plane.

"Yeah . . . I've dreamed it a hundred times! Anyway . . . look . . . there's Makurdi up ahead!"

Sure enough, about forty miles ahead, you can barely make out the white buildings of the town. You can also see the railroad bridge crossing the river.

In seventeen minutes, we pass overhead Makurdi airport on the east side of town, and take up a southeast heading to intercept the Gboko-Takum road.

'Hmm . . . Still having that tailwind.' The clouds are beginning to thicken.

Soon a red laterite road appears, winding its way through the sparse trees. We follow it. I trim the plane for descent, but I don't cut back the power. Up ahead the sky is beginning

14

to darken . . . sort of a dirty, greenish-gray with a purple-black tinge to it. The closer we get to the storm, the blacker it gets.

I cinch up my safety belt with the quiet words, "Storm up ahead."

You read the tone in my voice, the concern on my face, all business now . . . you tighten your belt also.

We are down to 500 feet above the ground. You can see the tall grass and the trees swaying violently as the warm, moist air feeds the storm. Sharp gusts buffet the plane. Hopefully, we can beat the storm to Takum, and get tied down before she hits. If not, it's seventy miles back to Gboko for the night.

"There she is!"

I head for the shining pan roofs of the Takum hospital, buzz overhead to announce our arrival, which also puts us on a left downwind leg for the airstrip. Just as I get the plane slowed down, a gust hits us so hard the plane literally shudders and flops all over the sky. I fight for control. We are coming under the edge of the roll-cloud that protrudes out ahead of the storm. The windsock is waving wildly from its pole. Have to be extra careful. To the east, a gray-green, black wall of water is approaching fast. There's a blinding flash of lightning, off the right wing, as we turn final. KERBOOOM!!

I touched down solidly on the end of the airstrip, braked sharply, and swung the plane around to quickly backtrack to the tie-downs. I jockeyed the plane into position, tail to the storm, cut the engine, and set the brakes hard. I scrambled to the back seat for the ropes.

As I'm tightly securing the tail, Ray Browneye rumbled up in his truck. He gave me a big grin, as he grabs a rope, and heads for the left wing. I go for the right . . . tie it tight. To the front of the plane . . . swing the prop to the horizontal position. In the cockpit . . . tie the controls . . . grab my bag . . . lock the doors.

Ray and I stood there for an instant, watching, listening to the roar of the on-coming rain. Jagged lighting strikes! Instant booms of thunder shake the ground! We jump into the truck. The deluge hit us! The truck shudders! The pounding rain drowns out our yells. The plane dances violently on its springy landing gear. We can hardly see. Ray moves the truck to the back of the plane to form a windbreak. We sit there, feeling very small. We pray. Flash! BOOOM!! The world shakes! The sun is gone! It is dark.

As the violent part of the storm passes . . . we just sit there for awhile . . . awestruck by it all. I look at Ray, "Man, you really got some mean storms down here!"

"Yeah . . . Well . . . we're just trying to impress you with one of the joys of living down here!", Ray laughs . . . "By the way, thanks for coming!"

"What did I come for?"

Ray cranks up the truck, flips on the lights, and starts down the two-track to Lupwe. "It's Ken Bergsma's little boy, Stukey . . . he's been unconscious for two days now . . . they think he's got cerebral malaria. We've just gotta get him to Jos!" Ray's voice has a catch in it.

"Okay man, we'll do that, first thing in the morning."

Ray gives a sarcastic laugh, "Fog's been thick in the morning . . . didn't clear up until noon today . . . you couldn't see a hundred feet!"

"We'll just have to pray. By the way, how much fuel do you have? I used quite a bit coming all the way from Ilorin."

"Ilorin . . . you mean you came all the way from Ilorin?"

So I filled Ray in on my flight to Ilorin to stay overnight . . . the phone call from Jos . . . the fantastic tailwind . . . just squeaking into Takum before the storm and nightfall.

Ray filled me in on the last couple of days. Working to a frazzle getting the roof on the hospital. Stukey getting sick, and going into a coma . . . too sick to travel by road . . . tinkering with the radio . . . trying to get a call to Jos.

"Jos must have heard me on the noon broadcast. That bulb with the loop of wire lights up just like you said it would . . . that's what did it!"

We stopped at the Bergsma's to let them know the SIMAIR plane had arrived. Ken and Eleanor jumped up, hope in their hearts, wanting to take off for Jos right away.

"No, we can't fly in the dark . . . first thing in the morning."

Eleanor began to cry. Ken took her in his arms. Both were completely worn out.

One look in the next room at Stukey showed me their grave concern. A small, pale, still form lay there. Doctor Gray and Anne Browneye were giving him a sponge bath, trying to bring the fever down.

Before I turned in that night, I stepped out on the porch, and looked up into the heavens. They were all ablaze with glory! Continual flashes of sheet lightning lit up the sky from one end to the other. Even the usual serenade of the tiny frogs, and all the night creatures, were in silence before it all. I bowed my head and prayed.

Next morning. Before the light of dawn. No fog! Not a single cloud in all the sky! We went out to the airport.

As Ray refueled the plane, I did the preflight with a flashlight. Passengers on board . . . Doctor Gray, and Ken in back, with Stukey laying across their laps . . . Mrs. Bergsma, and Debbie were up front beside me. We had a plane load. When I could barely see down the runway, I said quietly, "Okay, let's go."

Ray committed the flight to the Lord, and I cranked up the engine. We took off, and did a right turnout, climbing on course. As we passed over a small village, I noticed the smoke from the cooking fires was drifting toward the northeast, so we stayed low which would give us a quartering tailwind.

When we passed over the town of Wukari, I took out my calculator, "Fantastic! We have a ground speed of 137 miles per hour!" When we crossed the Benue River the ground speed had jumped to 141 miles per hour. I realized that the Lord was speeding us on our way.

Glancing to the back seat, I could see why. Doctor Gray's eyes met mine, and he shook his head. Stukey looked more dead than alive.

In another thirty-two minutes, we were approaching the Jos Plateau, and I began to climb, to just clear the edge when we got there. At 500 feet over the plateau, I could see the wind bending over the grass to the northwest. "Wow! The wind never blows that direction!"

Forty miles out . . . "Jos tower . . . Jos tower . . . this is Victor Romeo November Charlie Golf."

"Good morning, Charlie Golf . . . this is Jos tower . . . go ahead!"

"Roger, Jos . . . Charlie Golf at your boundary, inbound from Takum . . . flight level four five . . . estimating Jos at zero five . . . please contact the SIMAIR hangar . . . we have a medical emergency on board, and we will need a stretcher!"

"Roger, Charlie Golf . . . stand by!"

When I landed and taxied up to the hangar, the fellows had the station wagon ready to roll. The stretcher was laying on the ground nearby. Stukey was quickly loaded into the station wagon. Off they went in a hurry.

As I made out my logbooks, my mind went back over the flight. With the unusual tailwind, we had made it in record time. Then the tailwind from Ilorin to Takum, getting me there just minutes before the huge thunderstorm, then nightfall. The stomach cramps that kept me at Ilorin . . . the phone call from Jos . . . the call for help on a broken radio. The realization came to me that I had been used by God to be part of a miracle. Two days later, the little boy awoke from his coma, and opened his eyes! Stukey was going to live!

Over the years I often wondered whatever became of Stukey Bergsma. This letter answers that, and will be of interest to you.

Dear Mr. Schaffer, 4 June 1984

Ray gave me your letter of inquiry about the details of your response to our call for the medical emergency to Lupwe 26 years ago. Stuart, called "Stukey", was four years old . . . now thirty. He is married to Nancy White, and they have a nine-month-old daughter. They live in Troy, Michigan.

He does not really remember much of the trauma and happenings around this illness, other than what we have told him. We reminded him that God had given him to us twice, and must have a real purpose for him. He has often said, "I wonder how God wants to use me?" To which I responded, "He is using you, Stuart."

He has always had a keen sense of God's presence in his life, which spared him from going through much of the rebellion that so often goes with the teenage years.

He is a member of the Free Methodist Church in Ferndale and is married to a beautiful Christian wife. He attended Calvin College with a major in business. He is an executive in the Chrysler Corporation and witnesses to Christ in his open, honest, and sincere way of dealing with people.

He is a very special son. He has been an example to his three brothers that followed him, especially in the years following his father leaving the home . . . ending in divorce. He then asked the question—"How come Dad is violating all the things he told me were so important?" It created problems for him, but he came through a stronger Christian, mostly because he could see what this did to his father's life.

Dr. Den Besten (Lawrence) was the mission doctor, newly arrived, and was working at Gboko Christian Hospital. Dr. Herman Gray came from another station, Mkar, because he was called to help diagnose. Debra, Stukey's older sister, was the other passenger. She was six and was also ill with malaria, but a more mild version.

The morning we left Lupwe, the large school at Lupwe had a prayer service for Stukey. Two weeks later Stukey was back for them to see—alive and well. Their response to that was, "We have never witnessed such a quick answer to prayer!" From all medical history, Stukey should have been brain damaged. Praise the Lord, today, he is a beautiful 200 pound man!

It was a series of miracles and you were one of them. We thanked God for you then and we thank Him still. Thank you for giving me this opportunity to share . . . more than you needed, but important for me to do.

I am presently working in the Christian Reformed World Missions home office—right across the hall from Ray. If you come to Grand Rapids, come and see us! I wish you every success in your book.

Sincerely, Eleanor Bergsma De Graaf

An exciting kids version of The Stukey Bergsma Story was made for radio. You can obtain a copy of this tape from Rich Schaffer, 643 45th Place SE, Salem, OR 97301. A bit to cover postage and the cost of a blank tape will be much appreciated.

CHAPTER 4
JUST DOIN' MY THING

So what's it like . . . really . . . to be a missionary pilot? Certainly not all glory days like the Stukey Bergsma story. I should have kept a diary. I did one month and this is how it went:

August 6th. I flew Miss Sytsma, who recently returned from furlough, to her station at Wukari. From there, I hopped over to Gboko to drop off Mrs. Lambers and her three kids . . . one a spanking brand new baby. Also picked up Mrs. Bergsma and little Mark here. Boy, he didn't like airplanes at all! When I take Mrs. Bergsma back home, there will be two children instead of one. Ahh, these stork flights! Wasn't too bad a day . . . mostly flying the tree tops . . . sorta bouncy, but not that bad. Total trip—400 miles in 4:05 hours.

August 7th. Today I tried an early-morning takeoff, hoping to beat the thunderstorm buildups in the afternoon. Funny looking day . . . almost like there was "harmattan" in the air. I climbed up over the low clouds. It got too thick, so back underneath we went, flitting around the hills and rocks until we slid off the West edge of the plateau. My passenger was little Phil Blumhagen, just released from a two-months stay in the hospital. The clouds were getting a little bit low, so upstairs we went through a hole. Crazy thing, there is no horizon, so I go on instruments. Finally, I let down through another hole . . . just happened to break clear between two hills. After picking our way through the palm trees for awhile, we decided it was time to go back home. Flight time: fifty minutes.

One hour later, Johnny Clay buzzed in from Kano on his way to Lagos. "Looked nice up my way . . . maybe we can make it round about via Minna . . . you want to follow me?"

"Okay."

You won't believe this, but it was fog to thunderstorms in one hour. We fought our way out for fifty miles, and we fought our way back. It was like the Thompson Trophy air races chasing each other around those thunderheads.

Johnny says, "Well, tomorrow's another day!"

August 8th. And so it was . . . another day. We picked coconuts all the 245 miles to Oyi. "Hmm . . . field looks okay today." Ever since the day I sunk up over my wheels while taxiing down the runway to takeoff position, I wish the plane had some rubber boots, or something.

"Hang on Phil, we're gonna land in that mud puddle down there." Even though the ground was soggy from all the rain, it was good and solid underneath. Papa and Mama Blumhagen were so glad to see us, they even brought me a sandwich!

I hopped over the hills eighty miles to Ilorin. Picked up Mr. and Mrs. Paul Craig and their two children, who were returning from a two-week holiday. Mrs. Craig was scared of airplanes because of the last two hair-raising trips. This time, I gave them a good ride. The thunderstorms were far enough apart, we hardly got our wings wet all the 315 miles back to Jos. Flight time today: 6:10 hours.

August 9th. Solo 165 miles east to Kaltungo. No elephants in the swamp today. Oh, what a bumpy ride! I about gagged. Kaltungo . . . my favorite airstrip . . . rough as a cob . . . usually with 35 mile per hour crosswinds. Did a beautiful wheel landing. Surprise . . . jolly ol' Papa Nick wants to go along with Mama and little Nick Vanderduzen . . . all 205 pounds of him!

"But I gotta pick up Mrs. Beckett at Potiskum!"

"But I just gotta be there for that meeting!"

"Okay . . . get rid of some of that baggage then!"

It's amazing what people want to take along on some of these trips.

130 miles later at Potiskum . . . "Mrs. Beckett, how much do you weigh?"

Have you ever ask a woman that question? I learned to become a pretty good weight guesser.

"Let's see . . . six pounds per gallon . . . that means we will have to leave out twelve gallons of gas."

Potiskum to Jos . . . 190 miles . . . best flight I've had all week. Total time: 4:30 hours.

August 12th. Weather report says, 'Slight to moderate rain. A line squall affected Kano at 0630 . . . southern end unknown . . . may affect the plateau area later in the day.'

135 miles on my way to Oyi . . . I ran into another line squall and was unable to penetrate it safely . . . forced to return to Jos. It was a sad day, for I flew two hours and fifty minutes for nothing. Well, as Johnny says, "Tomorrow's another day."

August 13th. I was supposed to go on a medical emergency this morning to Kaltungo. But Johnny Clay took it so I could try the Oyi and Ilorin run again. Had rain mostly all the way, but I didn't have to fly under any trees to get there. Picked up Howard Dowdell and Sara Bakker at Oyi, and then slid over the hills to Ilorin for Marg Cook.

Going back to Jos was a picnic . . . nice tailwind . . . had to divert for thunderstorms six times, but plenty of room. Even saw some sunshine a couple of times. Total trip 640 miles in 6:05 hours. Left Jos at 0855 hours and returned home again at 1610.

August 21st. First flight in eight days. Spent four days in bed with some kind of flu. Had a good flight to Kaltungo. Saw a herd of 38 elephants in the reserve! Sure rusty on takeoffs and landings . . . ought to practice a little tomorrow.

August 22nd. One hour and five minutes of rust removing practice. Turns, 720's, chandelles, slow flight, stalls, pylon eights, short field takeoffs and landings. Lots of fun.

August 23rd. I met Bill Crouch as I walked into the guesthouse for breakfast this morning.

"Rich, we have a medical emergency at Oyi . . . Vic Carlson's got appendicitis!"

In twenty minutes, I was winging my way to Oyi, 245 miles away. Big, beautiful clouds were already mushrooming up, but there was plenty of room, so I went upstairs to pick up a nice tailwind. In one hour and forty-five minutes I touched down at the Oyi airstrip, ahead of schedule. I gassed up the plane, and waited. It was really hot and muggy.

Margaret Lang came out from the Oyi leprosarium with a thermos of ice cold lemonade. Oh, that was good! We talked about a lot of things . . . the flying, the weather, the leprosarium, home.

"I'm from South Dakota", Miss Lang mused.

I replied, "How about that . . . I was born in South Dakota!"

"You were? Where?"

"In Tyndall!"

"Why, that's where I'm from!"

It turns out that Margaret Lang came out to Africa in 1928 . . . the year I was born. She used to go over to my grandmother's house for cookies when she was a little girl. And we meet clear out here in Africa! Needless to say, she adopted me right on the spot.

Finally, the car arrived with Vic. He got out, picked up a couple of suitcases, and headed for the plane with a sheepish grin. I had missed my breakfast and "hi-ho Silvered" it all the way to Oyi, only to have my medical "emergency" greet me this way. Experience soon taught me to thank the Lord to have them this way, rather than almost dead. Dr. Oliver, who accompanied us on the flight to Jos, assured me that Vic really did have appendicitis.

Soon we were on our way. Almost scraped the trees at the end of the runway! Twenty miles out, we started diverting for this thunderstorm . . . then another and another and another. It was such a ragged, zigzag course, I finally found myself on the Minna to Jos run. "Thank you, Lord . . . always a hole big enough to squeeze through!" Even with all the detours, it only took us two hours and forty-five minutes to wind our way back home. That must have been a good tailwind.

The ambulance was waiting when we arrived. They removed an ugly red appendix which would have probably ruptured the next day.

August 27th. Looks pretty good today . . . so off with a plane load . . . and I do mean a plane load. Mr. and Mrs. Tadema plus their five kids. Total weight 503 pounds.

Slipped off the edge of the plateau, down through a beautiful lush green canyon . . . reminded me of the mountain flying we did with Mission Aviation Fellowship on a demonstration flight, with one wing hugging the canyon wall. We ran into a few small scattered rains, but nothing that I couldn't see through. We landed at the Gboko airstrip, 1:35 hours and a 175 miles later. Twenty minutes later, we took off again . . . this time with Mrs. Bulthuis and her two children, and Mrs. Dik and one child. By the way, all these people are with the Sudan United Mission. We lend a helping hand to the other missions when we can.

We climbed up through the same canyon on to the plateau. No trouble with thunderstorms today, but I had a strong gust of wind toss me into a steep bank while landing . . . that could be embarrassing so close to the ground! "Was someone praying for me today? Thank you!"

August 29th. 320 miles to Ilorin and back. Took Mabel Tyrrell back to her station. She is from Rogue River, Oregon . . . that made us automatic friends.

I always remember the flights with her over the years. Mabel would look out the window for awhile . . . then she would look the plane over . . . and then she would concentrate on me.

"Well Rich, how are you doing?"

I'd give her the standard answer that satisfied most people, "Oh, I'm fine."

She would bore a hole right through me with those dark black eyes, with deep concern in her voice, "No, I mean . . . how are you doing . . . really?"

That led to some of the most profound spiritual discussions that I have ever had with another person. She REALLY cared about me. That was just the way she was . . . she really cared about people. That was Mabel Tyrrell.

It was cool and smooth above the clouds for an hour until they got too thick . . . then it was bouncy-bounce underneath for two more hours. There was some heavy rain at Ilorin, so I skirted around it and landed downwind . . . prettiest feather-soft landing you will ever see.

Soon I was refueled and off for home base again. My passenger this time was Mary Ellen Bulander, who left the Moody Bible Institute the same year as I. Didn't know her there, but we knew lots of fellow students. After crossing the Niger River, I began deviating for the thunderstorms . . . two big ones, twenty miles in diameter. We were on the Minna to Jos track again . . . only this time we never made it to Jos. We squeaked into Zunkwa just ahead of a thunderstorm that covered the whole western edge of the plateau. There wasn't any turbulence, but the rain was very heavy, and the clouds hung right down into the rocks and trees.

As we waited for the storm to pass overhead, a large welcoming committee braved the rain to greet us. Hundreds of smiling faces came to see the metal bird up close. It's better than a zoo. Now I know what monkeys think of people who come to visit them . . . people are funnier!

Two old men, squatting under the plane, were in a very animated conversation. I learned later, they were trying to figure out if the plane was a male or a female!

Also Bill Neef came out in his little puddle jumper and invited us to his station for coffee. We ran out of gas on the way, and the battery was dead, so we had a good time, pushing in the rain. Finally, we took the carburetor apart to clean out the dirt and water. Forget the car . . . we rode the motorcycle back to the airstrip. Mary Ellen took all the mud in stride like a veteran missionary. Somehow, I always manage to make these trips as interesting as possible for the new ones . . . gives them something to write home about, you know! We made it home to Jos in time for supper at 1845. No overnight stop at Zunkwa this time.

August 31st. Took Mary Ellen back to Ilorin, along with Bill Crouch and Dr. Oliver. Went on top most of the way. Just one rain. Picked up Miss Carlson, who is going on holiday. Hopped up to Minna and picked up Mrs. Schalm who is going to have a baby soon.

Huge thunderstorms on both sides of the course, but no dodging around today. Just taxied up to the hangar when the clouds dumped a heavy down-pour of rain. Perfect timing by the One who governs every second of our day. Six hours of flying time and 630 miles.

Let's see, this is the end of the month, making a total of 49:50 hours of flying. This has been the easiest month so far. Next month's schedule looks like a heavy one, but there will be four pilots, too.

September 1st. Medical emergency to Gombe canceled. Missionary made rapid recovery during the night, thanks to advice given by Dr. Troup over SIMRAD, the radio network.

So you see . . . these new fandangled modern conveniences out here are not a waste of money.

In fact, who can say, how many lives have been saved, or life made a just little bit easier by the use of them, even during the short time I have been on the field? And we do it cheaper than a missionary can drive his own car!

Now that's what it's all about . . . winning souls to the Lord, planting his Church, redeeming the time, working until He comes, each of us using the talents He gave us in His service . . . what a privilege to have a small part in it! End of sermon!

CHAPTER 5
DADDY, TELL ME ABOUT WHEN YOU WERE A KID

How in the world did Rich Schaffer ever become a missionary pilot? Many a time I have asked that question, maybe in a little different way, as I'm dodging around the thunderstorms, or flying in the Harmattan dust so thick you can hardly see the ground fifty feet above the tree tops . . . "What in the world am I doing up here?" Or there's a hang-up in the schedule, and I'm waiting at some remote airstrip for my passenger to show . . . it's a hundred and ten in the shade . . . sweat is running in my eyes, and the flies are driving me wild . . . lots of time to think . . . "Why am I out here in this God forsaken dry and barren land?" Well, let's go way back to the beginning of time . . . for this kid, anyway.

Richard Lee Schaffer, born the second son of humble parents, William and Emma Schaffer, out in an old farm house near the small town of Tyndall, South Dakota. It's about fifty miles west of Yankton, and ten miles north of the Nebraska border . . . year 1928 . . . December 30th or 31st . . . baptismal certificate says the 30th, but Bonne Homme county clerk says the 31st when the U.S. Air Force wanted to see a birth certificate before they would take me. Don't remember any of that, so let's go on.

When I was quite small, the Schaffer family moved to Hot Springs, South Dakota, on the southern end of the Black Hills. My dad painted houses, did small carpentry jobs, or whatever he could find to do, as these were the rough Depression years. My mom worked in the kitchen up on Battle Mountain in the veterans hospital.

We lived in a small, one-room tarpaper shack. Newspapers were used for wallpaper over the single-board walls. There were two small four-pane windows, one in the south wall, and the other in the north. But we were rich . . . we had electricity! A single drawstring light bulb hung in the middle of the room. We also had running water, and a running toilet . . . you ran outside for both! The dipper in the water bucket was common to all. Dad and Mom's double bed occupied the northeast corner. It was fun jumping up and down on that bed when no one else was home. My brother and I shared a rollaway bed that was folded up during the day.

We even had some books! . . . high up on a shelf above the dish cupboard. One day my brother, Eugene, who was six years older, made me sit on a chair while he balanced on the back edge, to take down a book. Tired of waiting for him to make his selection, I got up from the chair. The results were fantastic . . . my brother went flying one way . . . the chair the other. And he got a licking to boot for making so much noise!

We had a large garden which was fun to water on a hot summer day. I always got wetter than the garden. I did a good job of thinning the carrots and radishes, trying to find one big enough to eat. One time, a neighbor boy and I were crawling around in the watermelon patch, cutting plugs out of all the green melons, hoping to find a ripe one. I really got a tanning for that smart trick!

One day when I was in the garden, I heard an unfamiliar droning noise. High up in the deep blue sky . . . three tiny specks were flying northward in tight formation. I watched those planes until sight and sound were no more. Nailing two sticks together to form the body and the wings, I went roaring after them across the prairie. From that day on . . . becoming an airplane pilot was my only dream.

The "prairie" was an empty block across the gravel street. The neighborhood kids played ball there, and kick-the-can at night. A worn path led to the small white Lutheran church, where we faithfully attended church and Sunday school as far back as I can remember.

Southward across another street was the race track, where I used to nose around in the empty stables . . . that was until I saw an Indian there . . . I made a streak for home.

Summer time was baseball time. The grounds keeper softened the diamond by dragging around a raft of planks behind his car. He would let me sit on the drag, and when he stopped, we would walk the diamond, picking up every little pebble that surfaced. One time he gave me a whole nickel for my help!

In the early morning, before the red ants awoke, my brother and I would paw around in their mounds, picking up the tiny Indian beads which the ants gathered from the prairie. Other treasures could also be found on the prairie, like the lavender crocus which announced the coming of spring. Waxy, bright-yellow flowers crowned the prickly pear cactus. Black choke cherries were picked in the summer. Round, green patches of clover gathered in the low places.

One lazy summer day, I lay in the cool grass in the ditch, looking up into the blue, blue sky. I watched the swallows darting after tiny insects. I dreamed of being a pilot, darting around in that same sky. 'Someday . . . when I grow up . . .'

My hand strayed to a small patch of clover. I picked a single clover and twirled it in my fingers, and it became a propeller. My mouth made the appropriate engine noises. I held it up to the sky and made a wish . . . "Someday, I will be an airplane pilot!"

But you can't make a wish with a three leaf clover . . . it had to be a four leaf clover! I rolled over to a kneeling position, and intently searched the small patch of clover. I went to another one . . . and then another. Lo and behold, in the third patch, I found two four-leaf clovers! Two! I could make two wishes!

I held one clover and tightly closed my eyes . . . "I wish to be an airplane pilot when I grow up!" I opened my eyes. Nothing happened. But nothing was supposed to happen, because my wish was for the future.

Then I got a bright idea for the other wish I had coming. I picked up the second clover, closed my eyes, and held out my hands. "I wish for an ice cream cone!" I opened my eyes, fully expecting to see a beautiful vanilla ice cream cone in my hands. But there was nothing there except the four leaf clover.

Maybe I didn't do it right, so I tried again, a little louder, and my eyes a little tighter . . . waiting a little longer. Nothing! Then I remembered someone telling me, I had to put the clover in my shoe. I tried that. No results. I tried the other shoe . . . I tried a clover in both shoes! No ice cream cone!

Now I was at that tender, naive age when you believe everything someone tells you. That day I had a revelation . . . someone had told me a lie. Why do people lie?

Then I thought about something my Sunday-school teacher said one time . . . "When you pray to God, you have to really believe that you will receive it, and He will give you what you ask for." (Matthew 21:22) So I closed my eyes and prayed, "Dear God, please give me an ice cream cone." I tried praying different words, but the results were always the same. No better than a four-leaf clover!

I came to some serious conclusions that day. It was shattering to my young soul. People tell lies! Even Sunday school teachers tell lies! Thus began my search for God and truth alone. Why ask others? You can't believe what they say.

I can recall many times down through my boyhood years of being alone, all by myself, doing nothing but thinking . . . asking deep questions. Is there really a God? Where is He? What is He like? Does He really love me? How can I really know Him?

Winter came, and it was cold cold outside. I watched the old Indian lady, who lived next door, sweep the front porch steps and go inside again. It had snowed a couple of inches during the night, and everything wore a fluffy white blanket.

"Why don't you go over and clean her sidewalks," my mother suggested, "maybe she will give you a cookie or something?" So I bundled up, and swept the front walk to the gate. She did not appear. So I cleaned a pathway clear around the side of her house, and swept the steps and back porch. Sure enough, the lady came out and gave me a cookie . . . and a whole nickel!

And with that nickel, I bought a vanilla ice-cream cone! As I ate it, I remembered that I had wished and prayed for that ice cream cone. I laughed . . . Maybe four leaf clovers do work! . . . Maybe God does answer prayers! . . . After all, I didn't say, 'Right now!'

(And so I have observed down through the years . . . God never answered my needs by my simply holding out my hands . . . but He gave me hands with the ability to work and to fix things! He met my needs the old fashioned way . . . I worked for it!)

One bitterly cold morning, I let Snowball, our small fox terrier, out to go to the bathroom. Later, I opened the door to let him in again. No Snowball! I called and called. He did not come.

I closed the door. Boy, it was cold! I watched from the window, but how do you see a Snowball on the white snow? So I went out to look for him. Three inches of new snow covered the old, and I could plainly see Snowball's tracks leading around the house and to the woodshed, where he dug at a hole where a mouse had scurried to safety.

I followed his tracks around the garden and across the road to the prairie. Snowball circled and sniffed at every mound of snow-covered bush for something to chase. I was really getting cold! His track led me clear down to Rosie Shep's place . . . then over to the race track. He jumped a rabbit by the barbwire fence, and Snowball was in hot pursuit. Up around the stables and through the fence several times . . . I followed their tracks to the choke cherry trees, where Peter Cottontail led Snowball on a chase around and through the bushes, trail upon trail, so many times . . . it was hopeless to figure it all out.

My hands and feet became so numb that I could hardly feel them anymore. Finally, I had to give up and head for home. I cried all the way. Snowball greeted me as I stumbled through the doorway. He had come home long ago! My mom stuck me in a hot tub of water to thaw me out.

My brother and I climbed Sugar Loaf mountain and cut a small tree for Christmas. We decorated it with tinsel and a few colored balls. We even had some real candles which you could fasten to the branches. On Christmas eve, we lit the candles and let them burn for a few minutes. What a beautiful sight. It's a wonder that we didn't burn the house down! I can remember one house on the hill that had a string of Christmas tree lights which bordered the eves of their house. They must have been awfully rich.

I don't remember this, but my folks said, one Christmas they gave me a small wheelbarrow. An hour later, they found me a half mile away, still outward bound. Guess I didn't know how to turn that thing around!

I remember one Christmas, mom took me downtown shopping. I had to stop and look at every window . . . oooh at this and aaah at that. At one window . . . "Oh mommy, get me that for Christmas!"

A strange voice answered, "It costs too much!"

Horrified, I looked up into the face of a perfect stranger with an amused expression on her face. Back down the street was my mother, holding her sides and laughing so hard, she could barely stand up. Somewhere I had grabbed the wrong hand!

And then there was this big tricycle. They sat me on it. I could make it go backward, but I couldn't make it go forward. From then on, all I could think of was that tricycle, but no way . . . it cost $5.50! My folks bought me a little red wagon for $1.98 that made me just as happy.

Seems there were always lots of kids in the neighborhood to play with. One evening on the prairie, the older kids played baseball, while us younger kids played a sort of rough-tumble game of tag. There was this one red headed kid, who was bigger than me, that seemed to get a particular joy out of picking on me. I could take him down and sit on him all right, but he always kept coming back for more. The rougher he got, the rougher I got. He would come sneaking up in the dark and grab me from behind. I would have to fight like the dickens to get him off me. Finally, I retreated across the road, and started bombarding the whole prairie with rocks, hoping to nail my antagonist between the eyes. Trouble is, I clobbered one of the big kids! Boy, I got it real good for that one!

Rosie Shep lived way down west a couple of blocks. We used to play monkey, climbing around in the crab apple trees. Her mother would give us canned crab apples that were just out of this world.

One day, we were playing in our garden. I knew little girls were different. She was about to show me 'how different' as she pulled her dress up high, so I could see her underpants . . . I heard a click, and saw a box camera poked above the window sill of the nearby house, recording the whole affair! I took off like a flash, leaving a puzzled little girl standing there!

It was a late summer evening. The potatoes had been dug and stored away in the root cellar. My brother and I were playing with some kids a couple of houses down the street. We were digging through the soft earth, picking out any small leftover potatoes and having a little game of war.

My brother took off, around the corner of the house, after the other kids. I was about to follow when I heard our mother call . . . "Supperrr!" So I stayed there, waiting for my brother to return. I hid behind a small, two-wheeled trailer from where I could ambush the enemy if they came back.

As I was waiting . . . slowly a cloud came down around me, so thick that everything was hidden from view! It became very quiet and still. I wanted to run, but I was glued to the spot! I looked up. Slowly it came . . . down through the cloud . . . a rod! Down . . . down . . . it stopped for a moment . . . just out of reach above me. Then it slowly went up into the cloud and disappeared! Then the cloud lifted up and everything was as before.

How long I was in the cloud? I'm not sure, but it was beginning to get dark as my brother and I walked home. The sun said goodnight to a cloudless sky!

As we walked along, I told my brother what had happened.

"Don't ever tell anyone what you saw . . . they will never believe you!"

But one thing I know . . . from that day on, I have never doubted the existence of God.

CHAPTER 6
I'M THE SHY MIXED UP KID

First grade was a traumatic experience. Five years old, very small for my age, quiet, and shy. Since there were two Richards in my grade, the teacher re-named me . . . "Dicky". I did not know how to write, so my teacher showed me how to write "Dicky" on a card.

"No Dicky, not with your left hand . . . you hold the pencil in your right hand!"

(So today I'm still the mixed up kid. I write right handed, and I erase left handed. I draw with either hand. I throw left handed, and I bat right handed. I play tennis left handed, and I play golf right handed. I use wrenches and screw drivers with either hand!)

Seems everybody knew their ABC's. Seems everybody knew their numbers. I didn't know a thing!. I was a dumb cluck . . . a real Dicky Bird, as the kids called me!

Grades one through three had recess early. Sometimes the older kids got out early, and jerked us from the swings, or kicked us off the slides. Being the smallest in my grade, I was always picked on. I got into several fights, which I won, but there was always some bigger kid, or a couple of them, who were determined that I knuckle under. So I learned to use my wits . . . and my feet! They would wait for me after school, so I learned different routes home. If they did see me, they never could catch me. I could run like the wind! It almost became a game.

MONKEY IN A CIRCUS!

Second grade was about the same. Somehow, somewhere along the line, I learned to do the numbers. I learned to read a bit. One day, as we took our places, the teacher announced, "Take out your reader and pick out a story that you would like to read to the class!"

That you would like to read to the class? Good grief! I don't want to read to the class!

I looked that book over from cover to cover, looking for the shortest story. But there were no short stories in my book! Somehow I had that feeling . . . you could bet money on it!

"Dicky, we will let you be first!"

I just sat there absolutely petrified! The teacher threatened me. I staggered to the front of the class, and began haltingly to read with a stutter . . . the longest short story I ever read in my life. It was about a monkey in the circus.

"Speak up, Dicky, we can't hear you!"

I mumbled the words. When I came to a word that I didn't know, I halted for an eternity.

"What is the word, class?", the teacher bellowed.

And the class would chime out the word with the intonation, which said . . . "you're the dumbest dicky-bird in the whole wide world!"

It became a mocking game.

I never finished that story. The recess bell sounded. I lay the book down on the closest desk and dizzily stumbled out to the hallway, where a few curious kids found me sobbing.

"What's the matter, Dicky?"

CHAPTER 7
WE MOVE TO GOD'S COUNTRY!

During the First World War my dad had been a cook in the army. In 1935, he received a Veterans' bonus, amounting to about $900, which was a fantastic sum of money in those days. It wasn't long until he was parted from one third of that money. A land shark suckered him into buying an acre of land, sight unseen, in Oregon.

"Covered with fir trees six feet in diameter and two hundred feet tall! A bubbling stream so clear . . . just full of salmon! Why, it's God's country!", the man exaggerated.

My dad also bought an old model A Ford, and a small two-wheeled utility trailer, into which the Schaffers loaded all their earthly possessions, and headed into the golden west to the promised land. Across the prairies, through Yellowstone Park, across the mighty Rockies, along the Snake River . . . we joined that caravan of the many, who left the dust bowl of the mid-west, emerging from the Great Depression with hope in their hearts for a new tomorrow.

One evening, after a hot weary day of travel, we stopped at a small town somewhere in Idaho. My dad paid a dollar to stay in the auto court.

My dad paid a dollar to stay in the auto court.

My brother and I set out to explore, while mom made supper in the small kitchenette. Steep rocky cliffs towered on both sides of the narrow canyon. Gene and I had climbed only a short way up the western wall, when we found some currant bushes, just loaded with red ripe berries. I stayed there while my brother climbed back down to get a kettle from the cabin. We almost had the container full of berries, when we saw a hawk circling along the eastern wall of the canyon. And then we saw it land!

My brother whispered, "Hey, I'll bet they have a nest!"

"Maybe we can get some baby hawks!"

We scrambled down the cliff, and took the berries to the cabin. Soon we were working our way up the eastern wall, along the edge of an old rock quarry. The cliff consisted of a series of ledges, almost like a set of giant stairs, some shorter, some longer than others. The climb was not difficult, especially for a couple of rambunctious boys, who had been cooped up in the car all day.

We were about two-thirds the way up the cliff, when we came to this certain ledge. My brother scrambled up with no trouble, but for me, it was different. It was too high for me to swing my knee up on, but it was to low for me to pull myself up with my arms. Gene turned around and saw my problem.

"Here, grab my ankle!"

So I grabbed his ankle and a small rock protrusion with the other.

"No, don't grab that rock . . . it's loose!"

I was about to make some smart remark, when suddenly the rock broke loose! Wheee!

I backward somersaulted down the cliff, bouncing from ledge to ledge like a rubber ball! As I rolled between two large rocks, I grabbed hold, but they started along with me. I let go. I dropped over one more ledge, and landed in a dead pine tree.

My brother came after me, flying down that cliff almost as fast as I did. He picked up my shoes on the way! I was covered with blood!

My screams really made the canyon ring! Everybody came running. They carried me down to the auto court. Inspection showed that I had a deep gash behind my right ear. No hospital in town, but someone said there was a horse doctor about three miles down the road. He used some kind of medicine on the wound, and used a torn bed sheet for a bandage. No broken bones.

They said that I had fallen over a hundred feet!

CHAPTER 8
GOD'S LITTLE ACRE

Our promised land turned out to be an acre of burned out stumps and fire-weed. No two hundred foot trees, six feet in diameter. No bubbling brook. My dad was so disappointed, that he wanted to turn right around and head back to South Dakota.

But mom put her foot down, "Look, I didn't want to come out here in the first place, but we're here, and we are staying!" With that declaration, we cleared a spot in the fire-weed, and pitched our tent.

My dad bought a couple of carrier loads of shiplap lumber for a dollar each, and we built a one room tarpaper shack. Not the prettiest thing you ever saw, but it fit right in with all the other tarpaper shacks just fine.

A well driller dug four holes and never struck water. Our money was almost gone. So my brother took a forked willow branch and, in fun, began dowsing for water. At a certain spot, fifty feet southeast of our new house, the willow stick would dip sharply, each time he passed over it. What could we lose? So we began digging a well by hand. At thirty feet, we hit water . . . some of the sweetest tasting water we have ever drunk in our lives!

Right across the road on the bay, sat the old pulp mill, which smelled like rotten eggs when the wind came from the west. It was especially bad when they vented the towers. My brother and I would go down there, and fish off the docks, using nothing but a green handline, a couple of hooks, and a sinker. We bountifully supplied the table with sea trout, perch, ling cod, and flounder.

One day I was lying on my belly, with my nose hanging over the edge of the dock, watching the jelly fish, or whatever, float slowly along on the incoming tide. A big salmon jumped clear of the water a couple of times over by the log boom.

"Wow! How would you like to get that guy on your line!"

Sometimes a crab would latch onto our clam bait. We found that if we teased them a bit, by tugging on the line, they would grab hold so tightly, that we could pull them right out of the water and up on the dock.

Suddenly, a fish jerked so hard on my line . . . twice . . . I was teetering on my belt buckle on the edge of the dock! Gene grabbed my legs, and saved me from the big splash! That was the last time I ever wrapped the line around my hand.

"Wow! Must have been that salmon!"

We dug clams, just south of the pulp mill, when the tide was low. Huge Empire clams! In a couple of hours we had our gunny sack so full, it took the two of us to carry it home. Mom would put them up in quart jars and sell them for a dollar a quart.

It was fun to play on the log booms. Jumping from log to log, or rolling them. Sometimes we would find a plank washed up on the shore. We used it like a surfboard, pushing along with a long pole.

One time, when dad stopped for gas in Charleston, a small mangy white Terrier with brown spots, jumped into our car.

The station attendant smiled, "Why don't you take him home with you . . . he's just one of the strays that hangs around here!"

"He" turned out to be a "she", and Tippy became her name. Tippy got doused with rubbing alcohol, once a day, which soon took care of the mange. She would whine and run around like crazy, but she did not run away. She knew that we were trying to help her.

No one lived to the east of us. Nothing but rolling hills and woods, crisscrossed by trails and old logging roads. Tippy and I practically lived in the woods, hunting for gray-digger squirrels, cotton-tail rabbits, and birds, with my old Daisy BB gun.

As we would top a rise . . . "Wow . . . does it ever look beautiful over on the next hill!"

And so we would go from hill to hill. Often we wandered so far away from home that I would miss lunch. No matter . . . I would eat my fill of wild blackberries, black and red huckleberries, and salmon berries. Mom never seemed to worry about me. One time we got so far away from home, we came to the deep dark woods. I heard some coyotes howling. That scared me, and I never went back there alone.

Cattle roamed these hills. They must have been wild, for there were no fences. One time I came around a bend in the logging road, and there stood old mama cow with her calf! She lowered her head and charged! Quick as a wink, I was sitting ten feet up in an alder tree!

There I sat.

There she stood . . . glaring up at me . . . pawing the ground! She kept me up in that tree for three hours!

Just south of God's little acre was the pulpmill dam, where the mill got its fresh water. My brother and some of his buddies cleared out all the dead snags, constructed a wind break, a fire pit, and made a diving board, for one of the finest swimming holes in the area. It's known as Schaffer's Dam to this day!

One day I found a log that had been cleanly split in half by lightning. It was about twelve feet long and two-and-a-half feet wide. The butt end even had a raised portion which made a fine seat. By balancing very carefully, I had myself a dandy canoe . . . a little on the heavy side, you might say, but once you got her moving, that log was like a battleship . . . nothing could stop it.

Tippy and I cruised Schaffer's Dam from end to end. It became our fishing platform. With a willow stick, a bit of string, a tiny hook, and some worms, I pulled a lot of fat native trout from that water.

One day, I eased the good ship "Lightning" up to a large snag sticking out of the water. A couple of large fungi were growing on the bark within easy reach. I attempted to remove them by banging the rotting wood with the butt of my cap gun. I skinned my fingers, and dropped the gun. Splash! I lunged for the pistol as it disappeared into the depths, and came very close to rolling my ship! And I couldn't swim a stroke! I imagined myself, down there thirty feet, beside my gun! Very carefully, I paddled to land, and took a shore leave that lasted for a long, long time.

CHAPTER 9
RED RUBBER HOSES,
MULTIPLICATION TABLES, AND PATTY HICKS!

As we came in from recess, the third grade teacher excitedly announced, "Quickly . . . take out a sheet of paper and write this sentence! See who can do it the fastest!" Then she turned, and jotted on the blackboard. I scribbled the sentence, and was one of the first to hand it in. But we had been tricked!

Later in the day, my quick production earned me a trip to the principal's office, along with another boy . . . Robert. We were taken down to the basement boy's room, where we were threatened with a long red rubber hose.

"Which one of you smart guys wrote these dirty words on the wall?"

Robert and I looked at each other with a big question mark. Immediate realization . . . neither of us had done it!

But Robert blurted out, "He did it . . . I saw him do it!"

The shock . . . I couldn't believe my ears!

"Okay, Robert, you can leave . . . when I get done with this scribe here . . . he will never write another dirty word!"

As the principal advanced with the rubber hose, I sprang back and crouched, ready to fight for my life. I spit out the words with intense conviction, "I did NOT do it!"

We glared at each other. He turned white, slowly lowered the hose, turned, and walked out. I clung to the wall and cried huge sobs. Truth had won!

Whenever we did something wrong, or bad, the teacher would make us stay in during recess and write the multiplication table . . . 1 X 0 = 0, 1 X 1 = 1 . . . 9 X 9 = 81. Thus I learned the multiplication table to perfection as I was always staying in for one reason or another. Then I got a bright idea. I wrote up a bunch of multiplication tables ahead of time. I would pretend to write for awhile, then hand in a 'ticket to freedom', and away I would go!

The school bell rang. I raced across the school ground, and ran up the long wooden stairs to the second floor. Just as I reached the top . . . Patty Hicks gave me a hard shove! I started to fall backwards, but managed to twirl around, stumbling down the stairs, taking four . . . six steps at a time. I wiped out at the bottom in the hard clay and gravel . . . my face, my hands, my knees!

Red rubber hoses, multiplication tables, and Patty Hicks . . . that's all I remember about third grade!

CHAPTER 10
LIVING IN GOD'S COUNTRY

School was over . . . Yippee! Sometime that summer, we moved back into the hills about fifteen miles from Coos Bay. Really out in the boondocks. Allegany consisted of an old time grocery store that had a little bit of everything. The Post Office was in the back corner. An old fashioned hand gas-pump was out front. The four room schoolhouse was stuck to the hillside across the road. If you blinked your eyes, you missed Allegany . . . that was it.

We lived about a mile up the West Fork of the Millicoma River, where we became the caretakers of Ripey's Ranch. It was sort of a semi-dude ranch . . . 640 acres of heavily forested hills with about 50 acres of farmable land in the valley. The arrangement was: Mr. Ripey would get the money from the four cabins and the six horses that people rented during the summer, and we would get whatever could be made from the farm.

There was an old flat-bottom boat on the creek. Riding trails and deer trails crisscrossed the hills. The place was pure heaven for my brother and me.

We ran down to the lower pasture and waded across the stream to see the horses. Brownie let us walk right up to her and pat her on the neck. Gene even eased himself up on her back, and sat there smiling down at me. There was Dan and Duchess . . . the retired race horses. Nig was a black cow pony with a white star on his forehead . . . and he was the leader. When he spotted us, he came running, snorting, and circling us. Nig let out a loud whinny and the other horses also came to look us over. I was scared!

Diamond was a huge red workhorse with four white boots, hooves as big as plates, and a white diamond on his forehead. Whenever people went riding in a group, Diamond would get so hyper that he even outran the race horses!

Diamond became my favorite. He would let me put a bridle on him. The saddle was too heavy for me to lift up that high, so I rigged up a pulley and rope, whereby I could hoist the saddle into the air, guide Diamond underneath, and gently lower the saddle on his back. I would lead him over to the fence, climb up and aboard. He was gentle and would do anything I told him, and he could run like the wind!

Then there was Little Chief. He was a coal black Shetland pony. I rode him most of the time, because I could lure him with a bit of sugar, catch him by the chin-whiskers, and put a bridle on him.

But he was mean. When you cinched up the girth, Little Chief would puff out his tummy. Then the saddle would slip when you tried to mount. I learned to kick him in the ribs with my knee as I tightened the cinch. He tried to step on my feet. He would try to rub my leg off on every fence-post or tree. He'd try to reach around and bite my leg. And then he would balk. When you tried to make him go, he would buck. When he ran, he deliberately jarred every bone in your body.

When I walked home after school, it was also my job to bring home the cows from the lower pasture if they had not gone home by themselves. One day I missed them, because they were hidden behind a small grove of trees. My dad angrily sent me back for them on the double. I caught and saddled up Little Chief. I jumped aboard at a gallop, but suddenly he bucked! Grabbing his mane, as I sailed over his head, I swung down to the ground. In to the saddle again . . . the same thing! The third time he bucked me off by a small Myrtlewood tree. Angrily, I broke off a switch and gave that horse the whipping of his life.

That did it . . . utter transformation! That horse took off at a gallop. No more bucking. No more biting. No more rubbing your legs on the fence posts. He would stop when you said, "Whoa." When you gave a gentle cluck in your cheek, he'd take off at a trot . . . a smooth trot. He would shift to a flowing gallop when you yelled, "Yeah!" From then on, all I had to do was carry a long blade of grass, wave it where he could see it . . . behold, the wonder horse! Little Chief became a joy to ride.

One day a friend and I were playing cowboys. I was on Diamond, and Ken was riding Nig. When I took a shot at Ken with my cap pistol, Diamond shied and took off on a dead run. I finally got him stopped after a half mile. No more cap guns!

Nig was a real cow pony. You just sat there and he would do all the work. If a cow tried to turn out, Nig quickly cut her off without any prompting on your part. When Tippy got tired, she would jump up and ride on Nig's rump behind you. We were quite a sight.

One time some hunters rented Nig for a pack horse. Out in the deep woods, the trail brought them to a large log spanning a deep gorge. They decided to continue on their own by caching some of their supplies and dividing up the essentials. They turned Nig loose to find his way home. The hunters carried part of the equipment across the log. When they turned around, there was Nig carefully inching his way across the log to follow them!

We heard that Nig could jump fences, so one day I raced toward a wire fence expecting him to take off. Just as we got to the fence, he made a quick ninety. I almost did a solo across the fence. I tried again . . . same thing. I know he could jump fences because you could put him in one pasture, and you would find him in another. But he could also work the latch and open the barn door. Maybe?

One day, we were lying on our stomachs with our noses hanging over the edge of the bridge, watching the small minnows feeding in the clear stream.

"What would you do if you saw a big . . . ?"

Suddenly there he was . . . a huge salmon!

No discussion what we would do! Three boys chased that poor salmon around that shallow pool until we literally wore him out. Then we were able to spear him with some branches we broke off the willow trees. We proudly lugged our prize up to the cabin.

"Look what we got . . . Look what we got!"

The salmon's sides were no longer silver, but were very dark and blotched. Dad cut him open. The flesh looked spoiled.

"He doesn't look quite right . . . better not eat it. Go dig a hole and bury him in the garden! And if you see any more salmon, leave them alone . . . they are coming up to spawn!"

The fall rains became more frequent and the stream began to rise a bit, and the salmon began their journey up the streams. They were followed by the cut-throat trout which fed on the eggs and the small fry which hatched from the eggs. The Schaffers had plenty of fish to eat, with surplus to smoke or to can in quart jars for the winter. Vegetables were also harvested from the garden. The fields of oats ripened. They were cut, dried, and wagon loads of hay filled the barn almost to the roof . . . food for the twelve milk cows. This was all accomplished with the help of Brownie and Diamond . . . no tractors here!

Harvesting the several acres of potatoes was a back breaking chore, but dad happily sold them in town for fifty cents a sack for much needed cash. Very poor reward for all the hard labor involved.

Also harvesting the apples was a real chore . . . beautiful crisp juicy apples with no worms. But dad couldn't get enough for them to even pay for the gas to run them into town! It was really discouraging . . . the Depression was hard on farmers everywhere.

The cows were milked morning and evening. The cream was separated, poured into cans, and they were picked up daily by the creamery truck. The skim milk was fed to the pigs, the calves, the chickens, the turkeys, the cats, Tippy, and us kids.

My brother caught a ride with the milk truck very early in the morning to Allegany. He jumped aboard the milk boat which dropped him off down river near the Coos River High School. He came home the same way at night, so I saw very little of my brother during the school year.

The school bus picked up Ken Johnson and me. We were the first kids on, so we had to ride the whole bus route up every canyon to pick up all the other school kids. It was a long trip. After school I walked home to save time.

My fourth grade teacher was Mr. Rogers . . . a man teacher. He also taught fifth and sixth grade . . . three grades all in one room. Seventh and eighth were in another room next door. First, second, and third were all together in the basement. When my class became boring, I tuned in on the fifth and sixth grades.

As I mentioned, I had learned how to multiply in the third grade, but when I got to the fourth grade, these country kids had already learned division! That really made it rough for me in the math department. Mr. Rogers must have thought I was the dumbest cluck that ever crossed his desk.

The school also had other ideas to make life interesting . . . such as skit night, where we little cherubs could display all our talents to our parents.

Nancy Lee giggled, "I can tap dance and sing . . . a tisket, a tasket . . . my green and yellow basket!".. She jumped up and went into her little routine.

Leo Hendricks stuck up his big hand, "I can play my mouth harp!"

Big Jim Poole grinned a buck-toothed grin, "Ahh . . . I can tell some funny jokes . . . ahhh!"

So one kid volunteered this, and another that.

Mr. Roger turned to me and smiled, "And Richie, what can you do?"

There was a complete dead silence. I was about ready to melt through the holes of the floor furnace when Ken volunteered for me, "Richie can yodel!"

"Oh, that's great!" Mr. Rogers chuckled, "Rich, would you yodel for the class right now?"

Yodel for the class? I shook my head and turned three shades whiter than I already was. No way!

"Well, you can stay after school and yodel for me then!"

Mr. Rogers was about to get an education on how stubborn a shy, dumb German kid can be. Oh sure, I could yodel all right. I loved to listen to cowboy music on the old battery radio . . . especially to those dudes who could yodel. I would copy them, and learned to do everything the big boys did. One problem . . . I was an ultra introvert . . . no way would you ever get me to perform for an audience . . . no matter what reward was offered, or whatever punishment was threatened.

I spent many a recess in that classroom, where Mr. Rogers tried everything in the books to get me to yodel. But I never yodeled . . . not one warble.

About a month later, while walking the road home from school, I did some yodeling that made the canyon echo back in fair reply. Ken Johnson heard me and promptly reported to Mr. Rogers. He was on my back again! That was the last time I ever yodeled, and so, I lost it. I sound worse than a sick crow whenever I try.

That winter, Mom was sick a lot with a heavy cough. When she found blood in her sputum, it meant a trip to the doctor's office, where she was diagnosed as having tuberculosis. She was put on complete bed rest at home. Everyone pitched in with the housework to make it easy for her.

One warm sunny spring day, while I was rummaging around in the Johnson's old house, (they had moved) I found parts to an old rickety wooden lounge-chair. "Boy, if I can just put this chair together, Mom can sit out in the warm sunshine . . . then she will get well!"

But it was beyond my best efforts. I had no glue, or nails, or screws . . . nor the tools. And there was hardly any sunshine that winter . . . just dull clouds . . . rain and more rain.

Spring came, followed by summer. School's out! Yippeee! But mom did not get better . . . in fact, she got worse! The doctor said they would have to send her to the TB sanitarium in Salem.

CHAPTER 11
WE MOVE TO TOWN

Dad could not cope with the farm alone so we moved back to town . . . to North Bend. We moved into a small house on the corner of 12th and Broadway.

Dad's room was the only real bedroom. My brother put his bed in the small storeroom that was tacked on to one side of the house . . . it had a nice work bench all along one wall. I put my bed in what should have been the living room. It was a funny room made up of doors and windows. One door opened to the kitchen, another to a clothes closet, two doors went out to the porch, and one went to my Dad's room. The only place my bed would fit was in a corner with all the windows.

The kitchen became the real living area. The former renters left a rickety antique table and four chairs. An old pot-belly stove warmed the whole house, and it could be loaded with huge chunks of wood. But we also had a wood cook stove. There was a sink in the corner with a cold water tap. A single light bulb hung in the center of each room with a pull chain. The toilet was outdoors, attached to the lean-to garage, and there was also a small woodshed.

Right across the street, a small patch of woods gave access to the sandhills which were covered with pine and fir for three miles out to the bay. This became my escape from civilization. I became familiar with every trail and road that crisscrossed the area.

I preferred to go alone most of the time, because my friends could not keep still . . . always talk, talk, talk . . . they broke every twig they ever stepped on . . . the birds stopped singing . . . the squirrels hid in terror . . . man was in the woods!

But we kids had our fun too. We would build huts with fir boughs, so warm, snug, and tight, that not even the rain could seep through. We played hide and seek . . . cowboys and Indians. We had fir cone fights, rock fights, sling shot fights, BB gun fights . . . when it got to air rifles, we decided that it was time to call it quits before somebody got hurt. But it seems that we could never play together peaceably. It was either Elton Cells and me against Sonny Hempstedt, or Sonny and me against Elton, or them against me.

We did a lot of wrestling. I was small, but quick and wiry . . . I could take down kids twice my size. My favorite move was to push and shove, then suddenly give way, flipping my opponent over my hip, falling on his chest, knocking the wind out of him! I also had a strangle hold that quickly put anyone out of action.

One time my big brother came around to show us his stuff. Push, shove . . . suddenly I fell back, put my feet in his tummy, and kicked him high over my back! WHAM! I took off, and he never caught me . . . I could run like the wind!

Right across the street there was a huge fir tree, so big around, it could not be climbed. But we found, that by climbing the cedar tree next to it, we could cross over to the fir tree, and climb clear to the top, which had been hit by lightning, which left a butt-end eight inches in diameter. Man, it was high! You could see for miles.

We got pretty good at bombing cars with the green fir cones as they passed along the street below.

BOWANG!

SCREECH!

The angry motorist would jump out to find not a soul in sight. We sat quietly up on our perch to await the next victim! One evening I was up there all alone. My brother called . . . "Supper!"

I started scampering down the tree. Suddenly, I slipped! I fell about three feet before catching another limb. If I had missed that limb, I would have fallen for a mile! I eased over and hugged that tree trunk for a long time. That was the last time I ever climbed that tree.

Up in the sand hills, there was a small pond where we built a raft. The deepest water was only three or four feet . . . water lilies everywhere. Somehow we always managed to tip the raft and get sopping wet.

One time, we built a fire on top of an old log right on the water's edge. Some of the embers fell down into the dry brush and started burning. A whole lake of water, and we couldn't get the fire out. We even tried carrying water in our shoes. The fire had too good of a start.

"Go get some help . . . I'll stay here!"

A man came with an ax, and a shovel, and a bucket. Soon the fire was out.

"Dumb kids", he growled as he stalked off, "But at least you were smart enough to get help. No more fires, you hear!"

One day, we found an old bathtub. We dragged it up to the pond. As we launched it, I noticed how unstable it seemed. So we put my dog, Rex, in the tub, and shoved him out a bit. He put his feet on the edge which started the tub rocking. When Rex bailed out, the tub tipped over and sank in four feet of water.

Rex was my constant companion. He was a collie-shepherd mix with all the collie markings, but he had none of the high brow personality of a collie. He was just plain solid dog, but he was really smart. It wasn't hard to train him. I just spoke to him like I would to another person. He understood and did whatever I told him. Stay . . . and he would stay. Sit . . . and he would sit. Heel . . . and he would never leave my side. Get'em . . . believe me, he would get'em! I was small and always the constant target for bullies, but nobody fooled with me when Rex was around.

One time we went up to Nelson's grocery on the corner.

"Rex . . . stay here."

When I came out Rex was gone. There was a car with some people sitting in it, looking kind of funny.

I yelled, "REX!"

He just about tore that car apart before they let him out! Evidently, they had lured him into the car with something, and were about to drive off.

"Hey kid, we'll give you fifty dollars for that dog!"

"Not for fifty million dollars!", I glared back.

Imagine them wanting me to sell my dog! That would be like selling my brother! Sell my brother . . . maybe, but sell my dog? Never!

Home life was not all that great without mom. My brother and I were always fighting. And when dad came home, seems that we would gang up on him. We were always arguing about something.

When I came home from school, my chores were to cut the wood, start a fire in the cook stove, and put some potatoes on to cook. When dad came home, he would cook some kind of meat, open a can of vegetables, and that would be supper. After supper my brother washed the dishes, and I dried them.

We always listened to the radio, like everyone watches TV now. I never missed my favorite programs: Little Orphan Annie . . . even had one of those message decoders . . . during the program they would give you secret messages telling you what to expect on the next program! Then there was Jack Armstrong . . . the all American boy. Batman. Superman. The Lone Ranger. The Shadow. The Green Hornet. I Love a Mystery. Fibber Magee and Mollie.

And then all the songs . . . my brother and I would whistle along. My, how we could whistle! All the warbles and the trills . . . just like Roger Whitaker!

On Sunday I always went to Sunday School at the little Lutheran Church. No one ever told me to go . . . I just went. That's where I learned about Jesus Christ from Martha Andrews and Maybelle Velde.

I also loved to listen to the Haven of Rest, the Radio Bible Class with Dr. DeHaan, and my favorite was the Old Fashioned Revival Hour with Charles E. Fuller. But somehow, I never really seemed to make it personal . . . until one night.

It happened on the night I learned that Mom had died. Reverend Mathiasen, from the Lutheran Church, came over and gave us the shattering news.

He gave me a Bible. In it my mother had written, "Read your Bible, Richard . . . this is your mother's prayer." September 16, 1940. That night I went sorrowfully to bed. I lay there and did a lot of thinking. I thought about my mother dying. I thought about ME dying! That really scared me.

Then, it was as if God said to me, "But you don't have to be afraid of dying if Jesus is your Savior . . . you do believe in Jesus, as your Savior, don't you?"

"Yes . . . I do!"

Then, I just rolled over and went peacefully to sleep. Jesus Christ became my personal Savior that night!

But life was not easy in those days. My dad was a house painter. The Oregon winters are often so wet, there's hardly any work to be found, except for a few indoor jobs. Sometimes my dad could get a package of flour or corn meal from relief. I grew up on bread and milk . . . condensed milk mixed with water . . . real milk cost too much.

As I said, my brother and I fought a lot. In one particular blow-out, we were arguing about the dishes. I threatened him with a paring knife, but he stood his ground.

He growled, "And from now on, you will not only dry the dishes . . . you will wash them!"

So from then on, I also washed the dishes . . . plus swept and mopped the floors . . . and chopped the wood. I wasn't much of a housekeeper. Never knew what a fridge or a washing machine was in those days. Oh, how I hated ironing clothes!

My dad never stuck around much. When he did, we fought. I never ever saw my dad drunk, but he had to have his bottle of beer or a glass of wine. I'm afraid that he went off to the bars, where he played cards and lost a lot of what little money he did earn.

One time I thought I would really fix him. I heard that if you put aspirin in a bottle of coke it would make you drunk. So I put some aspirins in his wine bottle.

"I'll make him so drunk that he will never touch the stuff again!"

But the wine started foaming so bad that it spewed out the top all over the counter and down on the floor. I dumped the whole bottle down the sink. I really got it good for that one!

And he always had his cigarettes. During the war days he had one of those roll-your-own machines. "Well, I'll fix him!" So I took apart some firecrackers and rolled him some cigarettes with the powder in the middle!

"Wonder what would happen if I stuck a whole fire cracker in one?"

So I made one up and lit it! The fuse went SSSS! I tossed it! KA-BOOM! You couldn't find a piece of cigarette paper bigger than a quarter inch!

But I did sneak the powdered cigarettes into his package! One night, after supper, he lit up. He was puffing away contentedly. Suddenly, flames shot out over six inches from the end of his cigarette as he tossed it! He about killed me for that one!

The work bench really kept me out of a lot of trouble as I spent hours and hours making solid model airplanes, balsa gliders, and rubber band models. For the solid models, I got some beautiful white Port Orford cedar blocks from our next door neighbor, Mr. Hornet. For the wings and tail sections, I used white pine from the apple boxes that I salvaged from Nelson's grocery. I would look at an airplane picture in an aviation magazine and then draw up my own plans. The balsa gliders really soared. The rubberband models usually made their last flight loaded with a firecracker and a bit of gasoline.

Late one night, I was building a birdhouse. I had the sides and bottom together. When my brother came home from the movies, he kicked me out because he wanted to go to bed. I only had the top left to put on, but no . . . get out! Grumbling, I went off to bed.

Sometime later, my brother heard his door open. I came in and turned on the light. He could see that I was sleep walking, so he kept quiet to see what I would do.

The next morning he confronted me, "Guess what you did in your sleep last night!"

"What are you talking about?"

"Go in and look at your bird house!"

There was my bird house completely finished . . . the top was put on perfectly!

"Did I really do that?"

I desperately wanted a bicycle for Christmas. So my dad took me down to the Western Auto store, where I picked out a neat looking bike . . . black with cream trim. It even had a streamlined headlight on the front fender, and shock absorbers for the front wheel! The price was fifty-five dollars. My dad paid five dollars down. I got a paper route and paid the rest off at five dollars a month. For delivering the Coos Bay Times to about 120 customers, I earned about fifteen dollars a month.

Dad was always borrowing money from me to buy groceries. I cut a round hole in the wall, installed a bank made from a milk can, and hung a picture over it. I managed to save some of the money that way.

The North Bend airport was about a mile north of our little house with the sand-hills on the west, the bay on the north, and Pony Slough on the east. Just before the Second World War started, the government had a Civilian Pilot Training program in operation at the airport. My brother got a job working as a hangar boy. Naturally, I was right down there with him as much as they would let me.

They had a couple of Piper J-3 Cubs on floats which they would transport from the hangar to the bay on a low trailer. Riding on the trailer and helping to hold the plane down, was pure joy for me. One day, after helping out quite a bit, my brother talked one of the pilots into taking me up for a short flight. WOW! I'll never forget my first airplane ride . . . the beauty of the Coos Bay area . . . truly, this was God's country. He even let me hold the stick for a few seconds! That really re-enforced my life-long ambition to someday be an airplane pilot.

On the west edge of the Pony Slough were several old house boats. Just tiny shacks built on logs . . . people living there didn't have to pay any property taxes.

One day, an old hermit sold me an old leaky wooden john boat for 25 cents. It leaked so bad that you could not keep it afloat until I found an old bucket of road tar, built a small fire, and poured the melted tar into the cracks. Then I made a square sail from an old bed sheet. We had a great time sailing around on Pony Slough when the tide was in. It was fun to catch flounder, cover them with mud, and bake them in a bonfire.

One time during a deluge of pounding rain, we crawled under an old warehouse there at the water's edge. We started exploring around. We discovered several loose planks in the floor, which we lifted aside and gained entry to the warehouse.

What a fantastic collection of junk. Two whole stories of it! All kinds of rusty machinery, car parts, barrels full of unfinished Myrtlewood bowls . . . even an old Edison spool phonograph that actually worked!

It was interesting . . . in all the times we went into that old abandoned warehouse, we never stole a single thing. It never even crossed our minds . . . that place was like a sacred museum!

CHAPTER 12
BUTCH

Eldon Butcher was another kid that I used to play with quite a bit . . . that is, tried to play with. You see, his mother was a first class tyrant, and Butch was her little slave.

"You can go out and play after you do the dishes and mop the kitchen floor!"

After he got all that done, she would sometimes tack on . . . "Oh yes . . . also make the beds and wash the windows!"

Or it was chop some wood, water the roses, mow the lawn, or any other thing she could dream up. I never ever saw her do a lick of work around the place except trying to make life miserable for her son. Even with my pitching in with the work, it was impossible for Butch to ever get it all done. So the only way that Butch ever got to play, was to sneak off . . . disappear! Anytime Butch appeared at my place, it wasn't that he had permission, I'll guarantee you that. And when he went home, he really got it good. She had a wide leather strap hanging in the back porch, and she could really make it sing.

Sometimes Butch would show up in the middle of the night, and wake me up by tapping on the windows by my bed. We would go out exploring in the dark night. There were a couple of empty houses in the neighborhood. In one we found a bunch of empty beer bottles scattered in the junk. We sold these and went to the movies.

When we were rummaging around in the other house, my legs began itching like crazy. The flashlight showed dozens of fleas swarming up my legs! Shining the light around the room we could see hundreds of fleas all hopping straight for their meal. We got out of there fast.

We made life miserable for Mr. Hornet next door. We would pick the padlock on his garage door and just leave it open. After a couple of times he would change the lock. We learned how to pick the new lock and leave it open. After about four locks, he finally got one that we couldn't pick. We wrote a note and hung it on his lock . . . "Okay, you win!"

One time, when we were alone in Butch's house, he took me over to a glass bookcase. He pulled out a certain book and opened it up. In the pages were hidden ten one-hundred dollar bills! A couple of months later when I went to Butch's house, no one was home. So I went around to his bedroom and climbed in the window. I went to the bookcase and pulled out the book. There was all those one-hundred dollar bills! I counted them, put the money back in the book, and replaced the book exactly like I found it. I climbed out the window and went home. Yield not to temptation!

Butch said, "Someday I'm going to steal that money and run away!"

"You better not! No one will ever sell you anything for a hundred dollar bill! You'll get caught and they will send you off to reform school." Butch never ran away.

One day Butch was helping me deliver papers. He went down a trail through the woods to deliver a few papers on the next street. I finished my street and waited for him to return. I waited and waited. Finally I went flying down the hill. We crashed right at the sharp corner of the trail! I did a complete somersault, as I sailed over Butch and his bike, landing on my rump. When I turned around, there was Butch laughing . . . holding up his bike in two pieces! It had snapped in two at the gooseneck. The next day, he had the blackest eye you could ever see.

Butch had a small black and brown dog. He was probably a mixture of terrier, beagle and dachshund. But whatever he was, Butch made life miserable for that poor old dog. I guess he was just taking out his home-life frustrations on the mutt. One day, he was snapping the dog on the nose with his finger. When the dog would growl or try to retaliate, Butch would clobber him with his fists. Finally it made me so mad that I took Butch down and began snapping him in the nose.

"Hey, how do you like it!"

I doubled up my fist ready to bust him one.

He cried, "That stupid dog just doesn't know nothin'!"

"He's just dumb because you never trained him!"

Later on, the Butchers went on a vacation and they left their dog for me to take care of. By the time they came home, I had taught their dog to lay down, sit, sit up, shake hands, and to stay.

Butch exclaimed, "I never knew that you could teach an old dog new tricks!"

And he actually became proud of that mutt.

"Hey, look at what my dog can do!" . . . and he began to teach the dog other things too.

Butch and his folks moved to Alaska. Wonder what ever happened to him? I hear of this Butcher gal every year winning the Iditerod dog-sled race . . . could this be his daughter?

CHAPTER 13
BIRDS AND THE BEES AND STUFF LIKE THAT

With Butch gone it got rather lonely, but that was okay, I guess. I was the loner type. I rarely saw my dad except at night . . . the same for my brother. When I was done with the chores around the house, I was free to do whatever I wanted. Rex and I spent a lot of time out in the woods, exploring all the roads and trails that crisscrossed the sand-hills. I learned a lot from watching mother nature all around me. There was nothing better than being up on some sunny hilltop or down in the deep cool trees beside a tiny trickling stream. I learned to sit still and I learned to be quiet. It's amazing all the things you will see and hear when you shut up, open your eyes, and look around. The tiny gray mouse searching in the leaves. The flirty shy brown wren. The bushy gray squirrel scampering from tree to tree. The gentle wind sighing in the tree tops. The tinkle of the crystal stream . . . the rainbow trout almost invisible by the rock. The raccoon quietly feeling underneath the ledge for a tasty morsel of crayfish. The shrill cry of the hawk wheeling in the blue, blue sky. The cackling crow off in the distance. Sometimes I would answer him and we had a game of hide and seek. Once I even saw a bald eagle before he saw me! All what the Lord has created . . . I was in awe of it all . . . sometimes my quiet spirit would well up inside me to a thrill you cannot describe . . . and I would tell Him . . . "Lord, you really knew what you were doing when you made that . . .!"

I learned that Rex was a normal dog. As he grew into his prime, and when there was a girlfriend nearby, often he would go "visiting". Back in those days no one ever tied their dogs. They were free to run, and run they did. I guess I learned more from our animal friends about 'the birds and the bees' than anyone else. Seems that our mother cat was always having a batch of kittens.

Not that I never noticed a pretty little girl when I saw one, mind you, I was just too shy to ever get involved much. When I was in the third grade I remember Buddy's older sister and her girlfriend who were always trying to catch me. They never did because I was too quick for them. But I was too dumb, about why they wanted to catch me, until Buddy told me!

One time I was climbing trees with the Dexter kids, and Glenn teased his sister about not having any underpants on. Later on, I hung by my knees and grinned at Alice, "Hey . . . bet you can't do this!" She forgot and copied my antics. Her dress dropped clear over her head and there she hung, naked as a jaybird! I took off for home, laughing all the way!

Behind Butch's house, there was an old abandoned one-room shack which we made into a club house. We swept out all the junk and scrubbed the floors clean. We made furniture out of apple boxes and orange crates, covered them with gunnysack material, and stuffed them with soft grass. All the neighborhood kids played there.

Jacks were the big rage with the girls then. One day, I got into a pretty wild game of keep-away with Happy and Lucille. They started stuffing the Jack-ball down the front of their dresses, or sitting on it, daring me to get it! When I tried, they would squeal with delight. It took dumb me awhile to realize what the real game was all about . . . when I did, I took off out of there!

Lots of times the whole neighborhood gang would play Hide and Seek in the dark. It seemed that Happy and I often ended up together. Sometimes we accidentally touched in the dark, and I can remember the feeling, like electricity, going through our bodies. She was quite a gal.

One time Happy asked Butch and me if we had ever gone Jay hunting. Now, we knew the spoof about going Snipe hunting, but we had never heard about Jay hunting. She said that she would take us tomorrow, "That's when the boys pants the girls!"

For some reason I stayed home that day. Not long after that, Happy's folks moved away, and I guess it was a good thing they did.

As I said, I was just too shy and naive a kid. As I grew older, sometimes I would have a crush on a certain girl for months, often without her ever knowing. There was pretty blonde and blue-eyed Patty . . . there was Lucy . . . Darlene . . . and Suzzane . . . WOW! Was she ever a beautiful girl . . . with long soft wavy hair . . . and the blackest sparkling eyes you will ever see! I guess you could say that I was growing up in a sort of normal way.

My brother graduated from high school. Dad always raised us with the idea . . . "When you finish high school, you're on your own!" Gene could hardly wait for that day, and he enlisted in the Navy. He was sent to San Diego where they taught him to be a metalsmith. I moved into his room with the tool bench. I graduated from Roosevelt Grade School and became a Freshman at North Bend High.

Sunday morning, December 7th, 1941, the Japanese bombed Pearl Harbor, and the United States was hurled into the Second World War. The local airport was soon converted into a Naval Air base and the whole place became a beehive of activity. Our house was just off the south end of the big runway. We could sit on our back porch and watch all the planes come and go. Grumman Wildcat fighters, and Grumman Avenger torpedo bombers. Douglas Dauntless dive bombers. Consolidated PBY5A flying boats for submarine patrol. We even had a couple of Navy blimps once in awhile. It was quite a show.

One evening, we had just sat down to supper when we heard a terrific roaring noise. Dad and I ran outside to see what it was. And here came this huge Boeing Flying Fortress on final! It was so close, I could almost touch it. When we went back inside, there was Rex on the table, wolfing down our pork chops as fast as he could go! We could have killed him.

It wasn't long after that, that Rex was killed. He had a running feud with a big red German Shepherd. They were fighting all the time. One day, Rex didn't come home. The next day, we found him across the road in the woods. He had died, trying to crawl home. Rex had been shot and his neck was fiercely chewed. I cried as I buried him in the woods where we loved to play.

With mom gone, dad was a lonely man. I guess that's why he went off to the bars at night to play cards. And I guess it was normal for him to begin looking around for another wife. He was a shy man, but he evidently got brave enough to write a couple of women whose addresses he had gleaned from a lonely heart's club circular. Strange letters with feminine handwriting began appearing in our mailbox.

One time, while cleaning his bedroom, I found a couple of these letters and curiosity got the better of me. I read them. Pretty mushy, I'll tell you that, and it didn't take too much smarts for me to realize that one of these heartthrobs could soon become my new mother! Now that was the last thing I would ever accept. No one could ever, or would ever, take the place of my mother if I had anything to do about it! So from that point on, whenever one of these strange letters arrived in our mailbox, I steamed it open, read it, and filed it in the wood stove that happened to have fire in it!

Every day dad would check the mailbox . . . no letter! Another letter would come but he never got it.

One day, he asked me, "Have you ever seen any letters in the mailbox for me?"

"Letters?" I never was a very good liar and he read me like a book.

He threatened, "Don't you ever touch my mail again!"

It wasn't long after that, a woman arrived with three teenage kids. They moved in . . . I disappeared. I spent the day out in the woods, only coming home at night.

The lady tried to be friendly, but I never gave her a chance. I made it plain, "You're not wanted around here!"

The girls, I'm guessing, were about 17 and 15. The older one was pretty nice, but the younger one was a jerk. One morning, she came into my bedroom and tried to crawl in bed with me! Thanks, but no thanks!

The boy was bigger than me, but he had a bigger mouth. Why, there was nothing he didn't know. There was nothing he couldn't do. I had a makeshift basketball hoop out by the garage, and we had some wild one-on-one basketball games. He was a dirty player, but I gave it right back to him. He just loved to swarm all over you, or deliberately hack you when you came in for a shot.

One time I was going for a lay-in. As I went airborne, he gave me a big shove that sent me sprawling in the dirt. I'll get that guy! The next time he came charging in with the ball, he intended to run right over the top of me. He went airborne . . . his feet flailing. Instead of getting out of the way, suddenly I ducked, clipped his legs, and flipped him on his head on the hard ground!

"Smart guy, eh?" He picked up the basketball and threw it out into the street, "There you go sonny . . . get your ball!"

I glared at him, "You get it!"

He stuck his nose in my face and started making noise like a chimp. I swung for his chin, but I hit him hard in the throat. He fell back against the garage wall with such force that it knocked a couple of the boards loose! He fell to the ground gasping for air . . . shock and rage all over his face.

"You dirty so-$@#!" He staggered up and charged like a bull.

I flipped him over my hip and fell hard on his chest. WHOOF! I sat on him.

When he got his breath, he roared, "You God-da%&*$#!"

I hauled off and hit him with my open hand, so hard it almost tore his nose off. Then I doubled up my fist and stuck it in his face . . . "You shut up!"

He glared at me in rage, but he didn't make a peep.

I finally let him up . . . "Now you . . . get the ball!"

Instead of getting the ball, he started running toward town, cursing me as he went!

I ran out, retrieved the ball, and then I started after him. I caught up in a quarter of a mile, and then I just stayed behind him . . . "I'm gonna get'cha . . . I'm gonna get'cha!"

He ran like a man running for his life. When he began to stagger and fall, I stopped and let him go. As I walked home, I realized that this was my first real fight, and I had triumphed victoriously! Yahooo!

I took the quilt from my bed, packed some clothes and food, and took off for the sand-hills where no one would find me. For sure, I didn't want to be around when my dad came home. I built a snug hut of fir boughs, dug a small cave in the sand bank to stash my supplies, and gathered a pile of dry firewood for the evening. After supper, I lay there by the campfire, watching it grow dark. I think I was probably the loneliest kid in the whole world. A million million stars came out that night. And I voiced my thoughts to the heaven . . . 'The future looks mighty bleak, but God, if you can take care of all those stars up there, I know that you can take care of me.' I put the fire out, rolled up in my quilt on a soft bed of fir boughs. Soon I was fast asleep.

Three days later I went home. The woman was gone, and her three kids with her. My dad and I had some harsh words, but surprisingly, he didn't beat me. "What in the world did you do to that sorry kid!"

I told him what had happened.

He sort of hid his smile . . . "Well, don't you ever do that again! And you can go out and nail those boards back on the garage!"

One evening, about three weeks later, my dad announced, "I'm gonna move to California . . . look for work . . . winter's coming . . . always rains up here! You'll be movin' in with Edna and Pearl, and goin' to school up here!"

In a couple of days my dad was gone, and I went to live with my aunt and uncle.

CHAPTER 14
HIGH SCHOOL DAYS

Aunt Edna, my mother's sister, was a tall caring woman who was always taking in strays, whether they be dogs, cats, or kids like me. Uncle Pearl was a quiet gentle man who worked with his hands . . . there was nothing he could not make or do. There was always a kid or two around to help fill up the table. They had just adopted Ardy, a beautiful little girl of six. So when I arrived on the scene, there really was no room in their small two bedroom home, but they set up a bed in the storeroom . . . after all, "this is just a temporary deal until I find work down in California!" My dad promised to send money for my keep, but I doubt that he ever did. Anyway, Edna and Pearl made me feel at home, and soon I was part of the family.

They lived about a mile south near Dead Man's Curve where the straight road made a sudden right angle turn to the west, much to the detriment of the drunks who were trying to find home after getting soused in the bars of North Bend. You took the little dirt road just before the Curve, past Duree's place, the old log cabin, and there was Edna and Pearl's. The Duvall's lived next door, and the Barclay's across the way. This little cluster of homes perched on a high point overlooking Pony Slough. The back yard dropped off into a deep wooded canyon where we made the swing.

One day, Pearl brought home a long thick rope that he found lying on the dock . . . evidently left there by one of the ships bound for who knows where with a load of lumber. Near the bottom of the canyon was a tall cedar tree that grew outward, before growing upward, and thus it hung out over the trickling stream. I scampered up the tree about thirty feet and tied the rope securely. I think everyone from kids to grandpas in the area had a go on that swing over the years. You launched off from a steep drop-off, putting your feet on the big knot near the bottom of the rope. Down, down you dropped in a rush of wind, over the stream, then up, up until you kicked the leaves of the alder trees on the other side. Twist your body around for the return. Lightly step off when you reach the launch pad. What an exhilarating thrill when you did it just right!

The canyon also was my quiet place where I could quickly escape from the hustle of the busy world. I did a lot of thinking, and a lot of dreaming. I came back from there at peace, ready for anything the world could throw at me. Everyone needs a quiet place.

When I first moved in, the house wasn't really finished. I helped Pearl to nail the shakes on the walls. Then we painted the house white with black trim. We laid tongue and groove cedar on all the floors and finished them with a clear spar varnish. Oh, what beauty! We laid a white marble-like vinyl in the kitchen, and I scrubbed that floor every week trying to keep it that way. We dug the well deeper. The water was so cold and sweet . . . you almost drowned yourself trying to get enough.

Just off the back porch was a long lean-to garage that was just full of Uncle Pearl's treasures . . . man's junk . . . that you kept because "it just might come in handy someday!" There was a tool bench where we fixed or made things. If you needed a nail, or a screw, or a piece of wood, you could always find it somewhere in all that junk.

One day, Aunt Edna and I cleaned out the garage and tossed out a lot of real pure junk. Sure enough, a few days later, Uncle Pearl was looking for a number four thing-a-mabob and could not find it. We had thrown it out!

"Man, I've been saving that number four thing-a-mabob for six years, and you clean-up jokers throw it out . . . this stuff is like gold . . . don't you ever throw anything away!"

I sure got that drilled into me. For today, my garage, my house, even the attic is stashed full of man's junk that "just might come in handy someday!"

Back of the garage there was a garden and a small chicken coup. I learned how to keep the garden and tend the flock. There is a certain awe and satisfaction when you pick that first vine ripened tomato and eat it, or when you reach under a mama hen to gather that fresh warm egg . . . to realize that you are doing what other men have been doing for the past thousands of years. With sweat on your brow, man shall work. There is a pure pleasure in that.

And it was here that I first became aware of flowers. They had a Hydrangea bush with flowers of the deepest blue. They were that way because Uncle Pearl brought home brass and copper turnings from the lathe at the mill and scattered them under the bush. They had Dahlias of every color and shape . . . such delicate beauty.

One day Pearl and I were replacing some foundation timbers under the house that were beginning to dry-rot. This was caused by lack of air circulation under the house. When Uncle Pearl built the house, he didn't make any air-vents around the foundation. "First mistake I ever made in my life!", he said with a twinkle in his eye. I also learned another important lesson in life as he told me stories about days past.

"When we moved out to Oregon during the Depression, we first settled down near Klamath Falls. The only job we could get was digging potatoes for twenty five cents a day . . . plus all the potatoes we wanted to eat, mind you, so we didn't starve.

"Well, we were sorta feelin' sorry for ourselves. There's only so many ways that you can fix potatoes, and one day, I got to tellin' the good Lord about it.

"And the Lord told me what the problem was . . . `How do you expect Me to bless you when you're not giving Me a tithe?'

"So we began tithing five cents from the fifty cents we earned every day, and you know, we have never been in want to this day! And the good Lord will bless you too, when you learn to tithe."

As I said, they were always taking in some kind of stray. One day, this hungry looking black and white dog showed up, so Aunt Edna gave him a nice big bowl of bread and milk. He thought that was pretty good, and he just made himself right at home.

But that dog only lasted a couple of weeks. He had some bad habits that needed correcting, like bringing the garter snake he had just killed in on the back porch.

She gave him a good scolding . . . "Hey, you don't kill snakes around here, and number two, you don't bring them in on the porch!"

And so that he definitely got the message, she gave him a good swat on the behind with the broom as he went out the door! That was the last we ever saw of that bum . . . he decided it was time to move on.

One day, we were at the beach. There was an old house down there, that always had a bunch of dogs around. It seems the beach is where people dump off their unwanted pets, and they eventually found their way to this halfway house where these good people would give them a kind welcome. And people who wanted a pet would come by and pick out some mutt to call their own. This was probably the start of the Humane Society. Anyway, we picked out a tiny puppy from a litter of pups.

As we were going home, we stopped by the store and bought some worm medicine. Edna said, "Well, what ya gonna to name him?"

"Oh, I don't know . . . hey, what about Sargeant? . . . after these Sargeant's dog pills here!"

My aunt agreed, "Oh yah, that will be a good name!"

Sarge grew up to be a beautiful dog. Some people said he looked like a Scottish Shepherd. Some said he was an Australian Shepherd. And just like Rex, Sarge became my constant companion.

When we went hunting out in the sandhills, all I had to do was follow Sarge to the chattering squirrels. If I couldn't see the squirrel in the thick branches, all I had to do was look where Sarge was looking. Finally I'd see a little head peaking around a branch. BAM! Down tumbled the squirrel into the underbrush. Sarge would be there before he ever hit the ground. He would bring the squirrel out and lay him at my feet. It was so easy that it took all the joy out of hunting. So I stopped hunting!

"North Bend Bulldogs our hats are off to you . . ." The high school band played and the cheering crowd sang as another touchdown was made and the extra point was kicked against our arch rivals, the Marshfield Pirates. Fullback, Bob Sanders, was like a charging, raging bull. Coach Vic Adams' football science was quite simple. Keep it on the ground. End play to left, end play to the right, or find a weak spot in the line. Lead blockers each take out a man. AND give the ball to Sanders, who was virtually unstoppable as he ground out six, eight, twelve, or twenty yards every time he touched the ball.

Bob Sanders was one of the very few to become a four year letterman in football and basketball at North Bend High. He went on to play fullback for four years at the University of Oregon which also enjoyed phenomenal success while he was there.

I was such a small guy that I wisely passed up football. During the game I usually helped to run the mechanical scoreboard or the phones along the sidelines.

But I probably would have done okay. In Phys Ed, we played a rough brand of touch football. You had to hit the guy with both hands at the same time, hard enough for coach Adams to hear it, and he was hard of hearing! We wore nothing but gym shorts and tennis shoes.

Because I was so small, stopping the big guys was hard for me, until I developed a technique that usually put the runner in the dirt. As I hit the guy, my hip would catch him in the thigh. Down he went in a cloud of dust . . . Wham!

One day, Gordon Hart got the bright idea of stiff-arming, so no one could get in close enough to hit him hard enough for the coach to hear it. On his third touchdown run, he just about took my head off, and bloodied my lip. Okay, buddy!

The next time he was going full tilt down the field, I ducked his arm, and tackled him like you do in real football! It took off skin every place he hit the ground! I got a fifteen yard penalty for that one, but that was the last time I ever got a bloody lip from Gordon Hart.

I guess I also did a good job at carrying the ball. I could run, and I could dodge. I'd get whopped with one hand, but rarely two. In real football, I would have been so scared of being tackled that I would have made a touchdown every time they gave me the ball! Brag, brag!

When the weather got too bad outside, we played a type of free-for-all football in the gym. You made points by shooting baskets. There were no downs or huddles. Everything else was football. One time, Bob Sanders was running down the sideline with the ball. I cut in to take him out. WHOMP! I landed twenty feet away on my face as he threw me with one arm! I just crawled over to the side and lay there for awhile.

Twice a year we had a sort of decathlon. We threw the javelin, shot-put, discus, baseball, and football. We did the high jump, the long jump, and the triple jump. We did push ups, chin ups, and sit ups. We ran the hundred yard dash, four forty, eight eighty, mile, and the three mile. We also had an obstacle course that was a real killer. I did best in the endurance runs, and the mile became my favorite. My best time in the mile was 4:45. But George Hardcastle left me in the dust one time when he ran the mile in an amazing 4 minutes and 28 seconds! You had to be good to get an A in Phys Ed from Vic Adams . . . and man, I was goood!

In fact, I was so good that I went out for basketball, where I found out that I really wasn't all that good. In the Freshman year, I barely made third string B squad, where I played defense against the first string in practice. I had never officially played basketball before, other than the schoolground type, or one-on-one at the home basket.

In the sophomore year, I made second string B squad and coach Adams let me play in the games a few times. In my junior year, I made third string A squad where I honed my defense skills, and in my senior year I made second string A squad.

As I learned the plays, I became a real thorn in the flesh as I continually screwed up the first strings' offense during practice. Coach Adams finally figured that out. Whenever we played against another school, and someone started getting hot, he would put me on the guy.

One time, we were playing Marshfield, and Ken Johnson, a former playmate of mine, canned a basket every time he got the ball. Coach Adams put me in the game, "Don't let that guy make another point!"

I stuck to Johnson like glue. He never made another basket, in fact, he hardly ever got the ball. When he did manage to get the ball, I swarmed all over him so he couldn't get the shot off. Ken Johnson looked at me in utter frustration, "Who is this wild man?"

And we beat Marshfield on their home court by three points! During my senior year I got to play in enough games to just earn my NB letter. I never wore the letter on a sweater, as you had to buy the sweater, and it just plain cost too much.

Some of us got into playing quite a lot of tennis during the noon hour and on weekends. About our junior year, pert little Miss Sutton, the girl's Phys Ed teacher, organized us into a team which played the other schools. We beat everybody but Marshfield, which was pretty good, considering that we were such a rag-tag bunch.

Bob Swanson was always joking around. When he got everybody laughing...wham... he would slam the ball down your throat.

Bud Terry would get mad and then all his shots would go into the net or a mile long. Usually he could really whop that ball. When he got that first serve in, you hardly saw it, much less touched it.

Johnny Budiselich had a bad foot, so he couldn't cover the court very fast, but Mr. Accurate literally ran you to death with his place shots, pinpoint serves, and spin shots. One rainy winter day, I found him in the gym practicing his serve. His target was a tennis ball can which he hit on practically every serve.

That got me inspired, and I developed a wicked serve, hitting the corners with hard accuracy. Sometimes I hit my second serve harder than the first, completely catching my opponent off guard.

Tennis was never recognized as an official sport at North Bend until two years after we had graduated. At Marshfield, I think you could even earn a letter playing ping pong!

I wasn't too great on the academic side. School was a real struggle for me. But I guess, if I could have read what was on the blackboard, it would have helped. However, you were a real nerd if you wore glasses, so I squinted my way all through high school. I would have done a lot better in sports if I could have seen the basket or the tennis ball more than just a fuzzy image. I was a slow reader, so my eyes really took a beating. And I had to do homework almost every night to keep up.

During my sophomore year, I started getting hayfever. Walt, at the Pacific Drug Store, gave me some pills which helped some, but they also put me to sleep in class.

How in the world did I ever graduate fifteenth in my class, and fifth among the boys? It was macho for the boys to hate English, Literature, and American History, so I usually squeaked through those classes with a C minus. I secretly loved math and science, so I usually got B's and sometimes A's through a lot of effort. Shop classes and Mechanical Drawing were a breeze for me. Since we were in the beginning of the Second World War, we did our patriotic bit by carving airplane models from solid wood which the armed forces used for aircraft identification to know which planes were ours and which belonged to the enemy. I was also in the Civil Air Patrol Cadets, where we did a lot of marching around and learning how to take orders. We also practiced the Morse Code and First Aid . . . sort of a takeoff of the Boy Scouts.

My favorite teacher was Mr. Fred Shepman, who taught math. He really made us work hard, and he didn't stand for any fooling around in his class. One time, Fred Day was caught joking around with another classmate. Mr. Shepman turned around from the board and glared at him, "You get out of here!"

Fred grabbed his stuff and scurried out the door, and he didn't get back in the class for almost three weeks! We learned something in that class other than math, and that was an awesome respect for this man who really wanted the best for each of us. Another good teacher was Coach Vic Adams, who also taught chemistry. Five to ten pages a day . . . I literally memorized that chemistry book.

One day in lab, Bob Moore held up this beaker full of clear liquid, "Look Mr. Adams, I made some nitroglycerin!"

Vic Adams calmly said, "You can take that stuff and dump it in the sand out by the obstacle course . . . and when you do . . . pour it s-l-o-w-l-y !"

I was the rather shy introvert type of individual who tried to stay out of the limelight, especially when it was time to stand up in front of the class to give an oral report in English. Old Miss Biddle was great on that kind of torture. I would write out my report and memorize it. Then, when I got up in front of the class, my mind would go completely blank and I would make an absolute fool of myself.

I was also shy of the girls. As I said before, I would have a crush on someone for months without her or anyone ever knowing about it. Down in the school basement, they had a place for dancing during the noon hour. I was a wall flower who rarely ever got up nerve enough to ask a girl to dance. A lot of the guys were like that, so most of the time the girls danced together themselves.

The first girl that I actually dated was Shirley. At first it was just riding our bikes to school together.. Then it got so I was going over to her house at night. We did a lot of hugging and kissing, but we limited it to that. She always wanted me to say that we were going steady. We were going steady, so I couldn't see what all the fuss was about. But one night, I finally reluctantly said, "Okay, we are going steady!"

The next night, when I knocked on the door, her younger brother stuck out his hand and greeted me with a big smile on his face, "Hello, brother-in-law!"

Man, I turned around and took off out of there. And that was the last she ever saw of me! Fifteen years old and a junior in high school! Thanks, but no thanks!

A lot of kids did get married right after high school, and they made a go of it. Me? I was so immature that I didn't even have peach fuzz on my face yet!

The most interesting thing about our English class was the planes taking off from the Navy base first thing in the morning and climbing out low over the school building, completely drowning out everything the teacher was trying to say. One morning, we heard this Grumman Wildcat coming . . . he was lower than usual . . . and you could tell he was in trouble. The engine was coughing and sputtering. He came staggering up through Pony Slough, so low, we could look down from the school, right into the cockpit, to see the pilot frantically working the controls, desperately trying to keep the aircraft flying. A little later, here comes the pilot, walking right through the school yard, slapping his leather helmet on his leg!

"He ditched the plane up the Slough!"

All pandemonium broke loose, and the kids took off! Some of us went right out the window and down the ivy as the teacher frantically tried to bar the door!

Most of the kids chickened out when they saw the principal, but DeWitt Barclay and I took off across the football field. The last we saw of Old Baldy, he was screaming and waving his fists at us from the gym steps!

We flew down the trail. About a half mile up the slough, there was the Wildcat. The wheels had hit a small ditch and flipped the plane on its back!

"Hey, we're the first ones here!"

We walked around the plane; our eyes as big as saucers. I found a small air-scoop that came from the wing, and I kept it as a souvenir.

We really got it good for skipping, but it was worth it. All this air activity reinforced my dream to someday be a pilot. I could hardly wait to finish school and join the U.S. Army Air Force.

CHAPTER 15
ARMY AIR FORCE DAYS

I graduated in the summer of 1946 from North Bend High School. Bob Swanson and Bud Terry enlisted in the Army Air Force right away. I had the opportunity of working at the pulp mill, so I decided that would be a good idea as I wasn't old enough at seventeen to join up anyway. However, in checking with the enlistment officer, I learned that it would be necessary to sign up before the middle of September because Uncle Sam was canceling all World War 2 benefits after that date, and if I wanted to go on to college after the service, those benefits would make that dream a real possibility. "If your uncle will give his permission, you can enlist in early September . . . then you will be in good shape!" So that became the plan.

I was barely 18

"The most destructive war in history was over. Some thirty-five million people were killed in that war. Seventy million fought on both sides. Hundreds of billions of dollars of property was destroyed. Fifty seven nations had entered the war. World War 2 was actually two wars that became one. How did they start?"

Please excuse me . . . while I meant to write only a couple of paragraphs about the war as an introduction to this chapter, when I researched it, I became rather intrigued at what had happened on planet earth during those years . . . it must be a lesson that we never ever forget.

"The war in Europe started because the Allies never really finished the job with World War 1. When the victorious Allies sat down at the peace conference, neither the defeated powers nor the new Communist government of Russia even bothered to attend when the Treaty of Versailles was written. The treaty allowed Germany to keep most of its territory, but they were required to pay war reparations to the Allied nations. The treaty also was to restrict the German army to 100,000 men, and to forbid them from developing heavy weapons, air power, and large ships. The German people refused to accept this treaty.

Economic hardship increased after the war. By 1923, inflation was so bad in Germany that the people went to market carrying their money in wheel barrows. With widespread dissatisfaction with the existing government, this made Fascism very appealing. Because of the terrible destruction of the war, the victorious Allied governments were determined to never fight again. The hard times kept them busy with their own problems. They did form the League of Nations, but it never had any real power to enforce its mandates.

A new leader (Mussolini) came on the scene in Italy who gave the people a vision of a restored Roman Empire, and his followers in 1922 marched on Rome and took over the government. The League of Nations actively voiced their disapproval but did nothing.

Germany followed a similar path under the leadership of Adolf Hitler. Hitler promised to restore Germany's military greatness. He told the dissatisfied people that Germany was really not defeated in 1918, but they had been stabbed in the back by the treacherous Jews at home. Germans were the 'master race' who should rule over the 'inferior races' like the Jews and the Slavs. Hitler rode this 'superior race' campaign to power and became the chancellor of Germany in 1933. When President Hindenburg died the following year, Hitler took full control of the government, and gave himself the title of Der Fuhrer. He established huge public works projects which put the people back to work which began to solve their economic problems. The people enthusiastically rallied behind the Fuhrer. He began rearming Germany, and the other nations of Europe had little will to stop him. Germany pulled out of the League of Nations."

"Impressed by Hitler's boldness, Mussolini ordered an attack on Ethiopia in October of 1935. This caused the League to slap a war materials embargo on Italy, which did not include oil, so Italy continued its aggression without further interference.

In 1936, Hitler sent his troops into the Rhineland, a part of Germany, which bordered France. Again the League refused to challenge this action. So Hitler became bolder. He pressured the chancellor of Austria, forcing him to resign. Then he sent German troops into Austria to 'restore order'. Thus Austria became a part of Germany. Not a shot was fired. The rest of the European countries looked fearfully the other way."

"Over three million people of German descent lived in an area of Czechoslovakia called Sudetenland. Hitler demanded that the Czechs turn this land over to Germany. As the Czechs prepared to resist, a meeting was held by Britain, France, Germany, and Italy at

Munich on September 29, 1938, and they agreed that Sudetenland belonged to Germany! In 1939 more demands were made by the Axis nations . . . Germany and Italy, and Hitler took over the rest of Czechoslovakia and part of Lithuania. Italy seized Albania. Then Hitler began making demands on Poland."

"Britain and France began to realize that their appeasement to Hitler's demands were not going to satisfy him, so they too began to build up their forces. They appealed to Russia to join them, but they were too late. Josef Stalin realized that Hitler could offer a better deal than the British or the French. Hitler had secretly offered Stalin to divide up Poland and the Baltic states into German and Russian spheres in a non-aggression pact on August 29, 1939. Thus Hitler made sure that he would not have to fight a two front war. Britain and France promised to help Poland if it was attacked. The world was on the verge of another war."

"Midnight, September 1, 1939, the German Luftwaffe flew over the Polish border to massively bomb the cities, railroads, and airfields. At the crack of dawn, the Nazi troops stormed across the border in a Blitzkrieg, or lightning attack, to encircle and trap the Polish army. The world had never seen military action of such speed and mobility. On September 3rd, Britain and France declared war on Germany, but they were not prepared to mount an effective attack. Hitler had gambled by leaving the border with France poorly defended. And the French were content to stay behind their Maginot Line.

The Soviet Union also attacked Poland from the east and by October 5th the Germans and the Russians had divided the country between them. Stalin then demanded bases and territorial concessions of the Baltic states. All gave in but Finland. On November 30, 1939 the Soviets attacked Finland, but the Finns stubbornly fought back. They used Molotov cocktails to set the Russian tanks on fire. The ski troops encircled the Russian troops and cut off their supply lines. Stalin sent in a massive second attack and finally overran the country on March 12th, 1940."

"The rest of Europe fearfully awaited Hitler's next attack. He strengthened his fortifications along the French border. Britain and France were also building their forces. Germany needed iron ore from Sweden to keep the war machine going, so on April 9, 1940, Hitler attacked Norway. They overran Denmark the same day. The Norwegian troops put up some resistance. Britain and France also sent in some troops but had to pull out their units when Hitler moved against Luxembourg, the Netherlands, and Belgium. These small countries fell in just a few days. Norway also surrendered on June 9th. Hitler had the Luftwaffe heavily bomb Rotterdam, killing over 40,000 civilians, as an example to other countries not to resist."

"The German army Panzer divisions cut around the north end on the Maginot Line through the Ardennes Forest where the French thought tanks could not go, breaking a fifty mile wide hole in the French fortifications. The German troops poured through and stormed across France with hardly any opposition. The troops reached the sea in seven days, trapping the French and British troops to the north in Belgium. They valiantly fought their way to the coastal town of Dunkirk, where a makeshift flotilla of every kind of ship and boat came from England to successfully evacuate 335,000 soldiers from certain destruction at the hands of the German army. Hitler's divisions continued across France. Paris fell on June 14th and on June 17th, 1940, Marshall Petain, the head of the French state, surrendered. General Charles de Gaulle set up an exile French government in Britain. The British feverishly prepared their defenses for they knew they were next. The United States sent supplies as fast as they could."

"Hitler offered peace terms to the British which they turned down. and the Battle of Britain began on July 10th, 1940 when the German Luftwaffe, under the leadership of Field Marshall Hermann Goering, began bombing the air fields of the Royal Air Force in Britain. It would be necessary to establish mastery of the skies before Britain could be invaded."

"The British had a secret weapon which enabled them to thoroughly frustrate the designs of German planners, even though the Luftwaffe had more aircraft . . . that was Radar. This gave them the ability to detect and track the enemy aircraft from miles away, even in the fog and clouds, even at night. The RAF could surprise the German bombers and fighters every time they crossed the channel causing heavy losses to the enemy. The Germans tried to bomb the radar towers, but they were hard to hit, and they were easily replaced. They tried to catch and destroy the RAF on the ground, but with Radar, the British always knew when the Luftwaffe was coming and would be in the air to engage them. But the Germans with their superiority in numbers were beginning to wear down the opposition."

"Then on August 25th, RAF bombers pulled a surprise raid on Berlin, the German capitol. This absolutely sent Hitler and Goering into fits of rage. They had promised the German people that their enemies would never touch Berlin. In retaliation, the German Luftwaffe was ordered to concentrate in destroying the cities of Britain, especially London. This gave the needed breather to the ragged Royal Air Force, who continued to pick off the bombers as they came over the channel. The Blitz reached its peak on September 15th, when the Luftwaffe sent more than 1000 bombers and almost 700 fighters over London. Hitler thought the bombings would destroy the spirit of the British people, and they would force their new prime minister, Sir Winston Churchill, to surrender. The British stood fast. Churchill encouraged his people, "This is our finest hour . . . we will never, no never, give up!" Hitler was forced to postpone his invasion of Britain. Even though the cities of Britain were bombed throughout the war, the Battle of Britain was over. The RAF lost 790 fighters to the destruction of 1389 Luftwaffe planes of all types. The Battle of Britain was the turning point of the war, because it showed that the mighty German air force could be beaten."

"Mussolini, looking for another easy target, attacked Greece from Albania. The poorly equipped Greek army fought furiously. The Greeks counterattacked and by the end of December occupied one quarter of Albania. Greece asked Britain for help, and the British sent troops to protect their air bases in Greece. In April 1941, Hitler invaded Yugoslavia and Greece. The German Blitzkrieg overran Yugoslavia in just eleven days, but they met firm resistance in Greece. However, with their numbers, speed, and mobility the German forces overpowered their opposition. In another daring evacuation, 43,000 British were able to escape from Greece to the island of Crete and to Egypt. Hitler ordered an airborne invasion of Crete and drove the British from the island. That little operation was not without its price. Over 6000 Germans were killed or wounded and 170 troop-carrying planes were destroyed."

"Because of his rapid victories in the Balkans and eastern Europe, Hitler turned to his next target—Russia. This proved to be the biggest mistake that Hitler ever made. June 22, 1941, Germany attacked Russia with a huge army of over three million soldiers in three main thrusts along a front 1800 miles long. In vast pincers movements at lightning speed the advancing Germans were able to encircle units of the Soviet army destroying or capturing large numbers of soldiers. At first, the Russians were unable to slow the onslaught. On July 3rd, Stalin called for all Soviet citizens to resist the Germans in every way possible. He asked the people to follow a scorched earth policy, to destroy everything of value that the Germans might capture and put to their own use. In ten weeks the Soviets had more than a million casualties. The resistance cost the Germans 450,000 casualties. Hitler had expected a quick victory and had not made any provision for winter supplies. In early October, the fall rains slowed the German tanks to a crawl as they tried to reach Moscow with their supply lines over 1500 miles long. Winter came early that year in Russia. The temperature dropped to forty below zero . . . the coldest winter in one hundred years. The German war machine, not equipped for the cold, ground to a standstill. On December 6th, 1941, the Russian forces counterattacked, driving the Germans back. Hitler ordered that there be no retreat. Much of his army froze to death. The Russian counteroffensive also petered out. Both sides spent the winter fortifying their positions."

"All the while, there was also a war being fought in North Africa. The Italians from their colony in Libya planned to attack Egypt and capture the Suez Canal. However, while they were gathering their forces, the British pulled a surprise attack, which became a complete rout. They killed or wounded over 10,000 Italians and captured more then 130,000 prisoners. Hitler, alarmed at the failure of the bumbling Italians, sent his own crack forces under the leadership of General Erwin Rommel, the Desert Fox, and in a devastating attack, he pushed the British back to the Egyptian border. The battle then became a seesaw affair with both sides gaining and then losing ground. Finally in a gigantic tank battle, Rommel took Tobruk, and drove the British back to El Alamein where they managed to dig in their defenses. Britain and the United States rushed in reinforcements. The German forces repeatedly tried to break through, and lost their attack strength because Hitler could not send sufficient supplies to Rommel. The British now counterattacked with superior forces on the ground and in the air. They drove the Germans back to Tripoli. Then in November of 1942, American and British forces, under the leadership of General Dwight Eisenhower, landed in Morocco and Algeria, behind Rommel's forces. Rommel attacked the inexperienced forces, but the Allies were able to stop his advance at the Kasserine Pass. The Germans were now caught in a vise. Slowly they were forced to retreat to Bizerte and Tunis. Hitler ordered a fight to the end, and thus the Germans lost over 275,000 of their best soldiers."

"In the summer of 1942, the German army once more began their summer offensive in Russia. The first thrust was towards Sevastopol in order to gain control of the Black Sea and then head for the Russian oil fields. Sevastopol was in their hands by early July. The second offensive was on a broad front toward Stalingrad and toward the oil fields to the south. The Caucasus region was also the last remaining agricultural area in the Soviet Union. With its loss, the Russians would be in danger of mass starvation."

"By now the German supply lines were over 3000 miles long, and the Russian resistance behind the lines was fierce, continuous, and damaging. In the first month of the offensive, the Germans penetrated 300 miles, but as the lines approached the cities of Baku and Stalingrad, they did not have the troop strength to take both places.

Furiously, Hitler ordered an attack on Stalingrad. Stalin was just as determined that the city fight to the end. On September 13th, the Germans were able to break into the city, but they had to win it building by building, city block by city block. By the middle of November, the Germans had managed to take three quarters of the city. But then the Russians brought up reserves and encircled the city, trapping over 300,000 Germans in Stalingrad. Hitler determined that his army hold their position in the city. With the cold winter and no food, only 90,000 starving Germans were left when they finally surrendered on February 2nd, 1943."

"With the defeats in North Africa, and Stalingrad, the myth of Nazi invincibility died. The German victories were over, and in the spring of 1943, the Russians began pushing back the German lines. The Russian strategy was to press steadily against one section of the German line. When German reinforcements arrived in that section, then the Russians would shift their attack to a weaker section of the line. The German army reeled backwards, leaving behind thousands of irreplaceable soldiers and all their fighting equipment. It was only a matter of time and all of Russia would be liberated from the enemy. But the Russians did not stop there. They were headed for Berlin."

"The Allies gained air superiority over Germany and the American bombers were bombing the factories during the day, and the British were pulverizing the cities during the night, bringing the war home to the German people.

We were also winning the war on the seas as the United States was building ships faster than the German U-boats could sink them. The endless supply line of war materials, food, just everything, could not be stopped."

"With the Germans defeated in North Africa, the Allies took the island of Sicily, and then invaded Italy in September, 1943. The Italians surrendered in a few days and we began the slow fight northward. Italy is a mountainous country with many rivers, and the Germans were able to set up defenses that were almost impossible to overrun. However, this caused Hitler to squander his precious reinforcements which had to come from western Europe."

"And just as Britain waited for the Nazi invasion in 1940, now the Germans were waiting for the Allied assault on Europe. Hitler was frantically preparing his Atlantic wall. We were building up the largest amphibious invasion force in history.

On June 6th, 1944, D-Day began. At 2:00 A.M., paratroopers dropped like a cloud on Normandy. Planes bombed and strafed the beach fortifications. At 6:30 A.M. the first troops and tanks landed on the beaches of Normandy. Many died that day as we grimly fought for every inch of that beach, through the mine fields, the barb wire, and the machine gun fire. But on they came, an invasion force three million strong. That day we established a beachhead in Hitler's Europe that could not be stopped. By June 26th, the Allies took over the port city of Cherbourg through which they were able to pour in more troops and supplies."

"The Allies advanced in two giant thrusts. One engaged the main body of German troops around Caen. The second thrust broke out of Normandy to the south and then circled eastward toward the Seine river, trapping over 100,000 German soldiers. The larger body of German troops fled across the river, pursued by General Patton's forces.

On August 5th, the Allies made a second landing in southern France. With the Germans pinned down in the north, the second group of invaders made good progress, and were able to link up with Patton's forces by September 11th, 1944. By mid-September, most of France was back in Allied hands.

Eisenhower wanted more supplies before he launched the next offensive. The British had captured the port of Antwerp, but it was unusable until the Germans were cleared from the surrounding countryside. This was accomplished with heavy fighting by the end of November."

"Hitler was now fighting a two front war. With a massive strike, the Russians blasted a hole in northern Poland 250 miles wide and 250 miles deep. The German army managed to regroup to make a stand at Warsaw. But Warsaw was finally taken in January of 1945. The Russians relentlessly pushed back the German army all along the eastern front."

"During bad weather, Hitler tried a counteroffensive in the west, and managed to penetrate 60 miles into the American lines. However, when the weather cleared, the air force blasted the German tanks. Hitler had sacrificed 200,000 of his best troops and failed. In February 1945, Eisenhower directed a broad advance against Germany's Siegfried Line. In four weeks they broke the line and were able to capture intact the bridge across the Rhine River at Remagen which allowed the Allies to establish a position east of the river. Eisenhower continued his broad advance tactics and by April, the Ruhr Valley, the heart of Germany's industry, was in Allied hands."

"Rather than sending a narrow thrust into Germany, aiming at Berlin, Eisenhower was content to allow the Russians the bloody task of capturing Berlin. And a bloody task that proved to be as Hitler ordered a stand to the last man. The Russians fought their way to the Oder River, just 30 miles from Berlin, where the fanatical Germany army threw the Russians back."

"The Russians assembled a massive force and managed to break through the Oder River line. In six days, they crushed the German army and advanced to Berlin. The last desperate Germans, civilians and boy soldiers, made the Russians pay for every block. In return, the Russians savaged the populace. Hitler directed the German forces from his bomb shelter in the city."

"President Roosevelt died on April 12th, 1945. His name appeared in the casualty lists along with others who died in battle that day: "Roosevelt, Franklin D., Commander in Chief". Just six days later, on April 18th, in the south, American troops linked up with the Russians at the Elbe River. On April 30th, with the Russians only blocks away, Hitler committed suicide. On May 7th, General Alfred Jodl signed the unconditional surrender of the German army. General Eisenhower sent a telegram to headquarters: "The mission of this Allied Force was fulfilled at 3:00 A.M., local time, 7 May 1945. Eisenhower." YIPPPEEEEEE!"

"As the Allied armies fought their way across Europe, they uncovered the most horrifying deeds of Hitler's Third Reich. The names of these small towns will haunt the human world forever . . . Auschwitz, Belsen, Maidenek, Buchenwald, Dachau . . . for they were the concentration camps where people from all over Europe were sent to be tortured, starved, experimented upon, to be put to death, and disposed of in the ovens. The ghostly victims who were still alive shocked the liberating armies. The piles of corpses that the Nazis had not managed to dispose of, horrified the world. As the stories of the mass extermination of the Jews began to unfold, people's feelings turned to absolute revulsion toward the German people . . . how could they allow such crimes to happen against other human beings?"

"Yet Hitler had made known all along his intentions toward the Jews, the Gypsies, the Slavs, and the so-called other 'inferior' peoples of the world. From the very beginning, he made the Jews the scapegoats for all of Germany's ills. 'Exterminate the Jews', was his solution, made known as early as 1939. With the capture of Poland with its 3 million Jews, and with parts of Russia with another 3 million, and another half million more in Western Europe, Hitler's plans did not change."

You see, many of the Jews were the elite of the German community. For they were the doctors, the scientists, the lawyers, the teachers, and the shop keepers. They were not perfect in their relations with others, mind you, in fact, maybe they would like to stick it to you when they got the opportunity. So Hitler's final solution to this 'scum of humanity' was total extermination, just like you would rid your house of a termite infestation. Early in his rise to power he began to systematically separate the Jews from their positions in society. Those that could, escaped to other free countries in the world. Read Corrie Ten Boom's book 'The Hiding Place'.

"In 1942, a Nazi directive called for the complete elimination of the Jews. They were sent to the death camps where whole sections of Hitler's Nazi SS troops were devoted to the logistical problems of killing and disposing of millions of human beings. More than six million Jews were killed by Hitler during the war. It was a crime that was to haunt the civilized world, and shake people's faith in humanity."

We must never, never forget. And we have not forgotten, for we have been fighting brush wars ever since, wherever the bullies of this world try to inflict their evil wills against defenseless people. The United States has been the champion for democracy, loudly opposing and sometimes even resorting to intimidation or force against nations where violation of human rights is in practice. Some nations openly condemn us for trying to be the police force to the world. I would say they have forgotten what was allowed to happen in Germany.

Or have we, ourselves, forgotten? For how can we allow such violations of human rights to take place in our own beloved country? How about the siege at Waco? Or the standoff at Ruby Ridge?

THE WAR IN THE PACIFIC THEATER

Now we need to take a look at the Asian part of the war which was going on at the same time, for that was how we were reluctantly dragged from our isolationism into the world conflict.

"The crowded island nation of Japan began expanding its power and territory in the early 1900s. In the 1920s, Japan also suffered an economic depression with the rest of the world, and in the absence of a stable political power, the military took over the government. They built up their war machine in order to acquire more territory in the Far East."

"In September 1931, Japanese agents exploded a bomb on the tracks of the Manchurian railway. Japan blamed the terrorist act on Chinese bandits, and sent troops to 'restore order' . . . they took over the whole province!"

"Two years later, Japanese troops took over the province of Jehol. The League of Nations condemned Japan's aggression, and Japan responded by pulling out of the League. Friction increased between China and Japan with further incidents and, the Japanese sent in troops to once more 'keep the peace' . . . they took over Peking and Tientsin in 1937."

"On August 8, 1937, they attacked Shanghai; in a furious battle the Japanese were thrown back. Japan sent reinforcements and overran the city on November 8th. The troops, then in revenge, marched up the Yangtze valley and destroyed, looted, and raped the capitol city of Nanking. The rest of the world protested but did nothing."

"Over the next two years the war raged in China. By the end of 1939 Japan had cut off all supply routes into China except for the Burma road and through Indochina. These became the next targets. The United States responded by putting an embargo on all aviation fuel, iron, and steel shipments to Japan. In September 1940, Japan signed the Tripartite Pact with Germany and Italy, and a nonaggression pact with the Soviet Union in 1941. The USA responded by freezing all Japanese assets in America and levied a total embargo on all trade goods with Japan."

"On December 7, 1941, the Japanese pulled a sneak attack on Pearl Harbor, sinking eight battleships, three cruisers, and seven other ships. Of the 394 aircraft on the ground, 108 were destroyed, and 159 were damaged. Americans killed were 2300, with 960 missing, and over 1100 wounded. The Japanese victory would have been complete, except for the three American aircraft carriers that were not in Pearl Harbor at the time."

"The next day the United States declared war against Japan. Three days later, Germany and Italy declared war on the United States, and we responded likewise. The war now encircled the whole world."

"On December 7th, the Japanese also attacked the British colonies of Hong Kong and the northern end of the Malay peninsula. The inexperienced British were forced to withdraw to Singapore island which was well fortified and thought to be invulnerable. The Japanese bombarded the island with artillery and sent waves of bombers against it. In a daring night landing, the Japanese established a beachhead, and then fought their way across the island. On February 14, 1942, they captured the island's water reservoirs, and the next day General Percival surrendered. More than 130,000 British soldiers were taken prisoner, killed, or wounded."

"At the same time, the Japanese invaded Thailand and drove toward Burma and India. On March 7th they captured the capitol city of Rangoon, and by the end of April they cut the Burma road, China's last supply link."

"In December, the Japanese also overran the island fortifications of Guam and Wake. On December 7th, the Japanese also bombed Clark Airfield in the Philippines, virtually destroying all the American planes on the ground. They landed 60,000 troops on the main island of Luzon. The poorly equipped Filipino and American forces were no match against the seasoned Japanese troops who slowly pushed the island defenders down to the end of the Bataan Peninsula. It was impossible to break the Japanese naval blockade so they were trapped. With fresh troops the Japanese forced 70,000 American and Filipinos to surrender. Thousands of prisoners died in the Bataan Death March and in the filthy prisons. The island of Corregidor fell on May 6th. General Douglas McArthur was ordered to evacuate to Australia."

"The Japanese also seized the Gilbert and Admiralty Islands. They also established bases in New Guinea from which they could bomb Australia. Their plan had worked, for they now controlled almost all of the important islands of the Pacific west of Midway to the Philippines, plus large areas of the Asian mainland."

"However, on April 18, 1942, a squadron of American bombers pulled a surprise attack on Tokyo. The Doolittle raid stunned the Japanese who thought they were beyond the reach of American retaliation. Where had they come from? President Roosevelt jokingly said they took off from the mythical city, Shangri La, in the novel, Lost Horizon. Actually, they took off from the carrier, Hornet, 800 miles from the Japanese coastline. This raid was a real morale booster for the American people, and it forced the Japanese to keep large numbers of their fighter planes at home to defend the Islands."

"Then the American cryptographers broke the Japanese code, whereby they were able to learn that, Tulagi, in the Solomon Islands, and Port Moresby, in New Guinea, were to be the next Japanese targets. The Americans sent the only two available aircraft carriers, the Yorktown and the Lexington, to surprise them in the Coral Sea. The Japanese had a task force of eighteen ships, including three aircraft carriers. The Japanese carrier, Shokaku, was so badly damaged during the battle that it eventually sank. The American carrier was so badly damaged that it was eventually scuttled. The Japanese lost 105 planes, and the Americans 81. While it was a close fight, it was a moral victory for the Americans, because the Japanese never landed at Port Moresby, and never again, did they enter the Coral Sea."

"The Japanese now went after the American island of Midway. Because we were still decoding the enemy's secret messages, Admiral Chester Nimitz was able to reinforce Midway's defense with a fleet of 29 major ships and 19 submarines. On June 4th, 1942, Japanese bombers and fighters attacked the island. The Americans attacked the Japanese fleet, but the Zero fighter planes so effectively protected the enemy carriers that not a single torpedo-carrying plane or fighter could break through. However, while they were destroying our torpedo planes near the water, our dive bombers came over the top and were able to sink four of the Japanese carriers in the three day battle. Yamamoto ordered a withdrawal. His fleet suffered the greatest naval defeat in Japanese history, losing 275 planes, more than 4800 men, some of them were their most experienced pilots. The battle of Midway turned the tide. The Japanese would never take to the offensive again."

"The American forces began their counterattack by island hopping, avoiding the most heavily armed islands and attacking the weak islands, thus cutting the supply lines to the strong islands. This maneuver saved a lot of lives as the Japanese forces stubbornly fought to the last man at every point. It took us six months to take Guadalcanal with the loss of a lot of lives. The same for New Guinea. The island hopping now began in earnest with intense fighting for every tiny rock. Over 1000 Americans were killed in the bloody fighting to take the islands of Makin and Tarawa in the Gilbert chain. In February 1944, we took Kwajalein in the Marshall chain. With added air bases, the Americans destroyed the Japanese bases on Truk and Rabaul. When the American marines attacked Saipan, the Japanese fleet was sent to the rescue. The American air, surface, and undersea forces sank three carriers and shot down over 300 Japanese planes. Japan lost over 24,000 lives defending Saipan. We also took back Guam and Tinian."

"Then began the battle to take back the Philippines. For six weeks, American ships and planes bombarded the enemy bases. Air bases, naval ports, and supply depots were pulverized.

October 20, 1944, began the greatest naval battle in history. Our invasion forces were carried and protected by a fleet of 700 ships. The Japanese divided their naval force into three segments. The northern force was to act as a decoy. The central force would engage our attack. The southern force would enter the battle as it developed.

Admiral Halsey's Third Fleet attacked the central force and sank two ships. The next day, more of the central force was damaged, and the southern force was almost annihilated. Halsey then took off in hot pursuit after the northern decoy.

A couple days later, the central force which had been damaged, but not destroyed, headed for the American beachhead where General MacArthur and 100,000 troops had been left with hardly any naval or air support. A small fleet of escort carriers under the command of Admiral Sprague moved in between the Japanese fleet and the beach. By using delay tactics, smoke screens, and what firepower he could muster, they held off the enemy for three hours. The Japanese desperately turned to kamikaze suicidal attacks where the pilots crash-dove their planes into our ships. Five of our ships were sunk, and there was little hope of holding off the Japanese much longer, but suddenly the enemy turned and fled. In the battle for the Philippines more than 2000 Japanese planes were destroyed and 450 ships damaged."

"Unknown to the Americans, the Japanese had hardly any naval reserves left, and we could have easily begun our invasion of the Japanese mainland. However, we kept fighting in the Philippines, liberating the Islands in early 1945."

"For seven months, we heavily bombed the eight square-mile island of Iwo Jima, yet we could not dislodge the enemy. We had to take this island in order to attack Japan with our long range bombers. February 19, 1945, our troops invaded the island. Waiting for them were 23,000 crack Japanese soldiers in heavily fortified concrete bunkers. The fighting was savage, yet we took the prized Mount Suribachi on February 23rd, and the island was ours on March 16th."

"Okinawa was close to Japan, and this island would be needed for the invasion of the Japanese mainland. An invasion force, supported by 1450 ships and 1500 carrier based planes, was sent against this fortress. Kamikaze planes and boats were sent hurdling towards our ships. Banzai suicidal charges of enemy troops tried to throw us back into the sea. It took us over three months of intense fighting, where more than 100,000 Japanese were killed. We lost 7613 young men. What in the world would be the loss of life, to both sides, when we invaded Japan?"

"We began bombing Japan with our long range bombers, causing untold devastation to the cities and industrial sites. We gained mastery of the skies over Japan to where our planes were rarely challenged any longer. But the bloody fighting and the stubborn refusal of the Japanese soldier to surrender convinced the Americans that the invasion of Japan would be very very costly."

"At the beginning of the war, Albert Einstein, a refugee German Jewish scientist, wrote a letter to President Roosevelt, telling him about the possibility to build a super weapon . . . it was the atomic bomb. It was believed that the Germans were also working on such a bomb.

The United States spent over two billion dollars during the Manhattan Project to build the bomb. The bomb was tested in great secrecy in the deserts of New Mexico on July 16th, 1945 . . . the devastation was almost beyond description. By then, Germany had been defeated by conventional means.

The scientists who had worked on the project, did so, to fight the evil that Hitler had represented. But now, they were hesitant in using the bomb on the Japanese and they advised President Truman to not use it. However, realizing what a loss of life there would be on both sides in a conventional invasion of Japan . . . perhaps millions of people . . .

President Truman issued an ultimatum to Japan to surrender unconditionally, or face absolute destruction. Japan refused."

"On August 6th, 1945, the lone Superfortress plane, Enola Gay, dropped the atomic bomb on the city of Hiroshima. Another ultimatum was issued for Japan to surrender. They refused. Three days later another bomb was dropped on the city of Nagasaki. Both cities were absolutely utterly destroyed. Many of the people who were not killed outright, died later from burns and the deadly radiation of the bomb. On August 15th, the emperor of Japan told his people that the war was over. Japan surrendered unconditionally to the United States."

(The information of the Second World War was taken from the books: "The Story of the Second World War", by Col. Red Reeder, and "An Album of World War II", by Dorothy and Thomas Hoobler.)

Now, finally, back to my story

So I became the pulp mill flunky, which was doing all the dirty jobs that no one else wanted to do. But the $1.25 an hour pay was good and I jumped into every job with enthusiasm. I did Joe's job on the rock tower when he hurt his back. This involved loading huge limestone boulders into a two-wheeled cart. Some of those rocks weighed as much as I did. When the cart was full, you pushed it into the elevator and rode to the top of a seventy foot tower. Then you opened a trap door and dumped the load into the tower. One whiff of the acid fumes rising from the hole just about took your head off. I learned to hold my breath like a pearl diver. You also wanted be careful to not follow the rocks down the hole!

Sometimes they would try to run the pulp through the rollers too fast, so instead of drying into a long continuous sheet, it would come apart and drop down below the huge hot rollers. Guess who they called to clean up the mess? It must have been a hundred and thirty degrees under there, and you could get scalded when hot drops of water hit you. You loaded the pulp into a cart and dumped it into a huge wooden kettle where the beater mixed it into a soupy mess which was then recycled to the mainstream. What a job!

"Rich, the conveyer is getting clogged up again . . . you better go out on the pile." The pile was a mountain of wood chips and sawdust which came from the sawmill. All the wood that wasn't good for lumber went to a chipper where it was chopped up and then sent to the chip pile via a long conveyer. The chips would mound up where they fell from the conveyer and jam the works. You climbed up there and dug at it with a pitch fork until you caused an avalanche of chips to cascade down the pile. Then you moved on to the next jam, and so on. When they used the chips as fast as the sawmill produced them, then there was no problem.

Sometimes they would crank up a huge bulldozer, and with a couple of sweeps, they moved more chips than I could move in a week. One day, I pointed that out to the supervisor, and that was the last time I had to work on the pile.

One morning, I got word that the supervisor wanted to see me in his office.

"Oh, oh . . . wonder what I did now?" I ran to the office.

"Rich, we understand that you took chemistry in high school?"

"Yessir, I did."

"Well, our chief chemist has been sick for quite some time, and just the other day we got word that he has terminal cancer. So we are going to have to find someone to take his place. We are wondering if you would like to move into the lab? We could train you right on the job!"

Wow! I had seen the lab and it was really something. I hesitated, "Well, you know that I was planning to enlist in the Air Force . . . I'm hoping to get into Cadets and learn to fly . . . and then I would also qualify for the GI Bill so I can go on to college!"

"That sounds great, but man, you could soon work up to eight dollars an hour . . . and you would have a wonderful job for the rest of your life!"

We talked for quite awhile. Finally, I left the office agreeing to think about it.

That night, I told Edna and Pearl. They, of course, thought it was a wonderful opportunity. Pearl laughed, "Why, you could be earning double what I'm getting now . . . and I've been there for over eight years!"

I spent a lot of time down in the wooded canyon . . . my quiet place. Should I take the chemist job, or should I sign up? Everything said I should take the job, but I just had no peace about it. The short of it was . . . I turned down the job, my uncle gave his approval, and on September 6th, 1946, Pete Cowan, a high school classmate, and I enlisted in the U.S. Army Air Force at Portland, Oregon.

Our group was shipped off to Fort Lewis, Washington, where we were issued our army clothes, and they took our civvies. We were assigned to a barracks and we were taught how to make up our bunk beds, army style . . . how to hang our clothes in the locker, army style . . . how to have a GI party every night, army style . . . everything was done army style. We were marched off to the barber shop where we were relieved of a lot of our hair. We were marched off to classes where our brains were indoctrinated with all the aspects of army life.

In one of the classes, they showed us a real gung-ho rah-rah movie about the paratroopers. Right after the movie they had a place for us to sign up for the paratroopers. Being the real rugged type, Pete wanted to sign right up. I hesitated, "Jumping out of airplanes looks like a real fun thing to do, but once you are on the ground, you're nothing but a ground pounder . . . I think I'll stay with the air force . . . I want to get into cadets where I can learn to fly!" Pete reluctantly stayed with me, and four days later, they shipped us off to San Antonio, Texas, for eight weeks of basic training. Yahoo!

About a hundred of us were assigned to a two story barracks which was called a squad . . . a number of barracks made up a squadron. There was a keen competition between the barracks to be the best squad in the squadron which was rewarded with a two day weekend pass. The two next best squads were given one day passes. The rest were punished by having to do KP all weekend, and the squad leaders took out their revenge with hours of drill and GI parties far into the night, and then up at four in the morning for some more drill.

Guys who really screwed up were singled out for special attention for push-ups until they dropped, or were made stand at attention until they keeled over, or they spent the night scrubbing the latrine with their tooth brush while everybody else was sleeping.

We had a real sharp squad leader who whipped us into a sharp squad in short order. We won the drill competitions. We had the cleanest, neatest barracks, and we usually got the weekend passes.

Most of the guys went into town to booze it up and look for girls. Pete and I would go sightseeing; like the Alamo, a nice park, go to a movie, or sometimes have a nice meal at a good restaurant. Sunday mornings, I usually went to the base chapel for church, and then to the service club where I wrote a letter home, or sometimes played table tennis.

All the marching and rugged calisthenics were to whip us into condition. To Pete and me, it was rather a joke because we were already in such good shape from the intensive phys-ed training we had all through high school. Absolute obedience to authority was nothing new to us. Vic Adams had trained us well. Basic training just fine tuned us a bit.

They gave us all a good physical exam. We were immunized with every kind of shot imaginable, including the square needle with a hook on it! They gave us a lot of aptitude tests to see if we had any brains. My IQ score was 124. Pete Cowan's was 167! They said this was the second highest that anyone had ever scored!

One of the incentives they gave us to enlist was that we could choose the kind of school or training we would like to take after we completed basic training. And true to their word, near the end of our basic, they posted a list of the schools that were to be available to us. More than 100 types of training, but nowhere on that sheet could I find Cadet School. My heart dropped clear down to my boots!

Sarge yelled out, "Choose three of the schools that you see on the bulletin board . . . you will be sent to one of the schools when you complete your basic training!"

I chose three schools that would put me in as close proximity to airplanes as possible . . . Navigator, Radio Operator, and Weather Observer. I forget what schools Pete selected.

To graduate from basic, we had to successfully complete a three day bivouac where we were to take part in a mock battle. They trucked us out to some wooded hill-country for this little exercise. It was a joke. The enemy who was to attack us, got lost, and never did find us. We spent the time looking for scorpions under the rocks, and trying to dig out an armadillo from his den. The obstacle course was a breeze. For some reason they didn't have time to run our group through the gas chambers. The three mile run in formation was done at a walk. So much for bivouac.

When we graduated from basic, they also gave some of us a stripe. So I was now, "Private First Class, Richard L. Schaffer, AF19277057, Sir!" Only thing it meant was that I got a couple more dollars of pay a month.

One day, they posted our schools on the board. Every guy jammed around trying to see where he was going. Next to my name was—Tabulator Operator Mechanic School. "Tabulator operator mechanic . . . what in the world is a tabulator operator mechanic?" (I learned later, this was the beginnings of computers.) "Hey, I didn't choose that . . . where's the Navigator, Radio Operator, or Weather Observer schools that I chose?" I began to panic inside.

The dumbest guy in our squad was going to Radio Operator school, and he didn't even choose the school! No one was listed for Navigator or Weather Observer. And Pete? They were sending him to Military Police School! A guy with an IQ of 167, and they were going to make him a dumb MP? Good grief! Pete was so mad he exploded!

He grabbed me and just about slammed me through the barracks wall, "I wanted to go into the Paratroopers, and I let YOU talk me out of it! Now look!!" After that little episode, I decided they had made a good choice . . . Pete would make a real good MP!

In due course they sent me to Lowery Air Force Base at Denver, Colorado. Tabulator school was in session. I would have to wait six weeks for the next school.

To keep us amused, they had us police the grounds every day, stuck us on kitchen police (KP), or they would just about drill us to death.

After about four weeks of this baloney, ol' Sarge came over to the barracks and announced, "There are two schools open . . . Clerk Typists and Auto Mechanics . . . take yer pick!"

So much for the choice of schools! I chose auto mechanics and they transferred us to our schools the same day. I laughed to myself, "I don't know the difference between a spark plug and carburator (see, I can't even spell it!) Oh, I'll make a dandy auto mechanic, I'll bet you!"

Primary Auto Mechanics was a course of ten weeks. Actually, they made it so simple, anyone with an IQ of 10 could learn to be an auto mechanic. That included me, and I really enjoyed it! They used a training film on a certain part, say the transmission. They showed you how to take it apart, replace the damaged parts, and put it back together again. Then you did it with a real live transmission.

You opened it up to find all the extra parts the guy before you had dropped down a hole, because he couldn't figure out where they should go!

And you did the same. "Yessir, that oughta make that one run just fine!"

Those of us who passed the Primary Auto could elect to take the Advanced Auto course which was another ten weeks with just a little more detail . . . you ended up with less parts down the hole!

Early in my time at Lowery, I found the tennis courts at the city park in Denver. Down at the east end was where all the good players squared off. And that's where I hung out. I wore only a pair of tan shorts, so most of the guys didn't know I was GI until I pulled out my sun-tans to get dressed. We really had some good slam-bang games and I got pretty sharp.

One day, I and another guy were really whopping the ball. A couple of pretty little gals came up and asked, "Would you guys like to play some doubles?"

"Sure!"

We thought, one for you, and one for me. But no, they wanted to play against us! We sorta laughed, "Ya, sure!"

Anyway, those gals just about beat the pants right off of us. They could really sock that ball. And they were steady, man, they were steady. Sometimes that ball would go back and forth, twenty, thirty times, on a single point. They served like men . . . ZIP! . . . it was past you if you weren't in the right spot. We really had to work hard to beat them 9-7 and 8-6.

In our talk after the match, we wondered if they were a couple of pros. "No, we are just a couple of the nurses from Samaritan Hospital!"

I also went out for the Base Track Team and practiced for the mile run. The winners of each event would compete in the all Air Force Meet at San Antonio. They didn't have anyone for the broad jump, so a bunch of us tried out for that. I jumped 17 feet 7 inches, the best jump, but that wasn't all that great. Anyway, in the mile, I decided to run a smart mile. BANG! Went the gun. We took off. I dropped in behind the lead guy and just stayed there. I couldn't believe how slow we were running and I was tempted to take off, but I played it easy and let the lead man set the pace for three laps. At the start of the fourth lap, I took off like a shot . . . like you would run the four-forty. I won the mile, half a lap ahead of the pack. Time was a slow 5:20. They embarrassed me, by giving me a gold medal for that wondrous accomplishment!

We flew down to San Antonio in an old DC-3. On the way, I wandered up to the cockpit.

The Captain grinned, "Would you like to fly it?"

"Sure!" I jumped at the chance.

He put the plane on auto pilot and gave me his seat. "Here's the compass . . . keep it on 195 degrees. Keep your altitude at eight zero. Here's the turn and bank . . . and here's the rate of climb. Keep the needles in the middle and you'll do just fine!" Then he took it off the auto pilot and left.

A wing would drop a bit and the plane would go into a slight turn. So I'd turn the other way to bring it back on course, but I'd go past the 195 degree mark on the compass, and I'd have to turn the other way. So we were wandering all over the sky. In the turns the nose would drop a bit, and we would start to lose altitude, so I would pull it up. When the oscillations got too great, the copilot would take the controls and get it all settled down. Then he would hand it back to me again. After about fifteen minutes, I thought I was sorta getting the hang of it, when the copilot said, "You're forgetting to watch a couple of your instruments, aren't you?"

"Which ones?"

He pointed at the rate of descent indicator, which said we were going down at 500 feet a minute, and the altimeter was unwinding at a good clip.

I hauled back on the wheel. The guys in back, who didn't have their seat belts on, suddenly found themselves suspended in space up near the ceiling! Also the pilot suddenly appeared to relieve me of my lofty position. Thus ended my first flight lesson, but I was truly in my glory . . . "Someday, I'm going to be an airplane pilot!"

The track meet at San Antonio was a real fiasco for me. I waited and waited for the mile run. I couldn't wait any longer, and went over to a barracks to relieve myself. While I was gone, they called for the mile run! I got back to the track just as the gun sounded! Coach furiously climbed my frame. I was absolutely demoralized.

After a minute, the coach grumbled, "Well, maybe we can stick you in the half mile!"

"But I've never run the half mile run in all my life!"

Coach growled, "You just take off as fast as you can go . . . play like I'm on your tail with a baseball bat!"

And that is the way I ran the half mile. I took fourth place, which was actually pretty good, considering that I ran it in tennis shoes.

After I graduated from the Advanced Auto Mechanics, they shipped me off to Smokey Hill Air Force Base near Salina, Kansas, where I began working at the base motor pool.

One day, they put a couple of us to work on a Cleetrac, which is a caterpillar-like contraption they used to tow around and park the big airplanes.

You steered the thing by pulling on the brake levers. Pull on the left brake lever and you turned left. Pull on the right lever and you turned right. Great. Only trouble was, the brake bands wore out in short order. Every Cleetrac on the base had burned out brake bands, and it took two whole days just to get all the junk out of the way to even get at the brake bands with the knuckle-buster tools we used.

We replaced the brake bands and the ol' buggy steered like a charm. That's all we did for the next three months was replace those stupid brake bands. I could have done it in my sleep.

One day, they asked for volunteers to go to school for Heavy Duty Auto Mechanics. I declined. Someone told me, it would be about the same thing, only the junk we'd be working on would be about ten times heavier. Cleetracs were heavy enough for me.

One night, I was in the service club, writing a letter, and in walked Bud Terry! We were both on the same base and didn't even know it until that night. We played tennis every chance we got. Summer time in Kansas . . . you could have fried eggs on the concrete it was so hot.

Our barracks were makeshift tarpaper affairs with just a single outside wall and no ceilings. Because of a flu epidemic, they oiled the floors to cut down the dust. We had to climb on top of the bunks when we changed into our khakis to keep from getting all dirty. One night, one of the guys came back to the barracks drunk as a hoot owl. He amused himself by punching holes in the walls with his fist, until he hit a two-by-four and broke his hand.

They put us on a week of guard duty. My station was to patrol a huge ammunition depot, way out on the prairie . . . four hours on and four hours off around the clock. In the evening, it was fascinating to watch the hawks swoop down and give chase to the jack rabbits. You could hear the mournful howl of the coyote in the black night. There were a million stars in the milky way.

One night, the Sergeant of the Guard came snooping around. He refused to stop when I challenged him. I just about shot myself one smart Sergeant, and boy, did he ever get mad! "Just doing my job, SIR!"

Bob and Lu Swanson were stationed near Bellevue, Illinois, so one weekend, Terry and I got a weekend pass and hitch hiked there to see them. One ride was with the State Police who checked us out to make sure we were not going AWOL. We got another hair-raising ride across the whole state of Kansas with a salesman. Sometimes we were flying along at over a hundred miles an hour. Never saw a single police car.

We only had time for a short visit with Bob and Lu, so we went to some school ground to play tennis. The gate was locked. I snapped a good picture of Terry and Bob trying to pick the lock. We arrived late back at Smokey Hill, so we were confined to the base for the rest of our stay.

After about three months at Smokey Hill, they shipped us to an air base near San Francisco, staging us for shipment overseas. We could opt for a month's leave before going, and Bud Terry did that. I declined the leave so I could get out of the service a month early.

We were confined to the base to be ready to ship out at a moments notice. All our gear was to be packed and ready to move out.

One morning, we were ordered to form outside the barracks. "Okay, listen up . . . the guys I read off will be going to Korea! Adams . . . Anderson . . . Bentley!"

As each name was read, some unlucky guy would respond with a, "Yo!"

"Schaffer!"

"Yo!" "Yo!" Two guys answered!

"Richard Schaffer!"

"Yo!" "Yo!"

"Richard H. Schaffer!"

Some guy answered, "Oh Boy!"

He was shipped off to Korea, and I was shipped off to Japan! Many a time I wondered what ever happened to that other Richard Schaffer.

On that November day when our troop ship sailed out of San Francisco bay, it was sunny and warm. and the sea was running with a gentle swell. There were some 5000 troops on board. We were hardly out of sight of the Golden Gate bridge when most of the guys were hanging over the rail tossing their cookies. I thought it was rather amusing as I was feeling great. Four days out, we ran into a huge weather front. Then it was my turn to hang over the rail. The ship was tossed about like a small chip of wood, and the storm lasted for days. Everyone was sicker than dogs.

One night, the foul stench in our hold was more than I could stand. I went up and out on the deck to get some fresh air. It was raining hard and the wind was howling in the rigging. The ship was pitching stem to stern as it staggered over the mountainous swells and then abruptly fell into the next trough.

I pulled myself along a rail as I worked my way toward the bow. Suddenly, the ship shuddered violently and rolled toward the port side. I was slammed hard to the deck and started sliding toward the outer railing on my tummy. I desperately grabbed and clung like a leech to a steel girder as I went sliding by. Another six feet and I would have gone over the side! And no one would have ever known!

When the ship rolled to the starboard, I released my grip on the girder, and I was flung over against the bulkhead, where I staggered to my feet and jumped through a doorway. That was a close one!

As I made my way back to the hold, I could hardly walk . . . something was wrong with my right knee.

The next morning, my knee was swollen and hurting, so I limped my way to the ship's dispensary. The orderly wrapped it with an Ace bandage and told me to take it easy. After a couple of days, the swelling went down.

One day, another guy and I were fooling around, play wrestling. I hooked his leg with my foot to flip him to the deck. A shot of pain hit my knee and I was the one lying on the deck in agony.

They carried me to the dispensary where a doctor took a look. He put an ice pack on my knee. "Looks like you've torn some ligaments, Sonny, best you stay off that leg for awhile!"

They rubbed my knee with liniment and wrapped it up again with another Ace bandage and put me to bed. 'Bed', was the top canvas bunk down in the third deck of the troop carrier. I had a fun-time trying to climb up six bunks when my right leg would hardly support any weight. Believe me, it was much better to be up there, rather than down below when the guys were seasick! The air was so stale and foul you could hardly breathe.

It took us seventeen stormy days to reach Korea where 3500 GI's disembarked. I stumbled up on the deck to watch the Koreans unloading supplies from the hold. This one guy had a mean looking knife in his belt. He drew his finger across his throat as he glared at me with a wicked smile. Man, I was out of there fast! Our ship went back to Japan where we unloaded at Yokohama. With my bum leg, I really had a time carrying my duffle bag down the gangplank. They put us up in the barracks at a former Japanese cavalry base. The weather was damp and gloomy, and there was no heat or hot water in the place.

A couple of days later, we boarded a train for a two-day ride to Itazuke Air Force base which was located on the southern island of Kyushu, Japan, near the city of Fukuoka. The train slowly chugged its way through the beautiful pine covered hills. Some of the steep hills were terraced. Every inch of level ground was devoted to agriculture.

Whenever we stopped for a moment, swarms of children would try to sell us their wares. I'm sure they did very well, as we newcomers ignorantly paid the asking price. I bought a small bag of tangerines which were very sweet and juicy. I noticed how drab and poor the villages and the people looked. Everything was a dull gray, black, or dingy white.

I'll never forget as our train inched its way through what was left of the city of Hiroshima, which had been completely obliterated by a single atomic bomb. A portion of a concrete wall or smoke stack here and there. The utter destruction. The desolation. No one lived there. However, if we had not dropped that bomb, our countries no doubt would still be fighting one another.

Our train continued down the main island of Honshu. As we neared the south end of the island, the train slowed down to a crawl. Suddenly, the world went dark. We were entering the tunnel that would take us under the ocean for seven miles to the southern island of Kyushu! The Yellow Sea has an average depth of 58 meters. How deep was it between the islands? And how deep was the tunnel below the water? There were no lights on the train and it was pitch black. It gave me a very uneasy feeling. What if there was an earthquake? We were down there forever . . . maybe a half hour. Suddenly, we broke out into beautiful sunshine.

The train pulled into the depot at Fukuoka, and we were immediately loaded into the awaiting trucks which took us to the Itazuke Air Base. We arrived just after noontime so they took us over to one of the mess halls to eat lunch. The little Japanese girls already had the place cleaned spic and span. As we were standing in the food line, one of the girls came from the kitchen, carrying a heavy tray with bread-pans full of silverware. She slipped on a wet spot on the floor and landed with a resounding crash . . . the silver went every direction. Instantly, I leaped over and lifted the unfortunate girl to her feet. She was very embarrassed and blushed appropriately. She was simply beautiful. I helped her pick up the scattered silverware, and then I picked up the heavy tray and carried it to the table. When I turned around, everyone was riveted in place like statues . . . you could have heard a pin drop. I took my place in line and finally things started moving again.

Later, I learned that I had done a thing of wonder. Women in Japan are not treated with kindness by men. I had a lot to learn about the culture in this beautiful land. But I found that my small kindness paid huge dividends when I went through the line, as the serving girls would load my tray high with food!

I was assigned to the 5th Communications Squadron of the 5th Air Force. This squadron had its own motor pool, completely separate from the base motor pool, and we were to be ready to move out at a moments notice. We had four mechanics to maintain the four Jeeps, four Dodge weapons carriers, six GMC 6X6's, and a couple of radio communications trucks.

Photos of my 20 months at Itazuke Air Force Base Japan, as Auto Mechanic, 5th Communications Motor Pool, and our 4 Jeeps, 4 Weapons Carriers, and six GMC 6X6's.

We did a monthly inspection where we did a tune up, checked and fixed everything to keep those vehicles in tip-top condition. We had priority on parts over the base motor pool, therefore, we had some of the best running vehicles on the base. The base motor pool was always agitating to take over our vehicles.

Actually our whole squadron was one sharp bunch of fellows. They were the radio operators and the cryptographers who handled all the secret communications for the base.

I developed quite a close friendship with Charlie Accord. Not once did I ever get the slightest word about his job, but he usually got quieter than usual when something was getting hot. He and I hung out at the base chapel where we fellowshipped with a keen bunch of Christian guys under the able leadership of Chaplain Winston E. Sutterfield.

We hung around the chapel a lot

He and his beautiful wife, Marcella, often invited the whole gang into their home in the evenings for hot chocolate and cookies. They had three wonderful children; Alfa Jo, who was about thirteen, Tommy was about ten, and I fell in love with their little four year old, Alice Kay, who was every bit a Shirley Temple with her curly brown locks and dimpled smile.

My little Alice Kay

Often on the weekends, we checked out a 6X6 and went on outings to the beach, or maybe a Shinto shrine, or hiking in the hills. When Alice Kay became tired, I usually carried her high on my shoulders.

The Chaplain and his wife became known to us as "papa and mamma Sutter". Under his simple teaching of God's Word, and rubbing shoulders with these fellahs, I began growing in the Lord. We had morning and evening services on Sunday, Bible study Wednesday night, choir practice Thursday night, and Youth for Christ on Saturday night, so we had a lot of opportunity for Christian fellowship.

Chaplain Sutterfield   *Momma Sutter*

All I had was a GI issue New Testament, so I ordered from the States a Thompson chain-reference Bible like Papa Sutter used. It took forever to arrive. When it came, I began devouring God's Word. I memorized verses, even whole chapters like; Psalm 22 and 23, Isaiah 53 and 55, John 3, the Sermon on the Mount, Romans 8 and 12.

Guys in the barracks began calling me preacher boy as I sometimes voiced my convictions. As we went around on our tours of the beautiful countryside, we often dropped gospel tracts to the people we passed on the road.

About a mile northeast of the base was the highest hill in the area. One day, several of us climbed to the top. The beautiful slopes were heavily wooded and the trail was steep. At the very top was a Shinto shrine. There were three sets of long wooden stairs which led up to the shrine.

Just as we arrived, a ragged old woman came down the stairs. When she got to the bottom, she paid no attention to us, just as if we did not exist. She picked a leaf from a small bush, cupped it reverently in her hands, bowed humbly, and said a short prayer. Then she started up the steep stairs, bowing with little nods, as she went. Again she came down the stairs to repeat the whole ritual.

I went off to the side and climbed up to the shrine another way and hid behind some bushes to see what she was doing at the shrine. The old woman kneeled and prostrated herself to the ground, laid her leaf before the altar, clapped her hands, and prayed in a sing-song voice. Then she went hurrying down the stairs.

When she was gone, I slipped out from the bushes. Before the altar laid seven leaves. I picked up the leaves, and in their place, I laid a Japanese New Testament. Then I returned to my hiding place.

As before, the old woman came prayerfully bearing another leaf. She kneeled before the altar; her eyes opened wide when she saw the book! Joyfully she picked up the New Testament and held it toward the heavens, crying loudly with tears streaming down her face. She bowed and clasped the book tightly to her bosom and went flying down the stairs and off through the woods. You could hear her joyfully laughing and shouting along the way.

Dr. Paul Lanier Ogburn and his wife, Merlene, sang in the choir. Both of them also played very good tennis. However, we hardly ever finished a set because Lanny, as the base doctor, would be called off to the hospital for some emergency.

Lanny was born in Japan, the son of missionary parents, who lived most of their lives serving the Lord in this country. Lanny could speak Japanese like a local. One time, we were in town buying souvenirs in the small shops. You had to barter in order to buy things at a reasonable price. Lanny would start out in English and animated sign language. Suddenly he would switch to the most eloquent Japanese, and their mouths would drop open in shock! We could have walked away with the whole shop!

Being a Corporal, I felt rather strange hob-nobbing around with a Captain, and other GI's really gave us the eye. But Lanny was just a plain ordinary guy. When he lost someone in surgery, it was such a shattering experience for him that he could hardly cope with life for the next few days. I never saw such a humble considerate caring person in all my life.

We won several local tournaments which qualified us to compete in the finals at Tokyo. When we flew to Tokyo in an old C-47, the weather was really bad. We bounced all over the sky, and I got so airsick that I could hardly stand up. When we arrived over Tokyo, we just circled and circled for over an hour . . . the field was socked in with fog. Suddenly, word came from the cockpit, ordering us to put on our parachutes! We were running low on fuel, and we might have to jump! Good grief!! We hastily put on our chutes, and we were ordered to stand up and hook our straps to the line. I was the last in line. We just stood there and stood there. The plane bounced all over the sky. I got so woozy I thought I was going to pass out. So I unhooked my strap and laid down . . . "You guys go . . . then I'll follow!"

Word came from the cockpit, "Sit down and buckle up tight . . . we're gonna try one GCA approach . . . if we don't make it, you'll have to jump!"

Down, down we came . . . the fog was so thick that we could hardly see the wing tips. Suddenly, we broke clear of the fog just fifty feet above the runway. The plane flared out, and ker-plop, we were on. Ground Control had talked the pilot right down to the runway. I whispered . . . "Thank you, Ground Control!" . . . "Thank You, Lord!!"

The next day, I still didn't have my legs under me when I had to play my first match. I lost it badly to some guy that went clear to the semi-finals. Lanny was knocked off in his second match. The guy who won the singles was about six-foot-six and built like Charles Atlas. He hit his first serve so hard that you couldn't even see it. Lanny and I teamed up for doubles, and we got creamed in the first round.

Our squadron had a badminton tournament and I won the singles. Charlie Accord and I teamed up and we won the doubles. Our squadron won the base volleyball tournament, beating the commissioned officers in a real slam-bang two-out-of-three squeaker. We did pretty good in basketball too. One time, I was late for the game and got in on part of the last quarter. I was so hot that I made 17 points in about four minutes! Everything I tossed at the basket was a swisher . . . but we lost the game by one point.

I thought I was pretty darn good, so I went out for the base basketball team. We had a screwball coach with an oddball offense that kept most of the players guessing most of the time. I played second string and got to play in most of the games. I did okay in some of the games . . . in others, just so-so. One time, we toured all over Japan for about a month and did nothing but play basketball. Our team was known as the Itazuke Bums. We were really a rag-tag bunch, but we managed to take second place in all Japan with fifteen wins and five losses.

The base basketball team   *Receiving our medals*

A bunch of giants from a little radar base beat us out by five points. They played a zone defense on their micro-court that was almost impossible to penetrate. It might have been another story if that game had been played on a regulation sized court. They went on to play in the all Pacific tournament in the Philippines.

On our weekend outings, sometimes we would go to a small village to distribute tracts and Japanese New Testaments. The people would gather in the village square and one of the fellows would preach through an interpreter. As we were doing this one day, I got back late to the village square, and the meeting was already in progress. I stood in the background and listened to the sermon. I was thinking what a fine job the preacher was doing. The people were in rapt attention. And I heard someone behind me say . . . "And someday you will be a missionary!"

I turned around to see who was speaking, but there was no one there! A chill went up my spine. "But Lord, I could never get up in front of people to speak like this!"

"Maybe not now . . . but someday you will . . . don't worry . . . someday, you will be a missionary!"

I earned another stripe. As a Sergeant, that gave me an overseas pay of $120.00 per month. I regularly sent home ninety dollars to be put in my savings account, which had grown to about twenty four hundred dollars.

My brother learned of this tidy sum and asked to borrow four hundred dollars which he used to build their first house.

The extra stripe also gave me the privilege to move from the main area into one of the eight rooms situated on the ends of the barracks. That was really nice. I shared the room with a Catholic fellow, and we really got into some interesting theological discussions far into the night.

Chaplain Sutterfield's tour of duty was over and I drove them into Fukuoka to the train station. The night was black and stormy. The road was flooded with water in many places. With sad hearts we said good-bye to this wonderful family that so many of us GI's had grown to love. I returned to the base and went to the chapel where I kneeled in the darkness and cried until I could cry no more. My Alice Kay was gone. Chaplain Delbert Partin was a good replacement and he tried his best to fill "Papa Sutter's" shoes.

Chaplain Partin & Janie   *In the rice fields*   *Army days*

Things were getting hot in the Pacific theater. Planes from our base were bombing and strafing in Korea for six months before the people in America even knew that we were in another war. Our base was put on alert with blackouts every night. We took turns at guard duty. One night one of our guys took a shot at someone going over the wall near our motor pool. Some personnel from our base were shipped over to South Korea.

My tour of duty was coming to a close. One day, Lt. Hargins called me into the office, "Schaffer, you need to consider extending your tour!"

"I'd rather not, sir!"

We went round and round for over ten minutes. "Things are tough back home. People are out of work. You got it made here. We'll even give you another stripe!"

When he saw that all his arguments were fruitless, Hargins exploded, "Why in the world would you want to go home!"

"Well sir, I'm planning to go to college!"

"OH! . . . Why didn't you say so . . . I can't argue with that!" He warmly shook my hand and wished me well.

Our motor pool was combined with the base motor pool and we were moved over to the Eighth Motor Pool Squadron. I was assigned to a stall in the shop, and I had two Japanese mechanics working under me.

Not realizing how things were done in the base shop, I pitched right in, working just as hard and getting just as dirty as my helpers. With pigeon English and sign language they got across to me that I was supposed to be the big big boss, and they were my slaves. I was supposed to just sit, and they were to do all the work. I shook my head and got across to them that we were equal, and that I would work just as hard as they did. They must of thought, "Who is this strange white man?"

Most of the GI's did just sit around and let the 'gooks' do the work. But I learned from them and they learned from me. When I took a vehicle out for a road test I took them along and taught them how to drive. I taught them how to analyze a mechanical problem and then how to fix it.

Once a week I could buy a carton of cigarettes in the PX for a dollar. On the black market I could have bought a string of cultured pearls for one carton of cigarettes. I could have bought a Leica camera for twenty cartons of cigarettes. But sometimes I bought a carton and gave them to my helpers. They didn't smoke them, but used them in the market like money, which was equivalent to giving them an extra month's pay.

A couple of days before I was to ship out, they gave me some going away presents. One gave me a beautiful black lacquered photo album with a temple scene made with inlaid mother of pearl. The other gave me a pair of real silk stockings to give to my girlfriend when I got home! I gave them each a Japanese New Testament and a bunch of tracts. We parted with tears in our eyes.

I was on my way home three month's early because I never took any of my leave time. The skies were blue, the sun was warm, and the Pacific Ocean was as calm as a big lake. We were disappointed that our ship did not stop at Hawaii. It took us only eleven days to cross the big pond . . . the Golden Gate bridge was such a beautiful sight it that brought tears to my eyes. After twenty months, it was nice to be home again.

We were shipped to a regular army base to muster our separation. Boy, they really made it rough for us Air Force guys. One evening, we were forced to stand at attention for over an hour, facing into the setting sun. Some fat slob officer stood in the shade atop the barrack's fire escape, screaming every foul four-letter word invented. It was his pep-talk version as to why we should be re-enlisting into the army.

It must have been a hundred and ten in the shade. The sun was burning our eyes out. We didn't dare wiggle a hair. Guys began passing out, which made this idiot fly into an absolute rage.

They used every brain washing trick invented, trying their best to keep us in the service. Some of the guys fell for the propaganda. This harsh treatment only gave me more resolve to get out. They had to process us out which they did a little each day. After about three weeks of this circus, I was finally a free man . . . a civilian again! Yahoo!

I thought so much of the Sutterfields that I took a bus back to Palmyra, Missouri, to visit them for a couple of weeks before I went home to Oregon. Papa Sutter was pastoring a small Baptist church.

Sunday morning, Alfa Jo sang the solo, 'There is a Balm in Gilead' . . . She brought the house down as she sang the part, "When you cannot pray like Peter, when you cannot preach like Pa..!"

Tommy and Alice Kay had grown like weeds. Alice Kay's hair was now in curls and she was a carbon copy of Shirley Temple in every way. I spent two weeks with these wonderful folks and then I was on my way home.

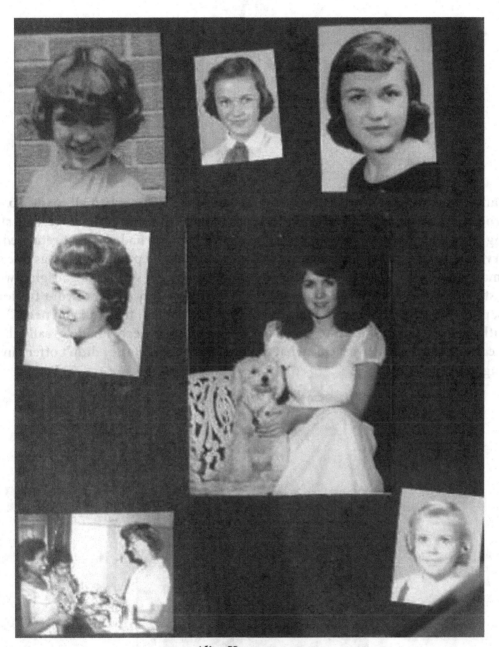

Alice Kay grows up.

CHAPTER 16
OREGON STATE COLLEGE

Edna and Pearl gave me a real welcome home, and they had my bed all made up in the store room. I figured that I didn't have enough money saved up for college, so I started looking for a job. I happened to bump into Bob Moore, who had also just returned from the service, and he was starting at Oregon State College in September. He was one of the real smart guys in my class in high school. "Rich, you better start college right away . . . if you start working . . . you will never go. The GI Bill will pay for all of your tuition and books, plus you get $75.00 a month for board and room. Man, that's all you need!"

With that pep talk, I was off to enroll at Oregon State College. I hadn't really thought about college and didn't have a clue what to major in. For sure, they didn't offer any pilot training here.

Oregon State College Days

My adviser suggested that I take a bunch of aptitude exams and from those they could give me some ideas. I got a score of 133, scoring high in the sciences and math, low in English and the liberal arts. But they also said that I had the vocabulary of a sixth grader, and a reading speed of 120 words per minute! With that handicap, they said that I would really have to buckle down and study hard. They suggested that I take a speed reading course, and that biochemistry should be my goal. So I enrolled as a chemistry major along with 250 freshman . . . most of them right out of high school.

I was assigned to room 203 on the second floor of Gatch Hall of the cardboard palace, a hastily built prefab dorm, that was to handle some of the expected swell of students, who were flooding the campuses of America, fresh from high school, plus a lot of guys from the armed services.

I lived in Gatch Hall on the 2nd floor of the "Cardboard Palace"

My roommate was Art Schlief from Hood River, Oregon, who was going to major in agriculture. I took the upper bunk of our 12 X 12 room, which was sparsely furnished with two beat-up old desks and a couple of rickety chairs . . . that was it. The mushroom painted walls were so thin you could talk right through them to Mitsuo Watanabe, next door, without hardly raising your voice. Board and room for all this luxury was $65.00 a month. The dining hall was a huge Quonset hut. While these facilities were meager, they really made up for it with all the abundant chow they fed us.

My classes were spread out all over the spacious campus, sometimes over a half mile apart, so I bought a bicycle, because you only had ten minutes between classes. The freshman chemistry course was just a refresher of high school. I loaded up with twenty one hours of classes. I took a speed reading course where I broke my lip-reading habits and increased my speed to 375 words per minute. Still I had to study twice as long to cover the same material as my classmates. It seemed that I was always studying while they were out playing. But I just loved to study. There was so much that I wanted to learn. I would go to college for the rest of my life!

This desire paid off with a 3.50 grade point the first quarter, while a lot of the freshmen goof-offs were put on probation. By the end of the next quarter, those who didn't settle down were given the boot.

Oh, I had my fun too. I took beginner's swimming in Phys Ed. In the spring I was on the freshmen tennis team. I sang in the men's glee club. I also joined the mountain club where we went climbing in the fall and spring, and skiing in the winter. I was also active in Intervarsity Christian Fellowship.

Like a good little Lutheran boy, I dutifully went to the Lutheran Church the first Sunday. It was next thing to walking into a funeral home. Dead! Now there happened to be a couple of live-wire, on-the-ball fellows in my dorm.

"Hey Rich . . . our youth group is having a hay ride this Saturday night . . . why don't you go with us?"

I went.

"Hi Rich . . . we're having a skating party Friday night . . . why don't you come with us?"

I did.

"We'll pick you up for church Sunday morning?"

"Okay!"

And The First Baptist Church is where I stayed. Before you know it, I was singing in the choir, going to prayer meeting on Wednesday night, to some youth activity Friday or Saturday night, and church Sunday morning and evening. A few times a year they had a spiritual weekend retreat at the beach or up in the mountains. Oh, I was a goody-goody little Christian all right, but there came that small wee voice in my conscience saying . . . "someday you will be a missionary!" But I kept that small voice way in the background with all my spiritual busy-ness. I also got diverted from my destiny another way.

One day, the mountain club went out to an old abandoned rock quarry where we practiced scaling the sheer vertical wall. You climbed with your fingers and toes, using every little crevice or rock protrusion to inch your way up the cliff. The rope around your waist was only there to catch you if you fell. It was fun. And there I met this beautiful girl, Barbara, with her sparkling brown eyes and long brown hair.

I met Barb in the Mountain Club

Barb and I started going on coke dates. We paired up when we climbed the Middle Sister and Mount Saint Helens. (We got up to the bulge where that mountain later blew its top.) These were usually weekend trips, or Sunday trips, which kept me from going to church like a goody Christian does every Sunday. Barb liked to go to the fun activities at the church, but I could tell she really wasn't all that excited about the church part . . . especially the altar calls they gave at the end of every service.

She also wanted to attend the dances held on campus, so we took a beginner's dance class. I took her to the school prom, and she looked 'oh so lovely' in her long flowing pink dress. We danced some fancy steps to a big name band. And that starlit night, we promised that we were going steady.

But it wasn't steady to church. In fact, it was getting less and less church all the time, and that really bothered me.

One warm sunny spring afternoon, we met under the trysting tree. But instead of giving her a ring, I gave her the gospel . . . very much to her disappointment. From that time on, both of us could see that our relationship was dead in the water, though we tried to keep it going.

School was over and we went to our homes for the summer. I visited her once, in Portland, and met her parents. We wrote several times, but the letters were cold and formal.

I got a job at Bill Morin's Shell gas station on the north end of Coos Bay. It was a busy place. Five us pounded the pavement, on the run, nine hours a day, six days a week, for three hundred dollars a month. We really gave first class service when we pumped gas. "Fill'er up, sir?" Big smile . . . "Yessir!"

While the pump was running, you checked the oil and water, the fan belt, and for any obvious mechanical problems under the hood that may give the motorist problems down the road. You washed the windshield and rear window squeaky clean. And you checked the air pressure in the tires. You ran to the till and back with the change. "Thank you sir, please come in again, sir!!" Big-big smile.

A grease job and an oil change for Chevrolet, Ford, and Plymouth cars was a dollar fifty . . . all other cars, two dollars. On the lube job, you also vacuumed out the inside, washed the windows inside and out, and you blacked the tires. A car wash was two dollars, where you also did all the extras. Fix a flat for two dollars. We always had races to see who could do the fastest job. Yessir, we really gave good, fast, and courteous service.

I bought my first car from one of the guys for a hundred dollars and my tiny Doodle Bug motor scooter. It was a baby-blue 1942 four-door Pontiac sedan that needed a lot of work. The paint was badly chipped and rusted. So I stripped it down to the bare metal and shot it with several coats of gray primer. Then I drove it over to a paint shop. They sprayed it with a new coat of blue for twenty five dollars. Wow! What a beautiful bomber!

I did a valve job, put in some new rod bearings, overhauled the carburetor, and did a tune up. It needed a brake job and a new set of tires. I dressed up the inside with a set of seat covers, rugs on the floor, and polished the wooden dashboard. That buggy was one fine car.

One time, I was racing with Bob Swanson. I got her up to ninety-five, with pedal still to go, when I chickened out. Second year students could have cars, so I took her to school.

Barb and I met again at school that fall. It was a no-go situation, so we mutually called it off. I bumped into her several months later, and she happily announced that she had fallen in love with a strawberry farmer, and they were going to be married next summer! That was great!

This experience made me rather gun-shy of the gals for awhile, as I learned a lot of girls were sent to school by their parents, hopefully, to nab a guy who had prospects of a better income in the future than say, a logger or a sawmill worker. I vowed that I would never get married until I had finished school. I dated some, but it was never anything serious.

Also I had to immerse myself into the second year of studies, as the honeymoon was over. Second year stuff was all new territory, and I was finding it increasingly hard to keep my grade point in the upper 10% of the class, where I had to stay if I wanted to get into research chemistry. But I just loved it. I studied, studied, studied . . . many times into the wee hours of the morning. Sure, I kept up on the church activities. And, in the spring term, I also won a spot on the varsity tennis team.

The tennis really took a lot of time . . . three to four hours every afternoon, five days a week, and then there were matches to be played on the weekends. Team members vied for place on the ladder where I was usually number five, or number three man. It made a difference, as the school provided free balls only to the first three men! You could wear out a set of balls in an afternoon with the type of slam-bang tennis we were playing, so there was real incentive to be in the top three. Balls cost money!

You could challenge two guys up on the ladder and they had to play you within the next three days. But when I was the number three man, I never had the guts to challenge the number one guy. He was an obnoxious intimidating little mutt . . . sort of like John McEnroe in temperament would be a apt description. And Megally was one of my arch rivals from Marshfield high!

But one day, when I was out on the courts early, this character showed up. Since there was no one else, he finally condescended to play with me . . . just hit the ball, you know.

And man, could I hit the ball that day! I matched him stroke for stroke . . . base line to base line. It worked into a full blown game as both of us had that fighting drive to put the other guy down. I aced him several times with my serve. I ran him all over the court.

Megally loved to charge the net and I would slam it down the line! He was going frantic. "You think you're hot . . . come on, give it to me!"

And I did! The next time he came to the net I drilled him right in the chest as hard as I could whop the ball!

"Ooops, sorry . . . hey, you're supposed to hit those!", I rubbed it in.

He slammed his racket so hard on the net that he broke it. Megally went absolutely berserk. He threw his racket at me, and stomped off the court! Yippeee!! I yelled after him, "Bet'cha I can clean your clock!"

I think the most interesting match I ever played was against a guy from the teacher's college. He was fantastically steady. Everything you put at him, he would just get it back . . . just get it back. Sometimes the ball would go back and forth, thirty, forty times a point. I would win the point only by slamming it so hard he couldn't get to it, or I would lose it by whopping the ball long or into the net. We started playing about one o'clock, and we were seventeen games all, still in the first set, when the match was called a draw. It was seven o'clock . . . everybody wanted to go home!

School was getting rough. I was burning the candle at both ends, and still I could not keep up. My grades were beginning to go down. And the Lord was speaking to me about this missionary stuff. But I was stubborn. I figured I could be a good little Christian just like everybody else, and yet, do what I wanted to do. But the Lord had other ideas . . . sort of like that line in the Hornet song . . . 'He just made them willing to go!'

Why, I could cram for an exam . . . know the stuff forwards and backwards. Then, in the exam, my mind would go completely blank. I would flunk it miserably. When I got outside, all the answers would come back to me! What's going on?

Quantitative Analysis was sure getting to me. You are cooped up for hours in those stuffy smelly labs, weighing those samples on the scales. Did I want to spend the rest of my life doing this? Maybe I was really an outside man.

The hand writing was on the wall. I didn't have to have too many smarts upstairs to figure that one out . . . I was gonna flunk it, and flunk it good! My grade point dropped to 2.33. But I was stubborn . . . I would switch my major to Geology. Thankfully, school was out.

SUMMER TIME

During world war two, when I was in high school, age fifteen, I got a summer job on the fire crew of the Coos Fire Patrol. There were no men around to hire. They had all gone off to war. So we high schoolers had a chance to do a real he-man's job. And what a job it was. That summer it was so hot and dry. We had some big fires . . . eight thousand, five thousand, and several three thousand acre fires, plus dozens of spot fires. We did the job just fine.

Anyway, I went back to the fire patrol, and they hired me as a warden. It was really a fun job. We had fourteen lookout towers scattered all over Coos County up on the high points of the coast range.

One of my jobs was to pack in the lookouts and all their supplies, open up the station, set up the radios, check the fire finder, clean out the spring, and anything else needed to make the place ready for occupation.

Thirteen of the lookouts were pretty young ladies! The only guy was a drunken bum they hauled out of the saloon every summer, got him sober, and stuck him up on his tower where he couldn't get to the booze. As long as he was sober, he was one of the best lookouts in the business.

I was on duty twenty four hours a day, seven days a week, for three hundred dollars a month. My bed was in a small attic room above the office. I went downstairs and monitored the radio at the crack of dawn until the dispatcher came, just in case a lookout called in early. Then I went off to breakfast. Boy, they really fed you! After breakfast, I got my pickup ready, hung around the office, waiting for something to happen.

Most of the time it was a boring job. But when one of the lookouts spotted smoke, I was sent to check it. Usually it turned out to be smoke from a burning permit that we had issued. When we did have a fire, I took a crew, built a trail around it, and then we put out the hot spots. That summer the biggest fire we had was a quarter acre! Coos County was nicknamed the asbestos forest!

THE THIRD YEAR

Geology was a whole new ball of wax. I really liked the courses, especially Mineralogy. Also the field trips were a lot of fun, as we studied the historic geology of the Willamette valley, the Cascade and Coast ranges. We dug fossilized gravel rocks and ancient sharks teeth from a bank on old highway 99, showing that the valley was once covered by the ocean.

I became active again at the First Baptist Church. After the Sunday evening service, the college and high school kids would get together for a sing. One night after the meeting, Jeannie and Patty had no way of getting home, so I offered the services of my blue bomber. I deliberately dropped Patty off first as Jeannie lived way out in the country. It was a beautiful moonlit night. Jeannie wasn't in a hurry to get out, so we sat and talked for a long time. Do you believe in love at first sight?

My Jeannie was the first true love of my life

As I drove home that night, I thought, "Man, she is really a wonderful girl!" And her one dream in life was to go to Bible school and someday be a missionary! "Oh boy . . . I really know how to pick 'em!"

We started seeing a lot of each other, but I didn't breathe a word to her about God wanting me to be a missionary! Its not that I had anything against missions or missionaries, I was just so backwards and shy . . . how could I ever be a missionary?

On a church retreat

At a beach outing at Oregon State College

The church was always having missionaries in, telling about their work and adventures. To me, they were all a bunch of gung-ho extroverts. They loved the limelight. They loved to be up front, talking to people. I really admired them. But me . . . no thanks . . . I could never be like that.

The missionaries always ended their presentation with a challenge to us young folks to give our lives to the Lord for missionary service. There was a lot of pressure by the church to come forward to the altar to dedicate our lives to the Lord. Jeannie had done just that, and she assumed that I had also, as I was so regular at all the church activities. I had her and a lot of other people fooled. I was one of those guys that sat up in the balcony, way in the back row . . . a back seat Baptist . . . but I had plenty of company. We hung onto those seats with all our might. Giving your life to the Lord, for whatever way He wants to use you, was a new slant for this goody little Lutheran boy. And go forward to the altar . . . in front of all those people . . . no way!! I was a good pretender, and I felt guilty as sin.

Late one afternoon at Intervarsity Christian Fellowship, we were shown a missionary film called "To Every Creature". It showed the hardships of missionary life in the jungle: how they sometimes spent days walking the muddy trails, or riding in narrow dugout canoes on rain swollen rivers. Sometimes they were cut off for weeks at a time, back in the jungle. And when sickness or an emergency struck, there was no way to help them.

Then the film showed how some mission organizations were beginning to use small light aircraft to aid the missionaries. A seven day trek through the jungle became only a 20 minute flight in an airplane. Short wave radios were being used for contact with the main base. The missionaries could stay on their station as the planes could easily supply them with food, mail, and medicine. It became a real morale booster to the missionary to realize they could be flown, in minutes, to a hospital when there was an emergency. I sat on the edge of my seat at the wonder of it all.

Then the film introduced how the Moody Bible Institute, in Chicago, was training young fellows to be missionary pilot-mechanics. It told about the four years of intensive training they received, preparing them for the often dangerous type of flying they would encounter in the remote areas of the world. And they were taught to maintain their own planes.

And then the Lord spoke to me . . . in that still small voice, "Yes, I know you are afraid to get up in front of people and talk. But isn't this something you could do for Me? You always wanted to be a pilot ever since you were a small boy!"

"Why yes, Lord . . . if You will get me in that course . . . I'll go!"

After the meeting, I went to the dorm and immediately wrote a letter to the Moody Bible Institute . . . in my excitement I even forgot to go to supper!

A couple of weeks later, a letter came from Moody. It contained a preliminary application to the Missionary Aviation Course.

They wanted to know everything about me. How I became and how long I had been a Christian. My Christian walk. My education, and work experience. My financial situation. My love life! Where did I hear about the aviation course, and why did I want to be a missionary pilot?

I wrote them pages, but I didn't breathe a word to anyone, not even to Jeannie. It was almost like a dream that I was actually doing this. Was I crazy to just throw away three years of college to go trotting off to a Bible school to learn how to be a jungle pilot? Maybe. So I figured that if I wasn't accepted, well then, I would just continue merrily on my way with the present course. "I'll fulfill my part of the bargain. Not accepted? Okay, Lord . . . I tried!" And no one would ever be the wiser.

One time there was this guy who went forward in church and announced that he had been called to be a missionary. Everybody thought he was so wonderful, and they made an absolute fuss over him. He just loved all the limelight and the attention. But when it came time for him go off to Bible school, he didn't go. His name became mud, and he faded from the scene. No, I would play it cool.

A few weeks later, Moody sent me a letter containing a formal application that was about six times as extensive. I spent over three weeks answering all their questions . . . all the heavy doctrinal stuff . . . what did I believe about God, the Trinity, the fall of man, salvation through Christ, who is the Holy Spirit, my prayer life, my devotional studies, how was I witnessing to others . . . on and on it went.

Tell us again about this vision of the rod when you were a small boy. Tell us more about your mechanical training in the air force. Tell us again how you were called to be a missionary when you were in Japan. Tell us again how God spoke to you when you saw that film on missionary aviation. Wow! . . . they were really looking me over! It felt hopeless that I'd ever be accepted.

Jeannie sensed there was something going on. I was acting so strange. "You're so quiet . . . what's happening with you?" I was sitting on pins and needles, but I just couldn't tell her about it . . . not yet, anyway. Naturally, I was wondering how she fit into all of this. Jeannie was just finishing high school, and with very little money, there wasn't a prayer for her continuing education. I got seventy five dollars a month, books, and tuition from the GI Bill. Married students going to Moody lived off campus wherever they could find an apartment. Could I commit myself to that? Questions. Doubts.

"Lord, You can work all this out." And He did . . . but hardly the way I expected.

About that time, a new guy started coming to our young people's group. Pat was an outgoing handsome fellow that really turned the heads of the girls. He especially caught Jeannie's eye at a swimming pool outing, with all his fancy dives off the low board. He really was a pro. And Jeannie was just nuts about swimming.

My Jeannie in pigtails

I missed a couple of meetings, and when I returned, I found that Pat had been taking Jeannie home. When I offered to take Jeannie home that evening, "Oh, Pat's taking me home!" I cried all the way home that night.

I finally heard from Moody again. They wanted a transcript of all my grades and courses that I had taken at Oregon State College. And they wanted me to take a physical exam, a timed monitored aptitude exam . . . and they wanted three references! "Oh me . . . now I'll have to tell some people!"

I talked to pastor Rodney Gould, and Bud Wildeson, the youth pastor, and told them what was going on. They were just pleased as punch . . . why, they would be happy to send in a good reference to Moody for me! "Don't tell anybody, okay?"

Youth Pastors Bud and Phyllis Wildeson

I wrote home to my aunt and uncle. They thought I was crazy, but agreed to send in a reference.

One of my geology profs monitored the aptitude exam. Wow! That was one rough exam! One of the local doctors gave me a thorough physical examination. Now it was the waiting game again.

The school year was coming to a close. Instead of going home, I stayed in Corvallis and rented a small apartment as I had the promise of a good job with a construction outfit. A whole two dollars an hour! It turned out to be a part-time job. They only called me when they needed another guy with a size fifty shirt and number two hat. It was a real back breaker.

Then I got on the brush crew with a bunch of kids from the church, clearing the right-of-way for a telephone company. One sixty an hour. That was a fun job.

Swinging an axe all summer long in the hot sun, my bronzed muscles became like steel. And a keen bond of Christian friendship formed between the guys on that crew.

When I got the letter of acceptance from Moody, naturally, I first told them the happy news. Jeannie got it second hand!

The next Sunday evening after church, she asked, "Could you take me home?"

The moon was big and yellow that warm summer night. We sat quietly for a long long time. "Why didn't you tell me?"

A long pause. "I don't know . . . I guess because it wasn't a sure thing . . . they only take twelve students a year . . . I figured there wasn't much of a chance for a guy like me. And you remember Joe . . . all the stir he caused . . . what a letdown!"

"But you could have told me . . . !" Jeannie cried.

"I'm really sorry . . . I should have told you."

I hugged her close for a long time. And it was during that time the Lord seemed to comfort us with the calm assurance that He had a plan for both of us . . . not the same plan. And that night, we humbly submitted to His will.

What Donna and Jeannie look like now

Jeannie and Pat as they are now

CHAPTER 17
MOODY DAYS

Four years in Moody's aviation course

Moody did not allow students to have cars on campus. So one weekend, I took the old Pontiac home, said my good-byes, and hitchhiked back to Corvallis, and continued working on the brush crew until it was time to go. I rode out to Jeannie's, gave my bike to her younger sister, Donna, and walked back to the highway to hitchhike all the way to Chicago. Jeannie was at work, so I missed saying goodbye to her.

"Gentlemen, welcome to Moody Bible Institute!" Mr. Paul Robinson, founder and director of the Missionary Aviation Course, spoke to us with authority and intense sincerity, measuring each sentence with a pause, giving time for our minds to absorb the words. "Four hundred and eighty seven young men applied for the Aviation course this year. Some of them had hundreds of hours of flying time . . . some had years of mechanical experience. We chose the twelve of you because we believe the Lord has already chosen you. We chose you only after much prayer and months of deliberation because we believe that you are truly sincere in your desire to become missionary pilot-mechanics who will go out to serve the Lord in that capacity. We are not interested in training you just to be pilots. We are interested in training you to be missionary pilots!" A long pause, as he looked each one of us squarely in the eyes. The air was charged with electricity. You could have heard a pin drop a thousand miles away. He had our attention. "If this is not your true intent, then you have no business here. If this in not your true intent, then we would ask you to step aside now, so your place can be filled by another who really wants to be a missionary pilot for the Lord!" Mr. Robinson paused again . . . no one moved a muscle. "In the next four years you will go through the most intense training in your lives. Only by God's help will you ever make it. Resolve to do your very best. Lives are going to depend on what you learn here!" Then a twinkle came to his eyes as he added, "that life may be your own!" WOW! What a guy!

The twelve chosen for the freshmen class of '52 were: Bob Cowley, Ollie Goad, Ken Huber, Ernie Krenzin, Johnny Lawless, Carl Mortenson, Norm Olson, Elmer Reaser, Jim Robertson, John Snavely, Lynn Washburn, and me . . . Rich Schaffer. Yippee!

The rest of the hour was taken up with pertinent information. The morning classes for the first two years would be strictly Bible school . . . after all, Moody was a Bible school. Our theological training was to be considered just as important as our technical training. Each quarter we would be assigned two Christian work assignments a week where we would put to practical use our spiritual training.

There were three technical schools . . . Aviation, Radio, and Photography. We would be taking classes in all three schools in the afternoons. Two afternoons a week we would be driven out to Wooddale Airport for flight training.

Goal for the first year was to have at least fifty hours flying time, and earn our Private Pilot's license. We would build up hours and cross country experience the second year. The third year we would move away from the school to wherever we could find a place to live, and that year would be completely devoted to our mechanics training to successfully earn our A&P license (Aircraft and Powerplant). The fourth year, we would go back to the flying, working toward at least three hundred hours of flying time, and earning our Commercial Pilot's license.

The twelve of us were so charged up we could hardly contain ourselves. By God's grace, we would become the best missionary pilots in the world!

Moody Bible Institute was right in the heart of Chicago. That year Moody enrolled 1350 students, about 100 more than they could house on campus, so they leased the whole sixth floor of the Lawson YMCA, two blocks east on Chicago avenue. My room was barely big enough to squeeze in a single bed, a desk, and a dresser. Just four feet outside my window was a brick wall . . . what a view! This country kid was beginning to get that hemmed in feeling. But I found Lake Michigan several blocks east of the YMCA, and a little bit to the north, along the shore, was Lincoln Park, where I could wiggle my toes in the green grass when I was about to go crazy. One day, some guy dug up a piece of turf from Lincoln Park, and put it in a coffee can. He set the can in the middle of the Moody blacktop, along with a little sign which read—Moody Campus! That was the only grass I ever saw at Moody.

All the skid row bums in Chicago lined the two blocks every morning at 0630 to greet us, as they soon learned that Moody guys were a soft touch for the, "Gimme a dime fer a cup a coffee?" routine. Along with the dime, I usually gave them a gospel tract, a cheery good morning, and a big smile. Several times, if they were in really rough shape, I took them to the local beanery on Clark street, and bought them a meal. I found they never threw my tracts in the gutter when I treated them like a human being. The hard cold winter wind that came howling off the lake really made life miserable for these guys who were "down on their luck".

The dining room at school was a thing of amazing efficiency. They could feed over a thousand students in one sitting in less than an hour . . . the men on the north end, and the women on the south end. Ten students to a table. Where you sat at the table gave you a certain duty to perform during the meal. The person at the north end was in charge and kept order. He made sure everyone got their fair portion of the main dish. Most meals were rather simple, and sometimes, just more food would have been a grand idea. So if refills were announced, survival depended on a person with quick feet to get there before it was all gone. Then one was assigned to keep the water pitcher filled. Another was to take the main dishes and serving dishes to the kitchen, where the student crew efficiently washed and scalded them. Dessert dishes, glasses, and utensils followed at the end of the meal. A number of students earned their way through Moody working in that dining room.

The evening meal was a dress affair. Because we were always getting back late from the airport, the fly boys were assigned a special table near the door at the women's end, where we could sneak in, and we were allowed to come in our grubbies.

Man, those gals were always pulling all kinds of tricks on us. Salt in the sugar. Sugar in the salt. Water sitting in our chairs. Glasses full of water turned upside down on our plates. But we gave it right back to them. I became a dead shot with a wadded up napkin into a water glass fifteen feet away! Yuk!

After breakfast, we had chapel in the basement of the would-be Torrey-Gray auditorium (the rest of the building would come when funds allowed). We literally raised the roof (or was it the main floor?) when over a thousand students sang in full chorus the wonderful songs of the faith: Amazing Grace, Wonderful Grace of Jesus, And Can It Be That I Should Gain?, He Lives, Onward Christian Soldiers, My Anchor Holds. WOW! It sent shivers down my spine.

It blew my mind to realize there were so many young people who were training to be servants of the Lord. And the Lord had chosen me to be one of them! We had some of the best of the spiritual giants in the world, who came to challenge us in that venture. God bless the school that D. L. Moody founded!

In the morning, we had Bible school for sure. Bible 101, Theology, Doctrine, Bible History, Church History, Missions, in depth study of the gospel of John, Personal Evangelism. There was so much to learn. But of all that I had at Moody, I learned more from the Christian Work Assignments than all of the classes put together.

My first two assignments were: Japanese visitation, and teaching a Sunday School class in a small black church on the south side of Chicago.

We had a group meeting for the Japanese visitation, where we were given a phone directory for all the Japanese who lived in the Chicago area. Then we were paired up in boy-girl teams. From the directory we were to obtain addresses, go out, and knock on doors at least once a week, find and talk to Japanese people about our faith in the Lord. Each week we were to write up a report on how we did. Oh boy! I was absolutely petrified! "Even now Lord, come quickly!" That was one of my prayers the good Lord never answered. I was stuck with it!

Because I had classes all day long, my partner, Jenny, and I decided to go visiting on Friday evenings. We took the subway to the south side of Chicago to an area where there was supposed to be a concentration of Japanese people.

It was spooky dark, and the streets were deserted. And it was cold. We used a flashlight to match names to an address. When we knocked on a door, it was rarely opened, and then, only a wee crack.

Moody Christian Work Assignment—South Side Chicago—Sunday School

"Hi . . . We're from Moody Bible Institute and we're lookin' for Sangi Yammamoto . . ."

"He don' liv heah!", and the door would slam shut in our faces. Of all the doors we knocked on that night, we only found two Japanese, and they did not let us in. We gave up.

The next Friday night, it was the same thing. But we stumbled upon a Japanese church, and found the parsonage next door. We knocked on the door, and it opened just a crack.

"Hi . . . we're from Moody Bible Institu . . .!"

The door swung open wide, he grabbed us, pulled us inside, and quickly shut and locked the door. "What in the world are you kids doing down here at night? Why, it's a miracle that you're still alive! Don't you ever, ever come down here when its dark!!" With that, he pushed us out the door, "Get outta here as fast as you can!" He slammed and locked the door . . . "of all the stupid!" . . . we heard him screaming as we left his porch. We were really shook!

As we rode the deserted subway back to Moody, we agreed, "Maybe Saturday afternoons would be a wiser choice?"

We gave up looking for Japanese. We knocked on every door and talked to anyone who was willing to listen to this brash impetuous couple. The best contact we had was a couple of high school girls who bombarded us with dozens of questions about our Christian faith. They were really hungry to know Him. If we didn't know the answer, we got the answer, and talked to them the following week. When it really came close for them to make a decision to accept Christ, we were told their parents did not want us to come any more. It literally broke our hearts.

Mr. Robinson called, "Brakes!"

I dug my heels into the brakes and returned, "Brakes."

He flipped the propeller through several times, and then called, "Contact!"

I turned the mag switch on. "Contact!"

As he gave a hefty pull on the prop, the engine roared to life. I eased back on the throttle a bit. Mr. Robinson came around, climbed into the front seat, and cinched down his safety belt. He waggled the controls all around to check their freedom.

"Okay, I'll taxi it out a bit . . . you follow me through on the controls!"

We started to move.

"Keep the stick tucked back into your gut. Sitting back there, you can't see over the nose, so when you taxi, you gotta keep weaving back and forth to make sure you don't run over somebody, okay?.. Now you try it!"

Wow! It's all like a dream. I sit here in front of this old computer, jogging my foggy brain back to Monday, September 9th, 1952, almost forty one years ago, to recall my first flight lesson in that little yellow Piper J-3 Cub . . . number 6875Hotel. I accumulated ten thousand, one hundred hours in my twenty years of flying on the mission field. (Man, I still have calluses on my rump! That's a lot of sittin' for a kid who never sat still five minutes in his life!) And having not flown a plane for the last sixteen years . . . yessir, it's just all like one big foggy dream!

I took over the controls and continued taxiing down to the west end of this lush green cow pasture called Wooddale Airport. The wind was blowing about ten knots from the east. The sky was a deep crisp blue. Little white puffy cumulus clouds covered approximately half the sky.

Mr. Robinson took back the controls and parked the Cub so you could see the incoming traffic. He ran through the pre-takeoff check, and then had me do it. Set the brakes, do the engine run-up and check the mags, check the gas gauge, check the instruments, and check the controls.

"Okay, I'll take you around the pattern . . . pay attention to the headings and the altitudes . . . and before you make your turns, look around, there are other guys up there tooling around, you know!"

He rechecked for incoming traffic, and taxied onto the runway.

"Follow me on the controls!"

He pushed the throttle full forward, and the 65 horsepower Continental roared to life. As the plane picked up speed, he pushed forward on the stick to pick up the tail. Then at the right speed, ease back on the stick . . . the little yellow Cub jumped into the air. Mr.

Robinson corrected for a slight crosswind and climbed straight ahead to four hundred feet. He leveled out, lifted the wing a bit, looked back and to the left before doing a left turn. Then he continued the climb up to five hundred feet, leveled out, cleared for, and made another left turn. We were now on the downwind leg.

"Here at Moody we keep the pattern at five hundred feet because we are so close to O'Hare Field. Even at that, keep your eyes open . . . we've had some of those jokers come through here even lower than that!"

At the end of the downwind leg, Paul looked around, turned to the base leg, and eased back on the throttle. We descended in a gentle glide.

"Always check to the right to make sure someone isn't coming straight in on final . . . I want that head of yours to be always swiveling around . . . every direction . . . you're gonna wish you were born with eight eyes in your head before I get done with you!" He turned onto final.

"Notice we have a slight crosswind . . . see how it wants to carry us off to the right of the runway? You correct for the wind by dipping your wing into the wind just the right amount . . . like this . . . see?" He dipped the left wing. "Or you can turn slightly into the wind." And he showed me that method.

"You pick a spot on the runway, and fly the plane right down to it . . . if you are dropping below your spot, add a little power . . . if you are moving above your spot, ease off on the throttle . . . slow her down . . . speed control's everything."

As we neared the ground, Mr. Robinson slowly cut the power, and eased back on the stick, while keeping the left wing tucked down to keep the plane from drifting sideways. We touched down three point, so soft, you could hardly feel it.

"Ahhh . . . just like sittin' on a cold toilet seat at thirty below zero! Hey, do ya think you can do that? Okay, let's give it a try!"

I taxied the plane off the runway and down to the end.

"Let's go through that pre-takeoff check."

So I did the check again.

"Okay . . . now when you make the takeoff run, add the throttle slowly. The prop torque will make the plane veer off to the left, so you need to add a little right rudder to keep it going straight down the runway. When you get up a little speed, push the stick forward to pick up the tail, and then just let'er fly itself off. Think ya can do that?"

I checked for traffic, and taxied out to the runway.

As I gave her the throttle, the little Cub started bouncing down the runway faster and faster. I picked up the tail. The plane started veering to the left so, I pushed hard on the right rudder pedal. The plane turned sharply to the right. I pushed hard on the left pedal and the plane veered to the left. Things were getting out of control when Mr. Robinson cut back the throttle, straightened us out, and eased the tail back to the ground.

"Hey . . . you're a little hard on the controls . . . just easy on those pedals . . . just the right amount of pressure! Let's go back and try it again!"

I taxied back to the starting point for another try. Down the runway we went. I added just enough pressure on the right rudder pedal to keep us straight. Up with the tail. The little plane jumped off the ground. We were airborne . . . my first takeoff!

"See how we're drifting off to the right . . . turn into the wind a bit so we climb straight out." He dipped the wing slightly and brought it up again. "See? . . . We're cocked a bit to the left now, but we are tracking straight according to the runway. Now when we get

103

up to four hundred feet, I want you to level off, and hold it there, before you make your left turn!" Sitting in the back of a J-3 Cub, the student has a hard time seeing past the instructor to the flight gauges. You try cocking your head, to the right and to the left, to cover all the gauges.

When the altimeter read four hundred feet, I put forward pressure on the stick to level the plane. By the time I got leveled out, the plane was at four hundred and fifty feet.

"Okay, look around, and then make your turn!"

I looked to the left and back, and started my turn. You move the stick to the left. The left wing dips down. Add a little pressure to the left rudder to keep the ball centered. Add a little back pressure on the stick to keep your altitude. You are turning. As you are coming to a 90 degree turn, you pressure the stick to the right to pick up your left wing. Add a little right rudder at the same time. You are level and climbing to 500 feet. As you approach that altitude you ease back on the throttle, and then a little forward pressure on the stick to put the plane's nose on the horizon. You make another left turn, and you are on the downwind leg. Ease back the throttle to slow the plane down . . . add a little back pressure to keep your altitude. Look for planes entering the traffic pattern.

You pass the end of the runway, make another left turn, pull on the carburetor heat, pull back the throttle, and you are gliding down on base leg. Check to the right for any planes coming straight in on final.

At the right moment you make another left, and you are lined up on final. Adjust for any wind drift. Keep the correct glide speed. Pick your spot. Fly the plane right down to it. At the right moment, you ease the plane to a three point attitude, just a couple feet off the ground. You hit your spot, soft, like a feather. "Ahhh, nice landing . . . "are you sure you have never flown before?" Keep the stick tucked back. Ease the plane off the runway at the end of your roll.

Mr. Robinson brings you back to the real world, "Well, praise the Lord, we got down in one piece . . . I see that we have about a hundred things to teach you . . . wonder if we can do it in the next four years?"

"Let's go around again . . . this time, try landing a little closer to the ground! Dropping it in from ten feet up is a little hard on the gear, wouldn't you say?"

We went around the pattern a few more times. The last landing really was soft . . . like a feather. An accident?

"Hey, that one was pretty good . . . maybe we'll be able to teach you something after all!"

We taxied to the gas pump, and refueled the plane. Mr. Robinson filled in the first entry in my log book . . . flight time, forty five minutes . . . familiarization . . . P. Robinson #139777.

I was so high I never came down for two days!

On Wednesday, we did it again. After a couple of times around the pattern, Mr. Robinson took me out west of the field to show me the boundaries of the practice area.

I practiced making turns.

"Come on . . . keep that ball in the center!"

I turned left. I turned right. I did 180's, and 360's.

"Okay, let's take her home!"

Home? Good grief! Where's that? I was so twisted around, I didn't have a clue where the airport was. He left me to flounder around for awhile.

104

"We came out west to get here . . . so where's the airport?"

"East?"

"Yeah, that's a good guess . . . let's try it!"

So I turned to an easterly heading and eventually found the Wooddale airport, entered the pattern on the downwind leg, came in, and landed. Forty minutes on my second flight.

On my fifth flight, we started out with the usual takeoffs and landings. I took off, and was climbing straight out, when at three hundred feet, Mr. Robinson suddenly chopped the power and yelled, "Forced landing!"

I promptly tried to park that plane right there! I pulled the nose up, the plane stalled sharply, and dropped like a rock. Mr. Robinson banged the controls forward . . . "STICK FORWARD!!"

I established a glide. We were about a hundred feet above the ground.

"Where ya gonna set it down?"

"Down there!" . . . I pointed to the field straight ahead.

At fifty feet Mr. Robinson added full power . . . "Okay, do the usual pattern."

When we got back on the ground, we pulled over to the side, and parked, where I got a good tongue lashing . . . something about trying to kill my favorite flight instructor, and myself included! "And don't you EVER try turning back to the field!"

When he got done, I felt about two inches high. I was shot for the day. But, no sir . . . I wasn't done for the day . . . we went right back up and did it again. Dumping the nose, establishing a glide, until picking my field became automatic.

On base leg he cut the power. I turned into the field early and set it down easy like.

"Hey, good job . . . if you really know that you can make the field, go for it! Yeah . . . we just might be able to make a pilot outta you yet! Let's call it a day!"

When I climbed out of the plane, I was soaked with sweat, including a wetter spot in the crotch of my pants! I had second thoughts about becoming a pilot.

October 23, was a notable day in my budding flight career. Eight hours under my belt. After four times around the pattern, Mr. Robinson exclaimed, "Hey, you're doin' pretty fair . . . take me up to the gas pump and drop me off . . . think you can take this buggy around by yourself?"

"You mean, solo?"

As I taxied back out to the runway . . . man, that front seat sure looked empty . . . am I really ready to go it alone? "Sure . . . just keep doin' what yer doin'!" And I did . . . no sweat . . . in fact, it was just plain wonderful to not have an instructor around, climbing your frame all the time.

I shot five takeoffs and landings as instructed, and taxied to the gas pump. Norm Olson was there to snap a picture of aviation history that every pilot goes through.

Some of the upper classmen were also there to perform another ritual event in history . . . the cutting off of my shirt tail!

I nonchalantly climbed out of the J-3 Cub. Suddenly, I rolled under the fuselage, and took off across the field with everyone in hot pursuit! I dodged, just as Chuck Bennett tried to tackle me; he went flying in the grass. But they finally cornered me in the hanger.

My shirt tail was added to all the other shirt tails hanging around the office wall . . . all the fellows who had soloed before me in the Moody Aviation course. Inscribed on my tail was, "Rich Schaffer—Soloed 23 October 1952." I added a little pair of pilot's wings. As

I looked at all those shirt tails, I wondered where those fellows were serving the Lord on the mission field. "And where will You send me, Lord?"

Norm Olson also soloed that day. After ten hours, Johnny Lawless decided the flying was not for him, and he transferred to the radio course . . . he had been a radioman in the navy.

We had some real bad weather come through the Chicago area, so we never got back into the air until November 13th, about three weeks later.

I was handed on to my next instructor, Mr. Paul Wertheimer, pilot's license #20371, for his assessment as to whether or not I was missionary pilot material. Oh me! This guy was tough . . . X-army air force tough, for that's where he had honed his instructing skills to army specifications and perfection. He was about like a Banti rooster in size and temperament. Under his teaching, I learned to fly all over again . . . the Wertheimer way . . . absolute perfection was the goal.

During the next few weeks, many a time, I wondered if I had missed my calling. This guy just wouldn't ease off. Whew!

Yes sir, it was like a breath of fresh spring air to fly solo. And I could do it . . . to perfection. But whenever that cocky little rooster climbed into the cockpit, I literally froze on the controls. I would screw up, and knew I was screwing up, but I wouldn't do anything, until he corrected me, as in the only way he knew how to correct someone . . . the Wertheimer army way. Wow! I had a real problem. If I ever was going to be a missionary pilot, I was going to have to learn to fly the Wertheimer way. Traumatic as that may be, I was determined to get past this guy.

As I look back on this time, I have to thank Mr. Paul Wertheimer for never giving up on me. For I learned how to fly the Wertheimer way . . . to perfection . . . and many a time that saved my life on the mission field. For the plane became a part of me. It would obey my every thought . . . my every demand . . . flying free like a bird!

When we weren't flying free like a bird, we were learning things on the ground, like: Civil Air Regulations, about the weather, cross country navigation, how to figure out your ground speed, estimate a time of arrival at a check point or destination by using a navigation slide rule, radio operation and regulations, basic maneuvers, and all the rules that made the Moody flight school what it was.

After I had about twenty five hours in my log book, they had me plot a cross country trip on my chart. And on 23 April 1953, Paul Robinson rode with me on my first dual cross country flight . . . Wooddale to Rock Falls to Howell and return to Wooddale . . . flight time, three hours and ten minutes.

The day was CAVU. (Ceiling and visibility unlimited) The air was solid like a rock.

I left the pattern and established my heading to Rock Falls. Adjusting for the wind, I hit my first check point right on the button, figured my ground speed, and gave my estimate for the next check point and for Rock Falls.

Suddenly, Mr. Robinson chopped the power and yelled, "Forced Landing!!"

I immediately established a glide and picked my field in less than three seconds.

Mr. Robinson approved, "Good choice . . . continue on your route."

On the way he asked me for my alternate airport, heading to it, and how long would it take to get there. Oh Boy!

So I drew a line on my chart and figured my heading from where we were to my alternate, measured the distance, and using my slide rule figured the time and direction . . . all the while keeping the plane flying straight and level to Rock Falls. He seemed pleased with my performance and we continued on to our destination. I entered the downwind leg of the pattern and landed at Rock Falls. No sweat . . . I had done gooood! Flight time: One hour fifty minutes.

We refueled the plane and took off for Howell. The strong wind was blowing us off to the left of course, so I adjusted my heading and that took us right over my first check point okay. I landed at Howell and topped off the tank. On the way back to Wooddale we picked up a good tailwind so we made it home in twenty five minutes. No problem.

"Hey Rich, you did pretty good . . . think you can do this by yourself?"

"Sure!"

"Okay, plan on it the first good day we have!"

"Yahoo!!"

The weather was so bad the next week we never even went out to the airport. On April 5th I went up with Mr. Wertheimer and shot takeoffs and landings, but the weather was so poor that we gave up after twenty five minutes.

On the 7th, the weather favored us again and I did my solo cross-country: Wooddale to Howell to Rock Falls to Wooddale. Three hours, forty minutes. Mr. Roger Allison signed my log at Howell, and E.V. Curry signed it at Rock Falls.

Whenever the weather was good enough, we flew out to the practice area to practice such air maneuvers as: 720's, stalls, around pylons, pylon eights, slow flight, forced landings. Sometimes I'd throw in a couple Chandelles when no one was looking. When the weather was el-stinko, we stayed close to the airport and shot takeoffs and landings. I managed to sneak in a couple more solo cross countries.

And then the big day came. On June 12th, 1953, I went on a radio cross-country with Bob Stockley, CFI #160610, in a Cessna 170B to Joliet via Chicago radio. Then Mr. Robinson gave me the recommendation ride for my private pilot's license. And Mr. Wertheimer gave me the flight test. So with 52 hours and 40 minutes, I earned my Private Pilot's license. Yippee!! School was out, and I headed home to North Bend.

SUMMER BREAK

That summer, I took up my first passenger, my cousin Ardy in a J-3 Cub that I rented at the North Bend airport. First, the guy wanted to make sure that I really knew how to fly the thing, so we went up for a little check ride. One trip around the pattern and he was satisfied, in fact; he became so interested that he offered me a job working around the airport, but I already had my old job back as Warden with the Coos Fire Patrol.

We flew down the coast, near to Port Orford, and took pictures of Bald Mountain, where a geologist, exploring the area in the 1800's, had chipped off a sample from a giant meteorite (estimated eleven tons in size). The area matched the description of the geologist's report that I had discovered, tucked away in the library at Oregon State College. He died while an expedition was being formed to retrieve the prize. They never found it, and no one has ever found it to this day!

(Later that summer, I hiked back into that area and looked around; my dream of fame and riches soon faded when I surveyed the vast area from the mountain side. You could hunt for a hundred years and never find that hunk of rock.)

When we got back to the North Bend airport, the wind was blowing so hard that I landed in about thirty feet. As I taxied crosswind off the runway, I had Ardy hang onto the outer wing struts. Even then, the wheel on the windward side was lifting off the ground. Ardy was also being lifted off the ground, much to her great delight. They saw me coming, rolled open the hangar doors, and beckoned me to taxi right into the huge hangar. Good thing I didn't flip that buggy over on its back.

We had a wet summer, and again, we had a very good fire season. A quarter acre was our biggest fire. I sold my blue bomber for fifty dollars to a couple of the kids on the fire crew. I told them the starter was going bad, but that didn't deter them. They just pushed it to get it started, jumped in, and were off to town for a good time.

BACK TO MOODY FOR THE SECOND YEAR

We lost a few more fellows from our class. Ollie Goad decided that he really wanted to be a preacher and transferred to the pastor's course. Lynn Washburn dropped out to get married. (He continued his flight training in Oregon where he got his commercial license and a sea plane rating. Lynn, and his wife, Gerry, later came back to Moody as a special student for the mechanics.)

Then, when Elmer Reaser took the entrance tests for the Aviation course, his monitor had let him take all the time he wanted. One of Moody's spiritual themes was . . . "The Lord cannot use you if you have sin in your life." Elmer got to feeling guilty about that, and had a little talk with Dean Broman. It was decided Elmer would have to take the tests again. If he passed, he could stay in the course. But Elmer flunked those tests bad, so he was out. He could take the regular missions course and sit the exams next year. Well, He finally passed those tests the year we graduated! Elmer went on to be a fine missionary pilot, and served the Lord admirably for years with MAF.

Also the photography course was out. The teacher got caught in some hanky-panky affair and thus ended his career. Too bad, for I really learned a lot about photography that first year.

Then let me tell you about the radio course. Ahh . . . the radio course! Besides not being a very good teacher, Rex tried giving the aviation guys all the radio theory as fast and heavy as he did to the radio majors. It bounced off my dome like water off a duck. So I was absolutely lost when I had to apply all that theory in the radio lab the second year. I managed to get a radio technician's license. I passed the course with a D minus . . . and that was an absolute gift. Praise God!

There was a lot of pressure in the Aviation course. It was a historical fact that four was the biggest class to ever graduate from Moody Aviation. Besides all our aviation subjects, we had the radio, the photography, all the Bible subjects, plus the Christian work assignments. Also we were cramming in courses in the first and second years so the aviation mechanics could be completed in a one year time frame during the third year. If we failed a subject, we were out until the next year.

One such subject was Physics. Even though I had Engineering Physics at Oregon State and passed it with a B+, I still had to take the physics course here at Moody. The guy teaching this course was an ex-missionary who really knew the stuff upside down and backwards, but Jim had a hard time passing it on to us. Every class ended with a homework assignment of four problems. We spent hours and hours trying to solve those problems at the expense of all our other homework . . . up until two or three o'clock in the morning, doing those stupid problems that had absolutely no bearing on aviation. I always missed one problem. Sometimes two, or three. So basically, when I went into the final exam, I was flunking it. Four of us were told that we could kiss the Aviation course goodbye unless we pulled a certain grade on the final. I had to get a 100! A 100!! Each of us got the exact score needed to pass! Thank You, Lord!

Mind you, we had our fun times at Moody. The second year, we lived on campus which put us more in touch with the rest of the students. Our floor had one of the scrappiest bunch of little guys to ever play on a basketball floor. The court was so small that you could shoot the ball from one end to the other, with very little effort, and make it! We played a full court press the entire game which drove our opponents absolutely wild with frustration. It was just a wonderful way to blow off steam, and vent all of our pent-up anger that we could never display in our classes.

Anger? At Moody? Yeah, at Moody. At Moody you wore your halo straight, forty-eight hours a day, ten days a week. And that's frustrating, until you learn that it is impossible to live the Christian life on your own . . . that's when you learn to let Christ live His life in you. And that's a lesson you have to learn every day for the rest of your life.

It took me quite awhile to get over my Jeannie, but for the record, let me tell you, there were some really nice girls at Moody. Not that I had much time for dating, but there were girls in some of my classes, there were girls on my Christian work assignments, there were nice beautiful keen Christian girls all over the place! There was Cathy, Norma, Phyllis, Mary Belle, Joyce . . .

And then, there was Greta. Wow! She had the bluest eyes, and hair of purest gold which tumbled over her shoulders in soft waves . . . sorta like Loren Bacall. She was so beautiful . . . all the guys went nuts over her. I just admired her from a distance. But we did sort of get to know each other. Just how that came about I don't remember. Anyway, we would say 'hi' when we passed each other going to classes . . . sometimes we even stopped and talked a bit. Why in the world I never asked her for I date . . . how dumb can you get?

One day in my mail was a little box. Inside the box was dead goldfish and a note from Greta . . . maybe you can give 'Herbie' a proper burial out at the airport? Since we wouldn't be going to the airport for a couple days, Herbie got a little ripe, so I flushed him down the toilet . . . oh well. I never did tell her.

Wow!

One time Carl Mortenson got a real bad sinus infection and ended up in the infirmary for a couple weeks. Sunday night while walking home from Moody church it was about zero degrees . . . really cold. I stopped in a little store and bought a couple of ice cream drumsticks. It was late so I went down into the tunnels and found my way up to the infirmary and snuck into Carl's room and gave him one of the drumsticks. We were chatting away quietly. Greta was on duty that night. Just about then we heard her coming down the hall, so I hid behind the door. Carl was looking where I was hiding. Suddenly she whirled around, "What are you doing here?" I stuck my drumstick into her hands and blurted out, "Here . . . I brought you this!" And I took off like a rocket. What a nut!

Sometimes on Sunday night Denny and I would go down to Tozer's church on the south side of Chicago. Greta would always be there down in front soaking it up, and my, how that Dr. Tozer could expound the Word. I should have taken her.

Speaking of Denny, he became my closest buddy.

Denny Huffman—best buddy at Moody

110

Awhile back I got an email from him reminding me about the time when we went on the yearly outing to some lake.

Denny and Dick Fuller went out on the lake in a canoe. And Denny ran around all day without a shirt and was burned to a crisp. Late that night I awoke to someone knocking on my door. It was Denny and he looked beet red and was really miserable. Because it was about one PM in the morning, hiking over from the Y to Moody to the dispensary was out of the question.

Outing to lake where Denny got sunburned

"What can I do? . . . I hurt so bad that I can't sleep!"

"Let's go back to your room and I'll help you."

So we went back to Denny's room and I had him lay on his tummy. I said, "Now what I'm going to do is talk you to sleep . . . You just listen to what I'm saying, and soon you will be fast asleep, okay?"

Denny nodded his head in agreement. "Okay Denny . . . listen . . . you are very sleepy . . . very, very sleepy . . . and you are going to go to sleep . . ." In a quiet monotone, I made these suggestions over and over, and soon he was fast asleep. What I did was to hypnotize him. "Now Denny . . . You will stay asleep until it is time to wake up in the morning, and when you get a chance you will check in at the dispensary . . . Also your sunburn will not hurt and it will not peel, but will turn to a golden brown." I went back to my room.

The next day I saw Denny between classes. "Hey . . . How's your sunburn?"

He shrugged is shoulders, "Fine, I guess." It did not hurt him, and it did not peel, and it turned into a golden brown! I had just practiced some of the hypnosis techniques I had learned while I was at Oregon State.

And then, there was another Jeannie . . . with the darkest brown eyes. What really attracted me to her was her love for the Lord. But she was destined to be a missionary in Israel, and a jungle pilot just did not fit into the program. Ahh . . . that's the way it goes sometimes!

111

One day I was walking home from downtown I noticed in the window of this florist shop a beautiful purple Cattleya orchid with a price tag of one dollar! I walked in. And for another twenty five cents they would make it into a corsage, box and all. Wow! Why in the world were they selling these twenty five dollar orchids for one dollar? Some of them were not quite perfect, or they may be perfect but they had more than they could sell before they spoiled. I left it at the desk of the women's dorm for Jeannie. Did that ever cause a stir! Everyone was wondering who her secret admirer was.

Then there was this special dinner that everyone went to . . . sorta like a prom night. And all the guys and gals who were interested in each other would sit together to enjoy this special night. The guys in there finest, and the girls in their long beautiful dresses. I went down to the florist shop and bought Jeannie another orchid and left it at the desk. And she wore it to the prom that night! When the dinner was about over I walked over to her table and complimented her on her beautiful gown and the orchid. No-one had a flower like that. It was then that she realized that I was the one who had given her the orchids. She blushed appropriately, "But you shouldn't have spent all that money!" I never did tell her what they cost. I laugh to this day. She was such a wonderful girl.

14 September 1953, first flight of my second year at Moody. Mr. Wertheimer took me up, and wrung my tail, but good, for fifty minutes. You might say I was a bit rusty and needed it?

The next noteworthy event was on 5 October 53, when I was checked out to fly an Aeronca Champion. Neat thing about this plane was that the student sat up front where you could see the instruments and everything outside with ease. A very liberating feeling. The second year was basically spent honing our flying skills to perfection and building up experience. During spring break I flew up to Rochester, Minnesota, to visit the Ogburns, who I had known in Japan. Lanny was specializing in surgery at the Mayo Clinic.

THE THIRD YEAR

24 May 54 would be my last flight for over a year. In the fall we entered into the mechanics phase of our training. Lynn Washburn rejoined our class, and Paul Lewis also joined us as a special student, so that brought our class back up to ten. Paul had spent some time as a missionary in Liberia and saw the need of aviation mechanics to round out his expertise. He was really a dynamic addition to our class.

Lynn Washburn fooling around . . .

Another big change was that we were through with our Bible subjects, and we had to move away from school . . . wherever we could find a place to live.

Moody also had a funny rule which said Aviation students could not live at home! This affected Carl Mortenson from Wheaton. So to make it legal for Carl to live at home, Moody reclassified the Mortenson house as a dormitory. He and I became the first occupants!

I think the Mortensons just sorta tolerated me as a necessary evil so their son could live at home. Could never quite put my finger on it, but I never felt at home there. Maybe it was their high strung Mexican Chihuahua that treated me like an intruder all time I was there? As for Carl's two sisters . . . ahh, let's forget that part of the story! The Mortensons did give me permission to dig a garden out behind the garage, but the only thing they would eat were the fresh peas. They snubbed their noses at the radishes, turnips, lettuce, beans, and the carrots. Oh well! On with the story.

Wheaton, Illinois, was a rich, beautiful, peaceful suburb about twenty miles west of Chicago. A college town full of churches and good Christian people. I attended the First Baptist Church where Pastor Gilbert so keenly taught God's word.

In the evening service, I noticed this bent old lady who always sat alone up front in the second pew. One night, I sat beside Mrs. Gustafson just to keep her company. I made a fuss over her, and she just loved the attention. So, whenever I saw her, I would go and sit with her. That just made her day. Little did I realize how important that would be to my future missionary life, as she became my most faithful prayer warrior for many years of my missionary career. How many times was my life spared, out there, because of her intercessory prayer??

For one of my Christian work assignments, Dick Sissel (a Wheaton student) and I, started a Boy's Stockade group at the church. We rode herd on about thirty five livewire junior high kids. Most of them were from a foster home. Wow! what an experience! We had some wild times with those kids, intermingled with harsh discipline, but with lots of love . . . sometimes we were even able to reach them with God's word.

Did any of it ever take? About thirty-four years later I re-met Craig Noll playing the piano for Jim's wedding (my second son) in Rhode Island. Craig still had his Stockade card with my signature on it! His parents were some of my most faithful supporters all the twenty years I was on the mission field.

Instead of the nerve-racking trip through Chicago, we had a nice fifteen mile drive through the country to the airport. Moody also bought out the airport manager and renamed that little cow pasture, Moody Wooddale Airport. They now had the whole she-bang.

Because we had to provide our own transportation, I hit all the used car lots and junk yards around Wheaton, looking for an old clunker that would do the job. Cars were expensive. But way back in the far corner of this car lot, I found a forlorn looking 1946 Chevy business coupe. It had that sorta desperate pleading "buy me" look to it. That car had not been on the road for years, so it didn't have any rust.

I offered the salesman mechanic a hundred dollars.

"Kid, yah gotta be joking . . . make yah a fair deal . . . it's yours fer jest a hundred an' forty dollahs!"

We dickered back and forth on the price. He finally got the message that a hundred dollars was all this dumb kid could afford!

"Look sonny, go back an' look'er over . . . mark down all ya find wrong with'er . . . an' maybe I'll let ya hav'er for a C note!"

I grinned, "You bet'cha man!"

A half hour later I came back with a list about two feet long!

He roared with laughter, "Sonny, she's all yours!" We dragged it from the corner. The battery was missing, so he 'borrowed' one from another old clunker. He put in a gallon of gas, pumped up the worn out tires, and cleaned three years of dirt from the grimy windshield. We had to pull it a long way to get it started.

I paid him the money, and I was now the owner of the sorriest looking car in the whole state of Illinois!

As I started down the road, all she would do was about fifteen miles an hour. She sputtered and bucked, and each time, it ran a little faster. By the time I got home, that ol' buggy would do about thirty-five miles an hour! The Mortensons came out and looked at that woeful pile of junk, laughed, and walked away, shaking their heads.

First I gave it a bath. Under all the layers of dirt the color was a dull black. "I'll do a tune-up . . . maybe that will help!"

The points were so burned, there were hardly any contacts. Then the center electrodes of three of the spark plugs were burned right up into the ceramic. "Wow! . . . I'll replace the points an' plugs, and this bomb will run like a million bucks!"

So I replaced the points and plugs. My tune-up made very little difference. So I rebuilt the carburetor, which made that pile of junk run a lot better, but it really idled rough.

It didn't have very much power. When I did a compression check on the cylinders, the readings varied from 25 pounds up to 90! So I ended up doing a valve and ring job. It purred like a kitten.

I found some used, but good tires at the right price . . . free! I recovered the ripped upholstery with white leatherette. I polished the imitation walnut dash until it glowed. I replaced the worn out shocks, the worn tie rods and ball joints, the U-joints, the muffler, and I did a brake job.

I think the Mortensons became rather proud of their newly adopted son as they watched the re-creation of that pile of junk into a right snappy, sassy running little car.

Carl had a 1940 Plymouth which he also transformed into a classic beauty.

We took turns about each week driving to school. Bob Stockley, one of our mechanics instructors, also joined our little motor pool. He gave me permission to use the paint shop to paint my car.

I sanded and prepped that bomber for over three weeks. Then early one Saturday, I drove out to the airport, masked the windows, chrome, etc, and sprayed on a couple coats of sandable primer, followed by two coats of black enamel.

I was just cleaning up the paint shop, after unmasking my black beauty, when Mr. Robinson appeared. "What in the blankety blank (literal words) are you doing here . . . who gave you permission to do this? You get that junker outta here fast! We gotta tour group coming through here any minute!"

Boy, was he ever mad! Evidently my newly painted car didn't fit into the definition of a spotless shop.

The paint was still tacky when I drove my car to the North end of the field and hid it behind the T-hangars. Every dandelion on the way donated their fluffy seeds. My bomber looked like it had been tarred and feathered! Oh boy! Moody Aviation would probably miss getting a big donation from some rich mucky-muck, and I could kiss my missionary career goodbye!

After the paint dried, I was able to rub the seeds off. From thirty feet, it looked pretty good!

An edict came down through the channels . . . No more painting cars at Moody Wooddale Airport. No more working on your cars around here . . . period! No more this, and no more that! Boy, my name was mud with the fellows, for all the guys were using the shop and equipment to keep their junkers going. I didn't get kicked out, but I kept a lo-o-ow profile around there for a long, long time.

Once a week the Snap-On-Tools guy came around with his van full of shiny new tools. Boy, they were expensive. They had a deep chrome finish, but according to the price, they must have been made of gold. Some of the guys bought the big fancy red tool box with the sliding drawers and every tool on Moody's required list. It cost a small fortune. I only bought a set of combination wrenches. The rest of my tools came from Sears, including a small tool box that only had a tote tray. I stupidly realized, after it was too late, that I could have bought all Snap-On-tools, and my GI Bill would have paid for the whole she-bang! My GI Bill school benefits expired mid-term that year, and now I was on my own. But I received five-and-a-half years of schooling for three years in the service. Not bad at all. Thank you, Uncle Sam!

Anyway, this Snap-On guy kept coming around every week, and every noon hour, we would go out and fondly paw through his van full of shiny tools. He tried his best to keep an eye on us, afraid that we might try to steal something.

One of the fellows ordered a roll-away. When it came, a bunch of us crammed his van full while a couple of the guys sneaked the roll-away out the rear door. When Bob sought to take delivery, much to the Snap-On man's consternation, the roll-away was gone! Disappeared! He didn't think it was very funny when we led him into the shop to show him Bob's tool box already sitting on top of the new roll-away!

One day I made up a little ditty, and we formed an impromptu quartet and sang with gusto.

> Snap-On-Tools are the tools for you.
> Cost twice as much as Craftsman's do.
> So if you wan'na get stuck . . .
> Run right out to the Snap-On truck!
> Dah-da-dee-dum-dum . . . dee dum!

Mr. Snap-On didn't take to our fun all that much . . . just a poor sense of humor, I'd say!

Another time he came around, espousing the virtues of a revolutionary new oil that Quaker State was selling. It was a 10W-30 oil which is supposed to be thin, like a ten-weight oil when your car engine is cold, for easier starting in winter weather, and be thick like a thirty weight oil, for better protection when the engine gets up to operating temperature. Blah, blah, blah. Good sales pitch. So when the weather started getting cold, and my Chevy began protesting, I bought a case of the stuff. Boy, it was expensive! But my car engine would really crank over and start every time. No problem.

But Carl didn't get any. We had this sudden cold front come though, and the temperature dropped down to twenty below zero. It was Carl's week to drive. Even though his car was in a garage, unheated mind you, that engine would barely turn over, and it would not start. We tried everything in the books to get that car running. Maybe the new engine rebuild he had done was still a bit tight.

I gave up and went to bed about eleven o'clock. "Look Carl, forget it . . . my car starts fine . . . we'll use it tomorrow!"

"No sir!! . . . It's my turn to drive!"

Carl is the most cussed stubbornest person that I have ever met on the face of this Earth.

Well, I heard this noise in the wee hours of the morning and toddled downstairs to the kitchen where I found Carl, trying to heat up a big pan of oil that he had drained from his car! It had the consistency of an icky green pudding. He was crying, and he was mad!

"Look man . . . you're gonna burn the house down . . . take some of my new oil and put it in your car . . .!"

"No way . . . I'll never use that stuff!"

I just shook my head and went back up to bed. No arguing with that guy. Even with the heated up oil, Carl's car would not start.

Next morning we went out to my car. It must have been thirty below zero. My buggy started up on the third crank. After school that night Carl slowly drained the pudding out of his car and put in some of my 10W-30 Quaker State. He finally got his car started . . . another convert to the new oil.

Carl was just a runny-nosed, wet-behind-the-ears kid, fresh out of high school, but what a guy. He was always so gung-ho to get things done. I tended to be rather laid back in my outlook on life, so he was always on my back to get with the program.

One day, he found this old abandoned gullwing Stinson Reliant rotting away at some back-in-the-sticks airstrip. Most of the fabric was just hanging in shreds. The engine was gone. He dickered with the guy and bought the whole pile of junk for a hundred dollars and his shotgun!

I was enlisted to get the thing home. We removed the wings, hooked it to his old Plymouth, and towed the fuselage home at three in the morning on the back roads of Illinois.

That old bomber sat out behind the garage until Carl finished the mechanics course. Then, in his spare time, he began rebuilding that old forlorn pile of junk into a beautiful airplane which he eventually flew down to the mission field in Ecuador.

When I said rebuilding, I should have said re-creating, for that is actually what Carl did with this plane. This runny-nosed kid did a number of modifications that had never been done before to a Stinson Reliant, and he got them all approved by the CAA! He covered the entire plane with aluminum instead of fabric. Fantastic! He modified a cargo door big enough to role fifty-gallon barrels into the plane. The Wright radial engine was gone. New ones were scarce, and cost a fortune. But Carl found some 300 horsepower Lycoming radials that could be bought from war surplus for fifty dollars each. He rebuilt one, and located an engine mount that would accommodate this engine to his Stinson Reliant. What a kid! But you ain't heard anything yet!

This kid married his high school sweetheart, and off they went to the jungles of Peru to serve the Lord under Wycliffe. Carl was flying Helio Couriers over the steamy jungle, and I guess he had some pretty hairy times. When your engine starts to running rough . . . well, there's just no place to set that buggy down in all those pretty trees. Carl calls them camouflaged telephone poles! He began thinking two engines would be sorta nice to have in situations like that. Just happens there weren't any twins around in those days that could takeoff and land on the short airstrips they were using.

Then, Carl came down with polio. While he was recuperating in the hospital, he began doodling around with twin engine aircraft design. If there's no plane that will do the job, why not make one that will? And that is exactly what Carl did. He took a leave of absence from Wycliffe, designed and built the Evangel. Where does a young jungle pilot kid get the smarts to design and build a twin-engine short takeoff and land airplane? I'll take a line from Rush Limbaugh, "Talent on loan from God", that's where! But the real talent that God gave Carl was his most absolute cussed stubbornness to start a project and see it through to completion.

Carl Mortenson "Evangel" prototype

The Evangel was the most ugly, uncomfortable, and noisy a plane to ever take to the air. It was so simple, the Evangel could be repaired in the field with ordinary hand tools. It was built rugged, like a square brick. To make it fly, he hung two powerful 300 horsepower engines on it. He bolted on some high lift wings and big flaps, jumbo tires and double-disc brakes . . . and presto . . . you got a twin-engine airplane that could land and take off on a dime! It really worked! Seven Evangels were built. But it was so ugly that no one really wanted to buy one. The company went bankrupt. But that didn't deter Carl. Back to the drawing board.

The next design was the Angel. This plane does essentially the same thing as the Evangel . . . land and take off on a dime . . . but it does so with style. The Angel is a sleek sexy-looking job compared to the Evangel. It took years to design and build the prototype, and finally, 20 October 92, they received the type certificate #A2W1 to commercially manufacture the Angel.

Angel Aircraft Corporation—Angel

(For information on this plane contact: Angel Aircraft Corporation, Municipal Airport, 1410 Arizona Place SW, Orange City, IA 51041-7453, phone 712-737-3344) As of Sept 93, Angel Aircraft Corporation has successfully raised the funds and are ready to begin production. As I write this, the Angel is on a demonstration tour in Europe and North Africa. Yes sir . . . this Carl Mortenson kid is really quite a fantastic sort a guy! Now back to MY story.

The upstairs classroom at the airport was so cold that you could see your breath. The old coal burner was going full bore. Mr. Stockley let us stand up and do calisthenics when we could no longer bear the cold. Evidently I had let this situation be known to my friends from Oregon State College, Ken and Madie Lair, for they sent me a wool-lined leather German Luftwaffe flying suit that Kenny had picked up in Germany during the war. Boy, that suit fit me perfect and was it ever a life saver!

I think Bob Stockley was the most patient instructor I have ever met. He had a real heart for his students, and sometimes he bent some of the Moody rules a bit to accommodate us, which eventually got him into big trouble. Anyway, a lot of us guys finished that grueling course of study only because of Bob Stockley, and let me say for all of us . . . "We are deeply thankful to you, and for all that you so wonderfully and masterfully taught us. Thank you, sir!"

The A & P Mechanic course (Aircraft and Powerplant) was some of the most intense schooling I ever went through in all of my life. I still have a stack of spiral notebooks over four inches high . . . detailed and intricate notes on all the phases of study that we covered in order to gain that coveted license in a time frame of one year. No small feat.

Aircraft phases were: shop practices, welding, sheet metal, rigging, instruments, appliances, electricity, radio, woodworking, inspection and handling, fuel systems, dope and fabric, and hydraulics.

The power plant phases were: primary engines, shop practices, lubrication, electricity, carburetion, engine overhaul, superchargers, propellers, trouble shooting, and Civil Air Regulations pertaining to all the above.

What we learned in the classroom, we demonstrated our proficiency hands-on in the shop. You had to pass a final exam, and acceptably do the shop projects for each phase. Failure of either meant that you were out of the course. So it was school all day and study all night.

Welding class

The pressure was a-building. Except for the grace of God and the excellent teaching by a dedicated staff, none of us would have ever made it. Ultimate perfection. And that's the way it should be, I guess. After all, in aircraft maintenance, one stupid little mistake on our part could lay people's lives on the line . . . and on the mission field that life could be your own, as we would be maintaining the puddle jumpers that we would be flying. Now that's an incentive for you! And Moody never ever let you forget it.

The phase I really enjoyed the most was engine overhaul, where a team of two actually overhauled a real live aircraft engine from disassembly, cleaning, inspection, measuring, magnafluxing, repairing or replacing parts, overhaul of all the accessories, and then reassembling the whole darn thing to where you started it (after being primed) with a single spin of the prop. And mind you, it had better start on the first spin . . . or it was Pepsi on the house . . . for every cotton-picking soul in the whole building! We goofed . . . ours started on the second pull . . . but did that little four cylinder 65 horsepower Continental engine ever run sweet!

The trouble shooting phase was a lot of fun too. The instructors would goof up an engine in some way . . . then you and your buddy would have to figure out why the stupid thing would not start, or why it would not run smoothly. Then you had to correct the problem, to make it start and run like it should.

They had an old bare-boned Stearman fuselage with no wings that they kept for just this occasion. They stuffed a whole army blanket in the carburetor intake to make it run with a rich mixture! On others they goofed up the timing on the magnetos. Or the mixture on the carburetor.

My notes list forty-two ways they could screw the thing up. Say that you narrowed the problem down to a rough idle as the problem. Now to fix it. First, check to see if you have too lean a mixture, or it could be too rich a mixture. Or the mag timing could be too early. It may have a too small a gap on the spark plugs, or maybe a fouled spark plug. It could have a weak coil or magnet in the magneto.

Ahh . . . you find they pinched two of the spark plug electrodes completely together. See how much fun this could be! And you are laying your scalp on the line with every venture! Or how about a combination of things they screwed up? They wouldn't do that to us, would they? Heh, heh, heh . . . who knows . . . what evil lurks in the hearts of men? The Shadow knows . . . heh, heh, heh . . .!

Of course, the great finale to all this effort was to take and pass the CAA (Civil Aeronautics Administration) exam which not only included the written exam, but also a practical exam where you actually demonstrated your expertise on any of the myriad of problems from which the examiner might choose.

He had me show him how to time the magnetos, how to safety-wire a turnbuckle, how to weld a cluster of aircraft tubing, how to pack a wheel bearing with grease, and how to clean, gap, inspect, and replace a spark plug. No problem. I passed the written with an 89. And on July 1st, 1955 I was issued my A & P License! Everyone in the class passed the first time around . . . Yahoooo!!

We were also officially graduated from Moody Bible Institute as part of the class of 55, even though we aviation students still had another year to go.

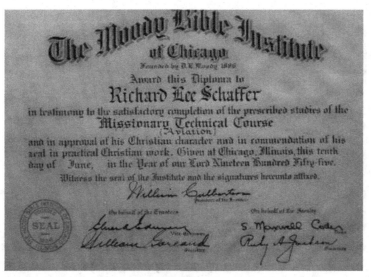

My diploma

With my license warm in my pocket, I applied for and got a part-time job as an aircraft mechanic at the Elmhurst Airport . . . a dollar-and-a-quarter an hour! I also moved over to Elmhurst where I lived in the basement of Bob and Virginia Cowley's rented house. I really learned a lot doing all the flunky jobs that a greenhorn mechanic can do without getting himself into too much trouble. Wash the planes, degrease the engine, do an oil change, remove and install the inspection covers, hose down and squeegee the floors at the day's end.

One day, I was washing a light green SuperCub. The fabric was covered with a stubborn grimy oil stain that just would not come off with the usual soap. So I took a little Ajax lightly to the fabric. Wow! When I got done it looked like a new plane! From then on, every guy at the airport was bringing their plane to our shop for "the wash job"!! The boss slowed them down a bit by jacking up the price from two dollars to twenty dollars!

I also proved myself with the spray gun, so they had me doing a lot of dope and fabric work. One day, a guy asked me if I could dress up the doggy interior of his plane a bit. I painted the floor black. I did the rest of the interior in three shades of gray, including a wrinkle finish of the instrument cover. It really looked great and the guy just went wild over it! They upped my pay to a dollar-and-a-half an hour! Wow!

THE FOURTH YEAR

I flew four times during the summer break to keep from getting too rusty. And in September, we began flying almost every day to build up our hours and experience for a Commercial Pilot's license. We also had all kinds of ground school classes such as: aerodynamics, weather, navigation, cross-country flying, radio, night flying, civil air regulations, missionary flying, even how to apply to a mission board! Man, we covered it all.

Going out to practice spin recovery

I also moved over to live with Mr. and Mrs. Victor Burnett in Bensenville which was just a couple of miles from the airport. Every year they opened their home to an aviation student. So I became one of Mom Burnett's boys. They were really wonderful people.

Fourth year students maintained Moody's small fleet of planes which gave us additional mechanical experience. I was also able to work two afternoons a week and all day Saturday at the Elmhurst airport which helped to pay my way.

One day while I was working on one of the planes at Moody, Mr. Robinson, who was leading a tour group around the facility, introduced me as being from Oregon, to a Captain Stabbert, who was the director of the Marine Medical Mission. Captain Stabbert greeted me very enthusiastically, and began telling me all about their Mission's summer program along the west coast of British Columbia. And they were looking for a pilot! I replied that I didn't have a seaplane rating, and that I was already considering another mission. The tour continued on its way.

On November 1st, I was up to 126 hours when Dirk Van Dam, CFI #1242214, started checking me out in the Cessna 140, which was a step up to a little heavier and sophisticated aircraft. It had a full IFR panel and radio which are needed for instrument flying. On November 14th, Bob Rich, CFI #1267209, started me in the required night flying. The same day Mr. Stockley started me out flying instruments under the hood in the Link trainer. That's a mock airplane mounted on a pedestal where the student can fly instruments and do radio work without getting into too much trouble. As you gain experience, the instructor keeps piling on more complex problems. You come out of that little box wringing wet with sweat, just like it was the real thing. Then at 142 hours, on November 29th, Mr. Wertheimer gave me some time in the Cessna 170B. So every day, every week, our flight experience was growing.

I determined that in my fourth year I would begin contacting all the various mission organizations which had an aviation program. My idea was to get moving toward the mission field as soon as possible. What better place to start than with my own denomination?

In one of my old spiral notebooks, I found the rough draft of the letter I wrote to Dr. Milton Baker, secretary to the Conservative Baptist Foreign Missionary Society. I smile, as I read it now, at the youthful ambition of a greenhorn who wants to serve the Lord. It goes something like this.

my address

11 Feb 56

Dr. Milton Baker
CBFMS address

Dear Dr. Baker,

Greetings in the name of our Lord and Savior Jesus Christ. In a few months I will have completed my training at Moody Bible Institute in the Missionary Aviation Course, and it is only logical to consider serving Him under my own denomination.

I know that you have under consideration my friend, Norm Olson, to possibly began the aviation program in Brazil. I have no intention of giving him competition for this position, but I was wondering if you would consider using a team of technicians for this project? From what I have heard of the future plans for this program, there would be many advantages in using a pair, or possibly three technicians. Or if you have another such aviation program in mind, I would be very interested.

I will be waiting expectantly to hear from you, or perhaps talking with you some Sunday night after church. (We were going to the same church in Wheaton).

in His service,
Rich Schaffer

And then I added about a two page PS to the letter telling him about all the wonderful training I was receiving at Moody . . . blah, blah, blah!

Well, I never even received an acknowledgment of my letter! One day, I heard that Dr. Baker would be speaking at such and such a church, giving a report of his recent tour of the CBFMS work in Africa. So I went to hear him speak. It was a glowing report to be sure. After the meeting, I approached him and introduced myself, and asked if he had considered my letter, offering myself to the mission for the new aviation program they were planning for Brazil.

He glared at me, spun on his heel, and walked off without so much as a word! Wow! What gives with this guy? (Several years later, I learned from Dr. Baker, when he was visiting me in Nigeria, West Africa . . . the night that I had tried to talk to him about missionary aviation, was the day he had received word from the Congo that their mission plane had crashed . . . killing all persons on board! One of them was his closest friend. Their aviation program in Brazil never left the ground. Norm Olson went with MAF.)

Next I wrote a letter to the Sudan Interior Mission. Yes, they had need of another pilot, and they sent me a preliminary "get acquainted" type of application which I filled out and returned. Happy with the information I sent to them, SIM sent me their official application. But like so many other Moody flyboys, I was actually hoping to go with Missionary Aviation Fellowship. They were the gung-ho organization! I would hold off filling out this application, at least until we did our cross-country flight out to MAF headquarters at Fullerton, California.

The purpose of this flight was to give us some real extended cross-country experience. MAF would also give us a taste of their hair-raising mountain flying course which they give to all their pilots. It gave us a chance to see the MAF headquarters, and it gave them an opportunity to look us over as possible recruits who could fill some of their growing personnel needs.

The crew for our flight was: Mr. Wertheimer, John Snavely, Norm Olson, and myself, in the Cessna 170B. Each student did the flight planning for the entire flight, but we would take turns doing the actual flying.

We left Moody Wooddale March 15th, and I flew the first leg to St Louis . . . two hours and ten minutes. The next day I flew the Dallas-San Antonio leg. On the 17th, Saturday, I flew from Marfa Alpine to El Paso.

When we got out to some of the remote dessert areas, we did some hedge-hopping. That was really something. Little did we realize, this was to prepare us for some of the hairy flying we would be doing in the Sierra mountains with MAF.

Sunday, March 18th, was one of the biggest highlights in my life . . . we attended the Old Fashioned Revival Hour! I was just absolutely enthralled to actually hear, in person, the choir and the quartet, to hear Charles E. Fuller preach, and to listen to Mrs. Fuller (Honey) read the letters. It took me back to those years when I was just a little boy and I sat by that old radio and listened to the broadcast every Sunday night. My . . . what a wonderful program . . . where so many people listened to the faithful gospel preaching, and responded to the invitation to be saved. Oh man . . . it brings tears to my eyes just to think about it now!

Mountain Flying

Early Monday morning, we took off from Fullerton airport for the high mountains in MAF's Piper PA20 Family Cruiser. Illinois is flat like a table, and we didn't have the remotest idea what flying around mountains was like. Hoby Lowrance talked to us for a couple of hours about mountain flying before we took off. From that we had a fair idea that we were going to get our tails wrung today.

The first lesson was how to cross over a low spot in a ridge. Hoby yelled above the engine noise, "You fly along the ridge instead of approaching it head on. Then, if you have any downdrafts, you can easily turn away. As you commit yourself to the low spot, you fly along the edge of the ridge, so you have room to turn out and away in case it gets rough."

Snavely took us over a couple of ridges with no problems. On the third ridge, we got caught in strong down draft, where we were dropping eight hundred feet a minute, even though we were trying to climb at full throttle. We were correctly impressed. But we easily turned away from the ridge to escape.

Hoby then took us to a box canyon. "The object is to fly up this canyon with one wing hugging the wall so you can turn out if you have to . . . tell me when you think we need to turn!"

John started up the right side of the sheer rock wall canyon.

"No . . . come on . . . get a little closer . . . you're practically flying up the middle!" So John moved over a tiny bit.

"Here . . . let me show you . . . you tell me when we should make the turn!" With that, Hoby took the controls, and put the end of the right wing about four feet off the canyon wall!

Now that got our attention! We are flashing by solid rock at a hundred and twenty miles an hour! The canyon is getting narrower. John yells, "Make your turn . . . make your turn!"

Hoby quietly replies, "No . . . we'll go a little further!"

Norm and I are sitting in the back seat, hanging on for dear life. We hit a bit of turbulence.

Again John yells, "Let's turn . . . MAKE THE TURN!!"

Hoby just keeps going. It looks like we are trapped. Suddenly, he throws the plane into a near vertical bank. Our wheels almost kiss the left wall. We swing around in the tight canyon. We're headed out . . . our right wing tip is just a few feet from the cliff! Whew!!

Hoby says to John, "You wanta try it?"

"No way, man!", John shakes his head.

"Good choice . . . but you'll do it just fine when you finish the mountain course!"

Next, he took us to a finger-like ridge. On the end of the ridge was a small air strip. As we circled overhead, Hoby asked, "How would you land on that airstrip down there? It's 600 feet long . . . sorta like a strip we have out in Irian Jaya!"

We studied that little strip of ground. There was no wind sock. The west end dropped off over a sheer cliff. Some scrubby pine trees defined the east end. There were also a few trees along the edges of the narrow runway.

John was still shook with the box canyon experience. He made no bones about it. He looked Hoby square in the eyes and firmly said, "I wouldn't land down there for a million bucks!"

Hoby chuckled with laughter.

Norm says, "Lets go down for a closer look."

We dropped down until we were about a hundred feet off the west end. Now we could see that the strip had a steep up-grade to the east.

I said, "Looks like you would have to land west to east . . . come over the cliff with good speed control . . . watch out for downdrafts . . . plop it on the end, and slam on the brakes . . . but once you're committed, there's no go-around!"

Hoby glanced back at me, "Right on, man! . . . and what about takeoff?"

Norm chimes in, "Take off east to west, down hill, and out over the cliff!"

"Yeah, you got it . . . okay, lets go to Big Bear Lake!"

The Big Bear was a 5850 foot long abandoned airport up in the high Sierras at an altitude of 6748 feet.

On the way, I spotted a reflection on the mountain side. We went over for a closer look. It was the remains of an airplane. On one of the wing panels, there was a big black X painted, indicating the plane was a known crash site.

We landed at Big Bear, got out, and had a good stretch.

"Up here we'll do some high altitude short takeoff and landings. This is the kind of stuff you would be doing over in the mountains of Ethiopia, or down in Bolivia.

"What I want you to do when you take off is to start at the stripe on the end, figure out the best way to get off in the shortest distance, gain the most altitude in the shortest distance over the ground, come around and land right on the stripe, and then stop in the shortest distance!"

I smiled within myself. We had done a lot of short field practice back at Moody, so this would be old hat for us pros. Here was our chance to shine.

I let Norm volunteer to be first. I figured, as time went on, we would be burning up fuel, so the plane would be lighter and perform better when it became my turn. Pretty smart, aye?

Norm taxied to the stripe on the end of the runway. He set the brakes, revved up the engine full bore, and then let her go. Seemed like we went forever before breaking ground. It was the high altitude that was giving us such a doggy performance. We staggered off the ground and began slowly climbing. A road crossed the north end of the long runway with a telephone line running directly across our path. We cleared the wire by fifty feet. Just ahead was a small lake. As we went across the lake you could feel the plane sink. Norm brought the plane around the pattern, landed just beyond the stripe, and stepped hard on the brakes. We stopped in about five hundred feet.

Hoby says, "Not bad, but let me show you a few things which should up the performance a notch or two. First off . . . at a high altitude like this, lean out the mixture so the engine will run better."

He showed us how to properly lean out the mixture. "Then, instead of starting the takeoff from a dead stop, start your run downwind, swing the plane around, and give it the power. That will also save the prop from getting chewed up if you have some gravel on the runway. Lift the tail off the ground soon as you can, but just a little way. As you pick up speed, pull on a notch of flaps, then pop the wheels off the ground as soon as you can, climb up just a couple of feet and level off. Let her pick up speed, and continue your climb out at best climb speed.

Then, on your landing, use full flaps, make a power approach, drag it in just above a stall, fly it right down to your spot, plop it on the ground, and jam on the brakes!"

Norm followed Hoby's instructions to the letter, and really put on a good show. From the back seat I kept track of the air speeds which gave the best performance. After a number of trips around the pattern, "Hey, you're doing pretty good", Hoby encouraged, "let's give Rich a turn now!"

On my downwind run, I revved up to a good speed. On the turn around, I kept the speed up by making a wide circle from one side of the huge runway to the other. I smoothly added full power as we came around. Just at the right speed, I picked up the tail wheel a couple of inches. I popped on a notch of flaps just at the right speed, eased the plane off the ground a couple of inches, leveled off, and held it there until we reached the best climb speed.

On the landing, I really dragged it in, just above a stall, plopped it right on the stripe, and jammed on the brakes. I swung the plane around before it came to a complete stop, cutting off another twenty feet from the landing roll. We had landed in less than two hundred and fifty feet!

I gunned it around for another take off and repeated the performance, cutting the distance a few feet less each time around.

"Very, impressive!", Hoby says with emphasis, "you've flown a Family Cruiser before?"

"Not really . . . but it sorta handles like a J-3 Cub."

"Well, you are sure doing a great job. On takeoff now, I'll handle the throttle . . . I'm going to cut the power back to simulate takeoffs at even a higher altitude . . . okay?"

"Okay . . . I guess!"

On each takeoff, Hoby cut the power more and more until we were using up over half of the runway before we broke ground. The plane would barely climb.

"We're not going to clear that telephone line . . . you want me to go underneath?"

"No . . . just keep it steady . . . I'll show you how to clear that wire!"

We were heading straight for that wire.

"Man, we're not gonna make it!"

"Just keep it steady!!"

Just before we hit, Hoby pulled on the flaps. We barely floated over the wire! As he slowly released the flaps the plane began to sink. We were barely gaining altitude.

Next was the lake. "That downdraft over the lake . . . you better give me a little more power!!"

Hoby never said a word.

As we came over the lake the plane began to sink. Hoby added just enough RPMs to keep it flying. I dragged it around, and set it down in less than a hundred and fifty feet!

"Are you sure you never flew a plane like this before?"

We got out and had a good stretch. The place had a lonely beauty to it. Barren, like the back side of the moon. Hoby says, "It's getting late . . . we better head back to Fullerton."

I got to fly it back home. As we neared Los Angeles, the smog got thicker and thicker. The horizon disappeared. I was flying instruments to keep the plane flying straight and level, and I was trying to keep track of where we were going by things on the ground. But it was getting hard to distinguish anything on the ground anymore. I was flopping all over the sky.

Hoby says, "Just stay on the instruments . . . I'll tell ya when to change heading!"

So I settled down and flew instruments. It was just like flying the Link Trainer. While Fullerton airport did not have a tower, Hoby got an IFR clearance from Aircraft Control. Boy, this was a whole new ball game for us greenhorns. I was mighty happy when we got back down on the ground again.

THE BIG LET DOWN

That evening, Grady Parrot, president of MAF, talked to us individually. During my interview, he asked me dozens of questions about my background, education, training at Moody, my personal life . . . what my goals were.

"I hear you really did a bang-up job flying that plane!", he expressed enthusiastically, "we're looking for pilots like you! However, we have a problem . . . MAF already has two single pilots that we don't know what to do with. At a lot of our places, we need a man-wife team to make the operation work efficiently . . . are you sure there isn't some girl there at Moody?" Disappointment dropped clear down to my shoes. "Not really . . . the girl I'm interested in has her heart set on being a missionary to Israel!"

Somewhere in the conversation I let it slip that I was in correspondence with the Sudan Interior Mission and they wanted me to fill out a formal application. "Oh . . . if that's the case, I'd suggest that you go ahead with that. SIM is really a good mission!"

Thus ended my interview and my hopes with MAF! Somehow, I had an deep inner peace about it all. I would continue my application to SIM.

20 March 56. Early Tuesday morning, we started homeward to Moody Wooddale airport. I flew the first leg from Fullerton to Prescott, Arizona. Other legs that I flew were: Dalhart, Texas to Dodge City, Kansas, and Topeka, Kansas to Kirkville, Illinois. It was an uneventful flight.

A VISITING I GO

I had signed up to use the Cessna 140 for a flight to Statesville, North Carolina to visit the Ogburns during the Easter break. Doctor Paul had completed his internship at the Mayo Clinic. He and Merlene had moved to Statesville where he was the resident surgeon. However, Dirk Van Dam traded me the Aeronca Champion for the Cessna 140, so he could fly into some radio controlled fields on his trip home to Pennsylvania. That was okay with me. The Aeronca was slower, so I would get more time.

30 March 56. I took off for Statesville. It was a cold, dull, dirty-looking day. I landed at a small airport near Danville, Illinois. The wind was whipping across the runway at twenty five knots. When I climbed out of the plane it felt like it was going to snow. I huddled up to the pot-belly stove while they tried to get me some kind of weather report. The weather sounded better farther south, so I decided to push on. It was a bumpy ride as I stayed under the low scud. By the time I landed at Bloomington the clouds had lifted a bit and the wind had calmed down some. I went on to Junction City.

I was going to fly to Ashville, but I ran into a thunderstorm in the mountains and could not get through. It looked mean and black as I worked my way up the canyon. A sharp gust hit me . . . WHOP! . . . sounded like someone had whacked the bottom of the plane with a board. I got out of there fast, and went back to Knoxville to spend the night.

I asked the taxi driver, "Know any hotels around here that don't cost too much?"

He smiled knowingly, "Yeah kid, I know jus' the place!"

He dropped me off at this dumpy-looking hotel, and I got a room on the second floor. We were still out in the country somewhere.

'The Place' turned out to be the local play-house, with lots of activity going on that night! There was no lock on my door, so I was a bit edgy about someone trying to come in. I wasn't getting much sleep.

Suddenly, I woke up to angry shouts and cursing, "You @%&* bitch . . . I'll teach you to steal my wallet!"

There was a hard thud as this guy slammed his girl-for-the-night against the wall and proceeded to beat her up. It sounded like they were trashing the place. She scratched his eyes and bit his nose, broke away, and went screaming out into the hall with nary a stitch of clothes! I closed my door and shoved the bed against it. Wow!

Things finally simmered down, and I managed to get a few winks of sleep.

I took off out of there at the crack of dawn, and started walking to the airport. A farmer gave me a ride and dropped me off right at the plane. When he saw the big Moody

Bible Institute sign on the side of my plane, he quipped, "Sonny, what's a nice preacher kid like you doin', spending a night in that sorry hotel for?"

"Honest man, I didn't know what kind of place it was!"

He just drove off, shaking his head. Oh boy!

I checked over the plane and took off for Statesville. The clouds were hanging in the hilltops. By staying low, I was able to snake my way through the canyons with no problems. The early morning air was smooth and solid. Beautiful country.

I landed at the Statesville airport and phoned the Ogburns. Merlene picked me up in their old Buick station wagon. Lanny was long gone to work at the hospital.

They were short of staff, so Paul got home about eleven that evening. He raided the fridge and wolfed down everything in sight. Lanny was very quiet and didn't really want to talk very much. Something was wrong.

Merlene rubbed his neck and shoulders, "Hard day today?"

"Yeah . . . just lost one of my patients . . . the Marler kid . . . died just an hour ago . . . stayed to comfort the parents. Jeez'.. these kids . . . when are they ever gonna learn to slow down!" (Johnny Marler had skidded off a sharp turn on Harper's road and rolled it a hundred and fifty feet down into the canyon. There really wasn't much left to work on.) Lanny just hung his head and cried. What a guy. I was to learn that Dr. Paul Lanier Ogburn really took it hard when he lost someone.

Next morning, he was gone before it was light, and home again late at night. In fact, I hardly saw Lanny all the week I was there at Statesville. I had hoped we could play some tennis.

On my trip home to Moody, I ran into some more bad weather between Ashville and Knoxville. There were thunderstorms all over the place, so guess what, I decided to give Knoxville another try. This time I got it across to the taxi-driver that I wasn't really interested in fooling around at their little play-house . . . all I wanted was a good night's sleep. And that's what I got. Boy, what a place!

I took off the next morning and flew to Junction City. Ran into some more bad weather, but finally managed to squeak into Louisville where I sat for a couple of hours. Things started clearing up and thought I would give it another try. Stopped at Bloomington and Danville. Got home to Moody with no more problems.

As I taxied up to the gas pump, Dirk strolled out to greet me, "Man, you should have kept the 140 . . . !"

"Oh, that's okay . . . I like this little Champ . . . we had a great time!"

"Yeah, but I flipped the 140 when I tried to land in some deep snow!"

"You did what?"

"I flipped her in the snow!"

"Oh man! . . . How did you do that?"

"Real stupid on my part. Didn't hurt the plane too bad . . . gotta go back and pick her up in a few days when they get it repaired enough to fly."

So it goes. Dirk was an exceptional pilot, but I guess, even the best have to make a few mistakes. We learn some good lessons, the hard way, from those dumb boo-boos we all commit. Thank you Lord, for your watch care.

"Oh, by the way," Dirk got a big smile on his face, "Sudan Interior Mission called a couple of days ago . . . they want you to give'm a shout as soon as you get home!"

"SIM? . . . wow! . . . wonder what they want?"

"Well, maybe you ought'a find out?"

THE FINAL COUNTDOWN

So I gave SIM a call. The conversation went something like this: "Yeah Rich . . . we're wondering how you are coming along with your hours of flight time? As you know, SIM requires a commercial license and 350 hours minimum . . . we would like to consider you for the candidate class in September . . . what do you think?"

When I finally came down from the ceiling, I replied, "Moody says that we should have about three hundred hours and our commercial license when we finish the course!"

"What are your plans for this summer? Would be nice if you could get another fifty hours . . ."

I thought for a moment, "I have this job as a mechanic at Elmhurst Airport and I could probably get some extra time here at Moody!" Then the thought came, "Marine Medical Mission is looking for a pilot for their summer program . . . but I would have to get a sea plane rating!"

We tossed the pros and cons back and forth. It was decided that I go with Marine Medical Mission for the summer . . . nothing like some real hands-on experience to round out my resume!

So I contacted Marine Medical Mission.

"Sure, we need you . . . just be here at Seattle before June 28th . . . that's when we head north!"

Wow! This kid needs to get his tail end in gear!

We were really having some el-stinko springtime weather. I now had 216 hours of flight time. We were flying every chance when it was good enough to get out to the practice area to run through the commercial sequence of maneuvers we would have to pass to earn our commercial license.

On April 23rd, Bob Stockley started giving me some time in the Cessna 170B, flying instruments under the hood. And by May 17th I had 252 hours. The next day Bob Rich gave me the recommendation ride for the commercial flight test, and late that same afternoon, Mr. Wertheimer tried to give me the actual check-ride.

A huge storm was approaching just as we got out to the practice area. The air was as rough as a cob and we were being thrown all over the sky. But this tough nut of a guy was determined that I perform to the absolute.

"Come on, Schaffer . . . where'd you learn to fly!"

A hard gust just about flipped us on our back as I was doing an on-pylon maneuver. That even scared the Banti rooster a little.

"Okay, let's get out of here!" . . . grumble, grumble, grumble.

Mr. Wertheimer huffed off to the flight room.

Oh boy! . . . I'd rather fly through a thunderstorm head-on, than fly with that guy again! What a bear!

The storm front finally cleared the area after a couple of days. On the May 21st, 1956, the air was solid like a rock, and I somehow managed to give Mr. Wertheimer a good enough ride (it's called absolute perfection) to pass my Commercial Test Flight. Yippee!

In fact, I gave him such a good ride that he must have thought it was an accident! Just to make sure it wasn't, he rode with me four more times in the next nine days!

We practiced such exotic things as special patterns, downwind crosswind landings and takeoffs, obstacle approaches, spot landings, speed control, one way strip practice, 90 degree crosswind takeoffs and landings in high winds, 360 degree overhead spot landings. He wrung my tail, but good.

"Thank you, Mr. Wertheimer, for never giving up on me!"

WE TAKE TO THE WATER

On July 1st, Dirk Van Dam started me on the seaplane training in the old Republic SeaBee. This has got to be the ugliest plane in the world. Big bulbous nose with a V-shaped boat bottom. As an afterthought they arched the tail up in line with the pusher engine that hung in the mid section behind the cabin. A couple of pontoons dangled from the ends of the wing. It was huge and it was heavy. All of this perched ungainly on a retractable landing gear. Yeah . . . this old goose could waddle on the land or splash down in the water.

Republic Seabee

You really worked up a sweat to fly this plane. The flaps, main gear, and tail wheel went up and down, by you, manually and furiously pumping the hydraulic handle mounted between the seats. You do this circus act while you keep track of where you are going, your speed, attitude, altitude, and make sure you don't run over somebody else in the process.

As you go around the pattern, you began to wish you were an eight-legged paperhanger, trying to get everything up and down, and in place, before you hit the ground again.

And then to make it interesting, Dirk cuts the throttle for a poweroff landing. That crate drops like a bomb. So steep, you literally stand on the rudder pedals. After an hour of this, you crawl out exhausted and wringing wet with sweat.

The next day we flew up near to the Wisconsin border to Fox Lake to do some basic waterwork. Takeoffs and landings, glassy-water work, turns, step-turns, docking practice. Neat thing . . . this plane has a reversible pitch prop. You can taxi right up to the shoreline and jump out the front door without getting your feet wet. And then you can reverse the prop and back out without turning the plane around! In fact, Dirk did that, and let me take the plane up for a solo spin around the lake. That old SeaBee proved to be a rather impressive airplane.

On July 15th, Dirk gave me my recommendation for the Seaplane Flight Test. However, there was no one else on the Moody staff rated to give me the test. I was running out of time. Dirk suggested that I take the check ride out at Seattle.

So I contacted Marine Medical Mission and they said they would arrange that for me. I said my goodbyes to all concerned, loaded my tools and junk into my old Chevy, and took off for Seattle.

As I drove westward bound, I had plenty of time for reflection. I had just successfully completed four years of the most intense training in my life.

"Thank You, Lord! Thank you, Moody Bible Institute!"

I felt like I was on top of the world. Yet I had a humble feeling about it all, realizing that I was still very green, and wet behind the ears. I only had 280 hours of flying. I had learned a lot, but I knew that I had so much, much more to learn. Someone has said, "The day you stop learning to fly, that's the day you better stop flying!"

"So Lord, what do You have to teach me at Marine Medical Mission? May I learn it well!"

CHAPTER 18
MARINE MEDICAL MISSION

I flew about 80 hours in MMM's
Luscombe Silvaire floatplane

The flat mid-west plains laden with bumper crops of corn and soybeans gave way to endless fields of wheat. Then my old bomber chugged faithfully up and down the Rockies and the Cascades. What a beautiful country! I arrived safely in Seattle on the evening of June 27th, 1956 to begin my new adventure with Marine Medical Mission. They were based on the southwest corner of Lake Union, right in the heart of downtown Seattle.

The ships had already left a week ago for the main base on Thetis Island, a tiny two by four mile emerald gem, hidden among the hundreds of islands that shimmered in the deep blue of Canada's Georgia Strait. Eighty kids from Christian Colleges and Bible Schools from all across the United States and Canada were going through their orientation and training, getting ready for the Mission's hectic summer program.

I walked down to the dock to take a look at the blue and cream colored plane that I would be flying for the summer. The Aeronca Sedan is an unusual airplane. The fuselage and tail are covered with fabric, but the wings are all metal. 1220Hotel (the registration number) had sort of a doggy look to it and I was thinking maybe it would be a good idea to do a 100 hour inspection on this buggy before we headed for the wild, wild north.

Charlie read me like a book, "She just had her annual re-license inspection, and we need to head out just as soon as we can get you checked out. We got you scheduled for your seaplane check-ride tomorrow afternoon at fourteen hundred . . . think you can handle that?"

I hesitated, "Yeah, I guess."

But I felt like I was getting the bum's rush. I had that uneasy feeling, but I was the new kid on the block. Maybe I could look the plane over when we got to Thetis Island?

Early next morning, Charlie rode with me as I familiarized myself with the Sedan. Flying a pontoon float plane was quite different from flying that ponderous Republic SeaBee.

After an hour of practice, Charlie suggested, "You're doin' pretty good . . . why not drop me off at the dock . . . I gotta lot of things to do before we shove off . . . you can do this stuff, solo! Just be sure you are over at Kenmore at two o'clock sharp!"

"Okay man, no problem!"

I went out for another hour of basic waterwork, takeoffs, and landings. You should see Seattle from the air . . . what a beautiful city! This was back in the days when the word smog had yet to be invented. Everything stood out sharp and crystal clear. The city, Lake Union, Lake Washington, the Cascades, Mount Rainier, the Olympic Range, the Sound . . . "Lord, you really knew what you were doing when you made all of this!"

I was over at Kenmore Seaplane Base at "2 o'clock sharp", and the examiner, Bill Fisk, license #403-17, gave me my check ride. We went out on the lake and did a bit of basic waterwork, shot a couple of takeoffs and landings, docked the plane a couple of times. That was it! He signed me off for my commercial seaplane rating. I never had an easier check ride in all my life.

The next day we flew up to Thetis Island. The place was humming like a beehive . . . college kids buzzing about all over the island. Everybody seemed to be in a big hurry. There was no more room in the big house, but I found a bunk on the Willis Shank. The ship was an old converted mine sweeper, the pride and joy of Captain Stabbert. They had a dental clinic on board, and when they stopped at an Indian village, or a small logging or fishing town, Marine Medical Mission offered free dental service to all. On board was also an electric organ. People could hear the Willis Shank coming over a mile away as Captain Stabbert played some rousing hymn of the church. And boy, could he ever play that thing!

Captain Stabbert—Founder and Head of Marine Medical Mission

'Cap', as everybody affectionately called him, gave me the royal welcome. During our conversation, I mentioned my desire to check out the plane. "Oh, that's already been done . . . just had its annual re-license inspection . . . need you to run me over to Vancouver right after lunch!"

So right after lunch, I pre-flighted the plane and waited for Captain Stabbert to show up. In the next half hour, several people came looking for Cap. Seems that no one did anything, or made any decisions around the place, without running it past the captain first. He certainly had the charisma. Tall and handsome in his trim captain's uniform. Deep tan, broad disarming smile, and a constant twinkle in his eyes, he commanded loyalty from a broad band of followers. But it didn't take you long to realize that this mission was a one-man show. Consequently a lot of people were just sitting around, twiddling their thumbs, doing nothing constructive, until they got the good word.

When I pre-flighted the plane, there was a bit of oil inside the cowl, and on the underside of the fuselage.

I muttered to myself, 'Might as well make myself useful while I'm waiting.' So I re-checked, without removing the cowling, to see where the oil was coming from. Also the oil looked very black, especially for a plane that had just come off an inspection. I decided to check the engine log to see when the oil had been changed. I couldn't find the engine log. I didn't find any of the plane's books!

After waiting for over two hours, I also went looking for the captain. He was tied up in a meeting. We would go just as soon as he could free himself. Another two hours went by. That oil leak was beginning to bother me, so I removed the cowling for a better look. Wow! The oil was oozing from a loose oil-line fitting! Just imagine what could of, would of, happened if I had not checked! I tightened the fitting and started up the engine. No more leak.

I thought, 'Boy, that oil is so black . . . now that I have the cowling off, might as well change it.'

So I was just draining the oil, and guess who comes and wants to buzz off to Vancouver real quicklike? Oh boy!

Captain Stabbert let me have it in no uncertain terms that I was screwing up the works!

I told him about the oil line fitting and the dirty oil. That didn't seem to make any difference.

"How soon will you have this thing put together?"

"Give me a half hour!"

Cap smacked his forehead and grabbed his hair as he grimaced and shook his head slowly with a hopeless look of despair, "Just not enough time . . . we'll go first thing in the morning!"

I also asked him about the logbooks.

"Logbooks . . . what logbooks?"

"The engine log, the aircraft log, the journey log . . . for the plane."

He stammered, "They are not here? . . . they must be in Seattle!"

(I also learned, later, that I had stupidly entered Canada illegally by not stopping at Sydney to go through customs and immigration, where I would have needed to produce the journey log for their scrutiny. Not knowing the ropes, it never even crossed my mind, and Charlie never breathed a word! Good grief! How dumb can you get!)

Next morning, I was up at the crack of dawn, had a quick breakfast at the big house, and went down to the plane at the dock. The Aeronca was sitting a bit low in the water, so I checked the pontoons where I found quite a lot of water in several of the compartments. I removed the water with the suction pump, rechecked the plane, and we were ready to go.

'First thing in the morning' worked out to be around nine o'clock, after Cap had taken care of a dozen little details that needed doing first.

"Cap, I pumped a lot of water out of the floats this morning!"

"Yeah, we usually keep the plane over on the skid in front of my house . . . we'll park it there tonight."

As soon as we were airborne, Cap gave me a smug look and took over the controls, "Jest like ta keep me hands from gettin' rusty!"

So happened there were a number of fellows in Marine Medical who liked to 'keep from gettin' rusty!'

We flew on to Vancouver where I landed in the Fraser River and tied up to the seaplane dock.

"Rich, you stay with the plane . . . be back soon as I take care of business!" Cap walked up the ramp and jumped into a waiting car.

He was back in less than an hour, and he was in a hurry! "Forgot some important papers . . . we gotta go back to the island!" I took off, flew back to Thetis, and tied up to the dock. Cap jumped out, "Be right back!"

Another dozen details and an hour later, Captain Stabbert was ready to go again.

Off to Vancouver we flew, where I settled down for the long wait, while Cap "took care of business." I had the plane fueled, checked the pontoon compartments for water, and checked the engine for oil leaks. Looks okay. Next time I would have a good book to read, or maybe a fishing pole, anything but just sit around and wait. Having something along to eat and drink would also be a grand idea!

Well anyway, Cap finally came back and we took off for Thetis. We circled over his house and landed east of the island. There was a long ditch that led you into a tiny lagoon at the house. It was narrower than the span of the wings. As I was carefully taxiing up the ditch, sometimes the mounds of sand, which had been dredged from the ditch, almost touched the wing tips.

"Here, let me show you how you do this!", Cap growled impatiently.

With that, he shoved the throttle full bore, romped the plane up on its step, and we went roaring up the narrow channel! Just as he got to the lagoon, he chopped the power, did a sharp ninety degree turn, hit the throttle again to slide us smartly onto the skid! WOW!

Only trouble was, the right pontoon failed to climb the ramp properly, which crumpled the tip of the pontoon and punched a three inch hole in the front compartment!

Cap looked at me and grinned sheepishly . . . "Didn't make it, did I!"

Then he walked off to the house, leaving me to figure out how to fix the stupid mess. Oh boy!

The next day was spent doing a quick fix. I glued on a patch of extra heavy canvas with contact cement and waterproofed it with some gray paint. Looked okay from thirty feet! The whole front end of the float would need to be rebuilt. Who knows when I would have time for that.

The next few days I flew some of the coordinators of the summer program to several of the nearby islands where the mission had Bible Schools for the kids in years past.

Information was gathered as to how many teachers would be needed, where they would be staying, what provisions they might need, and where the school would be held.

Everywhere we went, the kids and people flocked to the dock, as everyone recognized the plane. The Mission was held in high regard, and we were well received by all.

When everything was all set, the teachers were dispersed by boat or plane to the various islands where they conducted an intensive two week Bible School. For some kids, this would be the only direct Christian teaching they would ever get. The kids were offered a simple correspondence course which would further ground them, and help them grow in their new found faith. The parents were encouraged to get involved by establishing daily devotions in the home, and to reach out to others in the community. It really was quite a program.

While Phase One was going on, I flew the plane back to Seattle, found the log books, and did a proper repair to the damaged pontoon. That took me a whole week of precious time. What a job that was, but I made it good as new!

80 college kids volunteered for work on board MMM's "Willis Shank"

Phase Two was already in operation, and I caught up with the action at Alert Bay. I was to meet the Willis Shank here and fly the teachers out to the surrounding islands.

This is a fantastically beautiful country! Myriads of emerald green islands scattered everywhere in the crystal blue sea. Gems of every color, tiny lakes set in forested mountains all along the inland channel. Snow-capped mountains reached for the blue, blue sky.

But it is a place of danger. The weather can change in an instant to trap the inexperienced. The sea can be glassy smooth. Around the next bend, the winds have churned the water into frothy white caps, and there is no place to land.

As I was nearing Alert Bay, I could see the fog forming along the eastern hills. A half hour later, I had tied up to the dock at Alert Bay. The fog was so thick, sitting in the cockpit, I could not see the dock! It was scary quiet.

By noon time, the fog had lifted. Three hours later, you could hear the strains of 'Wonderful Grace of Jesus' floating across the water as the glistening white ship, the Willis Shank, came into view. What a majestic sight!

The people flocked aboard and listened to a rousing gospel sing led by the college students. They browsed the Christian bookshop. Some dropped into the dental clinic to have their teeth checked.

I was kept busy flying the teachers out to the nearby islands for their Bible school assignments.

One very memorable flight was to drop off a couple of teachers at a logging camp at the end of Bentinck Arm, about 200 miles from Namu. Landing on glassy-smooth water can be rather tricky because it is hard to judge your height above the water. During my seaplane training, I never actually encountered real glassy-smooth water, but, thank goodness, I remembered to put the plane in a touchdown attitude. What a shock it was, to touch down a few seconds later, when my eyes said we were still a hundred feet above the water! Believe me, that will raise the hackles on the back of your scalp!

I dropped off my passengers on the big log they used for a dock, and took off. I thought, 'Why not climb up and fly directly to Namu over the mountains, instead of the long horseshoe flight via the channel? Sure would save some time.'

I leveled off at three-thousand feet and had actually turned to fly direct to Namu, when that wee small voice sounded the alarm . . . I was breaking one of the cardinal rules of seaplane flying . . . "Always stay over the water, whenever possible, in case you have to make a forced landing!"

It's a good thing I chickened out! About seventy miles from Namu, the engine suddenly sputtered and died. In shock, I looked up at the sight-glass, for the right wingtank, to read that the full tank was now empty! I switched back to the left tank that still had a few gallons left. The engine came to life again. Oh. what a sweet sound! But there was not enough fuel to make it to Namu!

When the engine began to sputter, I cut the power and made a forced landing in the channel. That's the beauty of a seaplane . . . set it down anywhere . . . just as long as you obey that cardinal rule of staying over the water. After I landed, I climbed up on the right wing-strut to check the gas tank. The gas-cap on the Aeronca Sedan has a real fine thread. I had been warned, 'you can easily cross the threads, then the tank will not seal properly, and all the gas will siphon from the tank!' Guess what?

There was a gentle breeze that was carrying me down the channel toward Namu which was about ten miles away. Hey, how about that . . . I'll just sail the rest of the way home! So I dug out a couple of rain ponchos from the baggage compartment and tied them to the wing struts to increase my sail area. That worked great . . . until the wind switched and carried me right back to where we had started!

I thought to myself, 'Looks like a cove over on the west shore. Better get over there to spend the night. Don't want to get run down by some fishing boat out here in the channel.'

It would be dark in another hour. So I cranked up the engine and started taxiing toward the cove. Just about got there when the engine died. I climbed out onto the pontoon and gently rocked the plane, hoping to jiggle some residual gas from the wingtank down into the carburetor. It worked! But there were some huge granite boulders just under the surface in the cove, and all along the shore. The breeze carried me back and forth. There was nowhere to safely tie up the plane. 'Better get out of here before we punch a hole in the floats!'

So I cranked up the engine and taxied back out to the middle of the channel. 'What am I going to do? Nothing to do but sit . . . might as well go fishing.' So I rigged up a pole and fished until the sun was going down. Not a single bite.

As it was getting dark, the breeze died down, and the water became glassy-smooth. From off in the distance floated the lonesome cry of a loon. Up over the eastern mountains the full moon rose. 'Wow! . . . Just look at that reflection!' I was in absolute awe at the majestic beauty of this place.

As I humbly talked to the Lord that night, He said, 'You are getting so busy doing things for Me . . . why, you no longer have time for Me! Thought I would just slow you down a bit . . . to give you some time to see all this beauty I have made for you to enjoy . . . and to let you know that I love you!'

What a wondrous time of fellowship we had that night!

I turned on the navigation lights, and curled up in the back seat. Oh, I was so tired. But suddenly, I bolted wide awake! Way off in the distance . . . chug, chug, chug, chug, chug . . . a boat was coming!

I flipped on and off the landing lights three times . . . then, three more times as he came closer. He saw me, tooted his horn, and slowed to a crawl. I climbed out on the pontoon and frantically waved the flashlight.

He stopped. "Ahoy there . . . you have trouble?"

"Yeah . . . I ran out of gas!"

He was quiet for a moment. "Have boat gas . . . only five gallon . . . plane run on boat gas?"

"I'd sure be willing to give it a try!"

He eased the boat right up to the front of the plane. A dark Indian form handed me a jerry tin of gas. I clambered up on the wing-strut and carefully poured the precious fuel into the left wingtank.

As I handed him the empty tin, "Can I give you five dollars for the gas? . . . that's all I've got!"

He shook his head and jumped to the bow of his boat.

"Ah, come on . . . take it!"

He hesitated and smiled, "No way . . . you help next fellah, aye?"

"That's a deal . . . and thanks!"

The boat slowly backed away and soon he disappeared.

"Thank You, Lord!"

I cranked up the engine and began slowly taxiing toward Namu. 'Take me forever at this rate' . . . so I eased the plane up on the step. 'Wow! . . . the moon . . . you can almost see everythi..ng!!' Suddenly . . . a log . . . right across my path! I jerked on the wheel! 'Whew! I barely cleared that log by inches!' And I was airborne! 'Should I set it back down? . . . No, there could be more logs!' So I eased the plane up a couple hundred feet and flew on to Namu.

The tiny village, plastered to the hillside, was asleep. I circled around, lined up with the moon's reflection . . . you could see everything as bright as day. I landed in the moonshine, and taxied up to the dock. Not a soul appeared! Not a dog barked. 'Maybe they do this all the time, around here? This is all like . . . a dream!'

I walked up the hill to the missionary's house and went to bed. Suddenly, I realized that I was very hungry . . . that was no dream!

Early next morning, I went down to the dock and pumped out the floats, checked the plane over and loaded up with fuel. I was to meet up with the Willis Shank near Sandspit in the Queen Charlotte Islands to help distribute teachers to their various assignments in the Islands. About a half hour out, I ran into a solid bank of fog right down to the water. I flew parallel to the bank and tried to penetrate a light spot several times, but it was a no-go, so I returned to Namu. A couple hours later Namu was socked in with a fog so thick you couldn't see twenty feet. And it remained that way, and all the next day. What an eerie feeling!

The Willis Shank got word to me via the RCMP (Canadian Police). 'Urgent. Do not fly to Sandspit. Bad storm here. Meet the Nunivak (one of the power barges) at Bella Bella, morning of 7-22. Plan on immediate flight to Thetis. Urgent!' 'Hmmm . . . wonder what's going on?'

The weather was good enough for me to get to Bella Bella the next morning just as the Nunivak was arriving. I gave them a real buzz job. The water was calm in the channel, and the Nunivak stopped.

I landed and taxied along side. "Hi . . . long time no see!"

"Yeah . . . it's about time. Where ya been?"

"Sorry . . . been sittin' at Namu for the last two days because of the fog!"

"Just as well . . . Boy, it's a good thing you didn't make it out to the Charlottes . . . there would have been no place for you to land! We had waves twenty feet high. Just about sunk us!"

"Wow! . . . What's going on? Heard that I have to fly urgent-like back to Thetis!"

"Yeah . . . a couple of the teachers have to get home real fast . . . got word their dad was in a bad auto accident!"

"Oh boy! . . . Okay, I'm ready to fly . . . but why not take them straight to Seattle?"

"Charlie will do that . . . you come back with the Taylorcraft . . . we need you up here!"

"Okay, I guess," wondering at the wisdom of using a plane that could only carry one passenger and twenty pounds of baggage.

Jim and Ken hopped aboard, "Sorry guys . . . about your dad!"

"Yeah . . . thanks . . . we're not sure how bad it is . . . all we know is that he is in the hospital, and we're to get home as soon as possible!"

"Okay, let's do that!" I shoved the throttle to the wall. We had quite a conversation on the way.

In times like this you wonder why the Lord, who just turned you back from getting to the Queen Charlotte Islands, where there would be no place to land . . . why didn't He prevent this dad from having a car accident, so Jim and Ken could remain up here serving Him? Oh, we can ask that question in a thousand different ways, which all boils down to . . . "Why Lord?" And maybe we can all come up with a thousand different answers, which condense down to His answer . . . "No matter what happens . . . just trust Me!"

For sure, I will never pretend here to know all the whys and wherefores. But perhaps it would be a good exercise for you right now . . . to just think back through your life where you could have measured the difference between life and death by a thousandths of a second.

For you, who really belong to the Lord, though the way may not have been easy, your conclusion has to be . . . "Truly Lord, You have been so good to me!"

And for you, who do not know Him yet, perhaps life sucks. Isn't that how you express it? It's a real drag. But you can change that. "How? . . . you say." By repenting of your sins . . . ask Him to help you clean up your act . . . at the same time, ask Jesus to be your Savior . . . and then let Him be Lord of your life. Sure, you'll have to make some changes in your lifestyle, but you will find that it's really worth it. And He will help you. I challenge you to give yourself to the Lord. You want a life of excitement? A life that's really worth living? Give your life to Him and His service. I'll guarantee you, that you will have more excitement than you ever bargained for, when you really live your life for Him!

24 July 56. I took off early in the morning with the Taylorcraft for Alert Bay, via a gas stop at Campbell River. The little plane handled surprisingly well, but it took me three hours and fifty minutes to fly less than four hundred miles. This little buggy does pretty good, considering you got all that drag from the pontoons.

I spent the next two days taking one of the directors of the summer program around so she could observe the teachers in action. It was also interesting for me to see the flocks of kids being reached with the Gospel, and then to realize that I was also a small part in making this possible. On the 27th, I flew back to Thetis to get the Aeronca Sedan.

The next couple of days was spent picking up some of the teachers. It was interesting when I landed at the end of the South Bentinck Arm this time. Instead of glassy-smooth water, a strong wind was churning the waters to white caps. It took all my strength to hold the seaplane away from the log while my passengers hopped aboard. You never know up here what will greet you around the next bend.

The tiny logging village of Shelton hugs the mountains of B.C.

Charlie Ackley and Alice Johnson wanted to fly up to Kitimat to check on the possibilities of having a Bible School at this boom town next year. As we rounded the bend of Hawkesbury Island, a strong south wind was whipping the water to a froth. And when we arrived at Kitimat the conditions were no better. I circled around Minette Bay looking for a place to land. Over on the east side by Kitimaat Village Mission, a small point of land jutted out into the bay, providing a bit of calm water. I came in low over the dock, plopped her down, and taxied back to the seaplane ramp. We were welcomed by the pastor of the small Community Church who graciously invited us to lunch. Sure, he would be very happy to have Marine Medical Mission provide a Bible School at his facility. And he thought there would be very good possibilities over on the Kitimat side at a couple of the churches there, and he gave us the names of several people to contact.

Because the water was so rough, we waited around for over three hours, hoping for the wind die down. Charlie kept agitating, "Come on Rich . . . good grief, let's go . . . we can make our contacts, and then get on up to Prince Rupert before dark!"

"Boy, I don't know . . . it's really rough out there!"

"Look . . . we can't stay here all day!"

Because of the constant badgering, I finally agreed to go and take a look. We took off and flew over to the west side of the bay where I made several passes near the seaplane dock. I shook my head, "It's really rough down there!"

"Ah come on . . . set it down . . . for crying out loud!"

Against my better judgment, I came around and set down, planning to get stopped right at the entrance where the log boom provided shelter to the seaplane docks. But I skipped across the tops of several waves and hit with a resounding crash into a large wave that brought us to a shuddering stop. Water flew clear over the top of the plane! We bounced past the entrance, so I gunned the engine and brought the plane around to taxi back to the shelter. Suddenly I realized that the elevator control was partially jammed! I couldn't pull the control fully back to keep the tail down! As we sailed down a trough, I watched the fronts of the pontoons go completely under water before climbing the next wave! In the next trough, the plane up-ended. I cut the power when the prop hit the water. As we were going over, I turned the controls to bring the plane around.

I yelled, "Quick Charlie . . . climb out to the back of the pontoon!"

He scrambled out the door!

The tail settled back down and swung us around just as the wind carried us past the entrance to the shelter.

Suddenly, there was a loud explosion! The ball end of a throw-line crashed through the windshield! Charlie grabbed and secured the rope! A boat towed us to safety! WOW!!

We hopped out on the dock. The floats were half submerged in the water. One of the pontoon covers was missing and that compartment was completely filled with water. I pumped out the pontoons with the bilge pump.

Some guy said, "Boy . . . it's a good thing you didn't end up in the drink . . . glacier water's so cold . . . ya wouldn't a lasted six minutes!"

A friendly orderly at the nearby hospital let us sleep overnight in an empty wing of the hospital . . . "Just make sure you're outta there during daylight hours!"

So in the morning, we moved out and set up a hobo camp in the woods nearby. I went down to the dock to check the plane. I pumped out the water that had accumulated in the compartments overnight. There was a slight crinkle to the fabric on both sides where the front pontoon struts connected to the fuselage. I removed the inside covers and examined the areas with a flashlight. It was hard to see (without cutting the fabric) the whole extent of the damage. But it was evident that the tubing was buckled enough so the elevator control was partially jammed, hitting against something under the dash.

I checked the prop and engine for damage. They looked okay. When I started up the engine, it ran okay, but this plane would not be flying for awhile.

While I was tinkering around, an RCMP showed up and gave me some papers and requested that I file an accident report. Charlie asked him if he would try to contact the Willis Shank. They were expecting to rendezvous with us at Prince Rupert.

Charlie was fit to be tied. His quick assessment to what little damage he saw, "Man, there's no reason we can't fly this thing to Prince Rupert!"

Believe me, we had an exchange of words.

"Look Charlie . . . I'm not flying this plane . . . and neither are you!"

"But we're stuck here!", Charlie screamed and waved his arms in frustration.

"You bet'cha, man . . . we're stuck here . . . until somebody comes and picks us up! In the meantime, get off my back, sit down, and shut up!!"

I was really mad. To think I had allowed myself to be pressured into a flight that I knew was not safe to do.

(Little did I realize, that for the next twenty-one years of my aviation career, there would always be some 'know-it-all turkey' who would try to usurp my pilot-in-command authority, and DEMAND that I fly, when my training and experience said it was not safe. "Thank you Lord, for this hard lesson!")

I filed the accident report with the Mounties. To them it was no big deal. They were able to make contact with the Willis Shank. A power barge would pick up the plane.

Kitimat was quite a boom-town. Just like you would see in a wild west movie. The hastily constructed buildings and shanties lacked any semblance of permanence. The streets were a sea of mud, churned up by some ten-thousand construction workers and all their mobile equipment. Many of them did not speak English: evidently immigrants

143

from Europe, India, and Asia. The reason for all this activity was the hydro-electric dam they were building which would plentifully supply the cheap electricity needed for the new aluminum smelter under construction. Our clothes were dirty. Our faces grew quite a stubble over the days we waited for the barge. We looked like bums, but no one paid any attention to us as we blended in with all this hub-bub of activity.

The Nunivak showed up on July 7th. I taxied the Aeronca over to one of the docks where a huge crane easily picked up the plane like a small flea and deposited it on the barge. We immediately departed for Prince Rupert where I was to do a 'quick-fix' on the plane.

When I heard that, I blew up . . . absolutely sky high! "Quick fix? You gotta be kidding . . . why, this plane won't be flying for months! You guys haven't the faintest clue what needs to be done here! Everything in this cotton-picking Mission is just one quick-fix after another . . . and just what am I gonna fix it with? I don't have the tools or the materials or . . . !"

Ken interrupted, "Rich, take it easy . . . we got permission to use the PWA (Pacific Western) hangar facilities, and they are willing to loan you any tools you'll need!"

I simmered down a bit, "What kind of time frame you talkin' . . . it looks like I'm gonna have to strip some fabric just to see the damage. There's probably some cracked tubing. I'll need a welding outfit, and I'll bet'cha they don't have any 4130 aircraft steel tubing! And to redo the fabric . . . you wouldn't believe the time that will take!"

Ken just smiled, "Well, lets see when we get there."

When we pulled into the dock there was another crane which picked up the plane and set it gently onto a seaplane dolly which was then towed into the gigantic PWA hangar.

Everybody took off and left me to do my thing. I took the doors off the plane and removed the seats. Then I cut away enough fabric on the left side to reveal a crack in the vertical truss and a buckle in the lower longeron. The vertical truss on the right side was completely broken off and had collapsed about four inches. I cut away the fabric to expose the weld clusters and more of the tubing. There was a number of spots of rust on the tubing, so I checked these with a center punch. Wow! Some of the tubing was so rotten you didn't even have to hit it with a hammer! In a couple of places, I pushed the center-punch right through the wall of the tubing, just using my hand! I growled, "Good grief! What in the world was holding this plane together when we flew! It's a miracle we didn't fall apart in the sky!"

When they came back to see how things were going, I showed them the rotten tubing, and they concluded that this wasn't going to be a quick-fix.

"In fact . . . can this be fixed at all?"

"Yeah, well . . . it looks like all the fabric will need to be stripped off the fuselage to see the extent of the damage, but for sure . . . it's not a job to be done up here . . . and could you afford it? The labor costs will kill you! I could get the project started, but SIM's candidate class begins the first part of September! There's probably not enough time to do the whole job."

After a lengthy conference . . . "Well, we sure appreciate your offer to get it started. Dave can help you until school starts. There's a little shop there on Lake Union . . . we suggest the power barge take you and the plane down there as fast as they can go!"

So that was the plan. I made one more flight on August 10th, to Annette Island, the southern tip of Alaska, with the Taylorcraft. Then we headed south with the power barge. That last flight gave me a total of 344 hours.

When we got to Seattle, I called the Sudan Interior Mission and told them what had happened, and that I would like to stay as long as possible to repair the plane. After a brief conference, they said, "There's a special candidate class being held in December for three couples who can't make it to the September class . . . we'll plan on you for December, okay?"

Without hesitation, I agreed to that.

The little shop was just that . . . little . . . in fact, we had to remove the wings in order to get the fuselage into the room. At least I would be out of the weather. I began by cutting away the fabric to look for more damage and rust. I checked on the price for a whole new fabric sock that would slip on over the entire fuselage, and the Mission agreed that would be the way to go. So I stripped it completely. There she sat . . . just like a big model airplane kit.

I replaced fourteen sections of rusted-out rotten tubing. After each phase of the repair, I had a CAA inspector come and sign off the job.

"Where did you learn to do work like this!"

So I told them about my training at Moody Bible Institute and working at Elmhurst Airport.

"Well, they sure taught you right . . . wish there were more schools like that around!"

They took the rusted-out tubing for evidence, and said they were going after the base operator who had done the annual re-license inspection.

I shook my head, "There's no way he could have found this rusty tubing without cutting away the fabric!"

"No matter, we've been trying to nail this turkey for years for skimpy, shoddy work! Kick the pontoons, spin the prop, and call it an annual re-license inspection! Planes fly in from all over the northwest because they know they can get a quick inspection at a cheap price. We're gonna shut this joker down before somebody gets killed!" And so they did!

I got all the dope and fabric work done just before I had to take off for New York . . . it really looked beautiful. All that was left was to install the new windshield, drag it out, and attach the wings.

On the last night, there was a big send-off party for me. They presented me with a new stop-watch to replace the one that had popped off my wrist one day when I was pumping out the pontoons. Wow! It was hard to say goodbye, but it was also time to move on.

145

CHAPTER 19
CANDIDATE CLASS

My old buggy let me down on the Pennsylvania Turnpike. We were going along just fine when suddenly the engine began knocking loudly and started running very rough. We were unceremoniously towed off to a junkyard garage which cost me twenty five dollars. They were willing to fix it for a price, but I didn't have that kind of money. Their attitude was, "Well buddy, you're welcome to fix it yerself!"

They had that smug 'got cha' smile on their faces. Actually, they were hoping that I would just abandon the old bomber. I probably would have, except for my huge tool box full of tools which was too heavy to carry.

We were stuck in the middle of nowhere. There was no place to stay . . . no place to eat . . . and that December day, it was really cold. But I curled up in the front seat with my army blanket and shivered through the night. All I had to eat was a handful of grapes, and part of a huge head of raw cauliflower that I had purchased in Idaho for nineteen cents.. I called the Sudan Interior Mission, told them my hard luck story, and that I would be a day or so late. They were very perturbed with this unhappy news.

Early next morning, I jacked up the front of my car, setting it on a couple of old wheels. Then I drained the oil, and dropped the oil pan. I examined the connecting rod bearings. To my surprise, they were in perfect condition. What was causing the knock? You could plainly hear it as I turned the engine over by hand. Every second revolution . . . clunk?? All I had for a light, was my aircraft inspection gooseneck flashlight. And then I saw it. On every second revolution of the crankshaft, one of the big-ends would come around and just barely touch one of the cam lobes! Clunk! (Plain as mud, aye?) Just to make the story short, this was caused by five teeth which had broken off the fiber timing gear, allowing the camshaft to shift just enough for the parts to touch. They sold me a used, but good, timing gear for a buck and a half. I put everything back together again, and she purred like a kitten, much to the disappointment of my junkyard friends. I got to candidate school two days late.

SIM headquarters at 164 West 74th Street, New York City, was located in an old six story hotel whose glory days had faded long ago, although a huge crystal chandelier, marble walls, and stained glass windows greeted you when you walked into the lobby. That was where the glory ended. The dimly lit hallways led you to small dingy rooms that were furnished with dark antique furniture. I felt like I had stepped into a time machine that had transported me back a hundred years. SIM was not about to modernize this dinosaur. It was more important for the funds, donated by faithful Christians, to be used overseas to present the Gospel in every way possible.

What made this place come alive was the people in it, or those that passed through it. Everyone seemed to have that glow that comes to those who are in the service of the Lord. No matter how small their job, they still had that certain glow. And then to realize that you are to become one of them! Wow! Just how do you describe that feeling bubbling up inside of you?

Mr. and Mrs. Tom Miller acted as the gracious hosts to all who passed through the doors. They assigned various jobs, some not so nice, to us candidates, and then they observed how we performed the task. Did we display a willing attitude? Would we be a good prospect as a missionary working overseas?

Mr. Miller took a real shine to me when he found that I was a Mr. Fix-it. For sure, there were plenty of things around that place that needed fixing. From the washing machines and clothes dryers in the basement, to the leaking faucets and toilets, broken light switches and electrical outlets, fixing kitchen appliances and missionary's cars, Mr. Miller had me going every spare moment when we were not in a class. Little did he realize, that a lot of this junk, I had never seen before in my life. It's what you call winging it, and I did pretty darn good job, if I don't say so myself!

The three couples in the Candidate class were Jerry and Gladys Freisen from Dallas, Oregon, Dick and Kay Goss from Washington, and Jim and Eleanor Pelley from Connecticut? The things we didn't get into in that candidate class! It was a miracle that any of us were ever accepted into the Mission!

One day, Jerry and I were working down in the basement on one of the old washing machines that had overflowed and flooded the basement. Not a day went by that Mr. Miller sternly warned us to never put too much soap in the machines! Well, we had the machine tipped up, and Jerry was holding it, while I crawled under the backside to see what I could find. We were having a good time, joking around about our Scottish overseer. Jerry was talking in his best Scottish brogue, and I was answering in my best dumb German . . . "And yah, I vonder vhat vould happen if I put a whole box of soap in dis machine!"

A few moments before that profound statement, unknown to me, Mr. Miller had appeared on the scene. Jerry was sputtering, but it was Mr. Miller who answered me, "Young man . . . you better not try it!"

I stuck my head out from under the machine, "Oh hi, Mr. Miller!" My smile quickly faded. Mr. Miller's face was beet red, and he was NOT smiling! Oh boy!

I'm afraid that Mrs. Miller did not take a shine to me. And this dumb American kid rebelled against her oh-so-English ways. Every meal was a lesson in etiquette and authority. It bothered me the way she talked down to us. The way she held her tea cup just so. The way she rung her little bell when the server was to bring in the next course of food. And every day we got a sales pitch on how badly the Mission needed new chairs for the dining room . . . with the hint that we candidates were expected to donate toward this worthy cause! It got to be one of our little jokes. In my eyes, those antique chairs were so sturdy, they would last for a thousand years!

One day, while we candidates were clearing the table, we were discussing what a proper donation should be. I picked up the little dinner bell, rang it for attention, and in the best English manner that I could muster, "I think my donation will be . . . one dollar!" I waved a dollar bill around for everyone to see, and then I tied it to the bell's clapper with a rubber band!

The next morning, we all sat there with rapt expectation. We drank our juice. Mrs. Miller picked up the bell! She rung it once . . . twice . . . the shock on her face was something to behold when that familiar tinkle did not come. She turned over the bell and saw the dollar bill! Wow!

She put the bell down with a bang. "The young man who put that dollar bill in the bell . . . can pick it up after the meal is over!" With that, she stomped angrily from the room. Oh boy, I really did it! But one thing, the need for new chairs was never again brought to our attention.

And then, there was the mixing-bowl. Jerry was washing. I was drying, And Jim was putting the dishes away. "Here . . . catch!" He didn't! This huge beautiful mixing-bowl bounced off Jim's chest and to the tile floor where it exploded into a hundred pieces! I hunted all over New York city, desperately trying to find a replacement. Nothing came close to size nor beauty. The bowl I finally purchased was a very humble substitute to be sure.

Maybe it would be a wise thing if I just disappeared for awhile.

"Young man . . . you have a telephone call!"

To my surprise, it was . . . "Greta?"

She laughed, "I missed you in the September candidate class, and heard that you would be coming to the special class in December!"

"You mean that you are going out with SIM?"

She laughed again, "I'll be going out to Somalia just as soon as my support comes in!"

"Wow! That's great . . . Where are you now?"

"I'm at home in New Jersey . . . wondering if you would like to come and spend the weekend?"

"Mmmm . . . I'd like that . . . let me check and I'll call you back!"

No way could I get away for a week end, but arrangements were made to stop by after candidate class was over. Monmouth Beach would be on my way to visit the Ogburns in North Carolina. In the meanwhile, back to the here and now.

Not only were we there so the Mission could check us out as to likely missionary material, we were also there to learn about the Sudan Interior Mission. We had classes on everything imaginable.

We must have had six or eight sessions with Dr. Frame, the Mission's doctor, who gave every missionary a thorough physical exam coming back from, or going overseas. His word could end a missionary career, just like that.

He seemed to be hung up on psychoanalysis, at the moment, as he was always asking us probing questions, and then observing our reactions. One particular session, he was expounding on how our bodies sometimes become sick in reaction to our parental upbringing. Way out things like: "Why, your ingrown toe nails may have been caused because your dad beat you on the head with a belt buckle! Or you get those migraine headaches because your domineering mother stood you in the corner wearing a dunce cap! Or you come down with a cold or the flu just before you're going to hit the boss for a raise . . . or just before that chemistry exam, you get sick to escape a confrontational situation! We abuse our children because we were abused when we were little!" Way out stuff!

Each profound statement was backed up by various studies and declarations by some psychologist whacko who proved it beyond a doubt. And the three couples were just lapping it up . . . pointing knowingly at their mates, as such statements recalled similar incidents in their lives where they happened to get sick just before blah, blah, blah!

I couldn't believe my ears, and I guess my reactions were quite evident to der' doctor. Suddenly, he stopped and bored a hole right through me, "Schaffer . . . what are you thinking?"

I didn't blink an eye . . . "I think you're nuts . . . absolutely bonkers!"

"Why . . . sputter . . . sputter . . . you know . . . !"

I interrupted, "Look . . . I took some psychology . . . and you jokers are ALWAYS trying to put everybody in a convenient little box . . . we do thus and thus, or we get this and that, because of some bad scene in our past. That aint necessarily so . . . there are as many reactions to a situation as there are people in the world. It's high time we take responsibility for our OWN actions, and quite trying to blame our parents or others for our OWN failures!

"And as for sickness . . . we get sick because of germs! You get a cold because you shook hands with someone who had a cold, or you grabbed a snotty door knob, and then you stupidly stuck your fingers in your mouth, or picked your nose . . . grrrr!!" I rolled my eyes, pulled my hair, and threw my hands into the air. Everybody was in absolute shock . . . thus ended the class for the day!

I thought, 'Boy, I'm in for it now!' But surprisingly, the doctor recovered quite well. Just like this encounter never happened, however, we had no more psychology lectures . . . we stuck to more conventional things, like the shots we would need before going overseas, and the importance of faithfully taking our malaria medicine.

We went through the SIM Manual, which is the Mission's rule book, which governs how everyone shall conduct themselves while they are in the Mission. Simple, easy to understand, and it answered a lot of questions. It's a green loose leaf notebook which is periodically updated when the need arises. Every missionary is required to read the manual and sign a statement that you accept its provisions and regulations and agree to live, work, and serve in accord with them. Let me give you a real life example.

In section 3, regarding Personnel, in the Preamble it states: SIM seeks to enable its members to utilize their gifts to meet the objectives which God has given to the Mission. (Eph 4: 11 & 12 . . . which goes something like this . . . "God gives to some of us special abilities to be apostles, some to be preachers, some to be evangelists, to be pastors, or teachers, doctors, nurses, computer operators, farmers, welders . . . and way down somewhere in the list is, airplane pilots and mechanics. God gives us these special abilities so that we can do a first class professional job!" (My very loose translation!)

Then in Section 3, VIII.A, as to Assignments it states: 1. Every attempt is made to assign missionaries to the task for which they have been recruited. All recruits should realize, however, that the demands of missionary service require flexibility and willingness to fit into changing priorities. Above all, missionaries should recognize God's over-ruling hand in assignments.

Well, one day, a missionary coming home on furlough from Nigeria, gave me some very disturbing news. He said that SIMAIR (the aviation department) didn't need another pilot! They only wanted me as a mechanic!

Whoa! I had already gone through this little game of musical chairs in the Air Force when I had signed up, hoping to get into Cadets. But they didn't need any Cadets. Instead, they made me into an auto mechanic! An auto mechanic I was, my whole military career!

I thought I was signing up with SIM to be a pilot/mechanic . . . not just a mechanic . . . maybe I better do some checking. So I asked for an appointment with the Home Secretary.

A few days later in Dr. Darrow's office, I explained to him my consternation over this unhappy news. He looked at me over the top of his glasses and growled, "And suppose they don't even want you for a mechanic?"

I stuttered, "Wha . . . wha . . . what do you mean?"

He sat up a little taller, and he exploded, "Young man . . . this MISSION is looking for MISSIONARIES!! Are you willing to be NOTHING BUT A MISSIONARY?"

I was absolutely stunned! I didn't know what to say. His voice got very fervent, "You specialists . . . seems like every day, specialist this and specialist that is going through these doors . . . I'm sick and tired of specialists! What this Mission needs is missionaries! Are you willing to be a missionary . . . nothing but a missionary?" With that, he pointed me to the door!

Wow! I was absolutely shattered. What was I going to do? Well, one thing, it caused me to re-examine very carefully God's call on my life, and where that had led me over the past seven years.

I was certain that God had called me to be a missionary. And I was certain that God had called me to be a missionary pilot-mechanic, for which, in the last four years, I had gone through some of the most intensive specialized training to become exactly that. There was never a doubt that this was to be my absolute service to the Lord.

Now, would I be willing to forget all this, and be willing to be . . . just a missionary? I wrestled with that question over the next couple of weeks, clear to the end of the candidate school, when we were to appear before the board for examination.

Now that was a day that I will never forget. They called in the couples in alphabetical order . . . the Friesen's, the Goss's, and then the Pelley's. Time was standing still. It was taking forever.

When the Friesen's came out, they were NOT smiling. The Board said that Gladys needed to take a semester in Bible to meet the Mission's minimum requirement. Then they would be accepted for assignment to Kent Academy, the missionary kids school in Nigeria.

The Goss's were in and out in short order. Big smiles. They would be going to Ethiopia.

The Pelley's would be going to work at the radio station, ELWA, in Liberia.

And then it was my turn. It seemed like forever before they called me in. What were they discussing about me? I felt like I had really blown it. What's the use?

When I entered the room and shut the door, Mr. Miller led me around the room and introduced me to each of the board members, some who warmly shook my hand and even gave me a smile.

Mr. Miller motioned to the chair in the center of the room . . . "Have a seat, Rich . . . we are certainly glad to have you here!" And then with his hand on my shoulder, he turned and spoke to the members of the board. "This young man has certainly created one of the most lively candidate classes that I will long remember!"

He went on to tell them about the washing machine incident, and about the dollar bill on his wife's dinner bell . . . the mixing bowl. What a story teller! He literally had the board members in stitches of laughter. "And this young fellow . . . why, he can fix anything! . . . all the junk he has fixed around here . . . I wish we could keep him . . . he will certainly be a big help out there on the mission field!" With that hearty endorsement, Mr. Miller sat down.

After a number of general questions and niceties, one of the board members said, "Rich . . . I read your testimony . . . I would like you to re-tell it to the board members here . . . would you start with your searching for God when you were a little boy."

I told them about the planes flying high overhead, and how, from that day on, it became my desire to someday be an airplane pilot.

I told them about the four leaf clovers, and what I wished for. I told them about . . . "praying to God to have my wishes fulfilled when the four leaf clovers did not work. The same disappointing result . . . no ice cream cone. With the shattering conclusion, I realized that people told me lies about four leaf clovers . . . and also lies about God answering our desires when we pray to Him. And so began my search for God . . . alone . . . after all, you could not rely on what people said . . ."

Someone impatiently cut in, "Rich . . . tell us about the rod!"

Because of the tone of his voice, I hesitated. Then I reluctantly told them about us kids playing . . . waiting for my brother . . . about the cloud coming down around me . . . and the rod coming down out of . . .

I was interrupted abruptly, "What do you mean . . . a rod?"

I turned and looked into a scowling face of disbelief. I shrugged my shoulders, "Just a rod."

"But, what did it look like . . . how much of it could you see?"

"Oh . . . maybe three feet or so. It looked like it was made of wood."

"And so you mean, it was like a . . . a . . . staff?"

"Yeah . . . like a staff!"

In a very skeptical voice, "A staff, aye . . . and who do you think was holding the other end?"

I began to get angry, (this was the man's purpose). "I don't know..!"

"You don't know . . . you know what I think? I think this is all a bunch of poppycock you dreamed up to make yourself out to be someone special! Do you think you are . . . someone special?"

I paused for a long time . . . "I believe that God created each one of us for a purpose, and every one of us . . . is special . . . in His eyes. As for the rod, I believe it was simply God's way of showing a small confused boy, who was honestly searching for Him, that He really existed! And to this day, no matter what happens in this crazy mixed up world, when nothing else makes sense, I can go back to this point in time, in my life, and know that God is for real, and I can trust He is in control . . . even when a certain Christian tends to make an ass of himself!" I bored a hole right through the man.

The man even smiled a bit . . . "Touche! . . . and I suppose this was when you became . . . a Christian?"

151

"No . . . I accepted Jesus as my Saviour on the night I heard that my mother had died!"

"Would you be willing to tell us about that?"

A long pause. "My mother was sent away to a sanitarium because she had tuberculosis.."

"When was that?"

"When we lived on the farm . . . it was after the fourth grade."

"Go ahead."

"They didn't have any antibiotics in those days . . . so she just wasted away . . . and died . . . I guess it took about three years . . ." It was hard for me to go on. "Our pastor came by and told us that Mom had died! He gave me a Bible in which my mother had written, 'Read your Bible, Richard, this is your mother's prayer.' When I went to bed that night, I couldn't go to sleep. I was thinking about my mother dying. I began thinking about ME dying. That scared me. Then God said to me, 'But you don't have to be afraid of dying when you put your faith and trust in Jesus! You believe in Jesus as your Savior, don't you?' 'Yes, I do!' And with that, I simply rolled over and went peacefully off to sleep."

"Rich, tell us about when God spoke to you when you were in the service."

"You mean . . . about being a missionary?"

"Yes."

"Well, I joined the Air Force shortly after finishing high school. After completing my training as an auto mechanic, they sent me to Japan. That's where I really grew in the Lord. There was a keen bunch of Christian fellows on the base and the Chaplain could really preach the Word. He and his family practically adopted us and took us into their home . . . just like we were part of the family.

On the weekends, we used go on outings all over the beautiful countryside. We would all pile into a big 6-by-6 or a weapons carrier. Off we'd go to the beach . . . sometimes to a Shinto shrine . . . or maybe a silk or pottery factory. And wherever we went, we would drop tracts to the people that we passed along the road.

Several times, we even went out to some of the small villages near the base and held evangelistic services, using an interpreter. We would fan out all over the countryside and invite everyone to the village square for a meeting. One time, I was late getting back. The open space was jammed with people, and one of the guys was preaching.

As I was observing all this, I was startled to hear someone say . . . "and someday, you will be a missionary!"

It was so real that I turned around to see who spoke to me. There was no one there. 'But Lord, I can't be a missionary! You know how I am when I get up in front of people . . . how..'

"But you will be a missionary . . . someday . . ."

Someone interrupted, "We are getting short on time, Rich, tell us about the time the Lord spoke to you when you were in college."

"You mean . . . what did He say?"

"Yes."

He said, "It's true . . . you cannot speak, but isn't this something you can do for Me?"

"And what was . . . this something?"

"We were watching the Moody film: "To Every Creature" . . . they were showing how some missions were beginning to use airplanes to help their missionaries in the hard-to-reach areas of the world . . . how a two or three week trek through the steaming jungle, for example, was now made comfortably and safely with a twenty minute flight in an airplane . . . how a dangerous four day climb over the mountains is now done with a ten minute flight in an airplane! And God asked me if I would be a missionary pilot!"

"And what was your response?"

"I said, 'Sure!'.. Being an airplane pilot was my one dream in life . . . ever since I was a small kid . . . but I had never heard of missionary pilots before!"

"And so . . . what happened?"

"Well, they told how Moody was training guys to be missionary pilots . . . so I told the Lord if He would get me into that school . . . I would go!"

"The Lord speaking to you . . . ah . . . is this an audible voice you hear?"

"NO!! It's God's Spirit within . . . doesn't the Holy Spirit ever speak to you guys?"

Everybody in the room looked at each other and smiled, and some began laughing out loud. "And so . . . you are not one of these charismatics?"

Bewildered, I said, "What's a . . . a . . . charis . . . matic?"

That brought the house down. Everybody just roared! When they finally settled down, the man who had been questioning me said, "Forget it, kid . . . just forget it!" (The Mission was becoming quite concerned about a few of its members that were speaking in tongues which was causing division within the ranks.)

Another man: "There's one other thing some of us are concerned about . . . ah . . . if you were accepted by the Sudan Interior Mission . . . would you be willing to go out to the field and be nothing but . . . a . . . a . . . missionary?"

I thought to myself . . . 'oh boy! . . . here we go again!' I looked right at Dr. Darrow, and I said, "If you had a heart attack and needed surgery to save your life . . . would you want ME to do that surgery?" Pause. "Now if you were out in the jungle somewhere, and had that heart attack . . . would you want Me to fly YOU to the hospital to save your life? I think you would! Just as a doctor spends years in specialized training to know how to do HIS job, I have spent years in specialized training to do MY job. I believe the Lord wants me to do that job under the Sudan Interior Mission. I pray that you will allow me to do My job, just as you would let a doctor do his job, or any other specialized person for that matter. I hope and pray that you will allow me to do the job the Lord gave me to do!"

When I was through, you could have heard a pin drop a mile away. I looked around at everyone in that room. Dr. Darrow said, "Mr. Schaffer . . . thank you for that profound statement . . . we . . . ah . . . would like to have a discussion within the group of board members . . . ah . . . we will call you back when we have finished that discussion."

I got up and walked out of the room.

All the candidates were looking at me. "Man, you were in there a long time . . . what's going on?"

I shrugged my shoulders, "I think we're gonna have a policy change in SIM . . . anyway, I sure hope so . . . otherwise you'll see me as a missionary to the uninhabited islands!"

Thirty-seven minutes and fourteen-seconds later, they called me back into the room. "Mr. Schaffer . . . I think that you will find that you will be doing more flying for SIM than you ever bargained for! SIMAIR needs you very badly. They hope that you can raise your support, and be out in Nigeria by April! That gives you about three months! The Lord bless you!"

WOW!

CHAPTER 20
DEPUTATION—JANUARY 1957

I drove down the New Jersey shoreline to Monmouth Beach to see Greta. She was living with her folks in this small village beside the sea. Her mother was a charming woman who greeted me warmly. Her father was a commercial fisherman who was somewhere out on the Atlantic plying his trade.

Greta was pleased to see me. She smiled, "Welcome to our humble home!"

"Thank you . . . it's really nice to see you! I never realized that you were going to Africa with the SIM!"

She gently chided, "You would have known if you had attended the Africa Prayer Band at Moody!"

I dodged her dig, "Us flyboys had so much homework all the time . . . I usually hit the books right after supper. Also I was thinking more of South America!"

"Mmm . . . and I thought you would be going with MAF!"

"I was hoping to, but they already had a couple of single pilots they didn't know what to do with. Their thinking is more along the line of a husband-wife team, with Ma on the radio at the home base, keeping track of Pa while he's out flying over the dangerous jungle!"

She teased, "And with all those nice girls at Moody, you couldn't find one that would marry you?"

I gave it right back to her, "Well, I thought of asking YOU, but I'm sorta bashful, you know! And it's a shame that you are going to East Africa!"

"Why's that?"

"Well, how in the world am I gonna make love to you when we are four thousand miles apart!", I laughed.

Her face took on a slight hint of blush as she held me with her deep blue eyes. She slyly cocked her head and pursed her lips with an impish smile, "Well . . . you can write to me!"

That evening I phoned the Ogburns. "Hi . . . Merlene?"

Merlene replied in her southern voice, "Yes-s . . . and who's this?"

I laughed, "It's Rich Schaffer!"

"Oh-h . . . Rich! Just a second . . . I'll get Lanny on the other phone!"

Doctor Paul came on, "Hi Rich . . . What's going on?"

"Hi Lanny! I just wanted to give you folks the good news that I have been accepted by SIM! The only problem is that they want me out in Nigeria by APRIL! That only gives me a couple of months to raise my support . . . I'm wondering if I should head straight for home and by-pass you folks? I sure would like to see you guys, but . . ."

Merlene cut in, "Oh . . . we sure wanted to see you! That means we probably won't see you for another four years?"

"Yeah, that's a long time isn't it?"

Lanny said, "Rich . . . what kind of support do you need before you can go?"

"Well, the Mission says that I need to have a hundred and twenty dollars a month promised, and to figure about five hundred to a thousand to buy clothes and stuff that I'll need out there for four years . . . I plan to use my own money for that. Then I'll need about a thousand dollars for my plane ticket and for shipping my outfit to Africa."

"Okay . . . Merlene and I talked about this . . . you can put us down for five dollars a month support for starters . . . is that okay?"

"Wow . . . thanks a lot . . . I really appreciate that . . . you are my very first supporters!"

"Where should we send it?"

"I'll have the Mission send you some information which will include that kind of stuff . . . okay?"

"Okay . . . we're sure sorry that we won't be seeing you like we planned . . . but we certainly understand that you are in a real bind for time . . ."

"Thanks, Lanny and Merlene . . . I really appreciate you folks!"

"Okay . . . you have a safe trip . . . we'll be praying for you . . . let us know how things go . . . okay?"

"Okay . . . I'll do that!"

Early the next morning, Mrs. Johnson was determined to feed me a good breakfast, and that we have devotions before I took off. I was so wired that I could hardly hold still. I already had five dollars of my support . . . only a hundred and fifteen to go! Where would that come from? I could hardly wait to get started.

After breakfast Mrs. Johnson handed me a Bible and said, "You can read to us your life verse."

"My life verse . . . what do you mean . . . my life verse?"

She looked surprised, "You mean that you don't have a life verse? Why, everyone should have a life verse! What's your favorite verse in the Bible?"

"Well that old stand-by, I guess . . . John 3:16!"

She looked dismayed, "Well, I guess you can read that to us!"

So without opening the Bible, I began quoting the whole third chapter of John . . . "There was a man of the Pharisees, named Nicodemus, a ruler of the Jews: The same came to Jesus by night, and said unto him, Rabbi, we know that thou art a teacher come from God: for no man can do these miracles that thou doest, except God be with him. Jesus answered and said unto him, Verily, verily, I say unto thee, Except a man be born again, he cannot see the kingdom of God. Nicodemus saith unto him, How can a man be born when he is old? can he enter the second time into his mother's womb, and be born?" And when I got to the sixteenth verse, I said with emphasis, "And now, this is my favorite verse . . . For God so loved the world that he gave his only begotten Son, that whosoever believeth in him should not perish, but have everlasting life!" I continued, "For God sent not his Son into the world to condemn the world; but that the world through him might be saved." I finished with the last verse of the chapter, "He that believeth on the Son hath everlasting life: and he that believeth not the Son shall not see life; but the wrath of God abideth on him."

Mrs. Johnson looked at me through moist filled eyes as she cupped her chin in her hands, and with a softened voice she said, "Yah . . . I guess that will do!"

I smiled, "I also love the Sermon on the Mount . . . would you like to hear it? Or how about the fifty third or the fifty fifth chapter of Isaiah? I really love the twenty third Psalm! And the eighth and twelfth chapter of Romans . . . oh man . . . they are really great!"

"You mean . . . when did you learn all those . . .?"

"When I was in the army . . . in Japan."

"Why, that's wonderful!"

Greta just sat there . . . watching this exchange between her mother and me.

"The verses that I have been working on lately is Romans chapter 10, verses 9 through 15 . . . 'That if thou shalt confess with thy mouth the Lord Jesus, and shalt believe in thine heart that God hath raised him from the dead, thou shalt be saved. For with the heart man believeth unto righteousness; and with the mouth confession is made unto salvation. For the scripture saith, Whosoever believeth on him shall not be ashamed. for there is no difference between the Jew and the Greek: for the Lord over all is rich unto all that call upon him. For whosoever shall call upon the Lord shall be saved. How then shall they call on him in whom they have not believed? and how shall they believe in him of whom they have not heard? and how shall they hear without a preacher? And how shall they preach, except they be sent? As it written, How beautiful are the feet of them that preach the gospel of peace, and bring glad tidings of good things!' I guess these verses are my incentive for going to Africa to be a missionary."

We joined hands and Mom Johnson prayed for me and she prayed for her daughter. This was her commissioning service committing us to the Lord and into His service.

Soon I was ready to go on my way. I cupped Greta's hands in mine. Her long golden hair glistened with the morning light as she held my gaze with her deep blue eyes. I gently squeezed her hands, "Yes . . . I will write to you!"

I drove three miles south to Long Beach and then turned west, working my way over to the New Jersey turnpike, and headed west again when I came to the Pennsylvania turnpike. The old bomber was ticking along fine just a couple of miles above the speed limit. The only trouble was that the ticking began getting louder and louder until it changed to a sort of clunking sound. I coasted over to the side of the highway and turned off the engine. Oh boy! I sat there for a while and had a little prayer meeting. Again, I was out in the middle of nowhere. After the engine had cooled down, I started her up and we slowly limped down the side of the road to the first exit which took us into a little town where I found a small Chevrolet garage.

The mechanic came out and turned on the engine. "Hmmm . . . sounds like you got a rod going out!"

"Yeah . . . that's what I thought. What would it cost for you to fix it . . . and could you do it right now . . . I'm really in a hurry!"

He smiled, "Well, I'm not doing too much this morning . . . Let's put it in the stall and see what we can do." He noticed the olive-drab blanket draped over my tool box, "You Army?"

"No . . . Air Force . . . 46 to 49 . . . in Japan twenty months . . . that's my aircraft handtools!"

He shook my hand, "I'm Ted . . . twenty-one trips over Germany when we got shot down . . . that's when I got this gimpy leg!"

I gave Ted a brief history on the car, including burning out the timing gear.

"Did you happen to clean the oil pump screen?"

"No . . . it never even crossed my mind."

"I'll bet you a dollar that the fibers from that timing gear clogged the screen on the oil pump so that you had oil-starvation to the number six connecting rod!" He slid under the car on his creeper. "You feed me the tools and we'll have this buggy fixed in no time!"

He dropped the oil pan and removed the end-cap from the number six connecting rod. "Yeah . . . just like I figured!" He slid out from under the car and showed me the end-cap.

I looked at the end cap which showed a bit of scouring on the bearing surface, "You're pretty sharp, aren't you!"

Ted laughed, "Experience is a first class teacher! We'll need to replace the connecting rod and dress up the crankshaft a bit . . . she'll be good as new!"

"That means you will have to remove the head?" I could see where this was going to cost me some bucks.

"Naw . . . I'll try to get it out from the bottom."

Sure enough, Ted was able to pull out the number six connecting rod and piston. "Does your car use any oil?"

"Not much."

"Okay, We'll use your piston . . . I'll see if I can find a rod in my junk pile." He went to the back room and soon appeared with another connecting rod. "Hey, I found one!"

"Praise the Lord!" . . . It just sorta popped out.

But it stopped Ted in his tracks and he looked me right in the eyes, "You one of them Christian fellahs?"

"Yeah, I am."

He stuck out a big grimy paw and grinned, "Me too!"

We had quite a conversation while he worked on the car.

In no time he had my old bomber purring like a kitten. We went into his cluttered office where he tinkered on a pad. I was waiting anxiously for the bad news. He scratched the back of his head and tipped back in his chair, "Well, with the missionary discount, it looks like you owe me twenty five bucks . . . think you can handle that?"

"Wow! Thank you . . . and what's this missionary discount stuff?"

"Oh I promised the Lord when I opened the shop that if I ever got the chance to work on any missionaries' cars, I would give them a good discount!"

"Well, I'll tell you that I certainly appreciate your generosity!"

As I climbed into my buggy, Ted said, "Do you think SIM could use a grease monkey with a gimpy leg?"

"I don't see why not . . . they took a joker like me . . . why don't you write to them and find out?"

"You know . . . I just might do that!"

"Okay Ted . . . and thanks again!"

Ted grinned, "You bet . . . and you drive careful now . . . there's a speed trap just over the first rise west of town!"

I gave him a look of mock surprise, "You don't think a good little missionary like me would break the law . . . do you?"

"Well buddy, you better get the move on if you're planning to be in Africa by April!"

I peeled out of there as fast as that old dog would go . . . not very impressive.

I stayed overnight with Jerry and Rita Gilbert in Lansing, Michigan . . . he was one of my GI buddies at the chapel in Japan . . . they took on five dollars of my support.

Then I stayed with Ma and Pa Burnett in Bensonville. I visited at Moody airport where I showed my slides of the flying program with Marine Medical Mission. The guys had a ton of questions for me.

I also showed my slides during the evening service at the First Baptist Church in Wheaton. I was absolutely petrified at the thought of speaking to this illustrious group of people, but when the lights dimmed low, I simply reinforced the story that was already being told in the pictures. I forgot about myself, intent on the information I was trying to convey to the audience. I ended with a challenge to the people: "This gives you an idea of what I have been doing over the past year, and hopefully will be doing in the near future in Africa. I'm thankful for the privilege to be a part of the team who were responsible in the winning of souls to the Lord. However, let me remind you of the 'countless thousands who are still without Christ, without hope, and many times without food or clothing. Let us rise anew to the challenge where we have failed to complete Christ's commission. Are we really Christian soldiers, moving like a mighty army unto victory? We can have victory only by following the commands of our leader, Jesus Christ. Without this obedience, we have already lost the battle. Let us ask ourselves: what right have I to know Christ's saving power . . . to be redeemed and have eternal life, while heathen lands race on to their last hour, and countless lives are torn with fear and strife. What right do I have to hold to my possessions . . . to be so heedless to another's need? This world is starving, begging, sinning, dying. Can I alone sit idle in my greed? Our Lord is calling us to deeper service . . . souls all about us lost eternally. Oh Christian onward . . . our command is given . . . our only right, to serve . . . to set souls free.' Oh Christian young people with lives to give . . . will you sit idly by? Rise to the challenge . . . take up the banner of Christ . . . be obedient to his commands. You can live a life that's really worth living. You will live an exciting life when you turn your life over to the Lord and go out to serve Him on the mission field! In fact, I'll guarantee you more excitement than you ever bargained for! Young people . . . Lets go out and change the WORLD!"

(Used with permission: Some of the words above were borrowed from my fellow Moody classmate, John Snavely, given as a ringing challenge in his video "Wings Over Zululand", where he paid the supreme sacrifice serving our wonderful Lord in Africa.)

I also visited dear old Mrs. Gustafson. She gave me a pint jar full of quarters, dimes, and nickels, plus a few dollar bills which she had earned from washing and ironing shirts!

"I want you to use this money to buy yourself a good record player, so you can listen to some nice music when you are over there in Africa!"

I just shook my head. I didn't know what to say. How could I take money from this dear old woman? She looked so frail . . . like she had been starving herself . . . just to save money for me? I almost broke her heart when I tried to refuse her gift! But with tears of love, she insisted that I take it. I'll tell you, that was one very humbling experience for Rich

Schaffer . . . which was many times repeated by all those who sacrificed over the twenty years so that I could serve the Lord on the mission field. I never ever took my financial support for granted, realizing from where it came.

As I headed westward, my heart was full of joy. Mom Burnett promised they would take on five dollars a month of my support. Mr. and Mrs. "Husky" Noll said they would take ten dollars . . . their sons, Craig and Mark had been in the Stockade group that Dick Sissel and I had started at the Wheaton First Baptist Church. And Dick and Sharon Sissel promised five dollars!

Reverend Berg had asked me to be sure and stop by to visit the two country churches under his able leadership. On Sunday morning I talked to all the kids in Sunday school, and to the adults in the morning worship service at the Martintown church. We were invited to dinner by one of the farm families who really put on a spread. Then I showed my slides in the evening service. Everyone was very interested and they continually interrupted my presentation with a constant flow of questions. It was a long but good service. At the close of the service Rev. Berg said, "We have had a wonderful day. I'm sure you will want to show your appreciation when you shake Mr. Schaffer's hand at the door!" And they did. As each person shook my hand, they had something in it . . . even the smallest of the youngsters! I had never had this happen before.

When we finally got back to the parsonage, Rev. Berg couldn't contain himself . . . "Well, how much did they give you?"

I laughed, "I don't know . . . I'll have to count it!"

So I emptied all my pockets of all the wadded up bills and loose change, and even a few checks. We began counting.

"Wow! There's a hundred and seventy eight dollars, and sixty seven cents here!"

Rev. Berg chuckled, "Truly these are wonderful people!"

"They certainly are!"

On Monday, Tuesday, and Wednesday we went visiting out on the farms and also a number of folks in the small town. Everywhere we went the people treated us royally and stuffed us full of good food.

Then at the Wednesday night prayer meeting at the Nora church I again showed my slides. And again, the people bombarded me with questions. The meeting lasted over two hours! The people were also very generous when they shook my hand!

And Rev. Berg said when I left, "I'll let you know as soon as possible what the churches decide about your support . . . you will be their first missionary!"

I gave him a big hug. "Thank you very much . . . you and your people are really wonderful!"

I stopped in Tyndall, South Dakota for an overnight surprise visit with my Aunt Bertha and Uncle Cliff Schweitzer, and also Uncle Ben and Aunt Vera Schmoll. Aunt Edna had mentioned me sometimes in her letters, so they were all ears to hear about my going to Africa to be a missionary.

I finally arrived home in North Bend, Oregon where Aunt Edna and Uncle Pearl greeted me warmly. They still had my bed waiting for me in the storeroom. It was good to be home again.

After settling in, I got down to business, writing letters to everyone that I had an address for. We didn't have a typewriter, so I carefully hand-wrote my first prayer letter in black ink and took it to a printer. Then with black ink I wrote in the person's name and added a personal note at the end. The whole thing looked just like a newsy hand written letter.

This missionary stuff was all a little new to my aunt and uncle. Oh sure, they knew the Lutheran church had some mission work going on in foreign countries, but they had never seen a real live missionary and had never heard one tell of his work. All they knew was that part of their tithe that they so faithfully gave to the church each Sunday, also supported the Lutheran mission work overseas. The idea that I had to raise my OWN support was the craziest thing they had ever heard of. In fact my aunt emphatically stated, "If you think people are going to send you money each month, for four YEARS, just so you can be a missionary . . . why, you need to have your head examined!"

But you know, that is exactly what happened. A couple of weeks later, I started getting responses to my letter. Ron Calhoun said he would take five dollars of my support, Mitsuo Watanabe took five, and Ken and Madie Lair said they would take ten. In fact, six of my friends from Oregon State college days took some of my support. Even Jeannie's mom took five dollars. And another of my army buddies, Ed Smiley, took on some of my support.

One day I got a letter from Eddie Siedlman, the gal that manned the Cougar Pass Lookout during the Coos Fire Patrol days. In it she said that she had just recently become a Christian. She mentioned that I was always a different kind of guy . . . now she knew why. And she took five dollars of my support!

Each day the trip to the mail box became an exciting adventure, especially for my aunt. She was watching all this crazy goings on. And in just a short time three quarters of my support was promised. One day my aunt said, "Why, if they can do it . . . we can do it!" And she also talked Uncle Art and Aunt Grace into taking five dollars of my support. She talked my brother and his wife, Aunt Bertha and Uncle Cliff into five dollars.

One day I got a letter from the Mission. Word had come from Nigeria that SIMAIR wanted me out there soon as possible . . . THEY would pay my passage! WOW! The Mission said they were working toward getting my passport, and suggested that I buy and start packing my outfit!

First thing I bought was a Webcor Hi-Fi Stereo record player with the sixty five dollars that Mrs. Gustafson gave me. I went to the Payless Drug store and bought a 20 piece set of pale pink Melmac dishes, some cheap silverware, some cooking pots, and a plastic ukulele for $1.98! Why that store had everything! They even had some records for the record player. I bought an even dozen . . . all classical! I bought shoes, socks, underwear, khaki pants, t-shirts, towels, bed sheets, and pillow cases . . . what else would I need for four years?

Wes Way invited me to the Baptist men's prayer breakfast where they asked me to share. From that group, Carl Nordin and Wes each took five dollars of my support. Maybelle Velde, my Sunday school teacher, took five dollars. My close buddy at Moody, Denny Huffman, took five dollars; they themselves were going to Alaska as missionaries. This all totaled up to one hundred and twenty five dollars . . . five dollars over the required support! Then I heard from Reverend Berg . . . the Martintown church would start with ten dollars a month . . . also Mrs. Krebs and Mrs. Bidlingmaier would be sending five dollars a month . . . the Nora church would be sending 200 dollars a year . . . Nathan and Betty Hale would be sending ten dollars a month!

It was time to go. I wrote a short note to all concerned. A letter from my Dad warned me to be careful of all the poison snakes and not to fly too high! I promised him that I would fly low and slow! I stuffed my outfit of four years into four old footlockers that I bought at the Salvation Army store for two dollars each and sent them to SIM via Consolidated Freightways. I gave my black bomber to uncle Pearl to use for a work car as their 1936 Ford V8 was beginning to give problems. We said our goodbyes. I was on my way.

"As we look over the past few years, remembering the victories that have been won, we think also of the countless thousands who are still without Christ, without hope, and many times without food and clothing, and we wonder why we have failed. Are we really Christian soldiers, moving like a mighty army unto victory? We can have victory, only by following the commands of our leader, Jesus Christ. Without this obedience, we have already lost the battle. And we can ask ourselves: what right do I have to know Christ's saving power, to be redeemed and have eternal life, while heathen lands race on to their last hour, and countless lives are torn with fear and strife? What right have I to hold to my possessions, to be so heedless to another's need? This world is starving, begging, sinning, dying. Can I alone sit idle in my greed? Our Lord is calling us to deeper service . . . souls all about us lost eternally. Oh Christian onward . . . our command is given . . . our only right to serve . . . to set souls free."

(Narration by John Snavely in his video presentation: "Wings Over Zululand".)

Bible quotations are from King James Version: John chapter 3, and Romans 10: 9-15.

CHAPTER 21
I Go To Africa

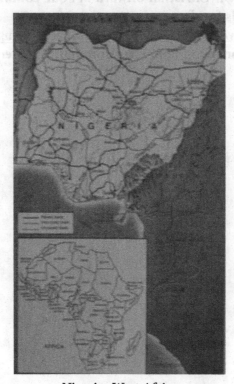

Nigeria, West Africa

The drone of the engines of the KLM Super Constellation lulled me into a semi-sleep . . . I was dead tired from the hectic pace that brought me to this point in time. I was actually on my way to Africa!

Africa . . . What would it be like? I never really gave it much thought before. It was what the Lord wanted me to do . . . and so I rested in that. Past experience had taught me that I could trust Him . . . with my life . . . with all the nitty gritty details we call living . . . everything.

But now, that I was actually on my way, I realized that I didn't have the remotest clue what I was getting myself into. All I knew was that the Sudan Interior Mission had an

162

aviation department and I was going be one of their pilots in a country called Nigeria, located somewhere on the coast of West Africa!

But to get to Nigeria, you had to go via Holland. We landed about one o'clock at the Amsterdam International Airport where there would be a four hour layover. It was a cold rainy day and the wind knifed through my suit as we walked from the plane to the terminal. On this 14th day of April 1957, Europe was still caught in the grip of ol' man winter. Although I could see the tulips were already forming flower buds, not one was brave enough to show its color. It was shivering cold, even inside the almost now deserted terminal . . . I sat on a hot water radiator trying to keep warm. That would be my last cold day for the next four years!

When I stepped off the old Douglas DC-4 at Kano Airport at five in the morning, it was already getting hot and sticky. It had rained sometime during the night and steam was rising from the small puddles of water on the tarmac.

Going to worship a dead and false prophet

As I walked into the customs area, a deeply tanned fellow clad in khaki shorts and an old t-shirt, approached me with a quizzical smile on his face, "Hi . . . I'm Johnny Clay . . . you're Rich Schaffer?"

"Yeah . . . that's right."

Johnny stuck out his hand and greeted me, "Thought you might need some help in going through Customs and stuff!"

It was hot and humid. The whole place was one of foul smelling bedlam, as people jammed toward the low inspection counter when the baggage carts were rolled into the area. Passengers and customs agents argued loudly over the price levied against the new radio or the camera they had purchased in Europe. Johnny pulled me into the background.

"We'll just wait awhile . . . do you see your bags?"

"There's the duffel bag . . . and . . . there's my brown Samsonite suitcase."

"That's all you got? . . . you travel light!"

Johnny waited until the place had cleared out a bit, and then he walked over to a customs agent who had just finished his inspection by throwing a passenger's clothes and stuff in wild disarray all over the counter, daring the man to say something.

Johnny smiled, "Good morning, Adamu!"

The man's face broke into laughter . . . "Ha . . . ha, ha . . . master John . . . how are you this fine morning?"

They shook hands warmly and carried on a loud conversation in some kind of lingo . . . I couldn't understand a word of it. Then Johnny introduced me, and the man grasped my hand with both of his hands and greeted me in very good English, "Welcome to Nigeria . . . I hope you will be happy here!"

"Thank you sir . . . I'm glad to be here!"

Johnny pointed out my bags, and they were brought to the counter. The customs agent didn't even bother to open them . . . he just smiled with a broad wave of his arm, "You may go!"

We picked up the bags. At Immigration and Health, it was the same. Everyone knew Johnny Clay, and Johnny Clay knew everyone. I was really impressed with the courteous treatment I received because of this man by my side.

We walked out to the parking lot and climbed into an old Volkswagen bus. I commented, "Wow . . . that was really something back there . . . you really know your way around this place!"

"Been there, done that . . . if you treat these people with courtesy and respect, they'll usually respond in like manner! But sometimes you need the patience of Job. No matter how hot it is, never try to push things through . . . if they think you're trying to hurry them along, you could find yourself there a long, long time."

"Speaking of hot . . . I'm already soaking wet with sweat . . . how hot does it get around here?"

"Oh, it might get up to a hundred and ten today . . . we had our first good rain last night so it is starting to cool down a bit . . . nice for you to get here just in time for the rainy season. We'll get you a room at the guest house. You can have a cool shower and get some cooler clothes on . . . breakfast is at 0630."

We stopped by the guest house and picked up a key for a room, and Johnny drove me around this long building and right up to one of the doors. "You look like you could really use some sleep . . . why don't you just flake out this morning . . . lunch at the guest house is at 1200 . . . then there's rest hour until 1400 . . . I'll pick you up about then and we'll take you out to see our hangar, okay?"

"Boy, that sounds like a good idea . . . I'm really beat."

Johnny dropped my duffel bag and suitcase on the narrow verandah and took off. I unlocked the door. It swung outward . . . so I propped it open with a large rock that seemed to be there for that purpose. The rickety screen door opened inward and cleared the floor by at least an inch. I surmised that every bug that landed on the screen would be ushered into the room when the door was opened . . . and the space under it was a sure invitation for every snake and scorpion looking for a shady place to hide. I carried my belongings into the room and put them on the bed. Then I searched every cranny of the interior looking for any unwanted intruders. I killed several mosquitoes hiding in the bathroom. 'Hmmm . . . sure is stuffy in here.' I unlatched the locks and swung the windows open wide. Not a breeze.

I took off my sweaty clothes and laid down on the creaky bed, continuing to survey my surroundings. An old yellowed mosquito net, draped over its support, hung above the bed . . . 'better use that tonight.' A couple of small lizards clung to the wall up near the ceiling . . . 'hey you guys, go to the bathroom . . . that's where all the mosquitoes hang out!'

Expanded metal reinforced the screen door and the windows, no doubt to slow down the thieves. You could see where someone had cut the screen in their attempt to unlatch the hook on the screen door . . . 'looks like someone had a visitor during the night . . . better keep the outer door shut and locked!'

I went into the bathroom to take a shower. The bathtub was made of concrete! There was no hot water tap. Actually it would have been more refreshing if the water had been colder . . . it was tepid. Before I got dried off, I was already sweating again . . . 'did he say it was going to get up to a hundred and ten today? Good grief!'

I stretched out on the bed again and looked up at that old mosquito net . . . 'maybe I ought'a try it!' When I pulled the net down, I was showered with a cloud of choking dust! I didn't know anything about the Harmattan dust that drifted off the Sahara Desert and smothered the land during the dry season . . . this was my first introduction. I took another shower, crawled under the net, sat on the bed dripping wet, and surveyed my world from the tent. As I lay down and drifted off to sleep, I muttered to myself . . . 'the Arabian Nights were never like this . . . '

When I woke up, it felt like my mouth was full of gritty sand . . . I was laying in a pool of sweat. The still air in the room was oppressive, just like I was in a bake oven. I took another shower, and pulled on a pair of khakis and a t-shirt. Suddenly I heard a rustling at the door. I whirled around. There was the most colorful lizard I had ever seen, cocking his head to the side, eyeing me cautiously. I froze. After a minute, he decided I must be okay, and so he came another foot into the room. This guy was almost a foot long. His head was orange, his shoulders and front legs were a dull yellow, his body was sort of a purple, shading into black. Again, the tail was yellow with a black tip. 'Wow . . . I'd like to get a picture of him!' I must have moved. The lizard scurried under the screen door, out to the verandah, where he did several push-ups, taunting me. I armed myself with my camera and slowly moved out the screen door. The lizard ran down the verandah several feet and stopped. I stalked him slowly and was finally able to get within six feet to shoot him with my camera!

I heard a bell clanging in the distance . . . I looked at my watch . . . 'Oh man . . . it's lunch time!' I hurriedly tossed my camera on the bed, locked the place up, and ran to the guest house. There must have been about twenty people gathering for the meal at the long tables. Not sure where I should sit, I hesitated. I was graciously ushered to an empty chair. Lloyd Wickstrom looked at me and nodded "I'd like to introduce to you our new pilot, Rich Schaffer, who just arrived this morning on KLM . . . please make him welcome . . . now let's pray."

Everyone smiled and introduced themselves when there was a chance . . . "Hi, I'm" . . . and they would give their name and make some comment like, "We are so glad that you're here."

Johnny Clay picked me up, and we headed for the airport . . . also in the bus was another pilot, Joe Swanson, and mechanic Bill Tuck, who welcomed me. They pushed open the hangar doors to reveal three Cessna 170's. One had the cowling and panels removed, as they were in the process of giving it a thorough 100 hour inspection. I dove right into the work, using some of Bill Tuck's tools. I learned that the other two SIMAIR planes were in Jos . . . the pilots there were Clarence Soderberg (Soddy), and Dick Vossler.

The first flight I recorded in my pilot logbook was on 18 April 1957 . . . flew from Oyi to Kano . . . evidently one of the SIMAIR pilots flew the plane from Kano to Oyi. (I only record the time when I actually do the piloting).

At Oyi Airstrip

The next flights were some dual time with Johnny Clay on the 22nd and 23rd to get me back in the saddle again, and to familiarize me with the Kano area. I was really rusty, as I hadn't flown for a long time.

On April 24th, Johnny and I flew 150 miles eastward to Nguru to pick up Dan Edwards, who had flipped his Jeep and had broken his arm. It was the end of the dry season, and things really looked brown and barren . . . in fact, it looked like a desert to me . . . dried up trees and bushes, and the brown, tan sand . . . everything looked the same. But as we went along, I began to pick up things that you could call distinguishing land marks, by which you navigate and fix that position on the chart . . . clusters of villages here and there . . . the dry riverbed that meandered the direction we were flying . . . and then the railroad . . . all we had to do was follow it to Nguru where it ended. There was a bit of Harmattan haze hanging in the air, giving us a visibility of three miles. No problem.

We buzzed over the Sudan United Mission station on the south side of Nguru and landed at the airstrip three miles southeast of town. In about fifteen minutes, a Landrover brought Mr. Edwards. He looked a bit frazzled with a grizzly beard and unkempt hair . . . his arm was in a sling and he looked like he was in pain. We loaded in a small mail sack and gently eased Dan into the back seat.

The next two days, I did some more rust removing practice, and I now had 351 total hours in my log book. SIM required 350 hours minimum flight experience to fly for SIMAIR.

So on the 27th of April, I took Dan Edwards back to Nguru by myself. The air was rather bumpy that day, and Dan was getting a little green around the gills, so I flew over the mission station at 3000 feet, descended quickly, and landed at the airstrip. We waited and waited, but no one came.

Dan suggested, "It's about rest hour . . . maybe they didn't hear us flying over that high."

"Yeah, I guess . . . well, let's go giv'em a real buzz job!"

So we took off, and climbed up to about 500 feet. When we got to the station, I peeled off, and dove for the roof tops. All I saw was a brown blob in my corner vision . . . BOOMMmm!! . . . there was this explosion! We had hit an Ungalu (turkey vulture)! The plane began buffeting wildly! I slowed the plane down, and fought desperately to keep it under control. There was a big hole in the right corner of the windshield. I glanced at my passenger. Ol' Dan Edwards was covered with blood and guts and feathers! What a sight!

We managed to stagger back to the airstrip and land. I took a bottle of emergency water, and washed the blood and gore from Mr. Edwards. Thankfully, it was not his.

When the Landrover arrived, I asked the missionary if he could loan me a cardboard box and some duct tape. He had to go back to the station for those. "Dan . . . come along with me . . . we'll get you cleaned up a bit!"

While I was waiting, I noticed some thorns sticking in the tires! The tires were covered with them! I worked them out with my jack knife . . . some were buried over a quarter inch into the rubber. Luckily, none had penetrated completely through.

When the missionary came back with the box and the tape, I used them to improvise a patch over the foot size hole in the windshield. Then I took off for Kano.

As I taxied up to the SIM hangar and climbed out, I put on my best sheepish hang-dog look, as the fellahs came out to assess the damage. When I told my story, Johnny and Joe nodded knowingly as they remembered the bird strikes in their past. This was not new to them.

Johnny quips, "How did the plane feel?"

"I could hardly control it!"

Then Johnny Clay blew his cool, "Well, let me tell you . . . if that hole had been one foot more toward the center of the windshield . . . you WOULDN'T have been able to control it, and YOU would have crashed! And WE'D probably be burying you tomorrow! I trust that this one will be a good teacher? . . . you got that?"

"Yes sir!"

"We happen to have a new windshield in the parts room . . . you busted it . . . you can fix it!" And off he stalked.

So the rest of the day and the next, I had the good pleasure of installing a new windshield onto one sorry looking Cessna.

29 April 57—Johnny came over early to my room, "Rich, we have a medical emergency at Minna . . . we'll pick them up and tak'em to Jos. Pack the stuff you'll need for the next couple of days, as you will be staying in Jos to take Soddy's place . . . he's going home on furlough . . . we'll fly the rest of your junk down on the first flight, okay?"

What could I say.

Picking up the Schalms at Minna ... going on their holiday at Miango. Rest and relaxation on the cool Jos plateau. Their kids can live with them ... Kent Academy is right next door. They'll also get their yearly physicals plus a few _____ to the dentist.

Picking up the Gottfried Schalms at Minna Airstrip, near their Adunu station

CHAPTER 22
JOS SWEET JOS

We picked up the medical emergency at Minna and delivered her safely to Jos. Johnny flew back home to Kano. They loaded the patient into the back of an old Ford station wagon . . . as there was no one at the hangar, I rode into town and got a room at the guesthouse.

The town of Jos is a hundred and fifty miles south of Kano, and four hundred and fifty miles inland from Lagos . . . roughly located in the center of Nigeria, ten degrees north of the Equator. It is located on a rocky barren plateau which is about fifty miles wide and seventy miles long . . . average elevation, 4000 feet. Ten miles east of Jos are the Sheri Hills at 5800 feet, the highest point in Nigeria, except for Mt. Cameroon on the coast. This area is a large producer of tin, as evident from the huge mounds of earth and lakes, left from the ravages of the open pit mining.

Also interesting are the huge granite rocks, some of them as big as houses, that are piled up on one another in fantastic formations . . . one, called Gog and Magog, is about three hundred feet high.

Look what God did!

It's a lot cooler and healthier on the plateau, which is a real boon to the missionary populace in Nigeria. The Sudan Interior Mission headquarters is at Jos. Nearby is Miango Rest Home and Kent Academy . . . during their vacation time, missionaries can gain a respite from the withering heat which is ever present at the lower elevations. Also their children attending the school can live with them during this time, which is really nice.

Because this is the hub of Mission activity, most of the flying originates or ends at Jos. Two planes, with pilots, Clarence Soderberg (Soddy) and Dick Vossler, were stationed at Jos. As I went exploring the SIM compound, I bumped into Soddy coming out of the BD (business department).

Soddy shook my hand enthusiastically, "Man, am I ever glad to see you! It's about time . . . what took you so long? Now I can pack my junk and get out of here . . . I'm done . . . finished!" And with that, off he strutted like a cocky banty rooster, dusting his hands in a matter of fact way . . . you could almost see an invisible load falling from his shoulders as he swaggered home. My mouth dropped open, but the words never came . . . 'what's with these guys?'

1 May 1957 . . . My first flight from Jos. I went the rounds with Dick Vossler to pick up the mail, medicines, and passengers for the days' flight. I would be flying Marg Dykstra to Zaria, and Mrs. Bell with three children to Sokoto.

As I was standing on the wing strut refueling my plane . . . "Hey Dick, what do you think of that storm over there?"

Dick walked to the front of the hangar so he could look where I had pointed. He yelled excitedly, "Let's get out'ta here . . . you can gas up at Zaria!"

A small thunderstorm was moving off the Sheri Hills and straight for the airport. Dick dumped in his passengers and took off. I let the gas drain from the funnel and dipped my tanks . . . I only had enough fuel for two hours flight . . . that would get me to Zaria with an hour to spare.

I did a quick pre-flight, loaded in the baggage and passengers, and taxied out to runway one zero, doing my pre-takeoff check on the way. The thunderstorm was just starting across the east end of the 4000 foot runway.

"Jos tower . . . Charlie India ready for takeoff."

"Roger . . . Charlie India is cleared for takeoff . . . winds are 270 at fourteen knots . . . gusting to twenty five!"

"Roger . . . Charlie India is rolling!"

The heavily loaded Cessna should have broke ground just after I topped the rise of the runway, but I was foolishly taking off down wind! There was not enough room to veer away and the plane was sucked right up into the storm! Visibility went to zero. The heavy pounding rain drowned out the screams of the women and children. We tossed around like a cork in an angry sea. Needle, ball, and airspeed . . . keep the plane right side up. Suddenly, we were spit out the side of the storm and into the beautiful sunshine. Wow!

I spent the next hour, as we flew on to Zaria, kicking myself for such stupidity. What I should have done was park the plane in the hangar and just wait for the storm to blow over. But I had let another pilot's 'Let's get out of here!' decision, hurry me into a choice that could have killed us all. Sometimes the Lord is gracious to us dumb, wet behind the ears, green pilots. "Thank you, Lord, for giving this one another chance!"

I landed at Zaria and taxied up to the fuel shed. "No . . . no petrol today . . . today big, big holiday!" No amount of pleading could persuade them to give me even a thimble full of av-gas!

Mrs. Bell suggested, "Maybe you can get some petrol at Gusau."

I climbed up to the wing and dipped my tanks with the fuel stick, "We have just one hour of fuel left. Gusau is ninety eight miles away . . . we'll be landing with only fumes in the tank . . . are you sure that we can get fuel at Gusau?"

Mrs. Bell shrugged her shoulders. "There's a mission station at Gusau . . . if we can't go any further, at least we will have a place to stay."

So we went on to Gusau. The missionary heard the plane going over and came out to the airport. Same story . . . today big, big holiday, but Roy Hirons kidded around with the refuelers, and gave them a copy of the African Challenge magazine, which SIM publishes. They happily topped off my tanks. Roy gave me several copies of the magazine. From then on, I usually carried some copies of the Challenge with me . . . seems everybody in Nigeria knew about the magazine . . . and almost everyone would do anything to get their hands on something to read.

A hundred and twenty miles on to Sokoto, and it was the same thing. So I offered them a Challenge magazine, and they also topped off my tanks!

I was now 330 miles from Jos. With full tanks, my plane had a range of 450 miles, so it was a good idea to have the hour plus reserve in case I had any detours in the road.

Sokoto to Jos

Little did I know.

I loaded up the mail and took off for Jos. Visibility was unlimited . . . in fact, when I was still over a hundred miles away, you could see the huge cumulo-nimbus thunderstorms building up over the Jos Plateau. As I approached the western edge of the plateau, it looked black and threatening. I dropped down to a thousand feet, hoping to find a weak spot where I could slide through. But there were no weak spots.

As I approached the heavy, greenish-black deluge of rain, the plane was suddenly slammed around like I was in a washing machine. Lightning flashed across the angry sky. I backed off. To the north and to the south, I tried . . . a solid wall of rain. No way was I going to get through or around this thunderstorm.

Big Black Thunderstorm

Okay, I'll just go back to my alternate and wait for this to blow over. So I landed at the little airstrip at Zunkwa, found the tie-downs, and began securing the plane to the heavy concrete blocks that were buried in the ground. People came from every direction when they heard the plane. Soon I was drowned in a sea of curious people. I gave out a couple of Challenge magazines. Eager hands pulled and clawed at me . . . a human wall pushed me hard against the airplane . . . I was almost crushed by the have-nots who surged forward in their eagerness . . . hopes of also getting a copy. What saved me was the rain . . . and the wind. Suddenly it came . . . the people scattered. I jumped back into the cabin of the plane. It blew so hard that I was literally airborne at times, flying on the ropes. The heavy deluge of rain came like an angry roar . . . a blinding flash . . . KER-BOOOomm!! . . . the earth shook . . . then another and another . . . the people were washed away . . . the pounding rain . . . "Oh God . . . help us!!!"

And as suddenly as it came . . . suddenly it was gone. The rain tapered off to a slight drizzle. I looked at my watch. Only a half hour of daylight left . . . 'maybe I can make it to Jos?' So I quickly untied the airplane and took off. I tried several places, but it was a no go . . . the clouds and the fog were hanging right down into the trees and rocks at the edge of the plateau. I reluctantly flew back to Zunkwa and landed in the last bit of daylight.

I secured the plane to the tie downs, crawled into the back seat, and rolled up into a little ball. It was pitch dark outside. I thought . . . 'not a soul in the whole wide world knows where I am . . . but God knows' . . . so I went to sleep.

Next morning . . . when it was light enough to see, I took off and headed for Jos. I met Soddy at the edge of the plateau, who was taking my scheduled flight to Oyi and Ilorin. Soddy says, "What happened to you?"

"Had to spend the night at Zunkwa . . . couldn't get in because of the storm."

"Yeah, that was a real bad one . . . glad to see you are in one piece . . . Dick will be using your plane for a flight to Kaltungo . . . better drop by the headquarters and let people know you are okay . . . plenty of people were praying for you last night, Buster!"

"Okay . . . will do . . . and thanks for taking my flight today!"

CHAPTER 23
My home in Jos

Soddy spent the next week packing, selling the household goods, and tying up loose ends. He was calling it quits. SIMAIR began shortly after the end of the Second World War, and Soddy was the first pilot, beginning the program with a Piper Family Cub. The program had progressed to five Cessna 170's, five pilots, and one fulltime mechanic when I came on board.

Dick Vossler would also be going home for good about a month later, bringing the pilot staff back down to four. He was one busy guy . . . not only with the flying, but in his spare time (is there such a thing?) he was installing better equipment and antennas for SIMRAD (radio department), trying to pack or get rid of his household goods, and trying to teach one dumb greenhorn pilot all the little extra jobs that need to be done to make the aviation program work smoothly and efficiently.

I would be left alone, doing all the flying in and out of Jos for almost three months until the Paul Rogalsky's returned from furlough . . . they would be re-stationed to Jos.

I lived in the catacombs of the guesthouse for about three weeks (so nicknamed because they were so dark and gloomy and damp during the rainy season). Then they moved me and Vic Stewart to a room above the Bookshop. There was an outside staircase, and a large balcony . . . where I grew some tomatoes in pots . . . they became loaded with luscious red fruit.

The Mission was in the process of building a two story apartment complex next to the Bookshop . . . four apartments on each end, connected by two couples' apartments in the center. I chose the lower southeast apartment, and my living room became a carpenter's shop. In my spare time, I built the kitchen cabinets, some cupboards, and a small built-in table. And then a full wall of cabinets, drawers, and a closet in the bedroom. All were made from beautifully grained mahogany plywood, which I finished with a dark oak stain and a clear glossy lacquer.

Sign by my front door

In the tiny bathroom, I installed a tea-kettle element in a fifteen gallon drum and hung it up near the ceiling above the shower stall. Up the side of the drum I mounted a glass tube which showed how much water is in the tank. You turn on the valve and fill the tank with about four inches of water, and then you plug the cord into the outlet. In about fifteen minutes the water is boiling hot. Then you disconnect the element and fill the remainder of the drum with water according to how hot of a shower you want. Oh, that was nice. I also built a beautiful cabinet around the sink.

I bought a small fridge and a wringer washing machine from the Vosslers. The mission provided a small electric stove. I hired a local carpenter to make two easy chairs and a couch from mahogany, also stained a dark oak, and finished with a deep glossy lacquer. I was able to buy some foam rubber for cushions in the market. The carpenter also made me a bed frame and a couple of kitchen chairs. The living room and bed room were painted a light blue . . . the kitchen and bathroom a light sunny yellow. I covered the concrete floors with a cheap colorful linoleum that one could buy in the market.

In about eight months my loads arrived in Lagos and came through customs duty free. 'Thank you, Lord.' Three weeks later, they arrived in Jos. Nothing had been stolen, and it was like Christmas time when I could finally unpack my things and really set up house. A couple of kettles and a frying pan, a toaster, a four place setting of Melmac dishes, and a four place set of stainless dinnerware, some coffee cups, and some glasses . . . what else did a bachelor like me need? (I ate lunch and dinner over at the guest house.)

I set the record player on the nightstand (a shipping crate) by my bed where it filled the apartment with the strains of the Nutcracker Suite and eleven other classical records that I had purchased through a record club.

The sewing machine, that someone had persuaded me to take, now came into good use. I purchased some heavy fabric from a Lebanese shop, which was patterned in a beautiful blue, gray, white, and black. With much difficulty, I sewed some fitted covers for the foam rubber cushions . . . and some pleated drapes for all the louver windows! And some drapes that hung from the ceiling to the floor to cover the wide space between the living room and the kitchen. Pretty fancy! This was my home until May 1963.

CHAPTER 24

SOME HIGHLIGHTS FROM MY FIRST FOUR YEAR TERM

6-7 May 1957—I flew Dr. Driesbach down to Oyi, and stayed overnight at Egbe which is roughly fifteen miles from the Oyi River Leprosarium. Did I say rough? That road gave me a fair idea as to why SIMAIR was appreciated so much.

At Egbe, SIM had a hospital and a teacher's training college. The compound was nestled against the hillside in a small valley overlooking the town. I was introduced as the new pilot to a number of people, and Barb smiles, "I'm having a couple of nurses over for supper tonight . . . would you like to come?"

"Sure!", I grinned, "about what time?"

"Oh . . . make it about seven thirty or eight?"

"Okay!"

Barb prepared a very good meal with candlelight, flowers on the table, and soft music in the background. We all had a very nice evening. But the interesting thing about this whole affair, was that news of this outing reached Jos before I returned the next day! Whoever handled the radio traffic at Egbe evidently thought this was a newsworthy event, and so blabbed it out over the airwaves for the whole SIM family to hear! Boy, during the next few weeks, did I ever get razzed about this wherever I flew. It made me realize very early in my missionary career that being a single male was something unusual on the mission field, and I soon learned to be very discreet with my encounters with the opposite sex.

So when I received a letter from Greta, who was now in language school in Somalia, I never breathed a word to anyone. She welcomed me to Africa and jokingly asked . . . "What took you so long?"

I sent her a copy of my first prayer letter which told about hitting the turkey buzzard at Nguru and about my first flight out of Jos, running into the line squall, forcing me to spend the night at Zunkwa . . . naturally I added a personal note, as I did to all prayer letters that were sent from Africa.

For the month of May, I flew 68 hours and 25 minutes, carrying 67 people . . . my flight on the 31st, being a medical emergency flight, Jos-Gboko-Jos for Mrs. Bulthuis.

Dick was really operating behind the curve. The Vosslers were to leave the next morning for Kano and home to the States, but their place looked a shambles with hardly anything packed. I helped Dick until 3 AM in the morning when he simply broke down and cried. Here was a wonderful man who never could say no to anyone. 'Dick, can you do this?

Dick, can you do that?' Never complaining, happy-go-lucky, dare-devil Dick Vossler, who flew his Republic Thunderbolt under the London bridge during the Second World War, who flew through all kinds of weather, who almost bounced his wheels on your rooftop whenever he gave you a buzz job. In the short time I knew him, I came to admire Dick Vossler. But now he was going home . . . burned out . . . his missionary career was over.

So now I was on my own at Jos. For the month of June, I flew 63 hours and 5 minutes, and 56 passengers. From June 19th through the 22nd, I flew some of the school kids home to their stations for the summer vacation.

What a day the 21st was! My pilot logbook entry says . . . 'Jos to Lakoja . . . Returned due to weather, low clouds near Keffi with 70-mph winds . . . lost!' That's a nice way of saying that I was trying to pick my way through the rocks and palm trees under the low scud for 2 hours and 45 minutes . . . twisting and turning this way and that, being slammed about, until I was thoroughly lost and beaten . . . as Johnny Clay said, 'Tomorrow's another day!'

So the next day, we made it to Oyi, where I dropped off Mr. G. Bartlett and Becky Playfair. Then we flew over to Lakoja. There were some goats on the airstrip . . . I gave them a good buzz job . . . Mr. and Mrs. Tobert were waiting by the fuel shed. Esther squealed with delight, "Ohh . . . there's Mommy and Daddy!" I quickly swung up and around and landed. She could hardly contain herself, jumping up and down. But her older sister, Carolyn, just sat there stoically. As we were taxiing in, Esther turned to her sister and burst out . . . "Look . . . act excited, so they THINK that we REALLY missed them!"

I ate my noon and evening meals at the guesthouse whenever possible. One day I arrived a bit late and people were just beginning to eat. I squeezed into my chair, bowed my head and prayed. When I opened my eyes, the girl on my left held a bowl of mashed potatoes . . . she smiled, "Would you like some?"

"Oh . . . thank you!" Next came some roast beef, gravy, a couple of vegetables, and salad.

Hmmm . . . I noticed that this girl was very nice . . . "I'm Rich Schaffer . . . and you are . . . ?"

"Margaret Shepherd!"

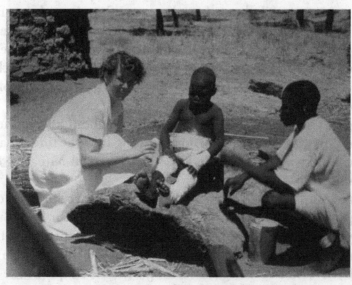

Marg at Bauchi Leprosarium

I laughed, "Oh really . . . an English shepherd! Well, I'm a German shepherd! . . . Schaffer means shepherd in German!"

"You're kidding me?" Her eyes just sparkled.

I chuckled, "No, I wouldn't kid you!"

We talked. Marg was from Canada . . . came out in 1955 . . . she was a nurse. After Hausa language school at Minna and Kano, Marg worked for about a year at Bingham Memorial Nursing Home in Jos, and then was re-stationed to Bununu for three months about the time I arrived on the field. Now she was presently working at the Bauchi Leprosarium.

When I got outside, I stopped short and said to myself, "Wow . . . was she ever nice!" But that was the last I saw of this beautiful freckle faced girl for almost two years. Little did I realize that one day . . . she . . . would become my wife!

Marg telling the Good News

For the month of July 1957, I flew 73 hours and carried 75 passengers. The rainy season was in full swing . . . two entries noted that I had to fly to my alternate airports because of bad weather. On the 16th, I noted that I flew a medical emergency flight for Mrs. Thamer and two children, however, I don't remember any of the details.

This brings me to the month of August and I kept a diary that month . . . you can refresh your memory of that month by re-reading chapter 4 of this book. My total hours of flying was now 610:05.

When the Paul Rogalsky's returned from furlough, they were re-stationed to Jos. Boy, was I glad to see them. They moved into the Vossler's house. I happily let Paul take over the flight scheduling, and Bea took over the books and the billing. It didn't take Paul too long to figure out that Jos was where the action was . . . the guys in Kano and the whole Aviation Department needed to be moved to Jos! So the need for housing instigated the obtaining of land on which three duplex houses were built with aviation funds. Soon after, a hostel was built on the Niger Creek compound for the high school students, who would be attending Hillcrest School, as Kent Academy only had grades 1 through 8. The move also necessitated the building of a new hangar and a shop for all five planes.

Rich Schaffer

Now that was a job, but builder Bob Shell and his crew of national workers did a good job. The concrete floor was as smooth as glass, and the 50 x 100 foot metal framework was hoisted in place and assembled in a couple weeks . . . every missionary in Jos lent a hand on that part.

Raising the steel framework for the new 50 X 100 foot hangar

Spacious rooms were built down both sides, the whole length of the hangar. Of course, we flyboys got into it whenever the schedule allowed. For instance, we took over the whole installation of the metal pan roof, because the nationals were installing it too crooked for our fussy perfectionist tastes.

I well remember the laying of the last 3 x 10 foot panel. We were having a heck of a time getting it in place. I got on it to get a better look. Paul quips, "Get off . . . it might slip . . . an' down you'll go!" We shoved and tugged and pulled every which way, and the darn thing just would not go in place.

Paul got on the panel to get a better look. I mimicked, "Get offf . . . it might slippp . . . and down you'll gooo!!" And that is EXACTLY what happened! Paul fell 25 feet down through the hole and landed on his back, barely missing two concrete building blocks! The heavy panel followed him like a guillotine . . . KER-CHUNK!! . . . it sliced into the wooden ladder just three feet above him! We just looked! Paralyzed. Paul was not moving!

Paul fell 25 feet from here on the hangar roof!

178

In a rush, we slid down to the edge and jumped off the roof, ran to the front of the hangar, and back to Paul. He was curled up in a little ball, moaning, trying to get his breath. After a while, he jumps to his feet, and up the ladder he goes . . . "Come on . . . let's get this stupid job done!" What a guy! Years later during a routine X-ray, it was discovered that he had a hairline fracture in his vertebrae . . . no doubt from the fall he suffered that day.

Simair hangars after completion, Jos airport

Wreck on the Jos Kagoro road

One day I was drilling holes in the concrete with a mason bit to install the metal parts which would hold the glass louver windows. To be at the proper height, I was balancing myself on the fuel stand. The drill had an electrical short in it. Suddenly, the fuel stand sank down on one side in the soft earth. I grabbed hold of one of the metal bars to keep from falling. An electric current instantly shot through my body from the drill to the bar! Try as I would, I couldn't let go of the drill or the bar! I was being electrocuted! The fellows heard my God-awful screaming and came running. Bill Tuck grabbed the cord and jerked the drill from my hand. It swung down, and cut a deep gash in his leg. I let go of the bar, and slid limply to the ground.

"Are you okay?"

I nodded weakly, but I just lay in the mud for several minutes. After awhile, I got up and continued my job, using a different drill. But later, I laid down again, weak as a jellyfish . . . the realization that I had almost been killed really scared me.

Yet, almost everyday, I was laying my life on the line. This greenhorn pilot was flying through some of the most horrendous weather that the tropics could manufacture. The awesome thunderstorms . . . the fog, the rain . . . around the rocks and the trees. I was a fast learner, but I was scared . . . and that was good . . . there are old pilots, but there are no old bold pilots!

One day I got a little package that contained about 25 Peanut cartoon strips that Greta had clipped from some daily newspaper . . . "thought you might enjoy these!" In another letter, she enclosed one of her prayer cards which had a beautiful picture of herself . . . I put that on my bed stand.

Greta's prayer card   *Greta at the clinic in Somalia*

Another time she sent me a box of Kodachrome slides. Every time I heard from her, she was at different station, and I mentioned, "Wow . . . they are really moving you around a lot!" It was then that I learned the Mission HAD to move her a couple times, because the men on the stations would all go gollywoggles over her, and that didn't set too well with the jealous wives! "Men are just a bunch of dumb creeps!", Greta summarized. Her beautiful golden hair and those deep blue eyes . . . ahh . . . the price of beauty!

Greta on the beach in Aden   *Greta at a clinic in Ethiopia*

What Greta looks like now

I bought an old BSA 125cc. motorcycle for fifty pounds (about a hundred and fifty dollars). It was in sad shape, so I spent my spare time fixing it up. The clutch and the kick starter were worn out, but I managed to get the parts to repair them. I replaced the spark plug, tires and tubes, and the torn boots on the front shock absorbers. Fixed the taillight. Got rid of the rust in the gas tank. I painted the bike a beautiful bright red with white trim, but the paint was no good. So I had to strip off all the paint and start over. This time I used some light Cessna yellow, and trimmed it in black . . . it really was beautiful and that bike purred like a kitten.

When I told my dad that I had bought a motorcycle, he wrote back real quick-like, "Suggest you stick to the flying and leave the motorcycles alone . . . they are dangerous!"

My Dad

And he was right. Even though I was very careful, I could write you a whole book on all the close calls I had over the years. One time I was forced off the road by an oncoming lorry . . . jumped the ditch okay, but crashed in a bunch of boulders . . . smashed me and the bike up real good. Repaired the bike, and my body healed over time.

I used the bike mostly on the weekends to explore the dirt roads and footpaths on the Plateau, passing out gospel tracts wherever they took me. It was fun and it was also a spiritual outlet for me, trying to reach people with the good news.

Passing out the little red booklets: "Hanyar Chato"—The Way of Salvation
"A chikin farko Allah ya halita sama da kasa"—"In the beginning, God made the
heavens and the earth".

By the end of the year, 1957, I had logged 825 hours in my pilot log, averaging 60 hours a month. When the whole aviation department moved to Jos, that didn't cut down the workload. We just took on more and more flying. All four pilots were averaging about the same hours. That increased the maintenance, and everything else that needs doing to run an efficient program. And Johnny Clay would be going home next July. So the Mission asked Soddy if he would come back for another term. He came back alright, but with a cocky attitude . . . "I'm here to rescue SIMAIR! . . . ta dumm!" That didn't set too well with the Kano guys . . . sparks flew. Finally Soddy gave up and quit . . . the Soderbergs were put in charge of the Hi-School Hostel where they did a very admirable job.

The 20th of May 58, was when I made the flight from Jos-Gboko-Takum-Jos. Go back to chapter 2 of this book if you want to refresh your memory about that flight. The miracle medical emergency flight for Stucky Bergsma in chapter 3 was made on 28-29th of May 58.

When the Clays went home on furlough on the 12th of July 58, Johnny was commissioned to find a plane suitable to replace the aging fleet of Cessnas. We wanted something that would go faster, and further, and carry more baggage, and do it cheaper. About that time, Piper came out with a new plane . . . the Comanche 180 . . . it was a sleek low wing four place aircraft that could cruise about 140 mph, carry 200 pounds of baggage, and had a range of 900 miles, but it had a retractable tricycle landing gear . . . would this plane really work out here on the mission field?

Well, we ended up getting four of these planes when Mr. Piper offered us a 'darn good deal' . . . "If you will buy ONE, we will GIVE you ONE, IF you will buy TWO more the following year! . . . and we'll give you 15% off on the ones you buy!!" (Piper Aircraft also gave us very substantial discounts on all of the parts we ordered down through the years to maintain these aircraft.) Thank you, Mr. Piper.

In 1958 SIMAIR switched over to the
Piper Comanche 180. Mr Piper said, "If you
buy one, we will give you one, if you will
buy two more within a year...and the ones
you buy, we will give you 15% off!
     These planes revolutionized our flying
in Nigeria. They will go 140 miles per hour,
carry four people and 200 pounds of baggage.
Had a range of 900 miles which meant
we could fly out and home again without
refueling...and no more balancing act when
we did need gas.

Piper Comanche 180 for $16,000!

I'll tell you right here, this plane absolutely revolutionized our aviation program. With double the range, many times we could fly all day and never have to take on fuel at a remote airstrip. Also being able to fly 20 miles faster saved us time and wear on the pilots. The ability to carry 80 pounds more baggage than the Cessna helped some . . . but get real folks . . . NO plane will ever be built that will carry all the junk that a missionary expects to take with him! As for the tricycle gear, once we learned how to maintain it properly, it was no problem . . . being able to retract the gear was the secret for giving us the extra speed at less cost.

Each plane came out to Nigeria via a cargo ship to Lagos in two big wooden crates . . . the wings came in one box and the fuselage in another . . . Nigerian Airways allowed us to use one of their hangars where we assembled them just about like you would put together a model airplane. My pilot log says that I had my check ride in VR-NCU on 17 December 1958.

When I call myself a 'greenhorn, wet behind the ears, runny nosed missionary', it was for a good reason. I guess every new missionary goes through this stage. We get out there and quickly size up the situation . . . the old time fogies are doing it all wrong! I expressed this sentiment to Lofty Grimshaw one day as we were walking over to the guesthouse . . . "If we all just packed up our bags and headed for home, and let the national church do the job . . . ."

Englishman Lofty Grimshaw curtly cut me off with these words as he glared down at me from his lofty height . . . "I say, brother . . . didn't the Lord call you out here to be a missionary?"

"Uh . . . ah . . . yeah!"

"And do you think maybe He called me out here . . . and all the other missionaries?"

"Uh . . . ahh . . . yeah, I guess . . . !"

"Well, if that is the case . . . and that it IS the case . . . don't you think we missionaries ought to stay out here until He calls us to GO HOME?" And with that stern rebuke he left me standing with my mouth wide open as he strode down the path on his long legs.

"Touché!" Ahhh . . . I just chuckle every time I think of this encounter with Lofty Grimshaw. What a fantastic fellow. Lofty was a tin miner working on the Jos Plateau when he was saved. He went home to England where he got some Bible training and came back as an SIM missionary.

Lofty lived in the apartment above me, when he lived in Jos . . . most of the time he would be out camping in his old VW van at the tin mines, preaching and teaching the miners about Jesus.

The water system in Jos wasn't all that reliable . . . many times the water would be shut off to make repairs. One day I came home to find water running out from under my front door and down the steps! I opened the door to find that my whole apartment was flooded with about two inches of water! It was running down the inside walls! I ran up the front stairs and pounded on Lofty's door . . . "HEY LOFTY!" No answer. I ran back down the stairs, around the building and up the back stairs. With all the ruckus, I finally raised a couple of neighbors from their rest hour.

It so happens that eight keys fit all the doors in the whole apartment building. I finally found someone that had a key that would also fit Lofty's back door.

I sloshed into the bathroom where the water was overflowing from the sink . . . the plug was in the drain. Evidently Lofty had come home, turned on the faucet, but forgot to turn it off again when no water was forthcoming. Not only did I have the fun job of drying out my apartment, I was the nice guy and also dried out his apartment! Who knows when he would be home again.

When Char Shaw came back to Bauchi Leprosarium from her year's furlough, Marg Shepherd was moved to Katunga where she taught a health class in the Bible School, and she also ran the small clinic for about nine months. To get into the station, it was a wild ride on the back of Ray Holly's motorcycle, on a road that was more like a trail. You had to wade the river and the swamps to get to Katunga in the rainy season.

On the head of one of the carriers was a small kitten in a basket. His job was to keep Marg from being lonesome when the river and the swamps got too deep and became impassable. As the little kitten grew up, it did what all cats do out here . . . they catch and eat lizards . . . only trouble is, this one would vomit the half eaten lizard on Marg's floor! That didn't set too well with Marg Shepherd . . . she has never liked cats since.

 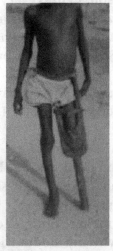

Marg cut off this leg to save the little boys life.

During the dry season, Marg came into Jos for her month of holiday. When I became aware of that, naturally I tried to figure out ways to be with her. But it was always in a group setting, like a bunch of us going on a picnic, or a hike. Marg was simply beautiful in every way. Here was someone who had no pretenses. But she showed no apparent interest in me . . . maybe that was what attracted me even more?

A long time later, I learned that while Marg was still at Bauchi, one day she and Alma Hixt had quite a lengthy discussion about their single state in life, with little hope of ever being married, because there were so few single men in the SIM compared to the large number of single women. Marg summed up the discussion with, "Well . . . if the Lord wants me to be married . . . why, He can provide me someone right out of the sky!" And so here comes this single pilot, Rich Schaffer! Was this in her mind every time she saw me?

Anyway, when Marg went back to Katunga, her cat was missing. She had left it with the pastor's family. One day she asked their little boy, "What happened to the kitten?"

Big big smile . . . "Oh, we ate him!"

My last flight for 1958 was a notable one . . . being the single pilot, it naturally became my lot to fly a medical emergency flight on Christmas day up to Upper Volta to pick up Florene Guess, who had an acute appendicitis. Dr. Warren took along his little black bag, just in case he needed to do a 'kitchen table' operation. We stayed overnight at Fada. Florene looked very pale, but she had a plucky spirit.

The next morning I went into Florene's bedroom and picked her up in her nightie and carried her out and gently laid her on the stretcher in the back . . . She was as light as a feather.

This was my first cross-country flight in the new Comanche, and to fly Jos-Kano-Niamey-Fada-Niamey-Kano-Jos took 11 hrs and 20minutes. In a Cessna 170B, that flight would have taken about 16 hours.

My pilot log now showed a total of 1430 hours . . . 605 hours were done in 1958. A couple of things of interest . . . December 6th, I gave a Father Goss a checkout ride in VR-NCI which means that we sold that Cessna to the Catholic Mission.

In January 59, we went to Lagos and assembled our second Comanche, VR-NCV . . . Victor-Roger-November-Charlie-Victor.

We also sold one of the Cessnas to the Sudan United Mission, but they would not allow Ray Browneye to fly any of their missionaries, because of his lack of experience . . . he only had about fifty hours. He tried to get into Moody Aviation as a special student, but there was no room. So I suggested, "Why don't we give you the Moody course right out here?" And that is just what we did.

SUM said that Ray could fly on his own, but whenever he had a passenger, one of us guys had to go along. Since it was MY bright idea, I was the one that did most of the 'going along!' And boy, we did it. 300 hours . . . through the Harmattan dust, sometimes so thick that you could hardly see the ground, flying fifty feet above the trees tops . . . through the thunderstorms, around the rocks and the trees . . . we gave Ray Browneye a flight experience he would never ever get at Moody . . . I should have logged the co-pilot time in my pilot log just for the record. But listen to me crow . . . he became one of the best missionary bush pilots in the world . . . cock-a-doodle-dooooo!

In February 59, Mrs. Holley was due to have her baby. So Marg Shepherd was also moved into Jos, where she worked at Bingham Memorial Nursing Home again until she went home on furlough in August of 59. But she made no bones about it, to me, and everyone else, including the munya . . . SHE wanted to be a BUSH missionary! So to keep her happy, the munya promised to let her go bush when she came back from furlough. And in deference to her wishes, I sort of reluctantly crossed her off my list, for who was I to stand in the way of God's will for her.

But one day, I took Marg and Belva on a hike to climb Gog and Magog. We tried to approach the rocks from the south, even though I had heard that you could only get to the top by coming in from the east. The closer we came to Gog and Magog, the bigger the rocks became. Naturally I assumed my proper roll in helping the girls up and down the rocks when the climb became difficult. There was that flow of electricity when our hands touched. You know what I'm talking about.

Gog & Magog

We came to this ledge. I eased myself over and dropped down. No way were the girls going to do this. Finally I coaxed Belva into coming to the edge, sit down, turn around, and I helped her slide down okay. But Marg tried coming down without turning around. She slid down through my arms, and ended up with her arms tightly around my neck, and I was tightly holding her around the waist . . . face to face . . . our lips almost touching.

I smiled and looked into her beautiful eyes, "My darling, may I kiss you now?"

She blushed, "Would YOU put me DOWN!"

"Oh . . . okay!" So I let her slide slowly through my arms until her feet touched before I released her.

Her eyes just sparkled . . . an impish smile stole from her lips as she slowly shook her head.

It was a nice shady spot, so we sat on the rocks, and ate our lunch. The rest of the day, whenever I caught her looking at me, she had that twinkle in her eyes . . . she would look away with . . . almost like she was laughing inside.

On the 28th of March 59, a new pilot arrived. Bob Ediger grew up in Dallas, Oregon and a number of his relatives still live in that area. He was a welcome addition to the aviation department. By the 28th of July we were now operating three Piper Comanches as VR-NCX joined the fleet. We sold another of the Cessnas to Dr. Dave Hilton who was stationed at Bambur with the SUM.

On the 12th of August, I flew Marg, Anna Lou Oursland, and Belva Overmiller to Kano to catch their international flight to Europe, where they would do a short tour of Italy, Switzerland, France, and England on their way home for a year's furlough. They had a lot of fun on that trip and consequently became very close friends even to this day.

On the 23rd of October 59, another pilot joined SIMAIR. Dave Rutt was from Pennsylvania, and graduated from the Moody Aviation course the year after me.

I was still corresponding with Greta. They finally shipped her off to Aden . . . "missionaries over here consider it like being condemned to Siberia!" I guess the mission figured she couldn't cause any 'men' problems there.

One day I got a letter telling about this 'wonderful handsome Englishman' that she had met at the club. From the next letter it sounded like this guy was literally sweeping her off her feet . . . she was even thinking about marrying him! "He's the only man who has ever treated me like a real woman!" From other things she said about him, I got the idea that he wasn't even a Christian. So I wrote her quite a lengthy letter about being unequally yoked to a non-Christian and suggested that she ought to break it off.

Wow! Did I ever get a hot letter back! She was mad! But surprisingly, she DID break off with the guy! "Who do you think you are . . . telling me who I can marry and not marry . . . why is this so important to you?"

I wrote back . . . "because I love you, and I want to marry you myself!"

I got the neatest letter back from her . . . "Rich . . . I feel honored . . . but it would never work out . . . you're just like a brother to me . . ."

And I had to agree with her . . . it would never have worked out . . . she was so beautiful . . . I envisioned it would be about like Abraham keeping tabs on Sarah when the foreign kings wanted her. Anyway, we remained good friends.

The guys had quite a running discussion about selling our remaining Cessna VR-NAF. We had a lot of extra Cessna parts and it would cost us next to nothing to have another plane around . . . except nobody wanted to fly it . . . the pilots groaned whenever they were scheduled to fly the Cessna . . . we were thoroughly spoiled by the Comanche 180.

One day, Dave Rutt and I took VR-NCX up for a test flight after we had completed a 100 hour inspection. I was flying, and Dave would write the results on the check sheet as we did the flight. We had been talking about how small the window was, next to the pilot. You could open it to let in some air when you were on the ground, or you could drop notes or small packets to people on the ground. That was about it. I was just breaking ground . . . "What if you had to drop out something bigger? . . . Wonder if you could toss stuff out the door?", I muttered.

"Let's see . . . ." and with that, Dave unlocked the door and opened it!

The plane gyrated wildly as the door popped open about two inches and began vibrating loudly. I fought to keep the plane under control. Dave tried with all his might, but he could not close the door! We staggered around the field and I plopped it on the ground. Dave gave me a sheepish look . . . "Wow, now we know why they have this sticker on the door! . . . DO NOT UNLOCK OR OPEN THE DOOR IN FLIGHT!"

I could have killed the guy!

But that settled the question . . . we would keep the Cessna . . . you could fly it with the doors off all day long. If we ever had to drop supplies, or whatever, to people on the ground, the Comanche was definitely not the plane to use!

17-18 Oct 59 . . . I made the first flight to Liberia where SIM has their radio station ELWA . . . 1500 miles one way. I flew Mr. Winterflood, plus two kids, the 450 miles to Lagos, where I stayed overnight.

We checked out of the country early in the morning and flew on to Accra, Ghana where we took on some av-gas.

My passengers this time were Reverend and Mrs. Howard O. Jones, and one child . . . Howard was connected with the Billy Graham ministries, and was a wonderful evangelist in his own right.

Everything was solid jungle inland, so we hugged the coastline to have the sandy beaches under us at all times. And so beautiful it was, with the deep blue water, the gentle white waves crashing the shoreline . . . palm trees right down to the water. White billowing clouds forming just inland. Sometimes we passed a small fishing village, where they would be dragging in the net with the morning catch. A few times, I flew just above the water. What a breathtaking sight. The people stared at us in wonder as we flashed by.

We buzzed the radio station to announce our arrival, and flew back to Payne Field. It was just a small airstrip along the beach. No customs or immigration here. We would have to do that in town. The whole 1500 mile trip took only 9:05 hours for an average cruising speed of 165 miles per hour! That's moving, even for a Comanche 180!

I tied the plane down and soon a vehicle arrived to pick us up. A lot of the houses at ELWA were strung out along the beach. They put me up in one which was being used as the guesthouse while the missionaries were home on furlough. The long, low, bungalow had lots of louver windows on both sides of the house, which were opened, to allow the gentle sea breezes to push the stifling air from the rooms. I was given a list of where I would be eating meals with various missionary families during my 5 day stay. WOW! . . . A five day stay! . . . in this lush tropical paradise!! . . . now this was going to be hard to take!

First chance I was alone, I wandered across the road, and down to the water's edge, only a hundred yards from the house. I dipped my toes in the water . . . it was luke warm! Jos was so dry and barren. For a kid who grew up near the ocean, this brought tears to my eyes. 'Oh man, how can these poor missionaries stand this day after day, year after year? . . . what a hardship to live like this!'

That night I had supper with the Tom Lowe family. He was one of the radio technicians. Naturally, I asked him lots of questions about the radio station. "We'll have to take you on a tour of the place!"

"And how's the fishing?"

"You like to fish? . . . not many of us fish on the beach . . . we go up a little river just south of the station . . . would you like to go sometime?" There was a twinkle in Tom's eyes.

"Sure! . . . when can we go?"

"Well, tomorrow first thing, someone will be running you and the Jones's into town for immigration and stuff . . . that may take all day. Best fishing is in the early morning . . . we'll figure a time before you have to leave."

Two days later, I rolled out of bed at 0400 in the morning . . . we were going fishing! I trotted over to Tom's house. He and Dale Graber were already drinking coffee. Tom poured me a hot cup, and I cooled it down with a big glug of canned milk, and killed the taste with two heaping teaspoons of sugar. Dale shook his head . . . "that looks more like cocoa to me!"

I ignored him as I downed my cup, "Ahhh . . . now I'm ready to go!"

The night before, they had loaded the 12 foot aluminum boat with all the gear onto a small trailer. We jumped into the Jeep and headed for the south edge of the compound where we disappeared through a small hole in the jungle wall. In the dark, we slowly wound around every which way on a very bumpy trail. I took it by faith that these guys knew where we were going. After backtracking a couple of times, we finally came to the river, which was barely discernable in the early morning light. We lifted the boat and slid it down the grassy bank. Dale handed me a stout pole which was rigged with a homemade wooden plug, "Let it trail about fifty feet behind the boat . . . and hang onto the rod, cuz they really hit it hard sometimes!"

"What are we fishing for?"

"Groupers . . . biggest one we ever landed was about twenty pounds . . . but we have lost bigger ones . . . they really put up a fight!"

Tom ran the small outboard motor, while Dale sat in the middle . . . I pushed off the bow and jumped in . . . with three guys, I noticed we were sitting low in the water. I tossed out my lure and let the line run out about fifty feet . . . the rod tip had a gentle throb to the action of the lure. Dale did the same on the other side of the boat. What a beautiful paradise . . . the lush green jungle right down to the water's edge . . . foggy steam rising from the winding crystal clear river . . . the sky was a low overcast with hints of blue here and there . . .

Something hit my lure, and I gave it a big yank . . . the plug came out of water and whizzed past my head like a bullet . . . "Wow! . . . missed him!"

Tom turned the boat around so we could troll over the same spot. This time Dale connected . . . "Fish on!" . . . Tom cut the motor. Dale's rod bent sharply as the fish made it's run against the drag. Suddenly the fish cleared the water with a spectacular jump . . . Dale lowered his rod and the fish stayed on. Dale gained back some line. Another run. The fish wrapped the line around a submerged log and broke the line like it was a piece of thread. Dale reeled in his line and muttered quietly . . . "now that was a nice fish!"

Dale and Tom switched places . . . Tom tied on another homemade lure. "Now, I'll show you how it's done!" A half hour later, and sure enough, Tom tied into another fish. This one gave him a real tug of war, but after a five minute battle, Tom eased the tired fish into the boat.

"Beautiful!" . . . I guessed maybe eight-ten pounds.

Dale quipped, "You gonna keep that smaaa-ll fish?"

"You bet'cha . . . we are gonna have us a fish fry!"

We fished for about another hour, but that was all she wrote. These guys had work to do, so Dale turned the boat around and headed back to the Jeep. We came around a bend. Up ahead, I saw something swimming across the river . . . "Hey, What's that?"

Dale gave the motor full throttle. As we got closer, I could see that it was a huge snake! We hit the bank just as it disappeared in the tall grass . . . I could have reached out and touched it's tail! In a flash, I was standing in Dale's lap ready to bail out! I just about swamped the boat! These crazy guys really hooted at me . . . "You're not scared of a little **Python**, are you?"

But honest . . . I could have walked on water, getting out of there, if that snake had come back . . . that thing was six inches in diameter and fifteen feet long!

We got back to the Jeep and slid the boat up out of the water and onto the tiny trailer. Now that I could see it, that was one sorry looking Jeep . . . they made some fenders and the rear end out of wood, because the rust had eaten the metal away. And that's the way everything was at radio station ELWA . . . being right on the ocean, it was a never ending battle with rust and corrosion from the salt laden air.

All good things come to an end . . . it was time to head for home. The return flight took 10 hours and 35 minutes. On the way I stopped at Abidjan, Accra, and Lagos. My passenger was Lois Williams, coming for medical and dental, and then a month's rest at Miango Rest Home.

On the 22nd of December, I took Lois back to ELWA. Again I was able to stay a few days at this tropical paradise. Tom loaned me a big pole and a sun helmet . . . and I wandered down to the beach to try some surf casting. I rigged up with a 3 ounce sinker and a big chunk of raw beef and tossed it out about 200 feet. What a beautiful lazy day. The early morning sun was hot, but there was a bit of wave and a slight breeze that kept it comfortable. The fishing was slow, but I didn't mind. It was wonderful to just relax and soak up my surroundings.

There was a couple of small tugs on my line. I hauled back on the pole to set the hook. Nothing. Nothing more happened. Maybe he stole my bait?

Suddenly something hit the rig so hard that it almost wrenched the pole from my hands! Three hard jerks. The pole responded double. I tightened up the drag as the line sizzled from the reel. I hugged the pole tight as my heels dug two furrows in the sand . . . I was literally being dragged down to the water's edge! Suddenly the line broke. I landed hard on my rump. The braided nylon line came zinging past my head . . . ZZzss . . . . ! I just sat there in awe. My right hand was a bloody mess as my forefinger had been cut to the bone by the line . . . I still have a scar there to this day. When I told Tom about what happened, he said, "You probably hooked on to a shark, or it could have been one of those big sea turtles . . . anyway, it must have been a big one because that line you are using is 50 pound test!"

The next day I was down on the beach again, fishing in the same spot. Nothing was happening. But up the beach about a quarter mile there were some low rocks that protruded out into the surf. Some gulls were circling there . . . some were diving down into the water. 'Hmmm . . . must be some fish feeding there . . . 'So I ran up the beach. I watched the waves as they sometimes covered the rocks. It was too far to cast out to where the fish were. 'Maybe I can work my way out on those rocks?..' so when the water backed off, I ran out. The next couple of waves covered my ankles, so I ventured out another thirty feet on the rocks and cast my rig. It hardly hit the water and I had a fish on! It was a big one. As I was playing the fish, it went down the beach which allowed me to begin pulling it in. And I began working my way back to the shoreline, not paying any attention to the waves. I heard this crashing noise and looked up . . . here comes a sneaker wave that's taller than me! No time to react . . . The wave literally picked me up and set me with a resounding thud on the dry beach! When I recovered, I had lost the fish, and my prescription sun glasses, and the pith helmet. I waded out and recovered the helmet . . . never did find the sun glasses. What fun!

They gave me a tour of the ELWA compound. The antenna field, the generators, and the shops. In the studio building I watched the actual operation of transmitting the good news to the far flung places of Africa. Who was listening at that very moment to the way of salvation being broadcast in their mother tongue? . . . 'Lord, may they understand.'

Tom said, "Here, let me show you something that will interest you." He played me an audio tape of a program called 'Miracles' that was put out by Bob Jones University. It was the story about one Rich Schaffer who had flown a small unconscious boy with cerebral malaria to Jos where he miraculously recovered! It was a very dramatic rendition of a prayer letter I had written about the incident that Eileen Erickson had put together in her radio communications class. (Go back to chapter two and three of this book to read the true version of the Stukey Bergsma story. If you would like, I can send you a copy of this radio version which really catches the imagination of young people. Would appreciate a small donation to cover the cost of the tape and for postage?)

On a nearby workbench there were stacks of extra large 16 inch diameter 33 RPM records of some old gospel programs that ELWA had transmitted over the air . . . most of them were of The Old Fashioned Revival Hour with Dr. Charles E. Fuller, and The Haven of Rest with Shipmate Bob.

"What are you going to do with all these old records", I asked.

"Oh, we just throw them away . . . you have to have a special turntable to play them . . . some people heat them up in an oven and when they are pliable enough, they drape them over a tin can and mold them into flower pots!"

"We have an old record player at the hanger that we play music on . . . wonder if I could adapt it so we could play these records?"

Tom smiled, "Be our guest . . . you can take as many as you want . . . there's some really good music on them . . . and good sermons too!"

So I reduced the stack of records by about four inches, which I took back home to the hanger. I also took along Dale Graber and his family for their month of holiday at Jos and Miango. That finished me out with 514 hours, and 508 passengers for the year of 1959 . . . 1944 total hours now on my sitter-setter.

Starting the year 1960, I flew a number of medical emergency flights. Jos to Yola to Jos on the 15th for an SUM missionary. On the 22nd I flew a medical emergency for Fran Edwards, Kaltungo to Jos. On the 28th-29th, I flew the Grabers back to ELWA, and turned right around with Mr. and Mrs. Jackson on an emergency flight. On the 11th of February, I had an emergency flight for R. Crowder, a Baptist missionary.

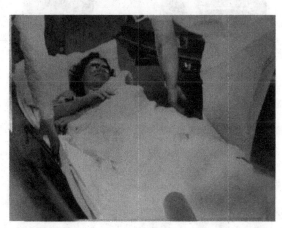

Medical Emergency Flight for Fran Edwards

191

As I study the entrees in my logbook, trying to jog the cobwebs of my memory . . . so many flights. It's all fading away. Sometimes when I run into an old time missionary, they will say, "You remember that time you flew me, and we ran into that big thunderstorm . . ." And I nod my head as if I do. And they began filling in all the little details, how black it was, how we got slammed about, and had to go back to . . . and sit down for a spell . . . you remember that flight, don't you?" I just laugh and shake my head. Twenty years of flying on the mission field in West Africa . . . it all becomes a blur . . . that's why I need to keep on writing this book before it all fades away like some amazing forgotten dream.

In August 1960, Belva, Anna Lou and Marg came back from their furlough within the year, and the munya, true to their word, sent Marg out to Gelengu to work in the clinic with Edna Alchin while Jack and Vera Nicholson's were home on furlough (You want an idea what pioneer missionary life is like? . . . read their book . . . "No Turning Back").

About three or four months later, they moved Marg to Kaltungo Hospital to fill in for Betty Van Dyken who was going home on furlough for a year.

On January 28th I flew Mrs. Hall to Kaltungo, a Miss Ober to Biu, and picked up Mrs. Shisler, and back to Gombe to pick up Elsie Lavery for Jos. On February 3rd I flew Mrs. Cooke to Kaltungo and picked up Mr. and Mrs. Hilker. These were quick turn around flights.

But on February 17th I flew Dr. and Mrs. Ockingay out to Kaltungo for a three day missionary conference where I was able to see Marg a couple of times. I walked down to the hospital compound every day during rest hour and knocked on her door. She was quite surprised and flustered to see me, but she made some ice-cold lemonade and we sat on her front veranda where we made small talk.

She told me about the fun time they had going thru Europe, and about furlough, and her folks. I talked about the flying, due to go home on furlough in April, things going on in Jos, and how I was fixing up my apartment.

My bush missionary

She had a battery powered record player that wasn't running at the proper speed . . . "Wonder if you would take a look at it?"

After tinkering with it for awhile . . . "Can I take it to Jos? . . . I think maybe I can fix it there."

"Okay."

In parting I said, "It was really nice to see you . . . only wish it were more often."

She looked at me, "Why is that?"

"Because I like you . . .", I smiled hopefully.

She looked down flustered as a pink glow appeared on her face, not knowing what to say.

On March 8th, I flew Dowdell, Cox, and Lewis to Kaltungo for a day long meeting. I wandered down to the hospital to see Marg and return the record player.

"Here she is . . . good as new."

"Oh, thank you very much," she smiled, "What did you find wrong with it?"

"Oh, I just took it apart and gave her a good cleaning, and oiled the motor and several other places . . . it really works good now."

I also gave Marg one of my favorite records which she was rather hesitant to accept. "Please take it . . . I'm hoping to bring back a whole bunch of new records! . . ."

"Well, thank you! . . . I'm sure that I will enjoy it very much . . ." Then she said rather seriously, "Do you think you will come back out here again . . . before you go on furlough?"

"I would like to, but I didn't see any flights on the schedule . . ."

She interrupted, "When will you leave?"

"I fly out of Kano April 15th . . ."

"Are you coming back?" sort of wistfully . . .

"Lord willing . . . in fact, I've signed up for some multi-engine and instrument flight training that is being offered to furloughing pilots who intend to go back to the field . . . so I have to come back in order to qualify for that training . . . Hey, you are going to miss me, aren't you?"

She didn't say the words, but the glow on her face, and the twinkle in her eyes said, "Yes!"

I had no more flights to Kaltungo. My last flight was Jos-Enugu-Jos on April 11th giving me a total of 2566 hours. And on April 15th, four years to the day, I was on my way for a year's furlough.

CHAPTER 25
Furlough Time

What does a missionary do on a whole year's furlough? Stick around and I'll tell you what this kid did on my first furlough. Back in the 'good old days', reentry back into the high flying American culture consisted of a brief contact with the munya at the New York office, and a thorough physical by der Doctor Frame. The Millers were still in charge of the home. He remembered my talents for being able to 'fix any gadget that ever was born', and he immediately put me to work whenever I had a spare moment. I had to disappear to get away from him.

I went down to the bank nearby and robbed my saving's account of the money I would need to buy a car to get me out to the west coast. In the car ads, I found an old Nash Ambassador that I thought would be a good idea, as you can fold the seats down to make a bed . . . I would sleep in the car going across the country to save money.

When I got over to New Jersey, the Ambassador turned out to be a pile of rusted out junk . . . I didn't even start the engine. They had a few other cars, but they were way out of my price range of $600. I was about to walk off the lot when I spotted a car way over in the corner. "What's that car over there?"

"Oh that? . . . that's a Studebaker Champion . . . we could let you have it for a thousand maybe . . ."

I walked over . . . this car had a 'please buy me' look to it . . . under the layers of coal dust, which indicated that it had sat for quite awhile, the body looked straight, and there was no rust. It had 37,000 miles on the odometer. The interior was fairly nice and showed hardly any wear. "What year is this thing?"

"It's a 57 . . . it's a nice little car."

I stuck out my hand, "Let's crank it up and see what she sounds like."

The guy handed me the key, "She's been a settin' fer quite a spell."

The battery was dead as a door nail . . . "I'll get the jumper battery . . ."

Even with the jumper, the car would not start until we poured a bit of gas down the throat of the carburetor . . . sounded like the buggy would have a heart attack, but finally it settled down to a nice even purr. We pumped up the tires and took it out on a little test drive. I was surprised how nice it handled, and the engine was very responsive.

Back at the lot . . . "Leave me alone with her for awhile and then I'll tell you my decision." I crawled all over and under that car and liked what I saw.

Then began the dickering . . . this guy didn't know the 'on the job training' this kid had out in Nigeria for the last four years . . . I scratched

the back of my head and pessimistically said, "This car looks terrible . . . best I can give you is maybe . . . $400."

The guy hooted, "You gotta be kiddin' kid! . . . $800 is our last price!"

"If you'll put in a new battery, I'll give you $450!"

"$750! . . . not a dime less!"

"It needs a new set of tires on the front . . . I'll give you $500!"

"You drive a hard bargain . . . $700 . . . that's it!"

I pulled out the six hundred dollars from my pocket and slowly counted the bills . . . "That's all I got . . . $600 . . . you steam clean the engine and wash off all that grimy soot . . ."

"Not a chance, kid . . . not a chance."

I shrugged my shoulders and slowly shook my head . . . "Okay." And I started to walk off the lot.

I didn't get twenty feet . . . "Okay kid . . . we'll do it for $650!"

I didn't budge . . . "look..$600 is all I've got!" . . . I held up the money.

"Okay, okay . . . $600 . . . jeepers @%XX*!!" . . . the salesman threw up his hands in disgust.

It took them awhile to get the car ready . . . under all that grime was a nice two-tone blue-gray and white colored car. They even blacked the rear tires, washed the windows inside and out, and put in a couple of gallons of gas! They got my $600 and I got a nice little car.

The next day I walked across Central Park to Dr. Frame's office for my physical. Awhile back some hood came into their office and robbed them at gunpoint. He made them take off their clothes and locked them in a closet so he could make his get-away. When I got to the office, I walked up to the receptionist's desk, pointed my finger, and yelled in my best gangster lingo, "Okay . . . this is a stick-up!"

Dr. Frame came flying out of nowhere. He angrily wagged his finger in my face, "Young man . . . you are NOT funny!"

I gave them my stool sample, and a urine sample, and a whole bunch of blood. He gave me a very thorough physical, and psychological exam, reluctantly, deeming that I was fit to be turned loose on the American public. (just kidding)

But I had to stick around for awhile until I was cleared to go. When Mr. Miller left me alone long enough, I went shopping . . . bought a slide projector and went through all of my slides and worked out a sequence that would tell the story of SIMAIR and what I did the last four years. I worked out a rough itinerary, and made contact with the people I needed to visit all across the States to California where a crop duster job was waiting for me.

My first stop was to visit Greta and her mom, who greeted me very warmly. We did a lot of talking and I showed them my slides . . . and Greta showed me hers. This gave me my first opportunity to practice my live presentation. That evening, Greta and I went out to a spaghetti place. She was as beautiful as ever with her long golden hair and those blue blue eyes . . . oh man. And we talked some more. But she was going to stay home. And I was slated for some multi-engine and instrument training and would be going back to Nigeria. That's life sometimes.

I drove on down to Statesville, North Carolina to visit the Ogburns where I stayed a whole week. That was really good as it gave me a chance to unwind. Lanny was as busy as ever at the hospital, but we managed to work in some good tennis.

One night they took me to a "Fiddle" contest. Now that was something I had never heard or seen before, but fiddle players from all over the state came to vie in this competition. Most of them turned out to be a small group composed of a fiddle, guitar, base guitar and drums . . . sometimes they also had a harmonica player which really caught my interest as I play, or thought I played one pretty good.

This was the time that Elvis Presley was becoming popular, so every other group had someone trying to act and sing just like Elvis, including all the hip gyrations. This missionary kid wasn't all that sure of this kind of stuff.

One guy dressed in oversize bib overalls was out front singing some filthy song, rocking back and forth with his hands down inside his pants. Near the end, he came right up to Merlene's face. Suddenly out pops his finger which he tried to stick in her mouth. Lanny and I jumped up and shoved this clown sprawling back into the band. The crowd thought this absolutely hilarious and that it was part of the act. When they realized that it wasn't, we picked up Merlene bodily and took our leave out of there, fast. Wow!

I drove up to Lansing, Michigan where I visited Jerry and Rita Gilbert . . . he was one of my GI buddies while in Japan.

I drove over to the Chicago area where I stayed with Mom and Pop Burnett in Bensonville. It was like being home again and did she ever feed me. The Wheaton First Baptist gave me the whole Sunday evening service to present my slides, which I ended with a dramatic missionary challenge to the young people. Can you imagine a large church allowing you an opportunity like that in this present day? This wonderful faithful church supported us all the twenty years that we were in Africa.

I also visited dear old Mrs. Gustafson who had just been put in a nursing home because her daughter could not take care of her properly anymore. She did not like it there, as she was having a lot of trouble with Alzheimer patients coming into her room and stealing her stuff. Also the patient care was not all that great . . . she complained that the nurse would not even cut her toenails! I had a clipper, so I cut her toenails. She was so thankful for me to do that. As I was about to leave, she gave me a pint jar that was jammed full of quarters, fifty cent pieces, and a few dollar bills . . . "I've been saving over the four years until you came home!", her eyes just sparkled. I tried to give it back, but it almost broke her heart. It also broke my heart. This dear lady was scrimping, saving every penny for me that she could . . . for me! Tears came to my eyes! How many other people were doing that so missionaries could be out on the field?

Ed and Carolyn Nowicki (the Burnett's daughter) invited me over for dinner . . . and they took on some of my support.

One night I woke up with a start . . . something was wrong . . . then I heard this crying noise. I jumped into my pants and ran downstairs. Pop Burnett had fallen and was wedged in the doorway of the bathroom . . . and with his Parkinson's, he couldn't get up. I gently pried him loose . . . nothing was broken . . . was he ever glad to see me at two in the morning!

I spent a couple of days at the Moody airport speaking and showing my slides during the noon hour to all the future missionary pilot/mechanics. They were really impressed with SIMAIR's aviation program which resulted in most of our future pilots coming from Moody.

Then I visited Rev. Berg and the two country churches in the northwest corner of the state. What a time we had. I spoke in the Sunday morning service at Martintown, and showed my slides in the evening service at Nora, and then showed my slides in the prayer meeting at Martintown on Wednesday. I met new people who took on some of my support, and all the people were very generous when they shook my hand which paid for all my cross-country expenses . . . I even had enough to sleep in motels instead of my car. God is so good.

I stopped a couple days to visit all my relatives in Tyndall, South Dakota, where I was born . . . Uncle Cliff and Bertha Schweitzer, Uncle Bill and Elsie Schmoll, Uncle Ben and Vera Schmoll and their daughters Myra and Lois.

I drove down to Ray, Arizona where Ken and Madie Lair worked for Anaconda Copper Company. Wow! . . . what a desolate place, but they were busy working for the Lord there. Madie had a special gift of teaching Bible, one on one, which usually resulted in the woman accepting the Lord. Out here, she had women scheduled for the next three years to take this course! These dear people supported me all the twenty years I was in Africa! As we walked around the huge open pit mine, I was able to pick up large chunks of the Malachite copper ore they were mining. Ken was in charge of the drilling crews that took samples from the earth to analyze the richness of the copper deposits.

As I drove across this dessert land, the sunsets were absolutely breathtaking. At one gas station, the guy commented on my car, "With that overdrive, I bet you really get good gas mileage . . ."

"Only getting about 18 or 19", I complained.

When he checked the water and the oil, he gave engine the quick once-over . . . "Have you ever looked at your air filter? Also that fan belt looks brittle." I was getting a sales pitch.

I did let him look at the air filter . . . it was almost plugged solid with dirt! He put in a new air filter. "Do you have a belt for this buggy?"

"Sure do", he gave me a squinty smile. After he put on a new fan belt, he rubbed his whiskered chin . . . "That battery . . . ."

"No, no . . . the battery's fine . . . she starts right up!"

When I pulled out of there, my wallet felt a few dollars lighter, but he was right . . . my gas mileage jumped up to 27 miles per gallon! I was the dumb head for driving practically all the way across the country with a plugged air filter!

As I was driving up the San Joaquin valley to Shafter, I saw this plane spraying a field, so I pulled over to the side of the road to watch. He dove down over some wires at the edge of the field and put the plane four feet above the ground and turned on the sprayer. At the other end, he zoomed up over the wires, did a sharp bank to the right, brought the plane around to the left, down over the wires, in exact line for his next pass. Back and forth, he repeated this procedure until he had completely covered the whole field. Wow! What a show. And this is what I was going to be doing? As I drove on, I noticed that all the fields were completely surrounded by wires!

I arrived at Putnam's Flying Service, only to be informed by the girl in the office that Mr. Putnam was over in Nevada seeding grassland, and that he would be gone for about two weeks! Now what do I do?

She smiled sweetly, "We were expecting you . . . here's the information that you will have to study in order to pass the written exam before you can do any crop dusting in the state of California." With that, she set before me on the counter a stack of manuals, bulletins, and pamphlets over two inches high! Oh boy!

One of the pilots took me out to the hangar to show me the operation. They had five old doggy looking double wing Stearmans that they had converted to sprayers and dusters. In our conversation, he soon discovered that I had never flown a Stearman before, and had never done any dusting! He sympathetically shook his head and proceeded to talk me out of taking on this job. In his matter of fact drawl . . . "Look . . . spraying and dusting around here is not for beginners . . . every field is surrounded by a jungle of wires . . . you gotta really know what you're doing . . ."

"Yeah, I can see that . . . when I was coming up the road, I saw this guy spraying a field . . . he put on quite a show."

"And that stack of manuals and stuff you're holding . . . you'll need to memorize them word for word . . . the chemicals we are using, it's poison . . . if a bit of wind carries that stuff over into the next field, you'll be up for a law suit, and so will Bill Putnam."

I didn't know what to say . . . "But I really need this job."

"Tell you what . . . I noticed on your resume that you are a mechanic. How would you like to build a sailplane for me? On the side, I have this sailplane school that I trying to get started, so when I retire from this flying circus, I'll be doing something that is a lot less dangerous."

"You mean a real sailplane?"

"Yeah . . . it's a kit . . . would you like to see it?"

"Sure."

We walked over to an empty hangar. In a large room was a bunch of boxes. Someone had started building one of the tail sections. I looked it over . . . whoever did it was a real craftsman.

He rubbed the stubble on his chin, "I'm really fussy . . . you think you can do work this good?"

I chuckled, "No problem . . . it would be about like building a model airplane kit . . . if you got the tools, I can do the job . . . in fact, I think it would be a lot of fun!"

"I'll give you everything that you need."

So for the next six weeks I built a Schweitzer sailplane. I got to where everything was ready to be covered with fabric when I got word from Lynn Wasburn that he required that his students pass the writtens for instrument and multi-engine before we came for the training. Better get my tail in gear, so I reluctantly left the sailplane unfinished and headed home to North Bend where Edna and Pearl still had a place for me in their storeroom. I acquired all the study materials and began to memorized it word for word. I wrote the exams and passed the first time around.

I showed my slides in Sunday School at the little Lutheran church where I grew up. Martha Andrews was thrilled that one of her boys had become a missionary . . . "if you had only become a Lutheran missionary!"

She felt better when I told her that we sometimes flew Lutheran missionaries out there.

I went to a little Conservative Baptist Church and they allowed me to speak in their church. I also showed my slides to the men's breakfast at The Hilltop House. The owner, Carl Nordin, and Wes Way took on some of my support.

It was time to go, so I said my goodbyes and drove down to Santa Cruz to pick up Paul Rogalsky who would also be taking the training. It was a cold and dreary February day when we arrived at the Wasburn's home in St. Louis. We talked into the wee hours of the morning as Lynn gave us a rundown of the training we would be taking and all that would be required of us during the next two months. No fooling around . . . we got the idea that we were about to get our tails wrung real hard.

A Dr. Brumme provided his Piper Apache to be used for this training to missionary pilots, including paying for the gas, oil, and the maintenance! Lynn Wasburn did the instructing (all for free!) whenever it fit into his flight schedule with Ozark Airlines, and that may be any time during the day or in the dead of night . . . we would each be flying one to three hours during a training session in all kinds of winter weather. (The heating system on an Apache has a lot to be desired . . . sometimes we came out of that plane absolutely numb from the cold, yet we were dripping wet with sweat from the intensive training that Lynn just put us through!)

The next day we moved over to where we would be staying the next two months in the warm basement of some folks in the church . . . and they housed and fed us for free! So here we would each be getting over $7000 worth of instrument and multi-engine training and it wasn't costing the Mission or us a dime! Thank you Dr. Brumme, thank you Lynn Washburn, and thanks to these dear folks who so wonderfully opened their home to us!

Our training started late one night and this is what I recorded in my Pilot Log . . . date-14 Feb 62, Aircraft license # N3485P, Aircraft-Apache, Engine make—Lycoming 160's, from Alton Field, IL, to St. Louis, MO, muti-crosscountry 1:30, night 1:30, instrument-hood :30, dual 1:30, daily total time 2567:40, Remarks: familiarization, turns, slow flight, climb and descents. Paul flew from St. Louis to Alton while I observed from the rear seat. (I always tried to fly second as I could learn from Paul's mistakes while Lynn had him cooking on the hot seat.)

The 15th was a cold miserable day, but we flew anyway. Today I was in the hot seat for two hours . . . 45 minutes under the hood and 30 minutes of actual instrument doing basic airwork, recovering from unusual attitudes (which Lynn put us into the extreme), climbs and descents thru clouds, getting used to flying a twin engine Apache airplane. To me, it was easier to fly actual instruments than it was under the hood where you peeked out of this sort of baseball type hat with an extra long bill that blocked out your vision above the instrument panel, and the goggle eyeholes blocked out all your side vision . . . it gave me claustrophobia. You were to concentrate on flying the plane only by the instruments.

The 16th was three hours of the same. Each day Lynn added something new. Today it was VOR tracking to and from a station, and Ground Control Approaches. Coming in to land at St. Louis, I did an actual ILS approach and landing. It was snowing like crazy. In every session, Lynn pushed us to our ultimate breaking point. If we did okay on one problem, then he would add something more to complicate it. He did this until we finally cracked. He called it, flying with your muddy boots on . . . "when you get your muddy boots off, then you can really fly!" (By the way, he happened to be the check pilot for all of Ozark Airlines pilots, so he was really qualified for wringing people's tails . . . and he wrung ours every time we flew with him!)

After we got done with our session for the day, we sat in that cold miserable airplane for another half hour to 45 minutes while he went over EVERY maneuver we did during the flight . . . praised us for what we did right, growled at us for what we did wrong, and asked us until we gave the right answer as to what we should have done . . . He went over every word that radio control said to us, what we said, or what we should have said in reply. And he did this ALL from memory alone! It just blew our minds. This guy was absolute perfection when it came to flying . . . and that is what he demanded from us. In just three days, we began longing for the day when we would be through with this guy. Yet we appreciated him for what he was doing, for we knew when he got done with us, we would be the best multi-engine and instrument pilots going.

On the 19th, it was at night and it was all visual flight, doing basic maneuvers, with a lot of unusual attitude recovery, spirals, VOR orientation, and finishing with a Ground Control Approach . . . just more stuff getting us used to flying a twin.

The 20th . . . more of the same, only during the day. The weather got to be very marginal, so we stayed close to the airport and shot a lot of take offs and landings.

February 21st, I repeated my clearance back to the tower, "Roger, eight five Papa cleared for take off . . . climb to and maintain 5000 feet . . . report reaching . . . report intercepting Victor fourteen to St. Louis VOR!" (This was ALL under the hood.)

"Roger, eight five Papa!"

I eased the throttles forward, reached takeoff speed, and eased the plane off the ground. Doing this under the hood and only on the instruments really had me sweating! I climbed up to 300 feet and did a left turn, climbed to 500 feet and turned to a heading that would intercept Victor 14 to track inbound to the St. Louis VOR.

I intercepted Victor 14, and established a heading of 140 degrees.

"St. Louis tower . . . 85Papa intercepted Victor 14."

"Roger 85Papa . . . report reaching five zero."

"Roger."

I leveled off at 5000 feet and called the tower. "St. Louis tower . . . 85Papa at five zero."

"Roger 85Papa . . . maintain five zero . . . contact Ground Control . . . good day."

"Roger . . . contact Ground Control . . . good day."

I switched the radio over to the Ground Control frequency . . . "Ground Control . . . 85 Papa . . . IFR level five zero . . . Victor fourteen to the St. Louis VOR."

"Roger, 85 Papa . . . IFR . . . maintain level five zero on Victor fourteen . . . report reaching St. Louis VOR."

"Roger . . . 85 Papa."

When we passed over the St. Louis VOR, the instrument needle swung 180 degrees. "Ground control . . . 85 Papa passing over the St. Louis VOR."

"85Papa . . . you are now cleared to the Monroe Intersection and hold at level five zero . . . report reaching."

Roger . . . 85 Papa now cleared to the Monroe Intersection to hold at five zero . . . report reaching."

And so the flight went. When I got to the Monroe Intersection, I went into a holding pattern and reported to Ground Control. I'm relating all this to you just to give you an idea of all the radio chatter that goes on between all the planes in the sky around you and the tower or Ground Control, so to maintain a proper separation between aircraft to assure their safety. It gives you an assurance and confidence that you are not going to run into anybody or they run over you.

Lynn took the mike. "Approach Control . . . 85Papa."

"85 Papa . . . this is Approach Control . . . go ahead."

Roger . . . 85 Papa holding at the Monroe Intersection . . . level five zero . . . requesting a GCA approach to Lambert Field."

"Roger . . . 85 Papa . . . stand by."

"85Papa standing by."

(A GCA approach is a procedure where they literally talk you right down to the ground in instrument flight conditions and it was el-stinko weather that day.)

"85 Papa . . . you are now cleared for a GCA from Monroe Intersection to Lambert . . . turn to a heading of one eight zero and descend to 3000 thousand feet."

"Roger . . . 85Papa cleared for GCA approach . . . turn to a heading of one eight zero and descend to 3000 feet . . . will report reaching."

"Roger 85Papa."

I turned to a heading of 180 and began a descent at 500 feet per minute. We were bouncing all over the sky and the instruments were doing likewise.

When we got to 3000 feet, Lynn called' "Approach Control . . . 85 Papa . . . level 30 . . . heading 180."

"Roger 85Papa . . . we have you on the scope . . . turn to a heading 255 . . . call St. Louis tower on 118.1."

"Roger 85Papa . . . turning to 255 degrees . . . changing to St. Louis tower . . . good day."

"85Papa . . . good day."

We changed the radio to 118.1 . . . "St. Louis tower . . . this is 85Papa."

"Roger 85Papa . . . go ahead."

"85Papa . . . GCA approach . . . inbound on 255 . . . level three zero."

"Roger 85Papa . . . you're cleared for a GCA approach to runway 26 . . . descend to one zero and report crossing Outer Marker."

"Roger 85Papa . . . descending to 10 . . . report crossing the Outer Marker."

I began a descent to one thousand feet. Gusts were buffeting the plane. For a novice like me in a strange airplane and flying under the hood, it was hard for me to keep the plane on the correct heading . . . I was sweating like I was sitting in a hot tub. We were actually descending through solid clouds . . . you could hear the rain pounding on the fuselage. But Lynn kept me under the hood to make it double hard. When we crossed the Outer Marker the needle on the ADF swung 180 degrees.

"St. Louis tower . . . 85Papa crossed the Outer Marker . . . level 10."

"Roger . . . 85Papa . . . change your heading to 260 . . . continue your descent . . . QNH 28.71 . . . winds 270 at 20 knots gusting to 35 . . . you are cleared to land . . . report field in sight."

"Roger 85Papa . . . cleared to land . . . QNH 28.71 . . . gusting to 35 . . . will call you field in sight."

I changed the altimeter to 28.71, slowed the plane down, and dropped the flaps one quarter . . . then I put the gear down and did a landing check to prepare for landing. We crossed the Inner Marker.

Lynn spotted the field, but told me to stay under the hood. "St. Louis tower . . . 85Papa has your field in sight."

"Roger 85Papa cleared to land . . . winds 280 . . . gusting to 40 knots."

"Roger 85Papa cleared to land."

Lynn said to me . . . "Okay Rich . . . I'll talk you down to the field . . . turn to 285 degrees to compensate for the cross winds . . . keep your air speed at 80 knots . . . descend at 200 feet per minute . . . now turn to 280 degrees . . . keep your air speed up . . . add a little throttle."

Lynn talked me right down to fifty feet above the ground. "Okay, take your hood off and land."

I jerked the hood off. There was the runway staring me in the face. I adjusted for the crosswind, flared out, and greased the plane on.

"85Papa . . . your landing time was 21 . . . you are cleared to taxi to the apron."

"Roger 85Papa cleared to the apron."

We taxied to the apron and I expected that Lynn would call it a night. It was starting to snow. I was absolutely bushed.

But NO! Lynn praised me, "Rich, you did good . . . okay Paul . . . let's switch seats and we'll go do the same thing!"

And so we did. We were bouncing all over the sky. Sitting in the back seat watching Paul do his thing, I got so air sick that I almost tossed my cookies. When we finally taxied back to the ramp about three inches of snow had accumulated on the ground.

Next morning, when we climbed out of bed, the wind was howling . . . sometimes the snow was flying horizontally past our window. The weather was so el-stinko that we didn't have another flight until the 28th of February. We had ground school instead. Lynn gave us a lot of navigation problems and gave us a very detailed idea what we could expected when we took our oral and flight exams with the CAA inspector. We spent hours and hours pouring over the study manuals.

The flight on the 28th was a night flight. We spent an hour removing all the snow from the airplane. It was bitter cold in the blowing wind. I was already numb to the bone when we climbed into the cockpit for another five hours . . . Lynn holding our feet to the fire didn't raise the temperature in that plane one bit. I came down with a terrible cold. March 1st wasn't much better . . . we flew in the morning and then again in the afternoon . . . honing our skills to perfection. Each day a little more was added . . . a little more was demanded. On the 2nd we started on engine out procedures. This was a doggy airplane with two engines working . . . cutting an engine on this plane, man, you didn't want to make any mistakes . . . if you did, you were dead meat! At any time during the flight, Lynn would cut an engine . . . no matter what maneuver we were doing, we had to keep flying the airplane . . . then figure out which engine had gone bad, cut the throttle, cut the mixture, and feather the prop, clean up the trim . . . do all this without hesitation . . . and continue flying the airplane no matter whether you were flying visually on a beautiful clear day, or when the weather is so bad you are flying by the instruments. This would be done on take off, or landings, or maybe when we were at our wits end just trying to fly the airplane. Any time when you are flying a twin, one of those engine can go . . . and when it does, buster, you better know exactly what to do, and do it precisely. Your life, and the life of your passengers, and also peoples lives on the ground that could be killed if you crashed . . . all because you didn't know exactly what to do. All this stuff . . . you keep doing it . . . keep doing it . . . until you just do it naturally, without thinking . . . like breathing. Every day there was something new to learn.

About half way through the course, Paul wasn't feeling so good and went to see a doctor. When he got back, I asked him how things went.

"I thought I was having a heart attack, but it's okay . . . he gave me a bunch of tranquilizers . . . I guess all this stress is getting to me."

Lynn never let up on us . . . this flying every day with his 'muddy boots on' philosophy to the breaking point was really getting to us. By the end of the course, I was begging tranquilizers from Paul! Both of us were ready to call it quits.

About that time, early in the morning, I got a phone call from SIM New York . . . "Rich, Grace Hiser here, SIMAIR is in the process of buying a new twin engine Piper Aztec B . . . would you be willing to fly it out to Africa when you go back?"

I went into shock mode. "You want me to wha . . . what?"

". . . . fly the plane out to Africa . . . a ferry pilot would cost us over 1500 dollars . . . we thought with the training you were getting, that maybe you could fly it out and . . ."

I cut her off. "Just a second." I told Paul what was going on. He just about flew straight off the bed. We talked it over and then I got back on the phone.

"Look, that sounds like a great idea, with the training Paul and I are getting, but neither of us really feel qualified to do such a thing. You just don't know what you are asking. You need somebody who is really experienced to do a job like that . . . we are just learning." It hit Paul and me like a ton of bricks . . . now we knew why we were going through all this agonizing torture at the hands of Lynn Washburn. The Mission was going to buy a twin engine airplane! Good grief!

Paul wanted to hear it for himself. "Here . . . let me have the phone!", Paul motioned to me.

"Just a second . . . Paul wants to talk to you." I handed Paul the phone.

"Yes Paul . . . SIMAIR thought with the multi-engine training you two were getting that it would really be a big help to the program if they had a plane that could carry more passengers and a bigger load at times."

Paul laughed, "That would be good idea maybe . . . but do we have that kind of money in the replacement fund?" (He was in charge of ordering parts for SIMAIR and for making sure that we operated in the black.)

"Yes . . . they will be paying for it with cash . . . and if Rich doesn't want to fly it out, would you like to do it?"

Paul shook his head, "No way . . . I got a wife and kids . . . you really need somebody who is qualified to do a Charles Lindberg across the pond."

"You got any ideas?"

"I don't know . . . Lynn Washburn, our instructor maybe . . . he's really sharp and he is getting into some pretty big equipment in Ozark Airlines."

"Why don't you ask him . . . and maybe Rich could fly out with him . . . that would save the money for his passage which could pay for Mr. Washburn's return."

"Okay, I'll talk to Lynn and get back with you."

And so that's how it happened. When Lynn heard what was going on he, really brightened up to the challenge. It would all depend if he could get a leave of absence long enough to do the flight. So Chapter 26 will be Lynn's detailed account leading up to and then the trans-Atlantic delivery flight to Nigeria, West Africa

We completed our training on April 6th. Lynn gave us our recommendation rides for the FAA multi-engine and instrument flight tests which we took and passed on April 9th with no problem.

CHAPTER 26
AZTEC FLIGHT TO AFRICA . . . A NORTH ATLANTIC CROSSING OR THE WAY WE WERE . . . FORTY ONE YEARS AGO

by Lynn Washburn and used with his permission

SIMAIR Piper Aztec flight to Africa—TransAtlantic route

Dear Mom and Dad,

As you may recall from my earlier letters, two of the fellows who took the Missionary Pilot Training Course here in St. Louis last February 14 through April 9th were Paul Rogalsky and Rich Schaffer. Paul has been on the field eight years and is from Santa Cruz, CA. Rich has also served in Nigeria four years, plus flying seaplanes for Marine Medical Mission in British Colombia, and he is a fellow Oregonian from Coos Bay.

Both are with SIMAIR, the air-arm of the Sudan Interior Mission which has an extensive flight program in West Africa with their main base located in Jos, Nigeria, presently including six pilots, two mechanics, four Piper Comanches and one Cessna 170. They have operated for over fifteen years throughout West Africa with a perfect safety record to date!

Last February Paul and Rich drove here from the coast for their training. They especially desired the instrument flying course as in Nigeria they experience the African Harmattan, a desert wind which blows a dense, but very fine dust that covers the entire Sahara and adjacent areas during the dry season, cutting the visibility down to as low as a couple hundred yards, a condition they have to operate in for several months each year. They were not particularly interested in the multi-engine rating phase we also offered, but they said they would take it anyway, as the training would be done in a twin engine plane. Interestingly, near the end of the training, they received a phone call from the Mission saying SIMAIR was in the process of buying a new twin engine Piper Aztec B, so with this coincidence, one might conclude that God was already preparing them for what was to take place.

They asked Rich if he would fly the new plane out to Africa as this would save hiring a ferry pilot at more than $1500, also would save Rich's passage costs. However, as Rich was not very well qualified for doing this, as up to the present his flight experience had been limited mostly to day VFR and pilotage type of navigation. Jonas Arms and the Piper distributor wanted SIM to at least hire a ferry pilot to take the plane to Dakar, Senegal, so the guys asked me if I would be willing and able to get some time off to fly the new plane over and then check out the other SIMAIR pilots in the new plane. This I agreed to do if the following conditions were met: 1. I would be pilot-in-command. 2. My expenses would be paid for including 25% of the return airfare (I could get a 75% reduced pass). 3. That the aircraft shall have the following equipment on board; two independent magnetic indicators, an HF long range radio with the proper frequencies, a minimum of 140 gallons of extra fuel, Canadian approved survival gear and life raft, and special trip insurance coverage. All my professional time I would offer at no charge.

Although the firm order for the new aircraft was sent to the Piper factory in early March, because of a three month backlog of orders for the Aztec B, SIM's delivery date was set for June 12th. Before learning of this date, I had initially started planning to fly the southern route . . . Miami-Trinidad-Natal-Monrovia-Lagos-Jos, as much of the year, icing conditions can be a problem for low flying non-pressurized light aircraft in the North Atlantic. The distances for both routes is very similar. But now that the delivery date would be mid-June and better enroute facilities exist on the northern crossing, the Gander-Azores-Dakar-Kano-Jos route was chosen.

When Rich and Paul completed their flight course, now both with freshly issued FAA Instrument and AMEL ratings, Paul left to tie up things at home for their return to Nigeria in June. Rich visited friends in North Carolina before returning to Mission headquarters in New York to oversee the ordering of radios, spare parts, emergency equipment, etc for the new plane.

Meanwhile I saw Capt V. C. White, Ozark Airlines chief pilot, who tentatively agreed that I might plan for a leave of absence for the month of July. So I seriously began the long task of flight planning which took $145 dollars and some 150 hours time which included writing 26 letters and 15 long distance phone calls to order special navigation charts from Denver, St. Louis, Washington DC, and Frankfurt, Germany to obtain US Coast and Geodetic Survey, Jeppesen, and USAF charts of every description. AOPA secured all our over-flight and landing permits which cost over $29 dollars for cablegrams. My passport, yellow fever, and small pox vaccinations were all current, so I only had to get a series of typhoid and para-typhoid shots plus some photos which I had to send to the SIM office who took care of our visas. Dr. Marvin Brumme (the Apache owner) got me some malaria pills that I soon began taking, and also he loaned me his Canadian Jepp charts.

Rich had all the special emergency gear sent via Air Express directly to St. Louis from Pan-Avion of Miami which included a brand new two man life-raft, day and night signal flares with firing gun, a US Navy VHF/UHF transceiver radio (Gibson Girl) which I briefly tested one evening, transmitting from the rear of our garden while Gerry listened for me on our own receiver in the house. It transmitted a strong signal on VHF 121.5 Mc and 243,0 Mc. Also included were two Mae West life vests, and 30 plus items all Canadian approved that were stored in the raft.

Transatlantic flight emergency and survival gear

On June 1st, during my third visit to our chief pilot's office, at last he finally gave his firm and written approval for my leave of absence for the entire month of July.

On June 12th Rich went to the Piper factory to observe the equipment installation at the adjacent Lock Haven Airmotive hangar, all nestled together in central Pennsylvania's narrow Susquehenna Valley, a place where I took an impressive tour in 1957.

This special equipment installation, we were assured, would take three days, so I arranged my Ozark flight schedule and at our Pass Bureau obtained a C-4 authorization on Eastern Airlines to go and inspect the completed installation. Then we would fly the brand new plane to St Louis. Everything would then be in position to begin the delivery flight immediately upon the completion of my last scheduled flight for June.

This equipment installation included; two Motorola VHF transceivers, each with 90 channels, one VOR nav receiver, one Motorola ADF (radio compass) receiver, a SunAIR ten channel crystal controlled long range HF transceiver with fixed and special reel-out trailing antennas. On this set up, a competent operator can easily talk 2000 mile distances and under ideal conditions I've talked over 4500 miles. In the Peruvian flight operation this was our primary means of communication. Additional special equipment was an RMI (remote magnetic indicator) fed by a compass located out in the wing tip away from disturbance, then the re-swinging of both onboard magnetic compasses (not too important for local flights, but very critical for ocean flights). Finally two special made 75 gallon ferry tanks, fabricated for Lock Haven Airmotive by a sheet metal shop in town, made of galvanized sheet metal soldered with internal baffling, each about 4' x 3' x 2 1/2' which would be positioned as near to the center of gravity as possible by removing the two middle seats and placing these tanks right up against the main wing spar directly behind the front pilot seats, requiring the seat backs to be straight up and unable to be reclined. These two tanks would gravity feed direct into the respective engine fuel systems, permitting full crossfeed capability through two brass flex-lines controlled by two water faucet style shutoff valves which connected to the regular fuel lines . . . a very simple installation that we would bet our lives on!

Instead of taking three days as promised, the plane was tied up for 13 days! By this time you might recall, Eastern Airlines had halted all operations due to a labor strike shut down, so my airline pass became useless! I could use Dr. Brumme's Apache to get me to the factory, but there would be a big fuel bill and a logistics problem, so I instead used a small two place Luscombe 8A . . . the fuel would only cost $30 dollars and another $25 dollars for lost wages to Paul Ettinger who went along to return his plane back to St. Louis.

So on June 25th at 5 PM, I completed my last scheduled Ozark flight for June, and by 7 PM Paul and I departed for Lock Haven, PA, landing at Terra Haute, IN for fuel. We flew on to Dayton, OH where we decided to stop for three hours of sleep in a couple of lounge chairs. At 5 PM we had a bite of breakfast and then took off at dawn, fuel stopping at Wheeling, WV and arrived at the Lock Haven factory at 0930 AM. At 10 AM the FAA inspector arrived from Harrisburg, PA to inspect and approve the installation and issue a special ferry permit.

Paul left for home. Rich and I followed shortly thereafter, flying VFR at 10,500 feet to test the fuel consumption at that level. We only had 20 gallons in each ferry tank, and on climb out we soon noticed strong gas fumes and then the sound of escaping air from the tank cap vents. This dilemma was alleviated by taking the caps off and then opening the little side window to draw out the gas fumes. Seems it might be good idea not to be a smoker if you plan a career as a ferry pilot.

We passed overhead Paul near the Bellaire VOR traveling 2 1/2 times faster. We had to frequently weave our way around the swelling cumulus clouds that were forming along a weak cold front which we paralleled on its North side. In addition to checking the operation of all the equipment and systems, I put on the hood and got some instrument time to become more familiar with this new instrument panel layout. This flight took just four hours . . . Gerry had a nice supper awaiting our arrival at home.

Aztec cockpit and instrument panel

Next day, Wednesday, June 27th, Rich and I went out to the airport where he got 2 1/2 hours of dual practice, then while he flew solo, I drove back home. Stopped by the Ozark hangar to check my company mail box and was shocked to find a general notice that ALL leaves for July had been canceled due to pilot shortage! The company had overlooked the scheduled MO ANG Summer Camp OPS at Volk Field in Wisconsin held each year in July. As our chief pilot was out of the office, I left him a message describing the fix this put me in, and I asked for: 2 weeks or 10 days minimum, or authorization to drop my first Ozark flight series in July, in that order.

(In 1962 I was a very senior First Officer on junior equipment, flying 10 to 12 day lines, a fleet of 25 Douglas DC-3s, and soon to become a bottom seniority First Officer on the Convair CV-240.)

I went back to the airport and picked up Rich. We stopped again at the hangar where I found in my mailbox a note granting me off the first 12 days of July, so I upped the schedule to leave that night for Moody Airport which was located near Chicago-O'Hare Field.

After an early supper, I called Dirk Van Dam at Moody Airport asking for permission to land and leave the plane there overnight. Then I called the US Customs Service office at O'Hare and arranged to have an inspector there at 6 AM tomorrow for authorization of our export license followed by an all tanks full take-off for Gander, Newfoundland.

Since we were not allowed to fly at night, our departure was planned for 7 PM, but due to all the last minute rushing, we didn't leave St Louis until 0730 PM. We climbed up to 9,500 feet to top the scattered cloud and haze level . . . also giving us a nice tailwind at that level. About 75 miles out we called Dirk on Moody's private frequency 123.3 Mc, and he said they would have a car with lights on at each end of the north/south runway to aid us in our 'illegal' night approach and landing. As we taxied up to park on their sod ramp, a few aviation students and Dr. Bumme were there to see the plane and its special equipment.

After securing the plane, we went to Dr. Brumme's house in Elmhurst, where lucky Rich got to sleep right away, but I now had to make up for leaving St. Louis days early. So

I began catching up all the last minute flight planning caused from our upset schedule. I got only two hours sleep before it was on to breakfast at Montana Charlie's 24 hour place on highway 83. (Gerry and I celebrated our 2nd wedding anniversary there in July 1955).

While Rich and Dr. Brumme were finishing up, I filed a 'legal' IFR flight plan with Joliet Radio. I had to again argue with the clerk concerning the 5N number in the Aztec's registration number (5N-ACF), and then had to repeat the lengthy routing no less than three times: ORD V100 Musky V193 Pullman V84 Peck V216 Toronto V300 Sterling V98 Saint John Direct Roxton Airway GREEN-ONE Fredericton V300 Charlottetown V300 Gander: before the clerk got it all down.

Dr. Brumme kindly dropped us off at Moody Wooddale Airport.

After saying thank you and goodbye, we flew over to O'Hare Field and taxied up to the US Customs Service ramp at 6 AM sharp. Because their office is normally closed until the afternoon when the international arrivals commence, we had to pay $12 dollars for his services, mainly to take care of the export license.

We called Skymotive Shell to refill us. He had difficulty filling the ferry tanks as the necks were such a small diameter, and we didn't dare spill a drop on the carpet floor . . . or we would have to breathe the fumes all day. So I ended up holding a big funnel and periodically checking the tank with my flashlight, while Rich monitored the meter on the truck.

Because of this tedious delay, we didn't taxi out until 0715 AM. Our tires looked a bit flat as we were well over the legal gross take-off weight, so I taxied ever so slowly over each tar segment on our way out to the run-up pad.

We switched the radio to the Clearance Delivery Channel, 124.2 MC, and we were issued the following clearance: "ATC clears Aztec 5N-ACF to the Gander Airport via V100 Musky V193 Pullman V 84 Lansing, Flight Plan Route, Maintain 4000' until further advised, Radar vector to V100."

After reading this back, we switched to the tower frequency, 118.1 Mc and were soon cleared for take-off on runway 09. We were airborne after a roll of about 1500 feet. We then switched over to Departure Control, 125.4 Mc who vectored us to Airway V100. We climbed at 130 MPH IAS and the rate of climb was very respectable even at our over weight condition. Our 4000 foot restriction was removed and we were cleared to 9000 feet which we attained before we reached the eastern shore of the 65 mile wide Lake Michigan . . . a rather humorous prelude to the 4300 miles of saltwater which lay ahead on this odyssey!

At about the same time, all the receivers began to intermittently cut out. Adding insult to injury, the right engine developed a little roughness that I couldn't seem to get rid of. We were flying in a heavy haze. Passing abeam Grand Rapids, Michigan we were instructed to contact Detroit Center. As we crossed the international boundary over Lake Huron just North of Sarnia, Ontario, our flight visibility improved so much that we could see all the way southward to Pelee Point which extends into Lake Erie.

I commented to Rich that if our radio and engine problems did not clear up by the time we passed Montreal, we would then turn South and head directly to the Piper factory to have things made right. About twenty minutes later, we discovered that the auxiliary mike which was hooked into the right microphone jack was the source of all the radio trouble, so after unplugging it all the radios worked fine. Also the right engine cleared up by over-leaning the mixture a bit.

Beyond Toronto about three hours after take-off the landscape began to change to wooded country, spotted with numerous small lakes. Passing Sterling, ON took us back into the USA and over Massena, NY right after we crossed the St. Lawrence Seaway. However, our route would soon take us back into Quebec Province just South of Montreal. Here the landscape turned into rolling farm country as we proceeded along the Green-One airway passing Magog and Sherbrooke.

Again we entered the USA to cross the entire state of Maine which was heavily forested and dotted with good sized lakes. The high pressure system in which we were flying was now centered behind us and a little to our right producing a light headwind. It took us just 45 minutes to cross the entire state. Shortly after our ADF needle swung around over the Millinocket Radio Beacon, we turned toward the Fredericton, Newfoundland LFR.

We re-entered Canadian Airspace near New Brunswick. Boston Center handed us off to Moncton Center who watched us for the next 200 miles on their radar . . . Off the right wing we could make out the blue Bay of Fundy where the world record tides change as much as 54 feet. For a short stretch we returned to Victor Airways, so I retuned the ADF receiver to some rather different, and interesting music.

Suddenly we were brought back to reality when the right engine sputtered. Rich quickly grabbed the right fuel selector and switched from OFF to OUTBOARD MAIN tank as I hurriedly turned off the right ferry tank valve. We had flown 7:35 hours which implied that we had a good 15 plus hours of endurance at this power setting. I squirmed around in my seat and peered into the left tank with my flashlight which showed that we would soon have a repeat. Ten minutes later that tank ran out. This computed to an average of just under 20 gallons per hour at a power setting of 55% which was good. With a little 'cruise control' this would give us an endurance of 16 plus hours, and a range of 2700 miles in still air!

Over Prince Edward Island we were re-cleared direct to Gander via St. Andrews LFR Airway Green-One. This new course put us right into a headwind out over the Gulf of St. Lawrence. Ahead we could see an extensive area of cloud, no doubt associated with the warm front we had been briefed about in our weather report at O'Hare Field. Our altitude of 11,000 feet would soon put us on instruments and in light rain. At the Red Cape intersection we were instructed to contact Gander Center, 119.7 Mc, when we arrived over the St. Andrews range.

Through the cloud breaks, Rich said he saw several good sized icebergs floating in Cabot Strait. Right on schedule the ADF needle swung around, so we gave Gander a call, but we were not getting through. On their alternate VHF frequency it was the same.

We watched the Outside Air Temperature gauge creep lower until it was below Zero Centigrade, and soon a white frost covered the windshield. A movement caught my attention on the left . . . the long HF fixed antenna wire that was attached from the left wing tip to the vertical fin was icing up, causing it to shake up and down vigorously!

Again we tried Gander of on HF 13354.5 Kc . . . all we got was a lot of crackling. On 8947.5 Kc it was about the same. The antenna was increasing in its vibration. We needed a lower altitude without delay, or we would lose our antenna! We did hear NY-Overseas Radio so we gave him a call . . . he relayed our request and position to Gander, and then relayed the descent clearance to us. Upon reaching 7000 feet the ice began breaking from the antenna and stopped vibrating.

Through another break we got our first glimpse of Newfoundland, a rugged and barren landscape . . . what caught our eye was the large white patches of old rotten snow still in the valleys in late June.

Passing the Island Pond Intersection, we finally got Gander on VHF 119.7 Mc and were given further descent clearance down to 5000 feet. This gave us better view of the bleak rocky island now interspersed with numerous long lakes bordered with scrubby looking trees.

Beautiful Gander Lake came into view. We switched to Approach control. 119.5 Mc, and were cleared for an approach to Runway 04. Even though we were in good visual conditions, I switched the VOR receiver to the Rwy 04 ILS localizer frequency, 109.5 Mc, not only due to the lack of any section lines, but also because of the nearly 30 degrees of magnetic variation. Abeam the outer compass locator (LOM), we switched to the Tower, 119.1 Mc for our landing clearance. Soon we were taxing up to the West end of Gander's huge South ramp.

Aztec at Gander, Newfoundland

After shutting down and finishing our paperwork, an Esso fuel tender came up to our small lonely airplane. In an interesting 'Newfie' accent, the guy asked what services we required. There were no tie-downs, so he blocked our wheels with two huge DC-4 chocks. We had flown almost 10 hours enroute, and had gone through two time changes, so it was now 0830 PM.

As we walked into the almost deserted air terminal, the sun was still quite high on the western horizon. After inquiring from a janitor, we finally found the Customs Service Office. The officer merely wanted two General Declaration forms and nodded at our suitcases. We called a taxi who took us to the Gander Hotel, the only place available.

With all the rush, I had had only an average of 2 1/2 hours of sleep during the past three days. (My, what gung-ho enthusiasm for a young 29 year old aviator!)

There were several things that needed to be done on the airplane. The MET office suggested that we stay over for another day, as this would give us a good tailwind after the LOW passed. So it became very evident that we should stay over two nights. It was certainly a treat I enjoyed, getting to sleep until 9AM the next morning.

Friday, June 29th . . . after a good breakfast, we headed back to the airport. We borrowed a bucket from the Esso man, so we could change the oil in the engines. The oiled from the right engine was much darker than the oil from the left. This engine used about one pint of oil and had a slightly higher fuel consumption, a higher cylinder head temperature, and higher oil temperature reading, with a slightly lower oil pressure. The oil from both engines had a few brass and aluminum flakes . . . (for new engines, that is quite normal). All the spark plugs were burning clean. Rich drained the fuel line gascolaters and cleaned the screens. He found some brass flakes and zinc Chromate flakes, some black dum-dum, and a clear-like jelly which we assumed came from the ferry tank installation.

When Rich was at Lock Haven, I phoned him to be sure that they would re-swing both magnetic compasses and make new deviation cards. Evidently they did not do this properly. You can cross the ocean without radios (Lindberg did), but it's not a good idea to try it without a good accurate compass. So we fired up the engines and got clearance to line up right on the center line of Gander's six ILS equipped runways. This meant that we could determine these six courses around the compass rose to an accuracy of one degree. We ran up the engines to near cruising RPM with all the radios on, and were able to read both compasses and the ADF azimuth dial to make up a new deviation card for each. Then we made a brief flight down one of these localizer courses to double check that everything worked okay. Back at the ramp we fueled up and added a little extra air to the tires.

Before going back to the hotel, we visited the MET office and requested a Route Weather Forecast Folder for a 0500Z or 0230 AM departure time.

We stopped at a grocery store in town and bought a small bag of apples, donuts, a large can of peanuts, two cans of pineapple juice, and two quarts of milk. In the aircraft, we already had two gallons of St. Louis drinking water.

That night, as we slept, the predicted warm front came through and the wind shifted to the southwest, which at our planned cruising altitude of 11,000 feet should swing around to the West. These were the thoughts going through my mind as I tried going to sleep.

At 1 AM on Saturday, June 30th, we were up and soon in a taxi heading for the airport. We had planned to get a quick breakfast, but forgot that idea when we saw the swarm of passengers that had just deplaned from a Douglas DC-6, and two Lockheed Constellations.

Instead we went up to the MET office and got a very thorough weather briefing which showed a warm front to be crossed some 250 miles out, and then a pair of cold fronts lying across our path about three quarters of the way. Winds at the 700 Mb level would be about 20 knots from the N-NW, shifting around to become light S-SW beyond the cold fronts to the Azores. This would figure to be about a 10+ knot tailwind component for today's entire flight. After computing these winds into my flight calculations, I carefully figured the two engine and also the single engine points of no return.

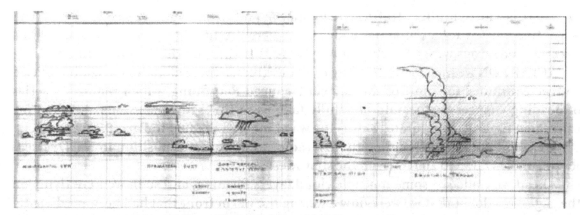

Transatlantic flight weather forecast sheets.

We then went to the ATC office and filed a rather lengthy IFR flight plan for flight level 110, requesting that OSV Delta (Ocean Station Vessel) turn on her radio beacon one hour before our estimated time of arrival over the ship. Finally we listed an estimated time enroute from Gander to Santa Maria, Azores of 0934 hours (computations all based on the forecasted winds), then we listed our alternative airports as Lajes and Lisbon.

(Rich talking here . . . As I am transcribing these very words on 1 February 2003, today the space shuttle Columbia broke apart during re-entry into the Earth's atmosphere in the skies over Texas 16 minutes before arrival to the Kennedy Space Center . . . a feat that has become so routine in our thinking that we hardly pay attention to these history making events anymore. And here we were about to embark on a little bit of history making ourselves.)

At 0420 AM (0650 Z), in the early morning dawn, we taxied out and were cleared to 'Santa Maria via Airway Blue-21 Torbay flight plan route, maintain 11,000. After takeoff, turn left on course. Report leaving 2000.' After a take-off roll of about 1500 feet on Rwy 27, we were airborne climbing out over Gander Lake. We passed over the St. John's range at 11,000 feet and tracked outbound on the LFR signal. This is accomplished by 'listening to the beam' which is identified by a steady hum. If you hear in Morse Code, a dit dah.—(A), or a dah dit—. (N), you are no longer flying on course. (On this 1997 update, I should explain that by 1962, though recently decommissioned in the USA, some of the old low frequency ranges still continued to be used elsewhere until about 1965.) This was the last occasion I had to use this 'audio beam bracketing', now certainly primitive and overdue for some museum!

On climb out from Gander, we again had a little tail buffet . . . the air speed would vary without much pitch change on my part, and the elevators did not feel as effective, so we were a little tail heavy in our attempt to get the CG right on the rear limit which increases the aircraft's efficiency at the expense of stability and control, resulting in maximum range possibility.

At 111 nautical miles out on the SW leg of the St. John's LFR, the TARPON intersection (46-19N/51-00W) was crossed and we changed our altimeters to standard pressure, 29.92 Hg, and maintained flight level 110. This fix is also the Canadian ADIZ boundary, a zone monitored by SAC radar to detect the penetration of any hostile aircraft toward North America.

There is a lot of military traffic hereabouts, and off to our right we passed abeam NAS Argentina located at Placentia Bay which was where President Franklin D. Roosevelt had a secret rendezvous with Churchill in August 1941 to draw up the Atlantic Charter.

At TARPON we turned to a heading of 131 degrees, as here all radio navigation ceased and we continued for most of the day via Deduced Reckoning, which requires a series of heading changes that should hopefully take us to the Azores, if winds aloft and my calculated figures are accurate. This is the way Linbergh made it to Paris 35 years ago.

We could not raise Gander on the HF radio, so we gave our position to NY Overseas Radio, on 8947.5 Kc, 1200 miles to the southwest.

Ahead we could see some multiple cloud layers forming, and soon we were flying on the gages. No doubt that we were now entering the warm front that had been predicted.

At 0945 Z, we gave our position to Gander Radio as 45-43N/48-00W. With the crystals we installed in the 45 watt HF radio for today's flight, we could talk with clarity to Gander, New York, the Delta vessel, Santa Maria, and Lisbon, by using the trailing antenna which could be reeled out to the exact wave length for the frequency being used.

About ten minutes later we came out of the clouds and we got our first good look at the North Atlantic proper. Ahead and to the right Rich could see a large ocean liner heading W-SW with its wake trailing out far behind. A fogbank running in a SW-NE direction lay off toward the East. On my left, I could see a smaller vessel heading northward . . . probably a fishing boat. We came overhead the fogbank. Further ahead it ended abruptly where we noticed that the color of the water changed from a light green to a bright blue. We realized that we were seeing the meeting of the cold southbound Labrador Current and the warmer northeast bound Gulf Stream termed the world's largest river. This most important river flows for more than 6000 miles from the western Caribbean Sea all the way to Scandinavia thus modifying the European climate dramatically.

At 1442Z we reported crossing the 45th meridian to Gander and they handed us off to NY-Overseas and we reported that we were entering their OCA (Oceanic Control Area). Right on schedule OSV Delta's powerful radio beacon (350 Kc) came on and our ADF needle swung around and pointed ahead. We asked New York to confirm Delta's position and in a few seconds he came back saying the vessel was ten miles east of their assigned position which confirmed what our grid map indicated. We no longer had a view of the surface due to the clouds below.

When we were an estimated 40 minutes from overhead we tried calling the Delta ship on VHF 126.7 Mc but got no reply. About 15 minutes later we did hear him faintly calling us as 'Pied Piper Aztec Five November Alpha Charlie Foxtrot', apparently an endearing term he used for us even though we never responded to him as such.

First thing we asked him for was our radar position and he said there was a target now coming onto his scope 85 miles to the W-NW. To this we replied that we were revising our estimate of overhead Delta as our computed groundspeed was an unhappy 120 knots. But he replied that he observed us making a good 140 knots! . . . then a little later he upped this to 150 knots.

After much figuring and re-figuring on both our parts, he said to stand-by as the ship's exact position would be computed. Several minutes later he calmly informed us 'that Delta ship had drifted some 40 miles further East . . . 'we roam around a bit out here'. Well this immediately solved all our concern, but he did give us a jolt, making us think that aerial navigation is even more an inexact science than we had feared.

Far ahead to the east we began to see that the horizon was covered with white . . . probably the two cold fronts that had been predicted for us.

Below, our USCG operator reported Delta's weather as: 600 feet overcast with visibility reduced to 2 1/2 miles in light rain and fog. He said that he was sending up a balloon which they tracked on radar so that we would know the exact winds aloft. As far as we were concerned, that would be tax dollars well spent!

The operator, who sounded a bit lonesome, asked us of what registry 5N was, and to please give a description of our Aztec. This I did . . . then commented that his RBn seemed awfully strong when it came on . . . 'wondering just how powerful it might be?' He replied, "That's classified information!" Then I asked if our 'ditching heading' hereabouts might also be classified? In less than two minutes he gave complete data on the local primary and secondary swell alignments, and the surface wind, and that our ditching heading should be 235 degrees magnetic, followed by, 'hope you don't have to use it!'

We passed overhead the Delta ship at 1235Z, gave our position to NY Overseas Radio, and then tried to contact Santa Maria with no success. We heard Lisbon working an aircraft. He relayed for us to Santa Maria that we had just entered the Lisbon OCA. Delta tracked us for another 90 miles on VHF until he faded out.

Our next position report we were able to give directly to Santa Maria . . . it went like this . . . "Aztec 5N-ACF, 42 diagonal 19 North 37 West at 1338 Zulu, flight level 110, estimating 41 diagonal 22 North 35 West at 1420 Zulu, flight conditions in between stratiform layers, higher clouds on the East horizon, temperature minus 5."

Santa Maria repeated the main elements back. On these two long over water legs we had some 18 of these reports using Latitude and Longitude co-ordinates. Passing the 35th Meridian, we were getting visibly closer to the back side of the front, where we could now see the towering CB's like a huge wall ahead of us.

To stay clear of the clouds for as long as possible we asked Santa Maria for flight level 13,000 feet, as the freezing level was predicted down to 8000 feet above sea level. As our confrontation with this 'hard looking' weather was about to happen, we turned 15 degrees to the left to make our penetration and passage as brief as possible. As we looked for softer spots in the wall, we got clearance to go up to 15,000 feet. When we entered the clouds it sounded like pea sized gravel hitting us . . . and we got the expected roller coaster ride. The Aztec became coated with a quarter inch of clear glaze ice. The bumpy ride continued for quite sometime with several more pea shots of gravel. Suddenly we popped out the other side into bright sunshine, and immediately turned to the right 30 degrees and flew this heading for the same number of minutes it had taken for the penetration, and before resuming our flight plan heading . . . all of this being precise 'hands on' flying as we had no luxury items like an auto pilot on this ship. Therefore, we were unspoiled purists, or in today's era of advanced technological times, we might be called 'brutes for punishment', but yes, having the time of our aeronautical lives, plus this was a navigator's delight!

Not long after, our ADF needle began to wobble, then pointed ahead. On the audio, in Morse Code, we heard the letters 'F' 'S', dit dit dah dit . . .-. dit dit dit . . . In a few more minutes the ADF needle had steadied, pointing at the powerful RBn located on little Flores, the northwestern-most isle of the Azorean archipelago. It was indeed impressive, and most satisfying, to see that it showed us exactly on our plotted track! Who said this was an inexact science?

Further SE of the front, we began seeing some breaks in the undercast. We asked for and were cleared down to Fl 90, putting us below the freezing level and we lost the rest of our ice.

At 1550 Z, way up ahead, we saw a rocky headland through a cloud break. Sure enough, at 1555 Z, our ADF needle swung around as we passed overhead Flores. We reported our position to Santa Maria. The sky cleared to scattered cumulous and we could see the small harbor of Horta on Fayal which in 1939 was an important refueling stop for Pan American's big Boeing-314 flying boats which flew from NY-La Guardia's Marine Terminal to Lisbon. We passed by Mount Pico, elevation 7,615 feet, the highest point in the Azores, on which lies the remains of an Air France Lockheed Constellation which crashed there on August 9th, 1954.

At 1732 Z, we passed abeam Terceira and reported our position. Santa Maria cleared us to descend to 3000 feet. Over Sao Miquel, we turned to a heading of 178 degrees direct to Santa Maria. Twenty five miles out we contacted the tower that we had the field in sight. We were cleared to descend and report on downwind leg for runway 05. We were cleared to final which took us out over the 300 foot cliffs that rose vertically from the sea on the strange looking volcanic island that had no beaches. We touched down 10:24 hours after lifting off at Gander, giving us an average ground speed of 146 knots . . . our gas consumption was just under 20 GPH.

We turned off the long runway to the right and a flagman parked us by the 91/98 octane fuel pit. As we very stiffly stepped off the plane, we were greeted by a half dozen Portuguese officials. In heavily accented English, spoken haltingly, we were asked to bring all our ship's papers inside, so while I took our documents inside, Rich stayed behind to supervise the delicate job of refueling the ferry tanks.

Soon I was talking Spanish as they responded in Portuguese which resulted in our conversation going more smoothly. I concluded that if one merely slurs Spanish words together a little and does not make an effort to pronounce the words distinctly, as the locals (hill billys) speak out in the sticks of Colombia where I grew up, this seemed to work best for them. Also by thinking in those 'outback' terms, my comprehension seemed to improve as to what they wanted. They were requesting to keep our documents in the safe overnight . . . my guess was to insure full payment for services before our departure tomorrow! Everyone seemed friendly and polite, so this Latin culture appeared more pleasant than the one I'd known 'south of the border'.

The Esso man kindly offered to drop us off right at the Hotel Terra Nostra, so we quickly put our luggage in his Land Rover and were on our way. The temperature was cool and the slight breeze was filled with the fragrance of wild flowers that bloomed on the hillside. The nicely landscaped grounds of the hotel was adorned with flowering trees. This very hotel was where my father stayed overnight back in 1950 when his Pan American flight had an engine failure on takeoff enroute from Madrid to New York. The hotel was on a gentle hillside a short way above the airport . . . near the shoreline was the village of Vila do Porto where the sun was now very low on the horizon.

After registering, we were shown to a front west facing room which was immaculately clean. We had left our cameras in the plane, so we dropped our bags and took a pleasant walk down a small trail that led across the flowered fields to the airport. A lot of the plants looked strange to us, but then there were others that were rather familiar, like the Indian tobacco that I tried to smoke when I was a teenager. Back up in our room we drifted off to sleep for a short nap to some beautiful music that I found on my small radio.

At 8 PM sharp we walked down to the dining room . . . we heard the sounds of an intense Portuguese Fado, a hauntingly sad melody in the minor key, reminiscent of a sad Mexican Bolero, which was being played by the Camo Acoreana, a smartly dressed group of musicians. They seemed to intersperse their renditions with American popular pieces which we could faintly hear from our table in the formal dining room, where we had been seated by a maitre-d wearing a white dinner jacket and gloves, and black slacks with a red stripe down the side.

Though I was at least wearing a white shirt and tie, Rich, to his horror, suddenly realized that all he was wearing was a grubby tee shirt and khaki pants, but we'd been seated anyway, and even helped with our chairs!

We were offered just one table-d'hote menu, again reminding me of childhood experiences up in very 'continental and dour' Bogata, Columbia, as also did the fancy china on which we were served along with the heavily plated oversized silverware. Our food was excellent indeed and the Filetes De Carne 'A Inglesa most delicious.

We felt a tinge of sadness, now at 9 PM, we saw only two other tables occupied by Saturday evening customers. The newly emerging Jet Age with its non-stop flights across the pond certainly is bound to greatly hurt the Azorean economy. Everything that was performed was formal and properly accomplished. Now, many years later, I'm sure we would have appreciated all this much more, as then, in our innocence, we were so tired that we hardly noticed. I somewhat cringe at the thought as to whether we left a proper gratuity for our waiter after such a nice evening's dining experience!

By 10 PM, lucky Rich again got to hit the sack, while I still had a good hour's worth of paperwork to take care of, including a review of tomorrow's flight details.

Next morning, Sunday July 1st, my alarm clock woke us up at 7 AM. We packed our bags and paid the bill. We took a few pictures of the beautiful setting, declined the awaiting taxi, and took our now familiar pathway across the field and down to the airport. It was too nice a morning not to enjoy the fragrant scent of the wild flowers as the shadows of a few morning cumulous clouds drifted southwards in the morning sky. We saw several family groups, dressed in their Sunday best, all heading to morning mass at the Catholic church . . . certainly making this seem to us as a totally unspoiled and isolated island paradise.

But we soon came back to reality as we viewed our plane squatting a mite low on her struts and looking a bit pregnant with such a heavy load of fuel on board. While Rich did the preflight inspection, I went to the Centro Meteorologico Principal where I received a very thorough weather briefing and was presented with a nicely made up Documentos De Previsao De Voo, a custom-made flightcast folder, looking even nicer than the one we received at Gander. This one even included a side view vertical elevation depiction of our route from Santa Maria to Dakar, divided into four zones pictorially showing cloud types, bases and tops, freezing level, precipitation types, and most important the winds aloft at the 700 Mb level for each of these zones, all this, very artistically done!

Our alternate airport for Dakar was Sal located on the Cape Verde Islands which is about 400 miles off the coast of Senegal. I had to sign a few papers and they handed me our passports.

Out at the plane I told Rich he needed to go in and pay the service fee, as on the entire trip he was to take care of all our finances . . . they charged us $30 dollars. We shook hands with everyone and donned our Mae Wests . . . Rich asked one of the English speakers to please take our picture before we climbed aboard.

Preparing to depart the Azores

On board we positioned the life raft and fastened our seat belts, arranged the various charts and manuals in proper order. Rich read off the check list as I did the start-up. The tower cleared us to taxi to Rwy 01 which has a total length of 11,000 feet. We did the engine run-up and we were given our IFR clearance: '5N-ACF cleared to Dakar via Echo intersection, Flight Plan Route, turn left after takeoff, climb to flight level 90, report passing through 30'. I read back the clearance and was cleared for take-off.

We were airborne again in about 1500 feet. Just as we rolled out, the tower controller excitedly said, "5N-ACF, you've got to return and land!" That's all he said.

We looked at each other . . . what does this crackpot want?

"CF . . . all your ship's papers are still here!"

Lynn replied, "Roger . . . stand by as we prepare for an over weight landing!" (Laugh here . . . we had no fuel dump valves!)

"Roger . . . after you land a car will bring you the papers!"

Lynn brought the plane around and slicked it on light as a feather. We rolled to a smooth stop and Lynn cut the right engine. The car rolled up and handed Rich the ship's papers.

"CF . . . you are re-cleared for a mid-field takeoff!"

Lynn replied . . . "Negative . . . CF will taxi back for a full field takeoff!"

"Roger CF . . . you are cleared to taxi!"

We did our run-up again on the way. "Okay tower . . . CF ready for take off again!"

"Roger CF . . . you a cleared for takeoff . . . have a good flight!"

218

We took off and turned left . . . reported climbing through 3000 feet and we re-set our altimeters to QNE (standard pressure, 29.92 Hg). For awhile we tracked outbound on the SMA RBn, then as the signal faded we listened to the Azorean broadcast station which was certainly more interesting and also provided us with some bearing information. Coming up to 33 degrees North, we tried tuning in the beacons at Funchal and Porto Santo located on the Madeira Islands, some 400 miles to the east . . . all we heard was a few CW code stations.

Right on schedule we encountered the Low pressure system as multiple layers of clouds began piling up hiding both the sea and sky from view. By changing our altitude and headings a couple of times, we were able to stay out of most of the turbulence.

At 1341 Z, we crossed the 29th Parallel. We could not pick up the beacons located on the Canary Islands . . . then it occurred to us that because it was Sunday, there probably was very little traffic from the mainland out to these island possessions, and so perhaps the beacons were also enjoying the traditional 'day of rest'?

However there was plenty of traffic on the HF radio which we monitored faithfully as we droned along on our heading of 182 degrees which would take us to the most Western tip of Africa, IF, the winds aloft numbers given to us by the Met officer at Santa Maria proved correct, and I had computed our course correctly.

At 1519 Z we reported crossing 25 degrees North to Dakar on 8820 Kc. As the afternoon wore on and the din of distant code stations cluttered the frequency, Rich suddenly gave a jump, as he heard Kano Radio, some 2300 miles to our S-SE, calling some aircraft!

About this time we flew into a heavy haze condition which obscured the sky and the sea below . . . occasionally a light rain peppered our windshield. We remained in this heavy haze condition for the rest of the flight . . . Harmattan dust coming off the Sahara Desert.

As we arrived at 23 degrees North, we finally picked up our first RBn on 359 Kc, Villa Cisneros located in Spanish Sahara. By timing a slow ten degree swing of our ADF needle, we surmised that we were about 220 NM off the shores of Africa . . . IF . . . our estimated ground speed figure was correct. There are just too many variables to know for sure our exact position, but that is better than nothing. Again, if I had to summarize this ferry flight in two words, it would be "Navigator's Delight"!

(To all you non-flying peons reading this, it must all be very BORING . . . but to the fly boys, this is what it's like to fly across the pond in a Piper Aztec B . . . this is how you do it!)

Out of curiosity, I tuned around on the radio broadcast band and finally picked up a French station playing some nice music. This diversion helped the time to pass as we droned along in the murky haze.

Down the line, we got a strong signal at 394 Kc from RBn Port Etienne located in NW Mauritania. As we passed exactly abeam the station, we were now able to compute our ground speed exactly, and therefore, our position to the West. From this we realized that our forecasted headwinds were a little lighter than what SMA predicted.

At 1720 Z, our right ferry tank ran dry. Soon afterwards we were able to pick up Dakar's long range beacon, YF, on 403 Kc and some 450 miles to the South. Passing 19-11N, we reported our position to Dakar that we were leaving the Canaries FIR and into Dakar's FIR.

Earlier we had set our VOR to Dakar, 113.1 Mc and put the course selector on a 180 degree bearing. As we crossed the 18N parallel, the flag began getting restless, then slowly worked its way down and out of sight, soon giving us a proper navigational signal. Once again, our day long Dead Reckoning track outbound had us right on course! Who needs enroute radios? Frankly, it sure paid off having carefully adjusted our compasses when we were at Gander! So we now homed in on the Dakar VOR. And when we reached a bearing of 120 degrees to the Saint Louis, Mauritania RBn, this fixed our exact position as 100 miles North of Dakar, and we reported our position to Dakar on VHF, 126.7 Mc.

Fifty miles out, they gave us clearance to descend to Fl 50, which put us just on top of a solid undercast . . . the sun faded away in the very brief dusk of the tropics. A full five minutes ahead of our ETA both the ADF and the VOR needles got noticeably jittery, then showed station passage.

We reported our position to Dakar who cleared us for an ADF approach to Rwy 30. So we reversed our course to take us back out over the ADF station and let down to 2600 feet. As we crossed over the ADF again, we let down further to 1800 feet. At three minutes we made our left teardrop turn coming inbound on a 300 degree track. At 1500 feet we came out of the clouds in the heavy haze and darkness. The air felt heavy and humid. The glow of the city lights appeared on our left and the high intensity lights on Rwy 30 were straight ahead.

"Dakar tower . . . 5N-ACF has your field in sight!"

"Roger CF . . . you are cleared to land!"

Our touchdown was at 1925 Z. We turned off the runway to the right and Ground Control directed us to a flagman who parked us at the fuel pit. Rich opened the door and the hot humid air flooded into our cramped cockpit. Welcome to the tropics!

After completing the paperwork, we stiffly staggered off the plane and took off our Mae Wests. Sitting in the same very upright position for the past 9 1/2 hours, we could hardly stand. Off to the left was a big sleek looking Air France Star-Liner, the latest version of the famed Lockheed Constellation. She was being refueled so we had to wait about forty five minutes before they would even look our way.

Off to the southwest we could see a lighthouse winking on a low hill . . . the most western point of Africa. This was a very interesting and different place as we were soon to find. All the newer buildings were of a bold ultra modern style . . . the control tower and the administration offices, even the Air Afrique hangar were most impressive. Dakar is indeed the show place and gateway to all the French West African colonies. Little did the builders realize that all of this would soon be nationalized.

Finally, the Shell fuel tender arrived and the Aztec was serviced in preparation for tomorrow's flight. Then we were directed to taxi to where we would be parking overnight. Soon as we shut down the engines, a vehicle drove up and placed four flare pots around our plane.

We unloaded our two small suitcases and my flight bag, and we hopped into another airport car who took us to the customs house. Inside we had to go through Passport Control, Customs, Health, and police inspection . . . each administered by a separate Senegalese officer, each in a separate booth. It was amusingly obvious that they weren't too sharp at all this bureaucracy, for often they would call over some French officer for consultation. At least they seemed to be learning. After they were finally finished to their satisfaction, we asked an Air France ticket agent to please call for a room for us at the Grand Hotel du Gor.

Outside several taxi drivers vied for our business. The cab which we entered said, "Four dollars!"

Rich replied sternly, "No . . . two dollars!"

They haggled back and forth . . . finally the driver agreed and off we went, heading southwest toward the huge hotel situated right at the water's edge, all dramatically highlighted with flood lighting. As we alighted, the taxi driver tried to charge us three dollars . . . Rich gave him the agreed to two dollars, and we started walking.

At the top of a very wide stairs were two majestic looking fellows dressed in long flowing white robes, turban covered heads, wearing sandals . . . sorta like something out of 'Ali Baba'. They whisked our suitcases right out of our hands, before we knew what was happening, and so we followed them up to the reception desk.

Rich asked the clerk what they had available for ten dollars. In reply he shook his head and said in very broken English, "only rooms for twenty dollars!" Rich explained that this was more than we wanted to pay, but he didn't seem to understand.

I joined in, "The current 1962 Pan American World Guide states that rates at the Grand Hotel du Gor, room for two, starts at ten dollars!"

The clerk just kept shaking his head. So we picked up our bags and started back out toward the wide entrance. The clerk shouted after us, "Okay . . . ten dollars!" After we registered, another Ali Baba picked up our bags, and we followed him up a very attractive live plant decked stairs, then down a long narrow dimly lit side hallway to the very end to a doorway sporting a number '1'.

As currently advertised, we now had our ten dollar room which reminded me of some 'back water' hotel room 'south of the border'. As we walked in I could feel a sandy grit on the bare cement floor . . . paint was flaking off the walls. Our beds consisted of two narrow swayback cots with mosquito nets, and of course, a 'sans bathroom and a French bidget which I had to admonish Rich to not use as a toilet.

After unpacking, we went out into a completely dark hallway to look for the communal lavatory. We fumbled around on the walls until we found the light switch. Halfway down the hall, the lights turned off and we were again in total darkness! We found another switch, and continued our search. We found the 'Les Toilettes Publique just as the lights went out for the third time. By now we surmised that the appropriate procedure requires pressing each and every wall button as one proceeds down the hallway. My, if we'd install such a system here at home, it might save us a small fortune!

Back in our room, Rich remembering our dining experience last night, changed into a suit and necktie. We walked down through the lobby, past the lounge, and found a spacious dining room with high vaulted ceilings and huge full length windows, all open to toward the sea. The long sheer curtains billowed in the cool breeze.

What startled us though, the place was filled with casually attired Frenchmen with shirts unbuttoned to the waist, dirty sandals on their feet, all talking and laughing loudly, sipping their wine through heavy black mustaches, and gesticulating wildly with their hands for emphasis. We indeed felt like a couple of men from Mars that had been dropped down into a strange alien world.

The unpronounceable special on the menu made no sense to us, so I ordered a 'bifteck a' point' from our Senegalese waiter who was dressed in billowy white shorts and sandals. I had to send my steak back to have it cooked a bit more, being afraid to eat anything very rare in this strange tropical place. Included was a vegetable selection of 'courgettes and haricot verts, pomme frits, and the best French fried potatoes I'd ever tasted . . . and the steak was also outstanding. This was my very first lesson that no one can top the French when it comes to cuisine!

The capper of the evening was when we ordered a Pepsi Cola. The waiter left with a perplexed look. The head waiter appeared and explained that even the vin ordinaire is much better, and besides the soda pop cost as much! I explained that we were too young to be drinking wine. The head waiter turned away in disgust, and under protest you might say, our waiter finally brought us two 45 cent bottles of Pepsi apiece.

After dinner we went for a short walk on the foggy beach. Then we returned to our hot dingy room to sweat it out for the night under the dust-laden mosquito nets. Our ears soon told us that the nets were a good idea.

My alarm clock woke us at 0730. While I finished packing, Rich went down and paid the hotel bill. In perfect English, the same desk clerk told him the airport limousine would be leaving for the airport at 9 AM. Rich complimented him in learning the English language in such a short time!

So just before 9 AM we walked outside with our luggage, but found no such limo, so several taxi drivers offered to take us for about 500 francs (about two dollars).

However, Rich in the meantime learned that the going rate was 70 francs (about 40 cents). All the local currency Rich had left was a 100 franc bill, but none of them would take us for that amount. I guess word had spread last night about the two 'American suckers'. So we started walking the two miles to the airport. About halfway there the limousine pulled up and we rode the rest of the way for free!

At the terminal we had to go through all of last night's procedure again. Half way through the process, a load of 'Panair do Brazil' passengers arrived en-masse, but they were held back until we had been cleared. We were given two Air France boarding passes and the big question mark evidently formed above our heads . . . 'What in the world are we supposed to do with these?' Several of the officials got in a huddle. Evidently they had mistaken us for airline passengers. Then one of them escorted us over to the other side of the terminal, to re-process us and 'get it right' this time.

Finally we got out to our plane. I suggested to Rich to put one of our suitcases in the front baggage compartment to see if that would get rid of the slight buffeting we experienced on the last three over weight takeoffs. Then he did the preflight while I went over to the weather office.

It was staffed with French officials dressed in khakis and sandals. They greeted me in French and it seemed that no one spoke English, so pointing to their maps and speaking slowly, they got a weather briefing across to me (I think). They gave me a briefing folder which showed a large tropical High would be centered over the western Sahara just south of the Atlas mountains at 27 degrees North. The Inter Tropical Convergence Zone would become active along the 10 degree North Parallel. An easterly N/S instability line was forecast to develop rapidly in eastern Senegal along the 14 degree W Meridian and move westward across our path. Winds aloft would be light southwesterly until we passed the instability line, then becoming easterlies at 35 knots for the next 250 miles, and 25 knots for the remainder of the flight. Scattered cumulus would develop east of the line with isolated thunderstorms possible. Though not as artistic, the data resembled the folder we got from Santa Maria.

At the nearby counter, I filed an IFR flight plan for 3000 feet. However, the clerk said he wanted me to fly at 5000 feet as ATC would lose radio contact on some segments. I replied that we were fully HF equipped with day, intermediate, and night long range frequencies, which is not dependant on altitude. But he said, 5000 feet finish! Having extensive flying experience in Latin America and dealing with the 'Latin mind', I merely nodded in the affirmative. Alternate airports would be Niamey in Niger, Fort Lamy in Chad. As I walked out to the plane, Rich was paying our airport service fee.

By now the morning air was becoming increasingly humid with a light sprinkle coming from the high overcast. Ground control cleared us to taxi out to Rwy 12 . . . then he gave us our clearance as: Aztec 5N-ACF cleared to Kano via ADR 537, flight plan route, maintain flight level 55 in control area, report leaving 20. At 10 AM we were finally airborne to began our longest leg of the trip . . . some 1840 miles, probably bucking a 15 knot headwind. This distance would be about like flying from St. Louis, Mo against a westerly wind out to Victoria, BC.

We gladly left Dakar's humidity and all the red tape behind as we climbed out over the city of 300,000 (800,000 by 1982). On climbout this time, we felt no buffeting, so our guess is that the one suitcase in front solved that problem.

We intercepted the centerline bearing of ADR-537 and tuned the ADF to Tambacounda RBn some 200 miles ahead. As we rolled out on course, I glanced back for one more look at the blue Atlantic that we had been over the last two days for 3400 miles, little realizing that for me this would be the first of 54 crossings in my airline career.

We reported to the tower climbing through 2000 feet, changed our altimeters to standard pressure 29.92 Hg, and reported to Dakar radio when we reached Fl 55. Ahead, the country was very flat, and dry, and soon turned into a desolate looking desert with hardly any population.

Thirty miles to the East the clouds increased and soon we were flying between layers in a light rain in very hazy visibility.

At 1103 Z we came abeam Kaolack Rbn, and reported our position to Dakar and left their controlled air space. Another fifty miles later our course followed the West African railroad track which links Dakar with all the French colonies. The clouds began thinning out and the visibility greatly improved.

Off to the South we could see the wide Gambia River winding its way West toward Bathurst . . . some 250 years ago this was a slave port where British ships arrived to trade trinkets for slaves, which then made the long journey to the Carolinas, where those who survived the voyage were traded for cotton and tobacco, which supplied Britain's industry with raw goods, as the American colonies were required to do.

The southwest wind that had been predicted for us never materialized . . . instead we were bucking a 25 to 30 knot direct headwind! At this rate we'd never make Kano! However, on the ground we could see smoke from several fires blowing from the southeast. When we came abeam the Tambacounda RBn, the railroad turned NE while we continued E-SE out over the trackless landscape. The dry sand gradually changed to a reddish soil and the vegetation increased as the surface elevation slowly sloped upwards. Off to our right on the south side of the Gambia River, the terrain rises to nearly 5000 feet.

At 1301 Z we passed overhead the Faleme River crossing the Senegal/Mali border. We were not able to obtain permission to over-fly this Communist country through the

AOPA, but was advised to go ahead as no other aircraft had been shot down so far while doing so.

The countryside began taking on a rugged appearance, and because of the strong headwinds, I gradually let down to 4000 feet which took us under the scattered cumulous. The ride became a bit bumpy, but we picked up five knots in groundspeed. This gave us a beautiful panoramic view of the small isolated villages with their garden plots, connected by footpaths which radiated out from the village like spokes on a bicycle wheel. The desert changed to bush country and then to tropical forest as the terrain rose into an area of jagged rocks and strange chimney formations.

East of the Senegal River there appeared a fault line running NW-ward to the horizon. The shadows of the cumulous clouds that were forming below us showed that we were bucking a strong headwind. Ahead we could see a thunderstorm growing in size. We descended to 3500 feet and diverted our course to go around it.

Even though our change in altitude reduced the effective headwind to 15 to 20 knots, we were by now so far behind in our schedule we decided that we may have to land at our alternate airport, Niamey.

Flying across West Africa, Dakar to Kano

At 1420 Z we caught our first glimpse of the 2500 mile long Niger River. As we flew by Bamako we could see the 6000 foot runway . . . three Russian Ilyushin 11-18 planes were parked on the tarmac. We reported our position to Dakar, now 650 miles behind us, and advised them to make Niamey our destination and Kano our alternate.

I snapped a picture as we crossed the Niger River looking downstream in the direction of Timbouctou, the famed lost city of the Sahara . . . a most isolated place of 7000 people.

We now changed our course to fly directly to Ouagadougou, capitol of Upper Volta. As fast as he could, Rich computed our new course and a revised ETA. This track took us along the southern edge of the vast desert. Along the southern horizon there was one continuous squall line of thunderstorms . . . the crackling noise of the lightning filled our headsets.

The panorama of the African continent unfolded before us . . . at such a low altitude it filled us with awe as our long range 'magic carpet' carried us steadily eastwards. We carefully checked our groundspeed as we passed the village of Dedougou and found that the headwind had dropped off substantially . . . smoke on the ground now showed there was a quartering tailwind coming from the southwest! So we descended to 1000 feet to take advantage of this.

We passed four miles North of Ouagadougou a full twenty minutes ahead of our ETA! We reported our position to Niamey and they gave us a weather report for there and also for Kano which indicated that we could count on this SW tailwind for the rest of the flight!

A quick calculation showed that if we now pulled our power back and using some cruise control techniques, we could fly a minimum of 8:15 hours for another 1250 miles . . . we could still fly to Kano and have enough to reach our alternate airports!

So I reduced the engines back from 65% to 45% power at a low 2100 RPM . . . then I used the Max Conrad Technique of leaning the engines (running the engine on one magneto while it is being leaned gives a sharper drop-off on either side of the best efficiency position and so helps to insure that the mixture control is in exactly the best position for maximum range, then the other mag is turned back on). At this setting, our fuel consumption dropped to less than 17 MPG, but still giving us a true airspeed of over 160 MPH.

We advised Niamey of our intentions to continue on to Kano, and on HF 8820 Kc we asked Kano to give SIMAIR our ETA. Approaching the Niger River now for the second time, Niamy advised us that his rotating beacon and runway lights were on. He couldn't seem to get it through his head that we were not stopping at Niamey.

We changed our course to cut corners and passed about three miles south of the field. The normal course from here, plotted earlier, was direct to Sokoto 220 miles ahead on a course of 108 degrees, then the course changed to 114 degrees for the remaining 220 miles to Kano. Since the Sokoto RBn only operated during daylight hours, we re-figured a direct course with a heading of 115 degrees to compensate for the SW wind.

Rich held this heading as I gave Niamey our new estimate. It was completely black outside except for the distant lightning all along the southern horizon. We tried to get Kano radio on the HF 5521.5 Kc but it was just one steady howl of static. On 8820 Kc we thought they might be trying to answer us, and it sounded like they said something about a thunderstorm approaching the station. Maybe we would need a little fuel to hold when we got there?

Our ADF was doing a better job as a thunderstorm lightning indicator as it alternately pointed this way and that, reacting to each stab of lightning that broke the darkness.

By dimming the instrument post lights so we could just make out the gyros, and turning off all other lights, we could make out occasional flickers of light as we passed over several villages. We wondered what they might have thought, being awakened by the drone of a low flying plane passing over at such a low altitude in the middle of the night.

As our night vision improved, I wondered if we might be able to see Sokoto when we passed by. So I dimmed the post lights even more and screwed out the amber 'gear up' light. Poor Rich, sitting on the right, could no longer see the two gyros, so I took over the controls.

Sure enough, at 2109 Z we could faintly make out a group of very dim lights off our left wing. We reported our position to Kano on the HF radio, but it was impossible to make out his reply because of the continuous static.

We increased our altitude to 4000 feet to make sure we cleared the rocky hills that Rich said were near Gusau 105 miles ahead.

As a pastime and an experiment, I turned off the panel lights completely, and had Rich try to fly straight and level by the 'seat of his pants'. After a two minute period, I turned the lights back on to find that we were in a shallow turn! Rich vowed, "I guarantee you . . . they will never ever get me to start any night flying out here!"

On schedule, the lights of Gusau flickered faintly off our right wing. We reported our position to Kano and gave them our ETA . . . this time we heard them respond . . . they cleared us into their airspace to maintain Fl 40. By now the ADF needle pointed toward the Kano RBn 376 Kc.

When we were fifty miles out, Rich, who was getting itchy, thought he could make out Kano's rotating beacon light, but I told him he was having hallucinations, as I couldn't see a thing out there. But sure enough, not long after, we both could make out the faint glow from the lights of Kano. We were now getting a strong signal from the Kano VOR, 112.5 Mc. Suddenly, with lots of extra fuel on board, I eased the power up to 75%.

The British controller cleared us for contact approach to Rwy 24. We touched down at 2140 Z, or 2340 local time . . . ramp to ramp time 11:32 hours. As we approached the parking ramp, I turned off the taxi light so as to not blind all the nice SIM folk who had come out at this late hour to welcome us to Nigeria!

We burned 214 gallons of fuel for an average consumption of 19.3 GPH, so we had 80 gallons or 4 3/4 hours remaining, so with the ferry tanks this was indeed quite a long range airplane.

Rich opened the cabin door, and we stiffly got out and climbed down from the wing. When I tried to stand up, I fell flat on my face . . . embarrassing myself in front of all our greeters!

As we were shaking hands all around, two customs agents ordered us to remove everything from the aircraft. Then they randomly had us open several suitcases and boxes for further scrutiny. This continued relentlessly until an officer asked Rich what was in our can of Planter's Peanuts, which we had purchased four days ago in Gander. Rich replied that they were 'ground nuts' . . . the agent opened the can and ate some. (Nigeria exports more ground nuts than any other nation in the world!) We asked him how he liked them. He said, "They are fine!" So rich replied, "Please take some more!" as we all laughed. Thus concluded our grueling inspection as he now told us to put everything back on board, and to bring our documents inside for inspection.

So Dave Rutt, one of the SIMAIR Pilots, attended to the refueling while we went inside where we had to face an array of Nigerian officials. They say that Kano is the world's worst for 'red tape' . . . now I believe them! Dave Rutt warned us that they were looking for any evidence that we had ever been in South Africa or Angola. When they finally let us go, we taxied the plane over to the SIM hangar to park for the night.

Then we were driven into the city to the SIM guesthouse. After taking a cold shower and getting ready for bed, we suddenly realized how hungry we were, for we had not eaten a single bite since our Pepsi Cola supper last night in Dakar! One could say this had been 'an enthusiasm powered performance' today!

7 AM Tuesday, July 3rd, we sleepily shuffled our way over to the SIM dining room for breakfast. Eating here reminded me a lot of Wycliffe's big dining room at their jungle base in the Peruvian Amazon.

When we went out to the airport, Paul Rogalsky had just arrived from Jos with a passenger. He and Dave Rutt said they would like us to all fly over the Jos compound in formation. So they took off in the two Comanches ahead of us as it would take them 1:15 hours to our 45 minutes to fly the 150 miles to Jos. So we filed our flight plan and took off after them. Rich talked to mission headquarters on their private frequency and gave them our ETA.

About 20 miles out of Jos we spotted the two Comanches below and descended down to their altitude and flew in loose formation. As we approached Jos we told them to hold their positions while we eased up between them, and together we flew a close V-formation over Jos and then the airport . . . then we, in turn, broke off and made a low pass over the runway, and swung up and around for a smooth landing on Rwy 28, followed by the two Comanches.

We taxied down to the SIMAIR hangar where a large crowd had assembled to welcome our arrival after this 8,125 mile delivery flight here to central Africa after crossing parts of two continents, and with an ocean in between. (Rich especially searched the faces of the crowd for Marg Shepherd, as he knew that she had been re-stationed in Jos again, but she was nowhere to be found.)

So that is about the end of this tale with no known detail omitted. (Rich talking here . . . I did cut this down a bit to eliminate a lot of the wordiness) What follows now is an account of the activities until I finally got back home to Saint Lewis.

The Aztec in front of Jos hangar

Jos, I soon found was quite a nice place. Easy to see why the British during World War Two, when it wasn't possible return home to England, would instead come here for their R and R. This was soon even more evident as I toured the town, where I viewed a number of attractive homes, including some that were English style thatched cottages, seemingly with most of the amenities of that green and pleasant land that were mustered here. Climate here, of course, is the main attraction, made bearable, just 10 degrees North of the Equator, by its location on a wide plateau 4300 feet above sea level, with the granite Sheri Hills rising to 5851 feet ten miles East of Jos.

The Mission compound reminded me of Wycliffe's big base at Yarina Cocha in Peru, though this one was even better established. And for good reason, I thought. SIM was founded in 1893 during the Victorian era, where as Wycliffe was founded during the Great Depression. Beautiful bushes and flowering trees made it a place of sheer beauty.

That afternoon, the SIMAIR fellows pulled the ferry tanks, and made a careful inspection of the engines, changed the oil, and did a landing gear retraction test, during which they adjusted one of the nose gear doors that was a bit loose.

Rich Schaffer with Aztec at Jos

The next two days I gave Rich and (mainly) Paul 9:20 hours of dual to make his transition from the smaller Piper Apache to this larger Aztec-B. This included a lot of instrument work and then perfecting their short field technique. The very extensive training ('muddy boots flying') they received in Missouri aboard Dr. Brumme's Piper Apache in which they passed both their FAA Instrument and Multi-engine rides, was now making this transition a 'real breeze'!

Aztec and three Comanche 180's at Jos

Our thanks certainly goes to Dr. Brumme who for five years donated the use of his plane so that more than twenty fellows like Rich and Paul could upgrade their FAA ratings and general flying skills. (and thanks too to you, Lynn Washburn, who spent hours and hours of your time into making us better pilots to serve the Lord). Now I, regrettably, had to hastily depart (due to my requested leave being cut in half), both Rich and Paul would be responsible for checking out the other four SIMAIR pilots on the particulars of the Aztec.

On Friday June 6th, I was invited to the Rogalsky home for breakfast where I got to meet Paul's wife and two sons. Afterward, Paul took me downtown where I purchased a new pair of English made shoes, as one of mine had unexpectedly lost a heel. Then he took me to the local museum where the history of West Africa is portrayed, including a series of terra cotta objects of the ancient Nok culture that was discovered on the SW edge of the plateau.

If Ozark Airlines had not canceled my month's leave, Paul would have taken me on a camera safari to the Yankari Game Reserve which is located about 135 miles east of Jos. Instead Paul and I flew back north in the Cessna 170 to Kano . . . this took more than twice the time it had taken Rich and me to fly in the Aztec.

At 1105 PM I departed Kano for Rome aboard a KLM Lockheed L-188 Electra, flight # KL594. KLM began their Electra service in December 1959. They are famous for their safety record and claim they are the world's oldest airline, founded 7 October 1919. I arrived in Rome at 5:20 AM.

(Lynn flew from Rome to Zurich to Amsterdam to New York and home to St Louis, all of which he described every detail in his descriptive language for another four pages.)

In conclusion, this trip report should help make it clear why, to a devotee, flying is never considered 'work'. To me, the greatest fulfillment has become, not in flying the aircraft, but rather, the challenge to better understand the laws of nature, the ever changing weather, and the logic and intricacies of aerial navigation in order to successfully complete one's flight. The result of extensive flight and travel experience, rewards one with an increased understanding of geographic, climatic, and cultural differences on this globe, and indeed most satisfying for anyone with any degree of interest and curiosity!

To now be in a position to direct some of these capabilities which are a result of this interest, and to be of assistance in some small way in spreading the Good News is certainly an ultimate fulfillment for a Christian!

It was certainly so, later to learn that 5N-ACF flew many thousands of safe hours in the service of the Sudan Interior Mission for the people of West Africa during the next 19 years until she was sold in 1981. As someone put it so well . . . "Your life is a gift from God . . . "What you make of it is your gift to God!"

And so ends this long epistle . . . please write soon to your wandering son . . . love, Lynn

ACRONYMS & ABBREVIATIONS FOUND IN THE TEXT

AOPA Aircraft Owners & Pilots Assn. SAC Strategic Air Command
SIM Sudan Interior Mission AM Amplitude Modulation
NYC New York City FM Frequency Moldulation
VFR Visual Flight Rules SSB Single Side Band
SIMAIR air arm of SIM OCA Ocean Control Area
HF High Frequency 1650 to 30,000 Kc FIR Flight Information Region
FAA Federal Aviation Administration ADR traffic Advisory Route
AMEL Airplane Multi-Engine Land CW Carrier Wave
OZA Ozark Airlines 1950 to 1986 ETE Estimated Time Enroute
Jepp chart Jeppesen IFR NAV Charts ETA Estimated Time Arrival
VHF Very High Frequency 108 to 137 Mc GS Ground Speed
UHF Ultra High Frequency 200 to 500 Mc USCG US Coast Guard
VOR VHF Omni Range radio navigation CB Cumulonimbus
OPS Operations Tstm Thunderstorm
NFLD Newfoundland, Canada NDB Non-Directional Beacon
STL St Louis Lambert Field, MO PAA Pan American Airways
QX Chicago O'Hare Field, IL MEA Minimum Enroute Altitude
SMA Santa Maria, Azores, Portugal AGL feet Above Ground Level
YF Dakar Yoff airport, Senegal ASL feet Above Sea Level
IFR Instrument Flight Rules NM Nautical Miles
Rwy 04 Runway 040 degrees (NE) LOM Locator Outer Marker
RBn Radio Beacon LMM Locator Middle Marker
GPH Gallons Per hour ATC Air Traffic Control
ADF Automatic Direction Finder GND Ground Control
LFR Low Frequency Range CAVU Ceiling & visibility Unlimited
OAT Outside Air Temperature GMT Greenwich Mean Time
VMC Visual Metrological Conditions Z = GMT
IMC Instrument Met. Conditions LR Long Range
ILS Instrument Landing System N/S North/ South alignment
MET Metrological weather office KLM Dutch Airline
700 Mb about 10,000 feet ASL TWA Trans World Airlines
1000' ASL feet Above Sea Level RPM Revolutions Per Minute
CG Center of Gravity ADIZ Air Defense Identification Zone

Rich Schaffer 503-363-7051 Lynn Washburn 636-477-9545
643 45th Place SE 414 Duckett Place
Salem, OR 97317 Saint Charles, MO 63303

CHAPTER 27
ROMANCE

It was good to be home and in my apartment again. I learned that Marg now lived at the other end of the building, so that evening after supper at the guest house, I went over and knocked on her door. When she opened the door, I stammered, "Go . . . good evening . . . I . . . I'm working my way through college, and I'm selling ma . . . magazines. Wo . . . wondering if I could interest you in a subscription to Ladies Home Journal? . . . I . . . ah."

She laughed and joined in the game, "You nut . . . sorry, I'm so busy that I don't have time to read magazines!"

"Then maybe I could interest you in this fine record?", I pulled out the record I was hiding behind my back, "It's really good listening!"

She took the record and studied the jacket, "Hmm . . . Montovani Golden Hits. Sounds nice, but I don't have much money at the moment . . . how much are you selling these for?"

"Oh no mam', the first one's free!"

"Nothing in this world is really free . . . what's the catch?"

"OK . . . only kidding . . . just thought you might like a nice record to play on your phonograph. But if you are afraid of receiving a gift, I'll trade it to you for an airform?"

Marg tilted her head slightly as if considering the value of the trade, "Hmm . . . stay put while I put the record on." She stepped inside, and soon the beautiful strains of Granada filled the air. Her eyes sparkled as she came out and sat on the steps. "I don't want to cheat you, so I brought you two airforms," she laughed.

"Well thank you, mam' . . . I appreciate your generous spirit."

We sat listening to the music. The night was warm and humid, but a slight breeze made it comfortable. After a few minutes, Marg offered, "By the way, welcome back to Nigeria . . . you sure were noisy when you flew over!"

"Thank you . . . it's nice to be home again. I missed seeing you at the airport."

"I was on duty . . . not everyone gets to run off to the airport, you know."

"I'll bet your sorry to be stuck back here in Jos again?"

"Not really." A long pause . . . "I asked to be moved."

"You what?" I couldn't believe my ears.

With emphasis, "I 'asked' to be moved!"

231

I waited for an explanation. Here my bushgal missionary now wants to live in Jos? It turns out that she was having the same kind of trouble that Greta had . . . some married creep at Kaltungo started making moves on her. It got so bad that she had to ask the District Supervisor to move her.

"I'm sure sorry to hear that, but I'm glad to see that you are here in Jos," I sympathized, "and I promise you that I will behave myself, okay?"

Marg studied my face for a long time, "I think you're a pretty neat guy."

I would have loved to hug her close, but wisdom prevailed, "Thanks . . . and I like you too."

The record had ended and Marg stood up to go inside.

"Uhh . . . I need to go . . . I'd like to get a letter written tonight to let people know that we got here safely."

"Okay . . . good night . . . I'll see you?"

"Sure." I think I floated about two inches above the ground all the way home!

The guys gave me a few days off to get my house in order and then the flying began.

9 July 62 . . . My first flight was an overnight to Lagos with the Aztec to register the plane with the Air Registration Board . . . only took 2:45 for the 450 miles. On the 11th I flew home via Ilorin with Annie Vanderbrand, Greta Jackson, Pat Erwin, and three kids.

The next day I flew Jos-Enugu-Jos picking up nine Hillcrest kids. The above flights would have taken two Comanches and two pilots to carry all these people and it would have taken much more time.

On the 13th I flew Dave Rutt to Kano and back to begin getting him familiarized with the new plane.

On the 14th and the 16th, I spent a couple hours getting myself used to flying the Comanche again, plus doing two cargo runs to Kagoro and Kwoi.

On the 17th I picked up Mr. and Mrs. Gilliland plus one at Bambur.

On the 18th I picked up Mr. and Mrs. Collins at Minna.

On the 24th and 25th I had a long trip up into French country . . . took Mrs. Ruten plus one to Diapaga . . . went up to Bogandi and picked up Miss Black . . . we stayed overnight at Fada. The next day we flew home to Jos . . . the flight took 12:55 hours.

I stopped by the radio room one day and talked with Heber Richins . . . he invited me over for supper, "Bring someone along if you would like."

"Okay thanks . . . I'll try to do that."

So I turned up on Marg's doorstep and asked her if she would go with me.

"Sure," she smiled, "about what time?"

"Oh . . . about six thirty . . . that's Friday, okay?"

"That will be fine." She seemed very pleased.

We sat on her steps and talked for awhile. It was a beautiful night and a full moon was rising above the trees. She stretched a bit . . . "It's almost bright as day . . . would you like to go for a walk?"

We crossed the street and took the path that led to the tennis court and past the Business Department and the Pharmacy. We sauntered slowly around the triangle. "I have to make out the papers for the flight up to Niger tomorrow . . . would you like to go out to the hangar and see the new plane?"

"Oh . . . that would be nice!"

So we stopped by Paul Rogalsky's and got the key for the SIMAIR VW bus. When Paul saw Marg, he gave me a smile and got a twinkle in his eyes. I nodded in return, but didn't say a thing.

I unlocked the passenger side and held the door for Marg. "It's a big step." But she hopped in with no problem.

We drove out of the BD yard and headed the three miles to the hangar. What a beautiful night. I had a little trouble opening the combination lock to the hangar door . . . it had been awhile. Our night guard, Abba, sauntered over from the open hangar to check us out. "Hello Abba," I greeted and then introduced Marg, "This is Miss Shepherd."

Abba bowed and greeted her in English. But Marg responded in Hausa which pleased him very much. Then I waited as they went through the long string of greetings. She, indeed, had a very good grasp of the language.

When I had a chance to break in, I said, "Marg, wait here and I'll go in and open up the hangar doors." I stepped in the small door and turned on the hangar lights. Then I removed the bolts and pushed the four big doors open with ease. After work, we had wet down and squeegeed the main hangar floor, so the place was really clean. While Marg continued talking with Abba, I went back to the radio room and put on one of the 'The Old Fashioned Revival Hour' records . . . the beautiful gospel music filled the whole hangar and floated out into the night air. Then I went into the office and dug out the General Declaration, Customs, and Immigration forms that I would need to type out for tomorrow's flight . . . four copies of each. I would be flying to Kano, Zinder, and night-stopping at Maine Soroa . . . returning the next day via Kano.

When Marg finished talking to Abba, she came into the office. "That music sure sounds nice . . . is that a tape?"

"No, it's one of those big records that I got at ELWA . . . I rigged up a record player so that we could play them." I took her back to the radio room for her to see. "We have some speakers hanging up in the rafters so we can hear it all over the hangar while we work on the planes."

Marg taking it all in, "Wow! . . . that's really nice!"

"Come on . . . I'll show you the Aztec." We went out into the hangar and I showed her the bright, shiny new plane.

As we walked around the plane, her eyes glistened like those of an inquisitive child . . . she was something to see. "This thing is a lot bigger than the Comanches!"

"Would you like to see the cockpit? Step here and then up onto the wingwalk . . . grab that handhold so you can pull yourself up." She did that with ease and grace. "Go ahead and climb in and scoot over to the pilot's seat." I followed her and sat in the passenger seat.

She slowly shook her head and her lips formed a silent wow as she looked at the maze of instruments and switches in the panel . . . her hands timidly touched the control wheel. I turned on the master switch and then the panel lights, which made it even more impressive.

I smiled, "Turn it to the left and look out at the left wing." As she did so, "That aeleron goes up which causes the air flowing over it to push the wing down, and you turn left. Turn the control wheel to the right and you turn right. When you pull and push the wheel back and forward, it makes you go up and down like this." I made the motions like my hand was a plane.

She looked at me and smiled with delight. I chuckled, "Now that you know how to fly a plane . . . how would you like to join SIMAIR? . . . we could use another pilot . . . you could be another Betty Green!"

She nodded and laughed, "Sure . . . I could do this!"

We sat there quite awhile as I showed her the throttle controls, the radios, the rudder pedals, and the myriad of switches, and I told her what they were for. It made her decide that maybe this could get a little more complicated than I made it sound. I turned off the panel lights and the master switch.

Then I suggested, "Watch me as I get out of the plane . . . it can be a little awkward until you get the hang of it." I then got out of the plane in one fluid motion. She followed but not quite right.

"I see what you mean . . . and maybe it would be better to have a pair of pants on?"

I teased, "That's okay . . . you have beautiful legs!" I offered her my hand to help her step off the wing.

"Why thank you sir!" She was blushing a little. "And you can let go of my hand?"

We went into the office. "I'd better get busy with those papers." But I went over to the fridge and held open the door, "Would you like a Coke, or a Pepsi, or an orange Fanta?"

"Mmm . . . I think maybe, a Fanta?"

I took the same and tossed a couple shillings in the coke box.

The orange drink was really ice cold and very refreshing on this warm humid night. I got busy with the typewriter and filled in all the forms. Then I made four stacks and stapled them together and sealed the staple with sealing wax as they demanded to be done.

We sat and talked for quite awhile. But tomorrow was going to be a long hot day. I turned off the music, rolled and secured the big doors, and tuned off the lights, and locked the small door.

When I left Marg at her door, I squeezed her hands. She said softly, "Thank you for the nice evening . . . I'll see you Friday?"

Wow! . . . I felt like I was in heaven!

But when you go to Niger, you feel like you are going to purgatory. It's hot and it is dry. Man, it is hot . . . maybe 130 degrees at times! And when you go to Maine Soroa you fly over nothing but sand everywhere. Sometimes the road from Zinder to Maine completely disappears and road travelers will make their own. Sometimes you will see a half dozen different tracks going parallel as people have wearily tried to pick an easier way through the soft drifting sand, eventually they come together again, and finally you find your way to Maine Soroa, some 250 miles from Zinder, SIM's most eastern station in Niger. I was flying in Mr. and Mrs. Beacham and their two children, and all their supplies to run the station while Cathy Jones and Lorna Downes were on furlough for a year. I couldn't imagine myself being here more than one day. And here we have the Lord's servants living here, day after day, year after year, and for what? Well, there's people out here. And they need the gospel. And so we go to let them know the "good news" of salvation. Why? Because Jesus told us to. And so SIM is sending people into all the corners of the world to give people the opportunity to accept Jesus as Savior and allow Him to become Lord in their lives. And a lot of these places are not very nice. Sometimes it is about as close to hell as you can get. It is hard. It is really hard. But we go. These dedicated people go. That's what missionaries do. And if you are a Christian, I would challenge you to go. Christ's great commission to go into all the world includes you. You! Someway, somehow, you should be a part of the program. And if you can't go, you can still have a part in reaching the lost. If you are not doing so, I would challenge you to personally and financially and faithfully take on the support of some missionary, take a real interest in them and their work, and then faithfully pray for them. You may not be able to do a lot, but you need to do it. And God will bless you for it.

I picked up Marg at about seven o'clock and we walked directly across the street to Richin's house. Phyllis Richins greeted us at the door with a big smile, especially to Marg, as I didn't tell them who I would be bringing. "I have a few more things to do in the kitchen . . . you make yourselves comfortable here in the living room . . . Heber-r . . . Rich and Marg are here!"

Heber came from a back room. He too seemed very pleased with my choice. He had a big grin on his face as he looked at Marg and then at me with a slight lift of the eyebrows. "Here . . . you good folks sit here on the couch . . . my, it's good to see you! . . . how are you kids doing?"

I volunteered, "Okay, I guess . . . I just got back from a flight up to Niger and Maine Soroa . . . I took the Beacham's out there to run the station while Cathy and Lorna are on furlough for the year."

"I hear that is quite a place . . . It would be nice if we could get a two way radio up there."

"It would also be nice if there was some kind radio beacon there that we could home in on. There are hardly any landmarks out there. All you can do is follow the car tracks. Yesterday even those disappeared for about twenty miles. Nothing but sand as far as the eye can see. I was wondering if you could design some kind of homing beacon that our ADF would pick up?"

It was almost like a you could see the idea come on like a light bulb above Heber's head, "Yeah . . . I think I could do that . . . how strong would you want it to be?"

Phyllis stuck her head around the corner, "Marg . . . come and help me . . . those two are just totally ignoring you!"

Marg went out to the kitchen while Heber and I tossed the idea around. "If we could pick up a signal at about five to ten miles out . . . that would really be a help . . . especially in the Harmattan . . . how much of a transmitter would that have to be? I've heard that MAF is toying around with the idea."

Heber scratched the stubble on his chin, "Well . . . let me do some tinkering . . . maybe I can come up with something."

Phyllis appeared again, "How would genius inventors like to do that another day. Dinner is being served in the dinning room!"

Wow . . . what a beautiful setting. Marg's eyes twinkled in the glow of the candlelight. Phyllis had put a flower in Marg's hair, and she looked so beautiful in her light blue dress. It almost took my breath away. As I made my way to her side, I took her hand, and she did not resist. Heber intoned the Lord's blessing on the food and on our evening. The meal was simple, but done in an elegant way. Phyllis and Heber had a real gift in fellowship . . . it could not have been nicer.

After the dinner and the table was cleared, Phyllis and Heber made themselves busy. "You kids make yourselves comfortable while we take care of a few things in the kitchen."

Marg and I looked at each other and quietly giggled, "Wow! . . . aren't they nice!"

"They sure are . . . someday, I would like to have a home just like this!"

I squeezed her hand to let her know that I felt the same way.

Heber and Phyllis came back and we had a roaring good time playing a game of Yahtzee. Phyllis served us some hot chocolate topped with a marshmallow. And when it was time to go, Heber read the Bible and closed the evening with prayer. In parting, "You kids are welcome to come over anytime and sit in our living room if you want . . . we knew how hard it was to be away from curious eyes when we were going together."

We looked at each other and laughed, "Thank you very much . . . and thank you so much for the wonderful evening! . . . It couldn't have been nicer!"

Marg and I were seeing each other several nights a week. Sometimes we did go over to Richins house. Sometimes we went for walks. Sometimes we just sat on her front steps and talked. What ever we did, we were very discrete in public. We never went or sat together in church. We never went to the guesthouse for meals together. We never held hands or showed any over affection in public. Very few of the missionaries even knew that we were interested in each other. Those that did, were for us all the way.

About November, Marg and Belva were invited out to Ringin Gani by Mary Haas. They decided they would ride their bikes the twenty-three miles out to the station. Marg asked me if I would come and pick them up on Sunday, as the return trip was mostly uphill. So on Sunday afternoon I drove out to Mary's and was invited to stay for the evening meal. On Mary Haas's last furlough she was on the Queen for the Day program. They gave her a new vehicle, a canopy bed, fancy china, and all kinds of nice household things. Her eyes just sparkled as she told about the program in detail.

When it was time to leave, I loaded the bicycles into the VW bus. Mary invited me out for Thanksgiving dinner and hinted that I bring someone with me! And I agreed to do that. So on Thanksgiving Day, Marg and I drove out to Ringin Gani. Mary just burst with laughter when she saw that I had brought Marg, "I thought she was the one you were interested in, but I just wasn't sure!"

And we had a wonderful time and a scrumptious meal . . . Mary was such a gracious hostess. It was late in the evening when we drove home. The moon was full . . . and it was like a magical night when I stopped the bus and proposed to Marg. She accepted! And we sealed it with our first kiss! WOW!

When we got home, we noticed the lights were still on at Richins, so we ran over and told them the happy news. They invited us in to hear how it all came about.

The next night we walked over to see Bill Crouch, our Field Director, to give him the news. SIM regulations require this be done for his approval. And from that date we would be required to wait six months before we could get married. It was quite a shock to him, but he gave us his hearty approval. And we asked if he would be the one to marry us, and he said he would be glad to do that. The date was set for May 4th 1963.

Our engagement picture

CHAPTER 28
WAITING FOR THE BIG DAY

Another SIM regulation required that engaged couples not live on the same station, so when Marg heard someone was needed to take Mary Stobbe's place at Okene while she came to Jos for an extended medical leave, Marg volunteered. On November 10th, I flew Marg down to Lakoja and picked up Mary Stobbe.

A couple weeks later I got a note from Marg, "What a beautiful place this is . . . I think we ought to spend our honeymoon here!"

I kept busy flying almost every day. All the places, all the names, they became a blur of memories. Of note in my logbook was a flight for SUM missionaries, Mr. and Mrs. Herniman plus two children and their dead baby. What a heartache for these dear missionaries.

On the 26th, the next day, I flew a medical emergency flight, bringing Helena Lowen up from Kwoi. On the 8th of December I flew a medical emergency for Mrs. Pickett plus one from Kaduna. As news of our engagement spread, everywhere I went, people wished us well. Naturally I invited them all to come to our wedding!

On the 12th I flew Edna Allchin and Mary Stobbe to Lakoja and to pick up Marg. But I stayed overnight at Okene to see this station. It was perched on a rocky ridge that overlooked the town and the surrounding area . . . You could see for miles. The breeze made it cooler than down in the valleys. Water was collected into cisterns to store for use in the dry season. When the wells went dry, then they begin rationing the water from the cisterns. Sometimes in a long dry season, they would have to buy and haul water from the town. The big thing was the maternity clinic where mothers came from miles around to safely deliver their babies.

It was good to see Marg again after being separated for a whole month. We went for a walk in the cool of the evening. Early the next morning, the Toberts took us down to the water reservoir for a pancake breakfast in a cool bamboo grove right on the water's edge.

Pancake breakfast at Okene reservoir

I learned that some resourceful person had planted Nile Perch and the record catch was 104 pounds! This indeed was a beautiful place. On the way home, I had to fly down to Ibadan to pick up Verna Pullen, and to Ilorin to pick up Edith Milloy.

Marg was glad to be back in Jos, but how long would she be able to stay? We remained very discrete in our being together, and we were happily surprised that she was able to remain the rest of the time right in Jos. This enabled us to be together for all the planning that needs to be done for such a happy occasion. We made arrangements to be married in Stirrett Memorial Chapel. And the Jos Guest House would be happy to host the reception. The ladies had a wonderful wedding shower for Marg there. The guys had a stag party for me where they presented me with a pair of red socks so that I wouldn't get cold feet!

As it was impossible for Marg's parents to be present for the wedding, Mr. and Mrs. Jack Nicholson agreed to act as her parents. Ken and Elsie Kastner agreed to act as my parents.

When I had the opportunity to stay overnight in Lagos, I went shopping for rings. What a shocker that was! The diamond on the engagement ring was so small you could hardly see it, and the price was a thousand pounds (2800 dollars)! Just a plain gold wedding band would cost over 400 dollars! Through our purchasing agent in the New York office, Grace Hiser, I was able to buy a beautiful 1/3 carat engagement ring and a diamond wedding band for a little over 300 dollars, and a wedding band for me would only be twenty five dollars! Grace promised to send them out with some missionary in time for the wedding.

Wedding clothes? Marg decided to sew her own wedding gown. Then she received word from her sister in British Columbia that a girl who knew Marg at Briercrest (Mrs. Lorna Thomas) offered to send her the beautiful wedding dress she wore when she got married. When it came, the dress fit perfectly without any alterations! The maid of honor and the bridesmaid dresses were made in a beautiful dark blue satin. The three flower girl's dresses were of light blue satin with dark blue sashes. I just happened to bring out with me a nice white dinner jacket. Bill Tuck, my best man, had a jacket to match.

There had not been a wedding in Jos for about five years, so everyone pitched in with enthusiasm to make this a grand occasion. Phyllis Crosby made a three-tiered wedding fruitcake, and Lola and Lois Brown decorated it. The seven girls from the high school hostel (Char Richins, Pauline Elizabeth Gross, Judy Giesbrecht, Anne Dreisbach, Gerrie Lou Thomas, Carolyn Tobert, and Joanne Soderberg) would serve at the reception. Jan Small made a large cardboard display . . . a blue cross with an open Bible with the words 'That we might be to the praise of His glory' . . . Ephesians 6:6 . . . Rich and Margaret, which was the theme of our marriage (all the years we were on the mission field, we had this display in our bedroom).

I learned that Dean Gilliland would be on holiday at that time, so I asked if he and Soddy would sing a lot of songs for our wedding and the reception. People would come to the wedding just to hear them sing . . . they were that good.

Bill Crouch had a small book of weddings and suggested we look through it to pick out one that we liked. When we looked at them we decided to pick things from several weddings and thus make our own. We memorized our parts so that we could say them by heart so we wouldn't have the pastor's, "Now repeat after me . . ." Several couples, who got married later, asked if they could copy "our" wedding because they liked it so much.

Another discussion came up . . . where would we live after we were married? Because of all the beautiful built-in cabinets, etc that I had made in my apartment, my thought was that we would live there. But No . . . they needed both our apartments for single folks . . . it was decided that we could live in the Pharmacy house during the year the McMillan's would be home on furlough.

Another thing had to be done . . . we had to post 'bans' at the court house in case anyone wanted to contest our wedding.

SUM bought a new plane . . . a Piper Comanche 250 which had a more powerful six cylinder engine which made it fly faster and could carry a heavier load. They also were getting another pilot, Gordie Buys, as their flying load was increasing to where Ray Browneye was flying over a hundred hours per month most of the time. Ray brought the plane up to Jos to do the first 100 hour inspection as they did not have the jacks needed to check the landing gear. We helped him do the inspection and then I went up with him to do the test flight.

Our flight load was also increasing and we would have another Moody pilot, Leroy and Charlotte Andrews, join us in April 1963. And another Moody pilot, Jim and Julie Wayner, would be joining us in January 1964, and Bob Swingle in May 1964. Joe and Lois Swanson went home to stay in June 1962. In our monthly hangar meeting, to prevent burnout, we hammered out a decision to limit a pilot's flying to a maximum of 80 hours per month, and a maximum of 25 hours in one week. If we flew a 25 hour week, then all we could fly the next week was 15 hours.

This decision was accepted with reluctance at the next council meeting. The idea was 'wish I only had to work 25 hours a week', as if that was all we did without any consideration of all the maintenance and everything else that is done to run a smooth efficient flight program.

What we do when we're not flying . . .

By the end of 1962 I had flown 3000 hours of which 137 hours was multi-engine.

For the month of January I flew 59:10 of which 22:30 was in the Aztec, carrying 87 passengers. Of note was a medical emergency flight on January 6th to pick up Virgil Kleinsasser at Keffi . . . Marg came along as nurse in case she was needed.

Leroy Andrews & Bill Tuck install emergency flight stretcher board

Then on January 14th I flew a medical emergency flight to pick up an E. Nicholson at Lagos. For some reason I went via Zaria and Ilorin, flying passengers: Betty DeLa, Edith Milloy, Mary Laity, and Edna Wiebe. Marg again went along as the nurse.

On the 26th, I flew a medical flight for Mrs. Ross Carson picking her up at Gusau. And on the 7th of February I flew a medical emergency flight to Keffi again to pick up Mary Kon.

I wonder how many medical flights the other four pilots flew during this time? Usually we sort of divided up these kinds of "glory flights" so that we would all have something exciting to write home about to our supporters showing how important and necessary the airplane was in the Lord's service, as if all the routine flying wasn't just as important. How many hot, dusty miles and days of road travel did we save our grateful passengers? How much time was saved? We were operating our aviation program cheaper than a missionary could drive his own vehicle. So how much money was saved? These kinds of statistics over the years would have been interesting.

241

When the missionaries brought out our wedding rings, they declared them in customs. They put on a charge of 100 percent duty! Wow! I decided to call their bluff and refused to pay. But they would not budge. So the rings were taken back to be held at the New York office. We never got our rings until we went home on furlough. Someone gave Marg a gold wedding band they had. I got busy and made my wedding band out of a piece of brass brazing rod, polished it up to where it really looked great. When the wedding dress came, the post office charged only a small amount of duty, and they didn't even bother to open the package for inspection.

On March 8th, I had a flight to Birnin Kebbi to pick up Don Williams. Shortly they would be going home to England on furlough, so he offered us the use of their 1960 Opel Karavan for the year! Wow!

On the 13th, I flew the McMillan's to Lagos to go on furlough. This flight continued on to Liberia with Bill Crouch.

West Africa Field Director Bill Crouch

We stopped in Ghana for a couple of days where I flew him, John Bergen, and Sam Goertz from Accra up to Kumasi for some meetings. On the 16th, we continued on to Monrovia where Mr. Crouch had more meetings with the ELWA missionaries. While we were gone, the Richins and Marg went over to look at the pharmacy house. The inside walls needed painting which they got busy and did while I was lolling away the time on the white sandy beaches of Liberia! Also the floors were quite bad, so Heber said that he would put down some new vinyl tile in the kitchen, the living room, and the bathroom while we were on our honeymoon! He said this would be their wedding present to us . . . wow . . . what more can I say!

We flew home from Liberia on the 21st and 22nd. We stayed overnight in Lagos. I dropped Bill Crouch at Oyi as he had to be at an education meeting at Titcombe College. The next day I took Mary Wyllie to Oyi and picked up Mr. Crouch, Pastor Gin, David Olatayo, and Howard Dowdell . . . stopped at Kagoro to pick up the Brooks child. The next day I flew back to Kagoro with Ken Kastner, and Pastor William for a meeting. Ended sitting there all day. As we took off in the late afternoon, the Harmatan was rather thick and I did an instrument approach into Jos.

On March 26th I flew a Mrs. Ferguson to Oshogbo. I ran into a big storm and tried to work my way around the North end, but it was a no go, so I went back and sat for awhile at Kaduna. It's unusual to have storms this early in the year. They brought out the mail for Jos. About an hour later we took off and were able to work our way down to Oshogbo. Then I flew back to Ilorin to pick up Jim Custer, Derrick Porter, and David Buremah. Amazing . . . it was a straight shot to Jos, and we even had a nice tailwind which got us there in 2:10 hours.

On the 27th I flew Larry and Shirley Fehl and two kids to Ilorin, and picked up Phyllis Crosbie. Again I ran into bad weather and had to stop at Kaduna for awhile.

The next day I flew Mr. and Mrs Henry Budd and two kids, plus Mrs. Butler and a new baby to Ilorin. Then I flew up to Kano where I did and instrument approach. Picked up Mrs. Kretchmer plus two kids, Dr. Oliver, and Pat Styran for Jos. There was a big storm covering the whole plateau, so I worked my way over to Bauchi to sit for a spell. We were definitely getting an early rainy season. We took off again and got into Jos just a few minutes before nightfall. It was a long day.

On March 30th I flew Jim Custer, Phyllis Crosbie, Charlie Frame, Derrick Porter, and David Buremah back to Ilorin with no passengers on the return. On April 1st I flew Mr. and Mrs. Beacham, and Mrs. Beacham plus two kids (my logbook does not list their first names) to Kano. Picked up Mrs. Wickstrom, Jillian Reynolds, and Mrs. Driediger plus two kids for Jos. On the 2nd and 3rd I had a long flight to Upper Volta with Mr. and Mrs. Lochstampfor plus two kids, and one baby. Stayed overnight at Fada. Took off early the next morning with Eleanor Beckett, and flew up to Mahadaga to pick up Florene Guess, and I picked up Bill Crouch at Kano for Jos.

Had a couple days of rest. On the 6th I picked up Dr. Oliver at Kaduna and flew him to Minna to check the leprosy work in the area. On the 8th I flew to Keffi to pick up Ernie Maxwell. On the 10th I flew Marg Cook to Kagoro, picked up Brooks and flew her to Oyi. Flew down to Lagos and picked up Laura Best and flew her to Ilorin where I picked up Vern Hurlburt, and Mr. and Mrs. Ernie Harrison for Jos. The next day I flew to Ilorin to pick up Laura Best for Jos and Henry Budd for Kagoro. Flew over to Oyi and picked up Brooks for Kagoro, and picked up Howard Dowdell and Marg Cook for Jos.

On the 13th I flew Derrick Porter and Ernie Harrison to Ilorin and Allen Moore to Lagos. I stopped at Ibadan on the way down to pick up Phyllis Crosbie for Jos, and decided to sit for a spell as the low clouds and fog were right down into the trees. We finally were able to hedgehop into Lagos where I picked up Mr. and Mrs. Ira McKie plus two babies for Jos. Getting home to Jos was no trouble.

On the 16th I had two flights. First to fly Mr. and Mrs. Hay, and Mrs. Hershelman to Kaltungo. And then the Aztec to Kano with Mrs. Kretchmer plus two kids, and Dorothy Kalloch. Picked up Mr. and Mrs. Christianson, Agnes and Margaret Hall for Jos.

On April 17th I flew Phyllis Crosbie to Ilorin and picked up David Buremah and Mr. and Mrs. Giesbreckt for Jos. No storms today and made the flight in 3:55 hours by flying down high and coming back low to catch a good tailwind going both ways.

Rich Schaffer

On the 19th I flew Paul Rogalsky, Bill Tuck, and Dave Rutt to Kano to welcome our new aviation couple, Leroy and Charlotte Andrews to Nigeria. It will be nice to have another pilot join our ranks.

On the 20th I flew to Biu to pick up Dean Gilliland, Mrs. Weekly, and Mrs. Welch and fly them to Bambur. There's a soft muddy area right in the middle of the runway, so the trick is to land and takeoff in the first third of the runway . . . no small feat with a Comanche.

I didn't fly again until the 29th when I had a flight to Niger. Flew Loyd Wickstrom, Mary Wyllie, and Mrs. Tewes and child to Kano. Flew Helen Peters and Della Watson to Maradi. Picked up Rita Salls and Esther Grant in Maradi, and M. Schneider at Kano. They were having a good rainy season this year, so it was nice to see all the green beginning to show up in Niger.

On the last day of April 1963 I flew to Ilorin with Greta Jackson, Pat Irwin, and Annie Van Den Brand, and picked up Mary Sauer and Reeser for Jos. This was my last flight as it was time to get ready for the big day in our lives . . . May 4th, 1963 . . . our wedding day!

244

CHAPTER 29
THE WEDDING

The church was packed and the music was playing and playing, but no bride appeared! Mr. Nicholson was to use Mr. Crouch's car to bring Marg to the chapel when she was ready, but he could not find where Bill had parked his car! Mr. Crouch thought Marg was still living in her apartment and thus left the car there. But Marg had already moved over to the pharmacy house. Jack had walked over to the pharmacy house which is a fair walk . . . no car!

Meanwhile at the chapel, John Barr, the organist got a signal and began to play the wedding march, but instead Bob Shell stomped down the isle with all his camera gear . . . he was to take pictures during the wedding. A titter of laughter broke out from the audience. Where was the bride? I was tempted to wave the 'red socks' in the air to show I hadn't gotten cold feet. To fill in the time, Dean Gilliland decided to sing a couple songs. Anyway, Mr. Nicholson finally found the car and drove over and picked up Marg and drove her to the chapel.

Marg and her three flower girls

The wedding march began again. The three flower girls scattered petals down the isle, followed by the maid of honor and the bridesmaid, followed by Marg in all her glory.

Wow! . . . Did she ever look beautiful. It was the first time I saw her in the wedding dress. To me she looked like an angel . . . and to think that this beautiful girl loved me and wanted to be my wife . . . and what a joy she has been to me down through the forty years we have been married. The Lord is so good . . . what more can I say?

And the wedding? We said our vows. We gave the rings. The pastor pronounced us man and wife. More songs were sung.

Suddenly it is legal for us to love each other like we have never loved before. It's amazing.

Saying our memorized vows to each other, Bill Crouch officiating

After we shook hands with all the guests, we went over to Bingham and visited all the people in the hospital. Then we went to the reception. When Bill Tuck read the telegrams and the radio messages, he also read a poem written by Willie McGill whom we had just visited in the Bingham . . . it brought tears to everyone's eyes.

Lofty Grimshaw read another poem he wrote which wished us well in our new life. In my response to Ken Kastner's toast to my wife, I also singled out Lofty by presenting him with the 'red socks' so he wouldn't get cold feet when his big day came! It brought the house down.

Speaking at the reception

One of the guys brought the Opel Kadett for our get away. As we took off about six or seven cars followed us all over town tooting their horns. I headed out toward the airport and down past the road to Miango where the others finally gave up. When I was sure that no one else was following, I turned east when we got to Bukuru and took the tiny backroads that led to the Jos reservoir and out to the road that would take us to Rigin Gani where we would spend our first night in Mary Haas's guest house. Everyone had thought we were going to Kwoi and on to Okene for our honeymoon. And no one bothered us on our first wedding night like some jokesters did to another couple in years past. As usual Mary was a superb hostess with a light dinner. We retired early and had a fantastic night.

After a scrumptious breakfast we went back to Jos to pick up Anna Lou who had no way to get back to Kwoi. These are her words in a recent email . . . "Yes, I traveled with you from Jos to Kwoi! I got a ride to attend the wedding, but had no way back to Kwoi. You stopped on your way back from Ringi and picked me up. I felt very foolish to go on your honeymoon trip, but I had to get back to teach. You two both made me feel so good about it. You stopped in the jungle just before we got to Kagoro and had a beautiful lunch. I don't know if Marg packed it (Mary Haas did) but it was very special. We found a big flat rock beside the road, spread out a blanket and we three ate your lunch. Thanks for being so kind . . . how long ago was that?"

We spent the night at Kwoi. No one soaped up the windows, but they did wire some tin cans under the car. We drove across the canyon and stopped on the opposite hillside where I shinnied under the car and got rid of the cans . . . gave them to a happy national who was passing by.

We had a three hour wait when we got to the ferry to cross the Niger River.

The ferry crossing at Lakoja

Then we drove on down through Lakoja and on to Okene, getting there early that evening where the Toberts graciously served us a nice supper. We spent the night with them and then they took us down to the John Holt Rest House which would be our honeymoon cottage for the next ten days.

Our honeymoon cottage

The Toberts sorta apologized for the shabbiness of the place. The Rest House was an interesting cottage with thick whitewashed mud walls and a grass roof which made it nice and cool. A string of small lights mounted up near the roof, circled the entire room. Electricity was supplied by a diesel generator. When I started the generator, to our surprise, the lights flickered so bad that it was like being in a disco dance hall . . . the loud thump of the generator supplied the music. We decided to forget all this and just use candles during the evening.

The furnishings were rather sparse and primitive. I lit the kerosene fridge and filled the ice trays with filtered water. The big lumpy bed was covered by a huge mosquito net which draped clear down to the floor. We thoughtfully brought a bit of foodstuff and a kerosene stove with us, and we were able to buy a few things in the small canteens. What the heck . . . we were so in love, and we were on our honeymoon . . . we didn't even notice what a dump this place was!

After we settled in, we drove down to the water reservoir where we spread a quilt on the grass and relaxed in the warm sun. Marg was content as she started working on her wedding book and writing thank you notes.

I put a small hook with a worm on my line and cast it out near the bank where I saw some small Tilapia. I caught several of them about two or three inches long and put them in a bucket of water to keep them alive. Then I put on a bobber and gently hooked a Tilapia behind the dorsal fin onto a big hook so he could swim around. I tossed him out where I had seen a big swirl in the water.

Fishing in Okene reservoir

I didn't have to wait long when the Tilapia began frantically swimming this way and that. Suddenly the bobber disappeared. When the line tightened, I set the hook. The pole doubled over and I was firmly hooked into a big fish. The line sizzled off my reel as he headed for the deep. Suddenly the fish jumped clear of the water violently trying to shake the hook. I lowered the tip of my rod to put slack in the line and the fish stayed on. He made another sizzling run bulldogging in the depths trying to wrap my line around some hidden obstacle. I began trying to retrieve some of the line but he was stubborn and wouldn't budge an inch. Out of the water he came again and again. Each time I countered by lowering my tip. Wow! He dove for the deep. Patiently I gained some line as the fish began to tire. When I worked him up near the bank, he saw me and made another frantic run, but he was done. I got him headed into the bank and slid him onto the grass where I pounced on him just as the hook came free!

My prize was a beautiful Nile Perch about sixteen inches long weighing maybe three to four pounds. His orange eyes glowed like fiery hunks of burning coal.

Nile Perch at Okene Reservoir

I put the fish on a heavy line and put him back into the water to keep him alive until we were ready to go, for he would be our supper tonight. The way this fish fought, I can't imagine what it would be like trying to bring in one weighing a hundred and four pounds on my small trout pole and eight pound test line.

I went back to the quilt and lay down next to Marg. She looked down at me and laughed, "Told you this would be a good place for a honeymoon!" I nodded my head in agreement. We just lay there and relaxed and talked. It was indeed good to be away from the flying and away from Bingham.

We went for a walk along the shoreline. When we rounded a point we came upon a small jon-boat that was full of water and completely submerged. I found a long branch from a Eucalyptus tree with which I was able snag the bow and pull the boat ashore. I ran back and got the bucket so I could bail out the water. "Wow! . . . wonder who it belongs to!" There was no rope on the boat, so it was obvious that it had been adrift until it filled with rainwater and had been here for a long time.

I cleaned the fish and we went back to our humble abode. That evening we had crisp fried potatoes al la Nile Perch, and a can of green beans slathered with dressing, with slices of homegrown tomatoes and carrot sticks. We drowned all this with steaming hot cups of coffee. Man, it was good!

The next morning we went down to the market and bought a couple boards of white wood, and went back to the reservoir where we sat on the quilt. Marg continued on her wedding book. With a small hatchet I hacked away at the boards to make a couple of paddles for our boat. I caught a couple small Tilapia for live bait and then we paddled out near a small island. I cast out the live bait and handed the pole to Marg. Then I slowly paddled the jon-boat along the shoreline.

Suddenly the bobber disappeared and Marg was hooked into a big fish as the rod tip bent right down to the water.

Fishing with Marg at Okene

She screamed, "Here . . . you take it!"

I laughed, "No way . . . it's your fish . . . hang on to the pole!"

The line was screaming off the reel as it headed for the middle of the lake as I started paddling after it. The power of this monster was awesome as he was literally towing us along in the jon-boat when the line was completely gone from the reel. Thankfully the line parted near the fish and we got most of the it back.

We paddled back to the island and went ashore. There was a couple big Eucalyptus trees and we spread the quilt in its shade to relax and talk. What a beautiful place. The lake was like a mirror which reflected the trees of the shoreline. White puffy clouds floated in a deep blue sky. We called it Paradise Island. But I forgot it all as I looked at this beautiful girl by my side. I loved her so much that I even forgot about the fishing.

My buddies who know me now can't imagine such a thing, for I do love to fish.

But we still had fish left over in the fridge so there was no need to catch another. We only caught what we needed plus a couple we gave the Toberts when they invited us up for a meal.

On our honeymoon at Okene

Time doesn't stand still forever and we had to drive back home and go back to work.

I moved my stuff over to the pharmacy house. Of our household goods where we had double, we either sold or gave away to other missionaries or to the nationals. Heber indeed did a beautiful job in laying the tile. We had them over for a meal in thanks and appreciation.

I began flying again on 22 May 63 with a flight to Kagoro and back.

At Kagoro Airstrip

Marg going to work at Evangel Hospital

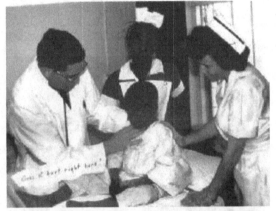

Dr. Lonnie Grant & Marg checking a sick boy

Getting ready to go

Lord, we pray for safety for this flight

On a flight to Oyi

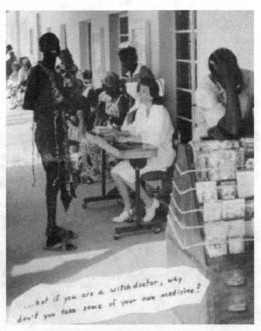

If you're a witchdoctor, why don't you try some of your own medicine?

Some little village somewhere

VFR above the clouds

Herds of elephant in Bauchi game reserve

Wikki Warm Springs in the game reserve

Marg loved to go visiting in the bush villages

Marg at the Jos Police Barracks Sunday School

Ken Kastner & Bill Grebinger with 3 National Pastorts

Ken's 27 lb. Nile Perch at Katsina Allah

Send-off party for Helen Griffin at Gure for 43 years

Jerry Swank on Jos-Zaria road120 miles, 50 minutes by air All day by road

Niger River in rainy-season flood—20 miles wide

CHAPTER 30
WE HAVE VISITORS

Here we go . . . back in the saddle again. Of the 38 flights that I made between May 22nd and July 10th, four of them were to French country. How many French country flights the other pilots made during that time I don't know. But early in the morning as we were getting ready to go, a military car bearing the Nigerian flag and three jeeps pulled up to the hangar. The soldiers jumped out with their rifles at the ready, began a systematic search of the entire hangar, as we stood there with our mouths open.

An officer appeared from the car and stiffly marched into our office and demanded, "Who's in charge here?"

Paul Rogalsky answered, "Can I help you sir."

"Call your men into the office!"

Paul went to the door, "Hey guys, come here!"

When we all gathered in the office, Paul again said, "And how can we help you, sir?"

The officer glared at us, "We are here to put a stop to your illegal flights across the border and your smuggling arms into the country!"

Without hesitation and with firmness, "Sir, we do NOT make illegal flights across the border, and we are NOT smuggling arms into your country! . . . If you care to examine the aircraft journey logs and our pilot's log books, and compare them to the General Declaration forms that we turn into Immigration, Customs, and Health each time we check in and out of the country at Kano or Lagos, you will see every one of our flights are proper and legal!"

He was rather taken aback with Paul's declaration, "Okay, let's see all your ship's papers, your pilot logs, and the declaration forms!"

Paul went to the file cabinet and pulled out a fistful of the most recent forms. He picked up the top set of papers and explained it to the officer, "This is the last flight we made out of the country. It was made on July 3rd, 1963, by Captain Schaffer in one of our Comanche's 5N-ACE."

With that he went over to the cabinet and pulled out the journey logbook for CE and found the entry I had made for that flight. I gave Paul my logbook and pointed to the entry I made on July 3rd. "You see here Mr. Schaffer's entries for this flight that day? . . . It shows he flew our workers (Beeba Speering, and Mrs. Tewes + 1 baby) to Kano, and then to check out of Kano for the flight to Parakou, Dahomey. There he picked up Mr. and Mrs.

Ed Morrow and flew them to Kano, where they checked into Nigeria and went through Immigration, Customs, and Health. If you will check at those offices at the Kano airport, you will find at each office a sealed set of papers just like these you see here. And if you checked at Parakou you would see the papers that we gave them each time we check in and out of that country.

The officer looked rather befuddled, so Paul patiently started all over pointing at each notation in my pilot log and explained what it meant . . . "3 July is the date this flight was made . . . 5N-ACE is the license number of the airplane . . . Comanche is the kind of airplane it is . . . Lyc 180 is the kind of engine and its horsepower . . . Jos-Kano-Parakou-Kano-Jos is where the airplane went . . . 7:25 is the number of hours the flight took . . . 3312:30 is the total number of hours that Captain Schaffer has flown when this flight was completed . . . XC stands for cross-country flight . . . B Speering, Mrs. Tewes + 1 baby, J-K, is the passengers that he flew from Jos to Kano . . . 1 + 2 E. Morrow stands for Mr. and Mrs. Morrow, P-K, is the passengers that he flew from Parakou to Kano."

The guy nodded his head like he was starting to catch on.

Then Paul went to the General Declaration forms showing him how each of the offices stamped and dated our copy verifying that we had indeed been cleared by each of these offices, giving us the clearance to make this flight.

The officer made a broad sweep with his hand, "We will take all these declarations for the flights you have made during the past year . . . and all the aircraft logs, and all your pilot's logs!"

Paul protested, "But sir, we need these books so we can accurately keep our records up to date . . . it's the law!"

"I am the law here! . . . and we will take what we want!"

And with that declaration, the military confiscated everything they wanted, but assured us that everything would be returned when their investigation was completed.

So from July 10th, 1963 until nearly a year later to June 13th, 1964 we kept the records of our flights in spiral notebooks. And all during that time I stupidly did not record the passengers I flew! I am sorry . . . I only listed the passengers on the passenger slips that we turned into the bookkeeper to do the billing.

But they did return everything just as they promised! And with them a letter, complimenting us for the accuracy of our records, and admitting they were fully satisfied with the integrity of our flight operation!

CHAPTER 31
A Flight to French Country

Paul called into town and told Bill Crouch what had just taken place.

"Did they ground us?", Mr. Crouch asked.

"No, they didn't."

"Well, let's go on with the flying until they do!"

"Okay . . . that's what we'll do." And so Paul gave us the word to get moving.

I called the radio room, "Heber . . . would you give Diapaga a new ETA of about 1300 on the noon broadcast . . . we're running late.. tell'em I'll buzz the station when we get there."

"Okay Rich . . . you have a good flight."

My flight was to Upper Volta (now called Burkina Faso) so I continued my pre-flight on the Aztec, grabbed my stuff, loaded in the passengers, and took off in a hurry. ETA's are given on SIMRAD on the early morning broadcast to all our arrival points and there are a lot of unhappy campers when we don't get there when we say we would.

When I had radio contact with Kano, "Kano . . . will you please phone SIM and give them my new ETA of 1040."

"Roger, Charlie Foxtrot . . . will do!"

"Thank you, sir!"

When I arrived at 1040, George Rendel was waiting for me with some stuff for Upper Volta. "What happened to you? . . . You know we got other things to do besides catering to you guys . . . I have to . . . ."

"Sorry, George." and I told him what had happened.

"Wow . . . that doesn't sound too good!"

Shell refueled the Aztec, then I went up and filed my flight plan and got a weather report, and took my passengers through Immigration, Customs, and Health, leaving a set of papers at each office. And they stamped my set of papers clearing us to leave the country. No problems.

I took off and climbed up to flight level 10.5 where we would have a good tailwind and set a course that would take us to Sokoto where I could home in on their radio beacon, and then track outbound to Diapaga.

I flew low over the station and then back to the airstrip to land. The flight took two hours and fifteen minutes. I gave the airport officer two sets of papers, and that was all that was necessary to check into and out of the country. He wasn't even interested in checking my baggage.

The missionaries there weren't too perturbed about our late arrival. For some people out in the bush, time doesn't seem to matter all that much . . . they were just glad to see us . . . they were glad to see anybody! I unloaded some mail and medicines for them, and took on the mail they had for Fada and Nigeria.

We talked for awhile and they were quite interested in my account about the unexpected visit by the military to our hangar. Any news from the outside was welcome to these people, so it was good not to rush off too fast. But they did listen to all the traffic on SIMRAD and that helped them keep up with the swing of things.

We finally took off for Fada where I would stay overnight. Bill Strong came out to the airstrip to pick up me and the passengers (sorry I didn't record their names in my spiral notebook). Eleanor Strong fed me a good supper and I visited with them for quite awhile. Then I went over and visited Eleanor Beckett (Gladys Tuck's older sister) as Gladys would always grill me when I got home as to her sister's welfare. (People in Jos were always asking me about their friends who were working out in the bush.) Eleanor and the Strongs were translating the Bible into the Gourma language. Al Swanson came up from the Bible School with their mail for Nigeria and it was good to see him again.

I took off for home, stopping at Birnin Konni, and then checking into Nigeria at Kano. It was always good to get home, especially now that I was married to the most beautiful girl in the world . . . I really had someone to come home to. And over the years I found that she was a wonderful pilot's wife, for she never worried about me, no matter how much danger I may have gone through that day. She just sort of accepted it that this was part of my job. That had a calming effect on me . . . yeah, it was just part of the job.

Marg bartering for vegetables   *Marg and her motor bike*

Shortly after we were married, Marg became pregnant. But one day when she was coming home from visiting on her motor bike, she hit a rut in the trail and took a hard spill. A couple days later she began bleeding and lost the baby. That was a hard thing. I sold the motor bike and began looking around for a car to buy.

I finally found a 1962 VW Beetle. It was a pile of junk that I bought for 200 pounds (about 560 dollars) from the VW dealer. (They overhauled the broken transmission and welded up all the cracks in the fenders.) I eventually overhauled the engine and repainted the car.

The Lord blessed us and Marg became pregnant again in September, and about that same time we were also blessed with a beautiful sixteen year old daughter!

Sharilyn Taves

Abe and Helma Taves, working in the country of Chad, were trying to get their daughter, Sharilyn, into Hillcrest School for her sophomore year, but there was no more room in the dorm. It was the same in our hostel and everywhere they tried. When we heard of their plight, we offered to have Sharilyn stay with us. That was quite a thing to do for a new married couple, but she was a joy to have in our home and it worked out okay.

On May 30th, 1965, after a hard delivery, little Mark Lee Schaffer was born.

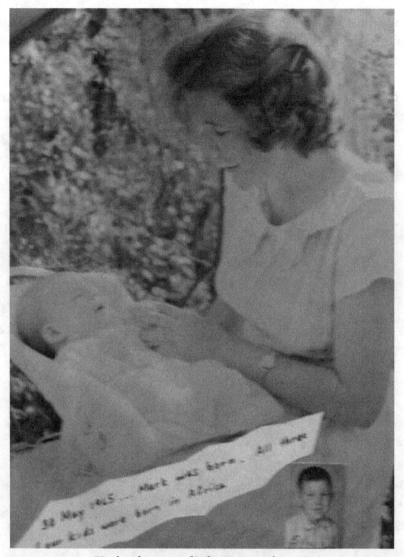

You're the cutest little guy, aren't you?
Our son Mark, and my favorite picture of Marg

Three weeks later we left on furlough. I had accumulated 4309:25 hours . . . 467:10 was multi-engine.

CHAPTER 32
YET ANOTHER FURLOUGH

Going on furlough—Mark just 3 weeks old.

What do I remember on this furlough? I remember that New York was having a heat wave . . . like 105 and high humidity, and not a breath of air. Little Mark broke out with a miserable heat rash and he let us know that he was very uncomfortable. His crying went on for hours no matter what we tried, until I gave him a little swat on the behind . . . wow! . . . he really cut loose then. But lo and behold, he fell into an exhausted peaceful sleep in a couple of minutes and we were so happy to join him.

As it became my custom, I went over to New Jersey and bought a car. This time it was a black 1959 Ford Thunderbird. Got a good car for a thousand dollars.

Our 1959 Ford Thunderbird

I remember driving down to North Carolina to visit the Ogburns. Lanny and Merlene were very pleased to meet my wonderful Marg and our wee baby Mark. We rested up there for a couple of days. I remember Merlene taking Marg to a beauty parlor to have her hair done in the latest fashion. Wow! What a spiffy babe!

My gal all dolled up with a spiffy hair do

Then we began our long journey up to Canada, first to Simcoe, Ontario to visit Marg's doctor brother, Dale and Barb Shepherd and their little Mark. Dale was into playing tennis, and boy, we played tennis . . . three-four sets at a time as he was determined to wear me down and beat me.

We swung down to Michigan to visit Jerry and Rita Gilbert, and then over to the Chicago area where we visited Moody, and stayed with the Burnetts. Again I had the opportunity to give a ringing challenge to the guys at Moody Airport and to the dear people at Wheaton First Baptist Church.

We visited the two country churches in northwestern Illinois where the good people smothered us with their enthusiastic love and good country cooking. And some more of them took on some of our support.

Dick and Sharon Sissel, and also Husky and Evelyn Noll had moved to Iowa, so they were right on our path to Marg's home.

So were my relatives in South Dakota . . . little did I realize what the rewards would be in the future from our short visits with these good people. For uncle Bill Schmoll, all down through the years, when he bought a savings bond, he would put some kid's name on it as a beneficiary . . . and this included our three! And Uncle Clifford Schweitzer did the same! So kids . . . pay attention to your relatives!

Then we headed up to visit Ken and Merle Moore, Vernon and Margaret Moore, the Ranum's, the Veysey's, and Mrs. Lenore Erickson . . . all friends from the Maryfield Camp days.

Marg tried to prepare me for the roads in Canada. It had rained a bit and when we tried to use a country road that didn't have enough gravel, our low slung T-Bird sank right up to the frame. That was my quick introduction to the black prairie gumbo of Saskatchewan. It took a friendly farmer to pull us out with his tractor.

We visited Marg's twin brothers in Saskatoon and then we headed to Marg's home in North Battleford where I finally met her wonderful Godly parents, and over the days, a host of other relatives. Jim and Gladys Shepherd had adopted four Indian kids. Their little house was full, so we lived out at the cottage at Murray Lake. The lake is about a mile wide and six miles long just full of Northern Pike and Walleye.

The twins had a beautiful fourteen foot boat with a 65 horsepower motor and they checked me out on how to operate it. I bought some fishing gear and had no trouble catching four to six fish in a couple hours every time I went out. Everything under 20 inches I released. When you learn how to pick out all the fine bones on these fish, they are quite good to eat.

Fishing at Murray Lake

During our six weeks stay, we were constantly invited out by various supporters, friends, and relatives where we had the opportunity to talk about our work in Nigeria.

One night we showed our slides in the evening service at Aunt Ellie's church. As I was gathering up my projector and slides, this guy came up and invited us to their home for pie and ice cream. Man, we were dead tired . . . it had been a long day . . . and they lived clear across the river in Battleford! But I said okay and we went.

While we were eating and having good conversation, Earl said, "I've got a good story to tell you folks!"

"What's that?"

"Well, we have some of the Lord's money that we need to give to Missions. But we didn't know who we should give it to, so we decided to put out the fleece . . . we said, 'the missionaries who accepted our invitation to come over for pie and ice cream would get the support!' Over the months we invited several missionaries to our house, and all of them made up one excuse after another why they could not come. But you came and YOU will get the support!"

"WOW! . . . that indeed is a good story!"

So Earl and Jean became another pair of our faithful supporters all through the remaining years of our missionary career. And when we came home and settled down in the work-a-day world, they became some of our good friends . . . Earl became my best email buddy. When I write a chapter of this book, he is the first one I send it to for his critique.

Jean passed away not long ago, and Earl is up in years now . . . his eyes are going bad because of macular degeneration, so it's hard for him to use the computer, but one or two times a week I'll get a good story from this wise old man, or maybe a poem that he has written. Not long ago he had a couple of bad falls, so we pray for him often, as he does for us.

As this is a 'how to' book, let me talk to you missionaries for awhile. Most of you are low on support, right? Maybe back there somewhere you turned down that invitation for pie and ice cream in the middle of the night? Maybe over the years, you just sorta took some of your supporters for granted? Maybe you don't even visit them when you come home? We'll skip 'em this time, you say. After all you're tired from all your hard work on the mission field. Yah, sure . . . I hear you. In fact you are so doggone busy, you hardly ever send out a prayer letter any more. And you are wondering why you are low on support? Good grief! I could make this a long sermon, but I'll spare the other folks who are reading this book.

One Sunday we were supposed to visit the Kelly's in Dodsland. It had rained hard during the night. As we were leaving the lake, I eased over to make room for an on-coming car and our black bomber sank right up to the bottom of the car! When I stepped out of the car my leg went half way to the knee in the black gumbo. No way were we going to get unstuck without some help. Marg and little Mark stayed put in the car while I walked back to the point. I finally found the maintenance man who had a tractor. Even with the tractor it was a hard, dirty job pulling the car from the mud. The car and I were so dirty that we gave up on the trip. I just waded into the lake to scrub off most of the mud from myself. Then I found a garden hose and washed the car, my shoes, and myself in that order. Later on we learned that if we had tried to get to the Kelly's, we would have never made it, as their roads were mucky mud going into their farm.

After about a six weeks stay, it was time to move on . . . heading west to visit Marg's sister, Sylvia and Bill Arnold who were living in the lumber camp at Crescent Spur, British Columbia. We also visited a number of Marg's supporters along the way.

Uncle Bill took a couple days off, and a helicopter took us up into the high hill country and dropped us off to hunt for caribou. This was my first ride in a chopper and for a fixed wing pilot that is quite an experience.

We set up our camp and about noon we hiked up a thousand feet to the top of a ridge. We sat there munching on our sandwiches. The sky was clear and it was a beautiful warm sunny day. A lone caribou stepped out from a grove of trees and started walking directly toward us. We froze. Suddenly he whirled around and trotted back into the trees. Evidently he spotted us or smelled us.

Bill whispered, "I'll circle around and try to intercept him as he comes out on the other side of those trees down there . . . you get yourself in a good position in case he comes back up the ridge!"

With that Bill dropped a little over the opposite side of the ridge to head for his vantage point. When I figured Bill was in position, I walked openly along the top of the ridge making a bunch of noise to drive the animal down towards Bill. Then I hid in a couple of trees in case the caribou came back up my way. About five minutes later a lone shot echoed among the hills . . . Bill stepped out and waved his hat for me to come on down. When I got there, he was busily bleeding the animal out. His shot had broken the caribou's neck right behind the head.

"That's a nice lookin' animal . . . how about a picture?"

So Bill held up the head and put his rifle across the antlers and I took several shots with my camera. Then he began dressing out the caribou, cutting it into quarters. He hung the rear quarters high in a tree to prevent the bears from getting them, and we lugged part of the meat back to camp. That was quite a chore . . . even though we were about parallel to our camp, it was a long hard hike along the side of the steep canyon wall with no trail to follow. By the time we got there, I was plumb tuckered out, not used to all this rugged activity.

The caribou that Bill shot

Roasting caribou meat over the fire

Bill cut off several choice pieces of meat for our supper, and then he went off about a hundred yards and tied the rest up in a tree. "Rich, you stay in camp . . . gather up a lot of dry wood for our fire . . . looks like weather's moving in . . . see if you can tie up this tarp. I'll take the pack-board and get another load of meat." And off he went.

I found several dead snags of Birch and easily gathered a huge pile of wood. I gathered a few poles to make a framework for the small tarp. At least we could get out of the rain a bit. I dug a fire pit and lined it with large rocks and built a small fire . . . rolled up a log so we could sit near the fire. Clouds blotted out the sun and it began to drizzle slightly. The helicopter was supposed to pick us up the next day. Bill finally got back and flopped under the tarp . . . completely bushed . . . on his pack was one of the huge hind quarters of meat.

I had skewered a couple chunks of meat on a stick and was roasting them over the fire. "Here . . . try one of these." I held the stick out toward him.

He stuck a piece with his knife and slid it off the stick. "Mmm . . . this is good . . . I hereby appoint you the chief cook of this wilderness adventure!"

I chewed off a piece and had to agree . . . "Yeah . . . this is good!" This was my first taste of caribou.

"Why don't you toss a couple of potatoes in the fire, and I'll go hang this meat in a tree somewhere."

"Okay, but take yer time . . . supper will be at six thirty."

I dug around in our supplies and found some potatoes, carrots and onions which I cut up into big chunks and laid the pieces onto a couple sheets of aluminum foil. I also added some chunks of caribou, a slab of butter, and seasoned the whole affair with salt and pepper. Then I formed the foil into sealed pouches and laid them in the coals of the fire. I also put some more chunks of meat on the stick to roast while a couple of gray Mountain Jays sat in a nearby bush begging for a handout just like our seagulls here on the coast. I filled a kettle at a spring and hung that over the fire.

Bill came back and sat down and held his hands to the fire. Clouds covered the ridge and the tops of the surrounding hills. Fog was forming down in the valleys. As we surveyed the scene, Bill commented, "If it stays like this, that chopper won't be picking us up tomorrow." The drizzle turned into a light rain.

A bit later I dug one of the pouches out of the fire and put it on a plate and opened the pouch so it formed a bowl. "Mmm . . . this is good . . . I hereby declare that supper is ready!"

Bill dug out the other pouch and opened it, "I say . . . this looks worthy of a prayer!" And with that we bowed our heads and thanked the Lord for this good bounty.

The water had come to a boil, so I poured some into our cups for a scalding drink of coffee. As it got dark we sat around the fire and chewed on hunks of meat, trading wild tales into the night. Finally we crawled into the tent and into our bags. I went to sleep like turning off a switch.

When I awoke in the morning, Bill was already up and had the fire going and the water boiling. It was rather cool so the fire felt good. We were really socked in with the clouds all around . . . we couldn't see more than a hundred feet. So we just bided our time sitting around the fire. For sure, that helicopter would not be coming for us today. Bill cooked up some eggs and bacon. He made some dough which he formed around the end of some sticks and stuck them over the fire which he rotated like cooking a hotdog. When they were done, he slipped one off a stick, stuck some butter into the hole, and handed it to me, "Here . . . try this!"

I took a bite. It tasted good. "That's quite an idea . . . I'll have to remember this one from now on when I go camping."

"They really taste good if you also put some jelly in the hole."

"What are you thinking about today?"

"Well, we need to go over and get that other quarter of meat. By then we should have a good idea if this weather will break. These guys fly in some pretty bad stuff at times, so we'll need to break camp in a hurry if he does show up."

So after breakfast Bill grabbed the packboard. "You better bring the rifle in case we bump into a bear or something."

We had a slogging good time hiking through the wet brush. Nothing had bothered our meat but you could see where something had been feeding on the entrails. "Hmm . . . looks like a coyote." Bill pointed at a couple of tracks.

I looked at the beautiful hide. "What about this hide? Have you ever tanned any?"

"Oh some . . . why don't you bring it along? . . . you could make a nice rug out of it"

So I rolled up the hide and put it in a garbage bag and carried it back to camp. We built up the fire again and sat around it to dry out.

Mountain jay stealing our caribou

Drying out around the fire

I spent a couple of hours cleaning up the hide, removing any fat or meat from the inside of the skin.

About three o'clock the weather cleared up a bit, and here came the chopper climbing up from the valley below. I doused the fire and Bill began dropping the tent. I took down the tarp and the tent. The chopper landed in a small clearing. Bill ran over to get the meat while I picked up stuff and carried it over to the helicopter. The pilot tied the meat and tent to the skids. We took off and slid right down the canyon wall to the valley floor. The weather was closing in again.

Then I remembered. "Oh nuts!", I groaned.

Bill looked back at me. "What's the matter?"

"I left the hide . . . I left the hide under the tree!"

Needless to say, with the heavy load we already had, we were not about to go back. I also noted that this was a smaller chopper than the one that took us up into the mountains. We found out why as we landed back at Crescent Spur. There was the other chopper sorta lying on its side. The canopy was cracked and the rotors were broken off. The pilot had been taking work-crews up into the hills to build heliport platforms where a chopper could drop off firemen when there was a fire in that area. As he was returning to land suddenly something broke and the chopper fell about fifty feet and landed very hard. It was learned later the pilot's back was broken in that accident, yet, he came back to pick us up. Wow!

The helicopter that brought us off the mountain

We visited some of Marg's supporters in Burnaby, Max and Gay Munday. Gay was one of the little girl campers at Maryfield when Marg was the nurse/counselor one summer while she was going to Briercrest.

Then we went on to Tacoma to visit Denny and Dianna Huffman. That year Boeing was hiring some 85,000 workers, gearing up for some big contract. (On a year's furlough, I tried to work part of the time so we could use the money to buy our next term's outfit, and hopefully to set aside a small nest egg.) I was hired and would be trained to be a template maker . . . starting pay $1.33 per hour.

Denny also put us in touch with Elmer and Anne Carlson who had a small house they wanted to rent to missionaries . . . fifty dollars a month! It was a nice two story fully furnished house just south of Boeing Field right on the Green River. As the Mission gave us a housing allowance of a hundred dollars, we gave them that. They could have easily rented it for twice that amount.

The house we rented from the Carlsons

Template school was fun. The work we did had to be accurate to 1/100th of an inch. In production, work had be to 3/100th of an inch. To locate a punch mark this accurate, we used a ten power magnifying glass.

One Friday night I was coming home in a deluge of rain . . . six lanes of traffic, and it was black outside. I was in the middle lane and needed to be in the inside lane, or I would soon be on my way to Tacoma on the freeway. It was hard to see out of the fogged up windows . . . the lights were blinding. When I tried to make my lane change, I hooked my front bumper in the rear part of the front wheel-well of a car that was driving with no lights on! I simply did not see him . . . the conditions were that bad. We slid over to the outside lane where I hit the rear end of an old station wagon. We tied up traffic big time . . . all three lanes! The three of us got out and bounced on the cars until we got them unhooked. And then the guy jumped into his car and took off yelling that he had a plane to catch! We stood there like a bunch of drowned rats.

All I did to the back end of the station wagon was bend his bumper a bit. He agreed to settle for fifty bucks and I gave him a check for that amount. One headlight, the grille, and the bumper on my Thunderbird were really messed up. So the next morning I looked at the car ads in the paper and found a couple of cheap cars for sale . . . I needed something to get me back and forth to school while my black bomber was being repaired.

I bought a 1957 Buick Century . . . a metallic copper and cream beauty with brand new tires for 360 bucks . . . it ran pretty good too. And it ran like a fine watch after I tuned it up. The Buick was a much better car than the Thunderbird, so I got rid of the T-Bird after it was repaired . . . and I sold it for what I'd paid for it! I was one happy camper.

Going to church in our 57 Buick Century

For our final in the template school, we were given a sketch of a template we were to make in a prescribed amount of time. Let me try to describe this for you . . . just try to follow me on this. On a piece of template material which is 3/32 inches thick with a black coating on both sides, you scribe out a 5 3/4 inch by 4 5/8 inch square.

Then you find the center and scribe a 2 1/8 inch circle and scribe a line down through the center. On the left side of that line, 7/8 inches away, you scribe another line parallel to it. On the right of the line, 3/8 inches away, you scribe the second parallel line.

Now up from the bottom of the square . . . on the left side, you scribe a line 15/16 inches parallel to the bottom, and another line 1 3/4 inches from the bottom. Then you scribe a vertical line 2 3/16 inches from the center line on the left side, and then another vertical line 2 inches from the center line on the left side. Then you scribe a line 1 3/4 inches parallel to the bottom on the left side which makes a little ear on that side.

Then to the right of the center line, you scribe a vertical line 1 7/16 inches. And then you scribe a line 5/8 inch parallel to the bottom on the right side. This completes the template drawing. Try to duplicate this on a piece of paper so you can really see it.

I handed this to the instructor for his examination. (I was the first to complete the layout on the material.) He checked it for square and exact size. He checked the exact position of the circle and its size. He checked all the vertical and parallel lines. He smiled and handed it back to me and said, "Okay . . . now cut out the square . . . and when you are finished, let me check it."

So I went over to the band saw and cut out the square from the material . . . then I carefully filed away the metal exactly down to the scribe lines. When I finished, I handed it back to the instructor.

He checked it for exact square and size. "Hey, you're doing alright . . . now I want you to cut away the circle and this bottom part . . . in other words, make this top part!"

I went back to the band saw and roughly cut out the circle and cut away the bottom part. Then with a half round file I carefully filed exactly down to the scribe line of the circle, and with a flat file, I filed down to the flat lines.

(I noticed some guys were handed another piece of material to do it over again, because they did not scribe the drawing within the 1/100th inch accuracy that was required in template making. Others had to do it over because when they cut out the square, it was not square, or the edges were tilted and not square.)

When I finished making the template I gave it to him for his inspection. He checked it very carefully. Instead of giving it back to me, he gave me another piece of material and said, "Do the layout again. And this time make the bottom part. When you are finished, it will have to fit exactly in the first template you made! And I will not be checking you step by step as you make it! If it fits like it should . . . you got a job here at Boeing!" WOW!

I took that second piece of material and again scribed out the drawing and made the second part.

And you know . . . when he took the second part and put it into the first part, it fit EXACTLY just like it should!

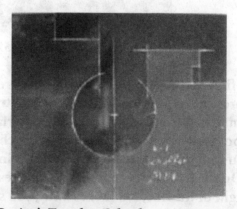

Test Project in Boeing's Template School

He held it up to the light and slowly shook his head, "This is the best work I have ever seen!" He held it up for everyone to see, "Hey look fellows . . . this is what you are supposed to be doing!"

Out of a class of sixteen . . . only three of us passed . . . and I did it faster! Cock-a-doodle Doooo!

Next Monday morning I started work in Renton at Building 2. It was a two story building about a half mile square. I was assigned to area 12. On each of the three shifts they had twelve of us guys. Our job was to make or repair or to modify templates that were being used in production. Another job was, if something was botched up on the production line, we were the guys who were sent to figure out how to fix it. Also, sometimes an Engineer would send a sketch of some tool that he designed . . . we were to make it and prove that it worked.

I was assigned to work with Zinzely who was to show me the ropes. I followed that guy all over that huge building . . . seems like we walked 20 miles a day. I came home at night absolutely pooped out. More often I followed him outside a dozen times a day so he could grab a smoke . . . man, what a waste of time this guy was.

One job we were given was to figure out why some of the mounting legs on the flap motor of the Boeing 727 were breaking. Suspect was that the spot-faces on the rear spar were not the same height . . . make a tool that can be mounted on the production aircraft to prove that this is the case . . . then figure out how to fix it!

We hung by our tails atop ten foot stepladders to figure out how to make and mount a tool that could accurately measure the depth of all four spot faces to an accuracy of a 1/1000th of an inch. Wow! Sometimes we found the difference in the depth of the spot-faces was as much as 1/10th of an inch! No wonder the legs were breaking!

We made aluminum washers of a different thickness and glued these, with a special glue, to the spot-faces so the end result was that all were exactly the same depth.

The rear spars were manufactured somewhere in the mid-west. So until the problem was corrected back there, Zinzely and I would have to go down to the production line, climb up on our ladders, mount our measuring tool, make the washers, and glue them to the spot-faces. We did this three times a week for about six weeks! That's how long it took the jokers back at the factory to get it right!

Another interesting job we had was to replace a damaged bearing for the rear spar bolt. This was a five inch diameter bearing that was pressed into the spar by a huge press at the supply factory. We would have to press a new bearing into the spar while it was in a horizontal position on a fully assembled wing. We carefully sawed the bearing in three places and removed the pieces. Then we froze the new bearing in a canister of liquid nitrogen to shrink it and pushed it easily into place with a press we jury-rigged from a couple of thick metal plates and some big C-clamps.

A certain top section of skin on the wing of the 727 was popping rivets and an engineer wrote an order for us to design a tool that you could set anywhere on the top of the wing panel to show that the curvature in the skin in that section was curved too much. His idea was that this pre-curved skin was curved too much in its manufacture . . . the rivets pulled the skin down to the ribs okay, but in flight, the undue pressure of too much curve and the flexing of the wing finally started popping the rivets as the plane was flying along. Not a good idea.

I was given this section of pre-curved skin which was about twenty feet long and tapered from about four feet at the butt end to three feet at the other end. So I made a tool to match the curve at the butt end. I also made a tool to match the curve of the rib where the butt end was fastened. They did not match and indeed showed that the skin was pre-curved too much.

When I set the tool on any other section of the skin, it did not match the curvature in that area. This was fairly obvious to me just by looking down the tapered skin. I showed my boss of Area 12 my findings, and he wrote a note to the engineer saying that we would have to make a tool for every section along the tapered skin section . . . how many tools did he want?

The engineer came down to Area 12 and scathingly read us the riot act, "You idiots . . . I want ONE tool!" He waved his finger in front of my boss's face, "One tool . . . see? . . . ONE tool, get it?"

We tried to show him how the tool worked at the butt end and would not work at any other section, but this guy just could not see it. He stomped off, "I want just ONE tool!"

We looked at each other and shrugged our shoulders. "Rich . . . make a couple of tools for the other end to see what that shows . . . then I'll go to his superior and see if we can get this joker off our backs!" So I made a tool to match the skin, and another tool to match the rib for that area. They were almost the same.

Then my boss had the superior engineer come down to see our findings. Eventually this skin panel was re-designed and there was no more popping rivets in that area. Hooray for our side!

One night I came home to find no one there. There was a note on the kitchen counter saying that Marg had taken Mark to the hospital. He had been having runny stools and a bit of fever. I went up there to find little Mark strapped down to the bed with an intravenous drip going into his arm. Six months old . . . Mark was one sick little guy. He looked up at me . . . his eyes said pathetically, "Daddy . . . help me!"

With blinding tears I shook my head as I touched him, "Marky . . . you hang on there . . . you are going to be alright!"

It took about three or four days for him to be alright . . . man, that was a tough one.

We were always getting work orders to repair a template. I would go down to the template storage area to check out the template in question. The templates were stored on their sides in racks. I gave the storage guy the number of the template and he went over to a certain rack and began pulling out the templates looking for the right one, sliding them out on their sides. The number for the templates are scribed somewhere in the center of the template, so he had to pull it out that far to see the number. When it wasn't the right one, he would slam it back into the rack and pull out another one.

Now some of the repairs to these templates was to repair damage done to the edges! I could easily see where this damage was taking place and the culprit who was doing it . . . sometimes he roughly slid ten templates back and forth until he found the right one.

I yelled at the guy, "Hey, take it easy! . . . you're gonna damage the templates handling them that way."

He glared at me, "You @*#gd idiot . . . what do you know about it? How in h#%l do you think I'm going to do it?"

I had to agree. It was no easy job. Some of those templates were over 4 X 8 feet in size. And sure enough, one of the repairs needed, was to repair the damage on the edge of the template! Over 1/100th of an inch was worn away from the edge.

I took the template back to Area 12. The way you repair edge damage is to place the damaged section on a heavy plate of steel and gently tap along that edge with a flat hammer which causes the aluminum to bulge out. Then you carefully file it back to it's original shape.

One day in the lunch room I noticed a suggestion box. Boeing would reward their employees for making suggestions that would save the company money or time or improve their product.

So I told them how the templates were being stored and how the edges of templates were being damaged in the storeroom by dragging them in and out of the racks.

Then I told them how this damage could be stopped and thereby save man hours to repair them or even replace them.

1. Put rugs on the concrete floor to provide a softer surface when the templates are moved in the racks.

2. Put the template number on the edges instead of in the center of the template. Then the storeroom clerk would not have to slide the templates in and out of the racks in his search for the right one.

Boeing adopted both suggestions and gave me a reward of $50.00! And Area 12 hardly ever had any more templates with damaged edges to repair! Yippee!

But we had to get our show on the road again. We needed to visit all our supporters and friends and relatives along the west coast, so I gave my superior my two weeks notice. We were due back in Nigeria in another three months.

"Rich, I'm really sorry to see you go, but I understand. If you ever need work, come back here again and you got yourself a job!"

"Thank you sir . . . this has been a fun job, and I really learned a lot!"

So I finished out the two weeks. I was surprised that in my final paycheck they had raised my pay to $2.78 per hour! Thank you!

We spent a couple weeks getting ready for the trip. We had become very good friends with the Carlson's, and when we let them know when we were going, they said they would take on some of our support! Also, Elmer said that he would sell our car for us so we wouldn't need to worry about that, and we could use it right up to the end.

We contacted our people to let them know when we were coming and how long we would be staying. When we heard from them, we worked out an itinerary that would take us down as far as LA and then back up to Seattle. Everywhere we went, we were warmly received by all.

When we got back home, we started accumulating things we would need for our next four years in Nigeria. I built 16 x 16 x 12 inch boxes out of 1/4 inch plywood as old trunks were becoming collector's items and cost too much. We received a departure date from the Mission, and we sent out a general letter to everyone on our mailing list letting them know we would soon be on our way. People responded and the support required by the Mission was fully met. We stored some household things with the Carlson's and they drove us to the SeaTac Airport to catch our plane to New York City. We were on our way! This indeed was a good furlough and we were again looking forward to our work for the Lord in Africa. Little did we realize how exciting the next term would be!

CHAPTER 33

THE CIVIL WAR AND . . .

We arrived back in Nigeria on July 9th, 1966. I was starting another term with 4309:25 hours under my belt. On the 11th and 12th, I went up in a Comanche to get myself back into flying mode. I was really rusty, but it all came back to me in short order. I noticed that soldiers were present at the terminal building.

We moved back into the same house on the Niger Creek compound and got our things out of storage to set up housekeeping. It was indeed good to be home again.

As I had sold the VW Beetle when we went home, we needed to have another car for Marg. Cars were scarce . . . however, an English couple who were going home had a little Morris Mini Minor they wanted to sell, but they needed to use it until their departure. So I plunked down the 270 pounds they wanted and then we waited for that happy day when it became ours. In the meantime, Marg rode to Evangel Hospital with Gladys Tuck who was working in x-ray. The married women had started up a little nursery where they could leave the children which allowed them to do their mission work. So each morning they would swing by the main compound to drop off little Mark and pick him up on the way home.

When we finally got the Mini, it proved to be the most fun car to drive that we have ever owned. With its little twelve inch wheels you rode about four inches off the ground. It's hard to believe, but one time Marg had four adults and nine kids in the car at one time! And off they went to the nursery.

One day Marg surprised me with the happy news that she was pregnant. And on April 7th, 1967, James Richard Schaffer was born after a long hard delivery. He was a good healthy baby and easy to take care of. Our little family was growing.

Marg and Mark with new baby Jim

In this chapter I am not going to stick to an exact time frame. I'll be jumping around a bit as I think of the things that took place during these exciting four years. I just shake my head as the memories of these days swirl in and out of my foggy brain. I need to capture them as they come to mind. It's almost like a fantastic dream.

Let me tell you about a rather interesting incident that happened on the 28th of November 1966. I had two flights to Kano that day. On the first flight I flew Mr. and Mrs. Schmidt and child to Kano and returned to Jos empty. On the next flight I had George Learned and a Mrs. Harris (I think from another mission) lying on a stretcher in the back.

When I was forty miles out I called, "Hello Kano tower . . . this is Five November Alfa Charlie Delta."

"Roger, Charlie Delta . . . go ahead."

"Charlie Delta at your boundry inbound . . . VFR . . . flight level eight five . . . estimating Kano at one three zero three."

"Roger, Charlie Delta . . . you are cleared to descend VFR . . . QNH 29.83 inches . . . the winds are two six zero at ten knots . . . call field in sight."

"Roger . . . 29.83 inches . . . Charlie Delta call you field in sight."

I had no sooner hung up the mike when suddenly the plane began shuddering violently . . . the wings began flapping like bird's wings! I chopped back the power . . . the shaking diminished some but not completely . . . we began losing altitude. I slowly eased on the power so that we were only dropping about 200 feet per minute. No matter what I tried the shaking did not stop. Ten miles ahead there was the lake where I could set it down in the shallow water near the shoreline. Not a good idea for my stretcher patient in the back, but better than crashing and burning. No roads. Everything else was trees.

"Kano tower . . . this is Charlie Delta."

277

"Roger . . . Charlie Delta . . . go ahead."

"Charlie Delta informing you that I now have engine trouble."

"Roger . . . Charlie Delta . . . what is your intention?"

"My intention is to try to make it to your field . . . I have reduced power and am slowly descending from eight five."

"Roger . . . Charlie Delta . . . are you declaring an emergency?"

"Charlie Delta . . . negative at this time."

"Charlie Delta . . . what is your position?"

"We are just passing over the South end of the lake."

"Roger . . . Charlie Delta . . . keep us informed."

"Roger . . . will do."

The engineers had built guard rails on top of the earthen dam making it impossible to land on it. The laterite road heading northward from the dam is overgrown by trees. Fifteen miles from Kano there is a dry river bed where I could possibly land on a sandbar. When I reached the river, I was down to 6500 feet. I noticed my oil pressure had dropped to zero, but there was no oil on the windshield . . . also the cylinder head temperature was normal. From the bridge on, the road leading to the east side of Kano was blacktop . . . it was wider with few trees along the sides. The traffic was sparse. I decided to head for the airport . . . I could land on the road if need be.

"Kano tower . . . Charlie Delta . . . fifteen miles South . . . have your field in sight."

"Roger . . . Charlie Delta . . . call right base for runway two eight zero . . . the QNH is 29.83 . . . wind is two six zero at fifteen knots."

"Roger . . . Charlie Delta . . . will call you right base leg."

I kept my altitude up until I was assured that I could reach the field with no power at all.

"Kano tower . . . Charlie Delta . . . right base for two eight zero."

"Roger . . . Charlie Delta . . . cleared to land . . . winds are two six five at ten knots."

"Roger . . . Charlie Delta . . . cleared to land."

I chopped the power . . . still there was a heavy vibration to the plane. As I turned on final I dropped the landing gear, slowed her down some more and put down the flaps. Up ahead I could see that the airport had all the fire trucks and emergency gear lined along the runway. I greased the plane on and turned off at the first exit.

"Charlie Delta . . . your landing time is 1321."

"Thank you Kano tower . . . request taxi clearance to the old SIM hangar."

"Roger . . . you are cleared to taxi."

Our SIM people who were meeting the plane saw that we were bypassing the main terminal and so they drove over to meet us at the old hangar. Needless to say, when I parked the plane, we had a short praise meeting.

As the people were removing my stretcher patient, I checked the engine. There was no oil on the belly, and there was no oil inside the cowl. I turned the prop over to check the compression. There was absolutely no compression on one cylinder. I got out the tool pouch and removed the top sparkplug from all four cylinders. Now as I turned the prop I held my thumb over a sparkplug hole until I felt the air compressing on my thumb. When I did this to the number one cylinder there was no compression at all to this cylinder.

"Kano tower . . . this is Charlie Delta."

"Roger . . . Charlie Delta . . . go ahead."

278

"Request you call Jos and have them tell SIMAIR to standby on SIMRAD for an urgent message!"

"Roger . . . Charlie Delta . . . will do."

"Thank you Kano for your help."

"No problem."

We drove into town to the mission compound and George Rendel got Jos on the SIMRAD radio. Then he handed the mike to me. I told the guys at Jos what had happened and what I found on the engine. They told me to stand by while they decided what to do. Then they came back on the air, "We'll be sending a plane to pick you up . . . Since Bill hasn't started to disassemble the old engine that we removed from Charlie Delta . . . he and one of the guys will load it and the hoist into one of the buses and drive on up to Kano, install the old engine, and fly it home."

"Okay . . . that sounds like a plan . . . what's your ETA for picking me up?"

"We'll be there about 1600."

"Sounds good . . . Kano out."

"Roger . . . Jos out."

Bob Swingle flew up to Kano. Bill Tuck would be coming in the bus. I flew Charlie Echo home to Jos. They removed the bad engine, and installed the old engine. Then Bob flew Charlie Delta home to Jos, and Bill Tuck came back with the old VW bus.

Bill mounted the bad engine to the engine stand and started to disassemble it. When he drained the oil, it was full of chunks of metal. Then he removed the exhaust pipe from the right side of the engine. He found a beat up piece of metal jammed in the pipe that led from the number one cylinder . . . this was what was left of the top of the exhaust valve. When he removed the number one cylinder, there were two holes in the piston head. Evidently the exhaust valve head broke off and destroyed the piston. When he removed the oil pan, Bill found the passage to the oil pump jammed full of small pieces of metal from the piston which accounted for the no oil pressure for the last fifteen miles of the flight. This was a newly overhauled engine that had only 57 hours on it when it failed. WOW!

What are some lessons we can learn from this incident? First is the absolute integrity of the Piper Comanche 180. With the violent shaking of the plane due to the imbalance caused by the damaged piston, there was no structural damage to this airplane or the engine mount. Incidents like this in other types airplanes have literally shook the engine off the airplane and the plane fell tail-first to the ground to its destruction and that of the occupants.

Second, was the wisdom of the guys to get me back up in the air the same day so I wouldn't "freeze up". SIMAIR has lost some valuable pilots because of some close call, or flying in the thunderstorms, or the Harmattan, or whatever.

Third, would be thanks to God for sparing our lives in this incident, and all down through the history of SIMAIR for that matter. We have had accidents. But not once has anyone ever been scratched or hurt or killed! (One pilot was killed because he broke the rules by not staying over the airport while he was doing 'slow time' on an overhauled plane and engine.) Sad to say, other mission organizations have lost a number of planes and people down through the years.

Fourth, would be to once again thank those at home who pray for us and the missionaries out on the front lines. Wow! When I hear of the things our missionaries are going through today, it is scary indeed. First thing when I wake up in the morning I say, "Lord, what is going to happen today?" You should see some of the e-mails we have received lately. We just shake our heads when we hear what is going on today out there. But like President Bush says, "We have a job to do, and we must stay the course . . . we will be there for as long as it takes!"

And then a question came to my mind. If I shut the engine off, could I slow the plane down enough so the propeller would stop windmilling and thus stop the vibrating? Then how far could I glide from 8500 feet to hopefully find a safe landing spot?

So one day I was coming home from Kaltungo empty. When I came over the Shere Hills ten miles out of Jos I shut the engine off and slowed the plane down. I had to practically bring the plane up to a stall before the propeller stopped turning. Then I established my glide to the airport. It was eerily silent as I sailed along. What a feeling. I was 500 feet over the airport when I restarted the engine and came in and landed. So from flight level 10,500 I covered ten miles using 6000 feet of altitude.

Then another day I did the same thing. But this time I came in and landed without restarting the engine! I did this without a hitch. As I was rolling on the runway, it hit me like a ton of bricks, "You stupid idiot! What if you screwed up? You could have killed yourself! You could have banged up the airplane! Of all the dumb stupid tricks you have ever pulled, this has got to top'em all!" I restarted the engine and taxied to the hangar and I never told a soul. I still shake my head to this day. Wow!

'When the Second World War spread to North Africa, and the Middle East, Nigeria became important to Britain and the Allies as a staging area for troops and supplies. Military camps and airports were rapidly constructed at Ibadan, Lagos, Kano, Enugu, and Maiduguri. Over 100,000 troops passed through West Africa.'

'Because the Allies could not win the European war without the help of the United States, Britain lost its position as a leading world power. The United States and Russia, with no colonies in Africa, pressured the European colonial powers to de-colonize.'

'So over a fifteen year period, Britain began a slow but sure turnover of the government in Nigeria until it gained independence on the 1st of October 1960.'

All the time we were out there it seemed like there was one political crisis after another. In the three regions, there was always the maneuvering by any means to gain predominance in power over the others. 'In a grasp for power, the political parties pulled all kinds of dirty tricks, intimidation, violence, etc. to achieve their ends. Graft and corruption were rampant. Then there was the continual bickering of the lesser tribes to have their voice heard. Gaining independence proved much easier than managing a modern nation-state, as the Nigerian leaders soon found out.'

'The state of affairs became so unstable that the military had to take over in January 1966. The leadership fell to Major General Aguiyi Ironsi and a predominant group of officers who were Igbos (Eastern Region). Ironsi soon learned that it was more than he could handle. Social pressures and political problems plagued the Ironsi administration, and he had no answers to the problems of ethnic rivalry. His regional governors failed to enact the radical measures which the people expected. There was no progress in the economy. The final straw was his Unification Decree put forth on the 24th of May 1966 which was to end Nigeria as a federation and inaugurate a unitary republic. Rumors filled the air that Northerners (Hausa) in the army would be eliminated and the Easterners (Igbo) would dominate the country.'

Less than a month before we came back, on the 29th of May 1966, riots broke out at the Amadu Bello University and the Institute of Administration at Zaria where Igbos (Easterners) were attacked and killed by the local Northerners. Many fled to the Eastern Region.

Then two weeks after we got back, on the 29th of July, a counter coup put an end to the Ironsi administration in which many Igbo soldiers were killed, along with other people who were not even associated with the Ironsi administration.

The Northern people began running down and killing the Igbos wherever they could be found. It was estimated that as many as 3000 Igbos were killed in the Jos area alone. We first got wind of trouble when I saw a man fleeing past our hangar with several youths hooting and hollering, chasing him down with clubs and machetes. They clubbed and hacked him to death just beyond the airport.

Early that morning Marg had dropped Mark off at some people's house on the main compound. I jumped into a VW van and took off for town. As I pulled up in front of the house, I saw a large bunch of hoodlums coming up the road from Kingsway, armed with clubs and machetes, and bows and arrows at the ready. Some of them were attacking a (non-mission) house across the street from the SIM Bookshop. I heard several gun shots. I jumped out of the bus and ran into the house to get Mark. When we came out, the group was coming up past the bookshop about a hundred feet away. They didn't seem to be interested in us, so we casually walked out to the van, jumped in, and took off for the airport.

When I got back to the hangar, I managed to call Marg and tell her that I had Mark. Evangel hospital was in a panic as the wounded who survived the attack flooded the compound which proved to be a safe haven. The same proved true for our hangar.

Suddenly a terrified guy fled into our hangar. The hoodlums screamed and cursed us, but they would not come into the hangar as if there was a magic barrier they could not cross. We yelled at them to beat it, and they did. When they left, we suggested for the guy to hide in a small grove of trees over yonder until nightfall and then make his escape.

Then another guy came and the same thing happened. Only this one refused to leave. Our hangar boy was really angry that we would protect an Igbo. We told him to go over to the other hangar. While he was gone we hid the guy up in the attic above our locker room. Adamu came back carrying a club with fire in his eyes. We sent him home for the day.

After a couple of days the police began trying to restore order. The Igbos fled to the police station for protection. When the missionaries heard they had no food, a number of us made food and took it down to them. It became a riot as people surged to get their share. Later these people were put on a train that was to take them to the Eastern Region, but we heard that the train was stopped in the lowlands and everyone was slaughtered.

'Lieutenant Colonel Yakubu Gowan, the most senior officer from the Northern Region, became the new Head of State. The counter-coup only replaced the fear of domination by the Igbos with a fear of domination by the Northern Hausas.'

'The Igbo military governor of the Eastern Region, Lieutenant Colonel Odumegwu Ojukwu refused to recognize Gowan's leadership.'

'In Gowan's first address, he proclaimed that "we should review the issue of our national standing." But this review process ended in war instead of peace. And on 26th of May 1967, the Eastern Region proclaimed themselves as a free state, naming themselves the Republic of Biafra.'

281

'Gowan immediately declared a state of emergency and assumed full power of the military and government and the civil war began. Gowan merely thought this would be a quick "police action" which dragged on and on for thirty months in which more than a million people died.'

'The strategy was to secure the control of roads and towns. When a town was captured by the Federal troops, the civilian population retreated along with the Biafran army which caused much suffering and starvation. The Federal Navy blockaded the Biafran coast to prevent sympathetic countries from supplying the rebels with arms and supplies.

And the Federal troops encircled Biafra and just waited for the people to starve to death or give up.'

'The war became international. When Britain and the United States refused to sell arms to Nigeria, the Russians stepped in and sold them the arms and aircraft, thus gaining another foothold in Africa. Egypt sent pilots to fly the Russian Migs. Anti-American feelings began to erupt in Nigeria.'

The military at Jos airport were given two anti-aircraft guns. Often these guys would train those guns on our aircraft as we took off or landed. An uneasy feeling to be sure. I was just waiting for some grasshopper to land on the back of one of these trigger-happy jokers and accidentally shoot us out of the sky!

The Egyptian pilots were first class cowards as they would fly over Biafra at twenty thousand feet, release their bombs, and then hightail it back to Nigeria. This caused absolute panic among the Biafrans whenever they heard a plane fly over.

One day, a couple of these Migs were returning to Kano. They decided to give the Jos airport a buzz job on the way home. We heard the planes coming. And they were long gone when the guys on the two ack ack guns started blazing away. They kept on, peppering the whole sky for over ten minutes! We just about died laughing.

Along with the trigger happy guys on the guns, we also had to endure the searches. We would load up at the hangar and then taxi up to the terminal building to have the military check the papers of our passengers and to inspect their luggage and our cargo. It was quite evident they didn't have a clue what they were looking for as they seemed to spend a long time pawing through women's undergarments and other things that had no bearing whatsoever on security of the nation.

My emergency gear was packed in a small military olive green knapsack. Whenever they asked what was in it, I told them it was my emergency gear if we ever had a forced landing. Not once did they ever look inside it! I could have had anything and everything in there. These procedures also took place when we landed.

Sometimes it got almost to the point of harassment depending on who happened to be on duty at the time. One day I landed and taxied to the terminal. Five or six soldiers came out to the plane and demanded that I take out all of the luggage. It had been a long day and I was bone tired. So I merely opened the door and showed the compartment jammed full of luggage, hoping they would be satisfied as they sometimes were. Not this time. One soldier . . . he was a little guy . . . always seemed to enjoy throwing his weight around. He shouted at me, "Take it out . . . take it ALL out!"

So I began to slowly take out the luggage. The baggage compartment is quite large and you literally have to climb part way into the compartment to reach things on the other side. As I did this, the guy was pushing and trying to see over my shoulder what I was doing. I must have snapped. I swung the portable typewriter hard as I came out of there. WHOOF! I caught him right in the bread basket! . . . sent him sprawling backwards, almost knocking down a couple of other soldiers.

"Ohh . . . I'm so sorry!", but I guess the smirk on my face suggested I really wasn't sorry at all.

He staggered up in rage and tried to grab a soldier's rifle . . . "Gimme the gun . . . gimme the gun! . . . I'm going to shoot this B@%$&d!"

A couple of soldiers grabbed him as he made a lunge for me.

I jumped to an aggressive stance, "Let him go! . . . I'll knock his cotton picken' block off!", I growled.

About this time the Lieutenant in charge stepped out of the Weather Room, "What's going on here!"

I shouted, "Sir . . . this harassment has got to stop!" I picked up a pair of women's panties and waved them under his nose. "Your soldiers have no business pawing around in women's underclothes or anything else for that matter! We're in your country trying to help your people, and you darn well know it! But we are getting sick and tired of all this stupid business, and it's high time you put a stop to it!" Boy, I was mad!

The Lieutenant was rather taken aback at my tirade, and he ordered his soldiers to leave. "I'm really sorry, sir . . . but I will see to it that this does not happen again!"

I simmered down, "Thank you sir . . . we would appreciate that very much."

I reloaded the baggage and my passengers and taxied down to the hangar. And things did simmer down for awhile. I never saw the little guy any more. When we taxied up for inspection, one or two soldiers would come out. Rarely did they ask us to unload the baggage, nor did the passengers have to deplane. Also the guys manning the ack ack guns no longer trained them on us. I rarely blow my stack, but this time it sure paid off.

On the 15th of February 1967, I had a flight to Chad, which is the country east of Nigeria. I had never been there before. I flew three hundred miles to check out of the country at Maiduguri. They had barrels blockading the runway, so I had to circle around the field until they removed them. Then I came in and landed and taxied up to the fuel shed.

I shut off the engine and picked up my pad to mark down the flight time. When I looked up, I was staring into the barrel of a rifle! The plane was completely surrounded by soldiers in full battle camouflage. All their guns were pointing at me.

I gave them a friendly salute and slowly reached down and unbuckled my safety belt. Then I slowly reached up, unlocked and opened the door, and stepped out on the wingwalk, plainly showing my hands to everyone that I had nothing in them.

They slowly closed in on me with their fingers on the trigger. The guy in charge motioned with his gun barrel for me to step down off the wing. I did. Then he motioned for me to raise my hands and turn around, which I also did.

They frisked me and took my billfold, my jackknife, and the keys to the plane. He asked me in very good but stern English, "What are you doing flying into Maiduguri unannounced?"

In an unthreatening tone, "Sir, we told Kano two days ago of our intentions . . . they should have notified you, sir."

"We have had no word from them . . . Where are you from and where are you going?"

"Sir, I am from Jos going to Moundou in Chad to pick up some missionaries who need medical attention."

He made me sit on the ground while they thoroughly searched my plane.

They dragged out my olive drab bag and everything else in the plane.. "What is this . . . are you a soldier?"

"That is my emergency kit if I have to make a forced landing in the bush . . . no, I am not a soldier . . . I fly for the Sudan Interior Mission."

They dumped my bag and looked at everything.

I explained what everything was for and he seemed to be satisfied. I picked up an African Challenge Magazine and offered him one. "This is our mission magazine which we send to hundreds of people all over West Africa . . . Would you like one?"

He took the magazine and thumbed through it. A smile came to his face, "Thank you, sir . . . I will read it!"

I offered him several more. "Here . . . you can give these to your soldiers."

"Oh, thank you very much!" And his face broke into a big grin.

That ended my hostile session with the soldiers.

The attendant refueled my plane and I was shortly on my way to Chad.

I hit the road and followed it south until I came to Moundou. The missionaries were waiting, so there was no problem with the airport authorities. "Sorry I am late." And then I told them what had happened at Maiduguri.

Moundou was the station of TEAM missionaries, Abe and Helma Taves, Sharilyn's parents, but they all were home on furlough.

Early the next morning we took off and headed for Maiduguri. My passengers were Mr. and Mrs. Benzanson and one child. When we landed at Maiduguri this time the soldiers were all smiles. The Corporal in charge had his Challenge magazine and pointed to a section, "Sir, it says here that I can get a subscription to this magazine!"

"Yes . . . you just fill in your name and address and they will send you a magazine every month."

"And then it says here that I can enroll in a Bible correspondence course?"

"That's right . . . they will send you the first lesson and when you finish it, you send it in. They will check it and then send you the next lesson."

"Wonderful . . . I will do it! But I will need a Bible?"

"I think if you go to the SUM station, perhaps the missionaries there can sell you one." I could see that maybe I should carry a Bible or two. Next thing you know I'll be a traveling bookshop. I gave him one of the little red booklets, "Hanyar Cheto", The Way of Salvation.

He thanked me profusely and we were on our way to Jos.

A month later I flew the Benzansons back to Chad from Kano after they were done at the Kano Eye Hospital.

Noteworthy in my pilot log was my first landing at our new Miango airstrip on March 20th, 1967. This strip proved to be a great help to people coming and going from the Rest Home and Kent Academy as it eliminated many of the long rough hard drives to and from Jos for whatever reason.

Also on the 10th of March was my first flight into our new airstrip at Igbaja. On the 24th of April was my first flight into Patagi.

Harry Eleaya preaching at Busali Airstrip

To greatly facilitate the work, we also built new airstrips at Omu Aran, Egbe, and then the airstrip near the Dahomy border at Gurai. Later on, a road company built us a better airstrip at Kaltungo. Harry Elyea cleared a bit of brush and we had an airstrip at Bursali. Another airstrip was built right at Galmi Hospital in Niger.

At the new Egbe airstrip

On the 15th of July 1967, I completed 5000 hours of flying . . . little did I realize on that day I had completed half of my flying career.

I have been stalled on this chapter for months. I am thoroughly frustrated for I have lost my pilot logbook covering this period of time in my life of flying! Missing is the logbook covering from 4 October 1964 when I had 4002:30 hours to 12 August 1971 when I finished with 6574:05 hours. We have searched the house from top to bottom dozens of time to no avail. I am going crazy! Where could it have gone? This was my brains! This is what brought to memory many of the stories I have spun out in this book! Now part of my life is gone! What am I going to do? A number of people have written saying, "When are you going to get chapter thirty three done?" . . . over 200 of you! Well, I'm just gonna have to get with it . . . memory prompter or no. So here goes . . . .

It was getting harder and harder to fly. The military was watching us like a hawk. Every flight had to be approved. Everywhere we landed we were searched and grilled.

One day I had a flight to Ilorin and I was right on time. I buzzed over the station and headed on toward the airport. As I approached the north end of the airstrip I saw a military plane just breaking ground taking off. So I dropped my gear and landed shortly behind him. When I taxied up to the terminal, the missionary car and the missionary who was to be there with my passengers was nowhere to be seen. What's going on? Where are they?

As soon as I shut off my engine, the military came pouring out of the terminal building and surrounded the plane with their rifles all pointing at me. 'Oh . . . oh . . . this does not look good.' I said to myself.

"Get out of the plane . . . get out of the plane!", the Corporal in charge barked.

I got out of the plane and stepped off the wing.

All the soldiers came around to that side with their guns ready to shoot me down if I made a wrong move.

"You did not have permission to land! . . . why did you land? . . . why did you land?"

"We radioed our time of arrival to our person in Ilorin . . ."

(The arrangement we had with our missionary in Ilorin was that we would give them our ETA and they were to go out to the airport right away and notify the military the time for our expected arrival so they could remove the barrels. SIMAIR was to circle the runway. If the missionary was not there, we were not to land.)

"But he is not here . . . and he never told us that you were coming!"

"I'm sorry . . . why he did not come out and tell you I do not know . . . and I should have circled the airport before I landed . . . but he should be here shortly because I flew over our place in Ilorin before I landed."

"We will wait . . . he better come."

We waited and we waited. The longer we waited the more agitated the Corporal became. From his mannerism it was obvious that he had been drinking a bit. He kept looking at his watch. "He better come or else . . ."

"Or else what?"

"Or we will shoot you!", the Corporal shouted angrily. He looked at his watch, "If he does not come in the next five minutes . . . you are a dead man!"

"Look . . . I'm sorry . . ."

He jabbed his rifle into my gut. "Five minutes!"

The next soldier in charge said to the Corporal, "Looka boss . . . you don't wanna to do dis thing . . . we getta in BIG trouble . . ."

The corporal whirled around, "Are you questioning my authority? How dare you!" He pointed his gun at the soldier menacingly. "You take him out and shoot him! . . . TAKE HIM OUT IN THE TALL GRASS AND SHOOT HIM NOW!"

The other soldiers began protesting. Just then the missionary car came around the terminal building.

The Corporal went over to the car, opened the door, grabbed the missionary by the scruff of his neck, dragged him out of the car, and roughly threw him to the ground. He pointed the rifle at his head and screamed, "Why didn't you tell us the plane was coming! If you screw up again, I'm going to shoot you! Do you understand? . . . Do YOU understand?"

The missionary cowered at this onslaught. His face was deathly white, his eyes full of fright, and he stuttered, "Ye . . . ye . . . yessir!"

And YOU mister pilot . . . you and your passengers . . . get the @*&%HELL outta here!"

We did! And believe me . . . we had no more problems with that new missionary at Ilorin shirking his duties . . . he had got the message loud and clear, and I didn't have to say a word.

Other of the pilots were having "incidents" and we were learning to fly high, dropping down quickly at our destinations . . . as everybody who had a gun was shooting at everything that flew over. Finally the military grounded us for our own safety, and we stayed that way from 7th of June to the 20th of November 1969. Missionaries were now forced to drive, but they were also having a lot of 'incidents' at the road blocks everywhere they went. It was a dangerous time to be a missionary in Nigeria. SIM began doing a lot of mission business over SIMRAD.

We spent our time catching up on a lot of projects around the hangar and on the planes. I started working more and more on missionaries cars as the word got out. Parts were expensive and hard to find, so I had to get rather inventive at times, but I was much appreciated when I could keep their ol' buggy running.

Parts of this chapter marked with "marks is information taken from a book called The History of Nigeria written by Toyin Falola. Greenwood Press 1999 . . . Westport, Connecticut

CHAPTER 34
LASSA FEVER!

As with any modern TV plot of today, you usually have two or three stories all going on in the same time period . . . and so it was with this term.

"This story begins in a tiny village south of Maidugari not far from the Chad border. It is Sunday and about three in the morning, 19 January 1969, Laura Wine is awakened by a sharp rapping at her door. As Miss Wine gets out of bed, her aching back is worse than usual, but she shrugs that off . . . almost seventy now, what are you to expect with the long hard workload she was carrying. She lights the lantern and gets dressed, picks up her walking stick and shuffles off into the hot and still African night to the small bush hospital. In the obstetric ward a village woman is writhing in her final labor pains, her body glistening with sweat. The Nigerian night nurse speaks soothingly to her as she waits for Laura Wine to arrive.

The baby arrives safely in the early morning dawn, and Miss Wine makes her way back to her house to get some rest. She feels more tired than usual and falls into a fitful sleep.

Dr. and Mrs. Hamer were quite surprised that Laura was not at the church service in the village that morning. She never missed a church service. However, she showed up at the usual Sunday meal with them. They noticed that something was wrong, for Laura lacked her usual sparkle and smile.

During the dinner, word came that a Margi tribeswoman had delivered a baby alongside the dusty road as she was making her way to the hospital. As it was her duty, Laura Wine rose from her chair to go out to the waiting Land Rover, but the pain in her back dropped her down into the chair again. Esther Hamer said she would go, and that she would drop Laura off at her house on the way.

Miss Wine did not protest which was very unusual for her. She had difficulty getting out of the Rover, shuffled slowly into her house, and dropped on the bed fully clothed. 'Neither she nor anyone else knew at the time that her malaise and backache would set in motion one of the most frightening episodes of modern medical history. It would reach from Africa to the United States in a series of unpredictable incidents that was to bring into action many of the leading medical scientists of the world"

(from the book "Fever!", written by John G. Fuller, 1974, Readers Digest Press)

"However, when she awoke Sunday evening she felt somewhat better. She merely shrugged off her setback to a flair-up of her arthritis and exhaustion from the long hours she was working in the obstetrics ward. She took her shift as usual. The sixty-two bed hospital was bulging with nearly one hundred patients. But not feeling well, Laura Wine left the hospital early that evening and walked back to her home and went to bed.

Early Monday morning she joined the staff for devotions, and then she took her turn at the short wave radio monitoring the news and information from the ten different mission stations of the Church of the Brethern. Her husky voice was noticeably weaker, but she completed her transmission with effort. After the broadcast she joined Esther Hamer in the drug supply room to fill prescriptions for the various wards. She mentioned that her throat was getting very sore. Esther suggested that her husband check it out.

When Dr. Hamer checked her throat, it didn't look that bad. Her temperature was normal. However, her complaint was a little unusual . . . the soreness was above and behind the soft palate. He told her to rest and take some aspirin, but she insisted that she had work to do. As the day progressed, the soreness in her throat increased. Dr. Hamer ordered her to bed. She began a course of Aralen because of the ever present danger of coming down with malaria when your defenses are weakened.

On Monday evening, the Hamers brought over some light food for her to eat. Dr. Hamer examined her again. She had several blisters on the front on her neck, but Laura said she had used a hot water bottle to relieve the pain in her throat.

At 6:15 Tuesday morning, Dr. Hamer stopped by again . . . Miss Wine seemed considerably worse. Her throat was so sore that she could hardly swallow. When he examined her throat he could see some yellowish ulcers with halos around them far back in her throat. They were different from anything he had ever seen. There were also some on each side of her cheeks. Her temperature was a little over 100 degrees. Dr. Hamer started her on a course of penicillin. If her condition continued, he would put her also on streptomycin.

Dr. Hamer took a blood smear, urine and stool samples back to the hospital to check them. He did the blood count himself. If the white blood count was high, it would indicate a bacterial infection. However, the count was low. The urine test likewise was inconclusive. As the urine output was low, he urged her to drink lots of fluids.

By Wednesday evening her temperature was 101 degrees . . . blood pressure and pulse were normal. He noticed a small hemorrhagic mark on her left arm just above the elbow.

On Thursday morning the oozing ulcers in her throat had faded a bit, but there was a swelling in her neck. Her temperature had dropped slightly, but she was drowsy and extremely lethargic. Dr. Hamer was stumped . . . nothing added up to a clear clinical picture . . . no known tropical disease seemed to fit . . . it had the possibility of some unknown stubborn virus. Laura Wine was not responding to penicillin or streptomycin.

Early Friday morning he was surprised to find that Laura felt a little brighter and her temperature had remained the same. Encouraged, he went about his usual rounds at the hospital checking and visiting over one hundred patients in the crowded wards. He finished about noon and came back again to check Miss Wine.

He was shocked at her condition. He could not understand her speech. Her kidneys were shutting down . . . her urine output was almost down to zero. She could barely swallow. Her face would alternately flush and then turn very pale. Her mouth was dry and caked like a patient who has been on a regimen of antibiotics for a month.

A new symptom appeared . . . a patch of discolored skin on her right thigh . . . minute veinlike hemorrhages beneath the skin. Convinced of the danger of the situation, Dr. Hamer decided he would have to move her to the Sudan Interior Mission hospital at Jos as fast as possible."

"On the five PM broadcast . . . "Brethern Lassa calling Brethern Jos . . . Brethern Lassa calling Brethern Jos . . . do you read? . . . come in please!"

Finally a very weak voice answered from Jos over 400 miles away . . . it was hardly discernable.

Dr. Hamer repeated his message a number of times . . . "Medical emergency! . . . Request SIM or SUM to send a plane with stretcher and nurse to Mubi! . . . send plane to Mubi . . . Emergency!"

The reply was so unreadable that he wondered if his message got through at all. Hopefully they would get a reply in the morning.

Laura Wine's condition was getting steadily worse . . . They moved her to the hospital and put her on intravenous fluids and put staff on round the clock shifts all through the night. There was no question that this would be a race with death even if the plane did come. What was this deadly virus? Where had it come from? How was it spread? And how could it be combated?"

"The next morning radio reception was not much better. However, after a number of repeats on both ends, the Hamers were assured that the SUM plane would be arriving at Mubi at about 10 AM.

The mission Land Rover was ready and waiting. Miss Wine feebly protested as they began preparing her for the journey. Gently they slid her off the bed and into a wheelchair. They had to give Laura oxygen to keep her breathing. She did not look good. By the time they were ready to travel, the air temperature was already over 100 degrees. It would take over one and half hours to drive the rough road from Lassa to Mubi which included fording two rivers. Mrs. Hamer rode in back with Laura trying her best to keep Miss Wine as comfortable as possible as they swayed and bounced and lurched along . . . soon they were all covered with the suffocating dust from the road. They came to a military checkpoint where they explained they were going to the Mubi airstrip to meet the mission plane. The soldiers were surprised that a plane was coming. Did they not know that the strip was covered with oil drums and other barriers to prevent any enemy plane from landing there?"

"Ray Browneye departed Jos on schedule and set a course for Mubi which took him over the Sheri Hills . . . the Harmattan was light and he settled down for the two hour flight. Fortunately, the military got word that the rescue plane was coming and had the barriers removed just as Ray got there. The Land Rover finally arrived . . . Laura Wine was more dead than alive. As they slid her onto the stretcher and into the plane, she could not speak, but expressed with her eyes her gratitude for the help she was getting. Such was the reward that we pilots got down through the years as we did our job . . . just part of the team in bringing the gospel to this hard land. Another part of the team was waiting . . . Dr. Janet Troup and Penny Pinneo with Bingham Hospital's Opel Caravan was there when Ray landed and taxied down to the SIMAIR hangar. They immediately put her on oxygen.

The stretcher and patient were quickly transferred to the Opel and they were on their way to Bingham where they lost no time getting Laura Wine on intravenous fluids. Together with the Hamers, they assessed the situation in detail."

"Signs of heart failure were obvious. Laura Wine was failing rapidly. Radical therapy would be needed to save her life. Lab tests were ordered and blood samples were put in the freezer that would be sent to Dr. John Frame in the States and also to the lab at the University of Ibadan. She was given injections of digoxin, and hydrocortisone. She was put on oxygen and phenylephrine. Tourniquets were rotated on her extremities to sacrifice blood to the limbs in favor of getting more blood to the brain and vital organs.

The blood picture did not look good. Miss Wine's leukocyte count was 21,900. Bleeding time was over eight minutes. Her blood coagulation time was twelve times over the normal rate. There was danger of massive internal hemorrhaging. Nurses were ordered around the clock. Laura Wine was dying."

"Charlotte Shaw, recently back from furlough, was out in the early morning cool of dawn tending the flower garden. She got a nasty jab from a rose bush. When she went to her apartment she washed her hands and dabbed on a bit of merthiolate and forgot about it. She would be on night duty so she took an extra long nap that afternoon."

(Marg was not involved in any of this as she was working at Evangel Hospital as the outpatient nurse.)

"The hospital wing was quiet, except for the labored breathing of Laura Wine. As Char watched, Miss Wine tried to speak. Char bent near to barely catch the words, "My throat." She examined Laura's throat and went to a cabinet for a gauze swab, wrapped it around her finger, and gently swabbed the thick mucous from the patient's throat. She felt a slight stinging and remembered the thorn prick. Char quickly disposed of the swab and washed her hands thoroughly with strong green soap, and then with antiseptic. Miss Wine was resting fairly well and the long night passed without further incident.

Esther Hamer was on duty the next morning. You could hear the beautiful hymns of praise drifting from Stirrett Chapel nearby. A wan smiled appeared on Laura Wine's swollen face. Without opening her eyes she said to Esther, "Oh, I'm so glad the hymns are in English today!" Then realizing that in Lassa the services were always in Hausa or Margi she exclaimed, "Where am I?"

Those were the last words she ever said. That afternoon she went into convulsions and then into shock. By nine that evening, she took a turn for the worse, and passed away into God's presence at 0933 PM. Laura Wine lived and died in the fulfillment of her lifelong dream."

"It was decided to bury her body at the Brethern Mission at Garkida. The body would not be embalmed so that an autopsy could be performed to gain some clues to this elusive killer. Dr. Hamer obtained the death certificate from the Jos officials, and on Monday morning SIMAIR flew the body to Bui, the nearest airstrip to Garkida."

"Dr. Hamer turned it over and over in his mind, 'What had killed Laura Wine in six days?' The symptoms definitely ruled out malaria and typhoid fever. It most certainly had to be a virus, but a virus that neither he nor Dr. Jeannette had never dealt with before. The peculiar rash and hemorrhaging just below the surface of the skin. The sudden high leukocyte count at the terminal stage. Normally this did not happen with a killer virus. Was this an exception?"

"The autopsy was done at the Mission's leprosarium at Garkida. It showed heavy internal hemorrhaging and kidney damage. Tissue samples were taken to be sent to the States."

"Eight days after Laura Wine died, Miss Shaw began getting severe back and leg pains. She also had a slight headache, but she sometimes had migraines and was used to that. When she began the chills, she was convinced that she was coming down with malaria and took a course of malaria medicine. Char told no one . . . certain that by next morning she would be feeling better. But in the morning there was no improvement at all . . . in fact, her temperature had shot up to 102 and she realized that she was in no condition to go to work.

Delores Rohe stopped by on her way to work and knew something was wrong the moment she saw Charlotte. Instinctively she knew this was not malaria and persuaded her to enter the hospital as a patient. Char was reluctant but finally agreed, since she also felt nauseated on top of the chills and fever.

When Dr. Jeanette and Penny heard that Char was sick, they went to her bedside immediately. They gave her a thorough examination and took specimens for lab tests. Her fever was now up to 103 so they gave her another stiff course of anti-malarials. (I remember what those were like . . . the cure was worse than the disease!) There was no discussion whatever about the thought that was on everybody's mind . . . Was there any relation between Charlotte Shaw's condition and that of Laura Wine that ended her life?

They were further disturbed when Char told them about the finger prick and about swabbing Laura Wine's throat. They tried to assure her that there was nothing to worry about as she had washed the cut and put antiseptic on it. All of them desperately hoped that this was nothing but a malaria attack."

"Penny followed the lab tests with intense interest. She and Dr. Jeanette looked at the lab report, and compared them with those of Laura Wine. The bloodwork was similar. But there were no ulcers in the mouth or throat . . . no rash or swelling of the face and neck . . . no subsurface bleeding. Char was considerably younger than Laura Wine and could be expected to withstand the onslaught of this disease . . . there was comfort in that. So they gave Char the best of attention with undue alarm."

"Over the next several days the patient's condition did not improve, nor did it worsen. Char's temp remained several degrees above normal. Then seven days after she became ill, on 10 February 1969, the macular rash appeared discoloring her face, neck, and arms. By that evening it spread to her trunk and thighs. Her temperature shot up to 104.8 and the strange ulcers appeared in her mouth and throat. The luecocyte count rose.

Two days later her face and neck were severely swollen and she had difficulty breathing. By midnight her skin took on a blue discoloration . . . her blood pressure dropped dramatically.

At 3:45 AM on February 13th, the eleventh day of her illness, Charlotte Shaw died.

The hospital staff was absolutely stunned as well as the whole Mission when the news was broadcast on SIMRAD that morning. Dr. Jeanette and Penny had to do an autopsy as hard as that may be on a co-worker."

"(If you want to know all the gory details of what an autopsy is like, get a copy of the book FEVER, however, I'll spare you that here.)"

"The body showed massive internal hemorrhaging and there was extensive lung, liver, and kidney damage. Specimens and blood were put in the freezer to be sent to Dr. Frame in New York. Services were held at Miango and Charlotte Shaw was buried in the tiny graveyard behind the church."

"What was this elusive killer? Where would it strike next? Or would it strike again? And if it did, what was it? No one knew the answer. Dr. Jeanette Troup and Dr. Hal White rehearsed the findings with newly arrived Dr. Dave Christensen. All agreed that they were facing something totally unknown."

"About a week after Char's death, Penny was having a hard time sleeping, feeling vaguely uncomfortable, and not quite sure why. It was three in the morning when Dr. Jeanette knocked on her door to ask her to assist her in the obstetrics ward. One of the Nigerian nurses on staff went into a difficult labor that would require that a Caesarean section to successfully deliver the baby.

As they made their way to the hospital, Penny felt weak and dizzy. She administered the anesthesia while Dr. Jeanette did a successful operation. Penny immediately went home and to bed. Her temp was a little over 100. The next morning she stayed in bed with a washed out feeling and headache . . . her temp remained slightly elevated. Despite the lousy feeling she dug out her portable typewriter, propped herself up in bed, and tried to write a letter to her sister Rose . . . "I'm not feeling very good today. We've had some difficult days here. On February 13th, one of our nurses, Char Shaw died after being sick for two weeks with high fever, bad throat and mouth and severe aching . . . some sort of viral infection that did not respond to antibiotics. A week before a missionary was brought here from another Mission who died within 24 hours with the same terminal symptoms that Char developed. Char was contaminated through a rose thorn prick in her finger. I'm wondering if I have the same thing? Appreciate your prayers for us here . . . ."

News trickled out that another nurse was laid low with strange and unidentifiable symptoms and concern grew to major proportions. The doctors noticed a small ulcer inside the cheek and the tonsils became red. Again the leukocyte count dropped. They gave Penny a strong dose of antimalarial and 1.2 million units of penicillin twice daily. They gave her gamma globulin along with the entire staff as a prophylactic measure.

Dr. Jeanette continually conferred with the other doctors. It was agreed to set a deadline . . . if her fever did not drop by Wednesday, February 26th, they would make plans to send Penny to New York where she could be treated at better facilities.

Dr. Jeanette typed up a detailed report covering the symptoms, the treatment given, and the time line of all three persons who were stricken with this strange viral disease. The report along with the accumulated specimens of tissue and blood samples would go with Penny on the trip. Penny did not get better and the plan was immediately put into action.

The logistics for the trip would be imposing. She would be flown by stretcher via SIMAIR to Lagos. Clearances would have to be obtained from Customs, Immigration, and Health. Permission would have to be obtained from Pan Am in New York for transporting a stretcher case, necessitating the purchase and removal of four first-class seats and the installation of curtains to screen off the patient. Someone would have to accompany Penny Pinneo on the trip who could give her the care required. Nurse, Dorothy Davis, who was due for furlough, was selected for this job."

"Dorothy began packing her bags, and also went to Penny's apartment to pack some of her belongings. She had been taking care of Penny's two canaries and decided first to feed them. Both of them were lying dead on the bottom of the cage! What had suddenly killed them? She reported this to Dr. Jeanette who included this fact in the report."

In the early morning dawn of the 27th, the stretcher was installed in the Aztec and Penny was brought out to the airport. A number of missionaries came to see her off. Out of deference to the desperately sick patient, the Nigerian troops came down to the hangar for their inspection and immediately cleared the plane for takeoff. Leroy Andrews taxied out to the runway and took off. He climbed up just above the Harmattan and leveled off . . . in two and a half hours they would be in Lagos.

"Nigerian health authorities were alerted about the flight by Pan Am and were waiting for the Aztec when it taxied in from the runway. Penny stayed on the stretcher as the hot tropical sun turned the plane into a bake oven. Dr. Stanley Foster, a U. S. Public Health Service official, heard about the impending arrival and was on hand to consult with the Nigerian authorities. The consultation was long and involved. Clearance from Pan Am in New York had not come through and there was not another plane for four more days!

They decided that Penny would have to be given a complete physical examination at the Lagos University Hospital and kept in isolation until she could be put on the next plane . . . IF she would be permitted to be put on the flight at all. There was a question of whether the plane was already entirely booked. Also Dorothy Davis had forgotten to bring penny's yellow health book! Finally Andy suggested to the authorities that the patient needed to be moved, as he did not want her dying in the plane because of the heat. That ended the conference.

The road from the airport into Lagos is sheer hell. Bumper to bumper diesel trucks and buses spouting noxious black fumes in the stop and go traffic. Countless cycles and pedestrians darted in and out of the traffic. Horns blared . . . the noise is deafening. It took over an hour for the ambulance to reach the hospital . . . it was like an oven."

"Penny was wheeled into the stifling emergency room which was jammed with outpatients where she lay for over an hour before she was examined by a Nigerian doctor, then a parade of them. They could find nothing specific so they had a consultation. After another hour they finally decided that she could not stay at the hospital! She would have to be put in isolation at the Pest House which was back out toward the airport an hour away! It was a crumbling building with a rusty corrugated tin roof set aside for people with contagious diseases. It was filled with babies and children with measles and chicken pox. As bad as the Pest House was, it was better than the former treatment when the diseased people were taken out into the jungle, given a bit of food and water, and then left to die.

Penny was carried in on her stretcher to a little room and was eased onto a bed. Word had been sent ahead that two American nurses would be arriving. There were no fans and the windows looked out to the naked sky. It was dark now, but the heat does not lift when night comes to Lagos. The room was dimly lit and suffocatingly hot."

"Dorothy checked Penny carefully, professionally. The rigors of the trip and the long hours in the van and the hospital had taken their toll. Her fever was up, her neck swollen, her throat ulcerated, and she had much difficulty in breathing. There was nothing much she could do. Would Penny live through the night?"

"Dorothy lay down on a bed close to Penny to fan away the hoards of mosquitoes which were coming through the open windows . . . there were no nets! A rat scurried across the floor, darting erratically back and forth, looking for food. Strange, but she was just too tired to even care anymore. An enormous loneliness came over her. She prayed."

"Then she became aware of the sounds of the crying children down the hall. A small baby suddenly convulsed and died. The mother broke into uncontrollable wails, shrieking out in supplication. Eventually they were taken away, but the cries of the other children continued on through the night. Lord, where are You? Does anybody care? Do you? Do you care enough to come out to the forsaken land to help?"

"Dr. Stanley Foster arrived in the early morning. Just his presence raised Dorothy's morale, but more than that, he brought over a half dozen bottles of intravenous fluid with all the equipment to administer it. It was rushed into use, but Penny's fever continued to climb, slowly and relentlessly. There was deep concern.

Then a further morale booster came later that day with the arrival of Dr. and Mrs. Herman Gray of the Christian Reformed Church. They were now stationed in Lagos. They offered to relieve Dorothy in her twenty four hour duty."

"The Nigerian nurses, who were shy at first because of the unexpected visitors, tried to do everything possible to help. It was the first time that the Pest House ever had anyone other than Nigerian. They tried their best to make them feel welcome. They closed the room off to new patients. In the evening, they came with brand new mosquito nets for each bed, some insecticide, and an ancient electric floor fan."

"But the heat still hung in the room. Penny's temperature was climbing. Dorothy prayed in despair. Mrs. Gray arrived to relieve and Dorothy dropped on the bed in total exhaustion and tried to sleep. But the cries of the children tugged at her heart. It was a hard night.

Sunday, March 2nd, Dorothy suddenly realized that it was now the 10th day since the beginning of Penny's illness. Neither Charlotte Shaw nor Laura Wine had lived much beyond that. Penny knew this also."

"But good news came . . . plane reservations had been cleared and confirmed!"

"When Dr. John Frame finally got news of the events going on in Jos, it was confusing. He received a cable from Jos saying that a second nurse had died. He knew nothing of a first nurse dying. Then he got a second cable stating that Penny was on her way to New York in very serious condition. Information was disjointed and he could draw no real conclusions from it. Then he got a phone call from the SIM New Jersey office saying they had received a letter from Jos which simply stated that a mysterious series of lethal illnesses had struck SIM Jos with a vengeance. There were no details."

"Dr. Frame called his colleague, Dr. John Baldwin at Columbia Presbyterian Hospital to arrange for Penny's immediate admission. Even with the sketchy information they had, he thought it wise to not take chances . . . strict isolation measures should be arranged. In his gut, he had a feeling that this was really serious. After dinner that night, Frame went over his notes and records and medical journals. His extensive knowledge of tropical diseases would enable him to quickly eliminate a wide spectrum of possibilities to narrow down the field. He was prepared for Penny Pinneo's arrival."

"It took some time for the letter that Penny had written from her sick bed to reach her sister, Rose, who was in Rochester, New York. Her elation faded when she read the letter . . . it was not like Penny to be sick, and if she was in bed, it would have to be something major. News of the two nurses dying, and that one of them felt that she had been contaminated while taking care of the first, Rose knew that Penny would have been in the thick of things and would have been involved in the taking care of these nurses. As a trained nurse herself, she was perturbed that the symptoms did not respond to antibiotics.

Two days after the letter arrived, on the 3rd of March, she got a call from the SIM office in New Jersey . . . "Penny will be arriving at Kennedy around midnight via Pan Am Airways as a stretcher case!" The gravity of the situation was immediately evident. She made reservations to fly to New York City the following day."

"John Frame got a similar message and quickly alerted Dr. John Baldwin at Columbia of Penny's arrival late Monday night. He also called the Yale arbovirus lab and got hold of Jordi Casals alerting him to the fact that a missionary who was quite ill would be arriving from Nigeria as a stretcher case with an unidentified fever . . . it would be wise to give special attention to the blood specimens that were being shipped with the patient in light that two other nurses had possibly died of the same disease."

"Isolating a virus is a long and highly complex problem. It involves tedious manpower hours, hundreds of laboratory mice, time for the disease to incubate, and careful preparation of tissue cultures for observation with an electron microscope, followed by repeated verification of it all."

"Everything done at the Yale lab would be of no benefit to Penny Pinneo. The only hope for her would be the most meticulous symptomatic and supportive treatment . . . another way of saying . . . keep the patient comfortable, the fever down, and the pain reduced."

"But Yale would have to search out the enemy in an attempt to develop a vaccine or plasma antibodies to help people who became stricken with the disease in the future. Rescheduling the work of the thirty-five man laboratory for a crash program was another problem. With more than thirty ongoing projects a year, a halt in the Yale assembly line could throw everything out of kilter. The number and variety of viruses under study at any one time was staggering. There were fifteen viruses alone starting with the letter C being researched at the lab. It is doubtful that more than a handful of doctors were familiar with most of these, much less the other 350 viruses that were under study at the arbovirus laboratory."

"When Dr. Frame arrived at the airport, Rose Pinneo and Trevor Ardill were already there. The ambulance was also waiting. The Pan AM plane arrived ahead of schedule. After the regular passengers disembarked, Dr. Frame, Trevor, Rose, and an official from the U.S Public Health Service boarded the plane. Penny recognized her sister, "Thought I would never see you again!"

"Penny was obviously a very sick person, and the health official immediately gave permission for her to be taken to the ambulance. Dr. Frame drew 10 cc of blood and put it in the Vacutainer. "Good to see you back safe."

Penny replied, "I can hardly swallow."

"He immediately went to a washroom where he scrubbed his hands as if he were preparing for surgery. He was taking no chances. On viewing Penny's condition even briefly, he was convinced that something serious was going on."

"Dorothy Davis took the luggage and equipment to Customs. The officer was sympathetic, "Please go right through." She saw her family waving to her from the balcony, but their reunion would have to wait until she saw Penny safely to the hospital. She rode in the ambulance with Rose to Columbia Presbyterian . . . the end of a long journey that started from Jos so many days ago. She wondered, 'How much can a person stand in this condition? . . . or in any condition for that matter? . . . but Penny did it!'

"The isolation ward of the hospital staff were prepared for the midnight arrival. They lost no time in getting Penny into her room and ready for the complex routine of diagnosis. Tests would begin right away."

"As a precaution, every staff member in the isolation area were gowned and masked. Rose Pinneo was permitted to stay with her sister as a relative rather than a nurse and they provided her with a gown and mask. Dorothy Davis went to join her family."

"John Frame stopped by at the isolation ward and was startled to find the staff were not wearing rubber surgical gloves along with their masks and gowns. He really shook them up . . . "Look here folks, this is a frightening disease! You should be handling this as if it were the plague!"

"Checking Penny's chart, he noted that her temperature was steadily climbing which was not a good sign. They needed to bring the fever down. The fever peaked at 107 degrees . . . many adults die long before that. It became a question of treating the fever and not the disease which continued to resist everything. Penny was packed in ice. Intravenous fluids were continued. She was put in an oxygen tent. Aspirin was given. Slowly the temperature began to fall. Even then, death could come at any moment, for her chest was filling with fluid. When Penny coughed, it was agony. She gasped for every breath. Her face and neck became more swollen. There was nausea. Penny thought, "Lord, how long can I take this? How can I bear it?"

"Rose Pinneo wasn't even sure if her sister could hear when she read to her from Psalms 103 . . . "Bless the Lord, O my soul, and forget not His benefits . . . Who forgiveth all thine inequities . . . Who healeth all thy diseases . . . Who redeemeth thy life from destruction . . . Who crowneth thee with loving kindness and tender mercies."

"But Penny did take it. And Penny did bear it through the night. Her temperature in the morning was down to 102. Would it stay down was the question. That morning, the doctors removed 170 milliliters of clear fluid from her lungs."

"Later on at his office he got a call from a jittery intern, "Can you tell me this . . . has anyone ever recovered from this disease?"

"There was no answer that John Frame could give . . . or anyone else for that matter.

Lab tests showed that Penny's blood work closely matched that of Charlotte Shaw and Laura Wine. Overall, there was still nothing to grab hold of. But they all agreed that this must be some kind hemorrhagic fever that was deadlier than anything known before."

"Wil Downs set the package holding the thermos of specimens from Africa on the table. It was agreed that only Sonja Buckley, Jordi Casals, and himself would be permitted to check these. No-one who had families would be permitted to work on the research."

"Downs and Casals began right away to work on their carefully bred mouse colony.

The infectious material was for the most part blood serum, pleural fluid from the chest cavity, and urine specimens."

"Sonja carried the specimens down to her laboratory and put them in the freezer unopened. First she would have to prepare her cell lines . . . tissue cultures . . . in a series of test tubes and bottles. Inside the bottles were carpets of living cells that they would later try to kill in various controlled ways with the infected specimens.

There were two kinds of living cells which were drawn from baby hamsters and from the kidneys of African Green Monkeys. The carpet of cells floated on top of the red nutrient fluid that kept them alive. As they grew and divided Sonja Buckley would draw off some to start another bottle. When she had 200 cell cultures completed she closed down the work for the weekend."

"For Wil Downs and Jordi Casals the picture was different. The blood and urine specimens would be injected into the brains of their purebred Charles River mice colony.

The mice were free from any other disease. Precautions were taken to protect the mice as they were being farmed and bred in order to die in the interests of science. They were housed in rows of metal boxes. Each box had its own ventilating system, creating a negative pressure which reduced the danger of the mice kicking up urine and feces dust. The foul air from the isolator is drawn out and incinerated."

"They decided to start suckling mice for their first batch of inoculations because there would likely be a faster response from mice at such a tender age. Was there a live virus in the fluids they were unpacking from the ice? If so, how many mice would it kill? Or would it kill any? You inject the mice and then you watch and wait for any damage to appear in the animal. You also set up the same number of mice as a control group. You assess the results of your experiment and then repeat it over and over again to tabulate the statistics. You never take anything for granted. You always allow for variables. It is slow, precise, and painstaking work.

Working with the mice is more dangerous. Cells don't move . . . mice wriggle unpredictably. Downs and Casals took no chances. They put the mice under deep ether anesthesia. Each took a syringe with .02 milliliters of straw colored serum from Laura Wine, picked up a baby mouse and plunged the needle into the cranium. They did this into the long hours of the night.

Casals usually commuted back to New York every evening, but he decided to stay with Downs in nearby Branford, Connecticut. Both were exhausted. Under conditions of pressure and crisis even the best of scientists makes mistakes. And neither realized that they had already made their first mistake which would cost them time . . . time that they could not afford to lose."

"On Monday morning, Sonja Buckley went to her lab to begin the first assault on her healthy tissue cultures. The experiment is a fairly simple one. She would expose the cultures with the blood serum from one of the victims. If any virus was lurking in the serum, damage to the healthy culture would show up in three or four days . . . moth holes would appear in the carpet, slowly at first, then multiplying until there was hardly anything left of the green monkey cells. She would have to wait."

"In the meanwhile, in Casals lab, nothing was showing up in the inoculated mice. They looked perfectly healthy. It would make you doubt there was any deadly viruses in the blood serum samples."

"On Tuesday morning Jordi Casals came down to Buckley's laboratory. "Nothing is showing up in the mice . . . how are you doing?"

Sonja replied, "Nothing here . . . but I'm not expecting anything yet."

Casals was pessimistic about the outcome, but there were plenty of things to do getting ready for the more complicated tests they would be doing."

"That afternoon, Dr. Max Theiler, who was credited for his work in developing the yellow fever vaccine, dropped by to have a cup of coffee with Sonja Buckley. He was interested in what she was presently doing, so she took a tray of the plaque bottles out of the incubator to show him. She was shocked at what she saw. Every single carpet of cells was covered with white spots or holes that made the carpet look like it was covered with chicken pox! She felt a chill go through her. She took down the second tray. It was the same! The virus was eating away with a vengeance. Sonja tried to remain calm. She went to the trays of matching control bottles. Not a single hole . . . these bottles were not

298

infected. She said to Dr. Theiler, "I wonder why Casals mice, who were injected three days earlier, have not shown anything!"

"Maybe my cultures have been contaminated with another virus . . . I'll have to make a second run. Don't tell Downs or Casals, okay? . . . I want to make sure of findings first."

"Theiler promised not to say a word, but within minutes after his leaving, Wil Downs bounded upstairs to her lab, "Well Sonja, I hear you have something to show me?"

She showed him the trays . . . there was no doubt that something radical was going on.

Downs got on the phone to Dr. Frame, "Looks like Sonja has something . . . it has hit every tissue culture in the first run! . . . but nothing has shown up in the mice . . . we are going to do a second run on everything."

"Frame was excited. Finally there seemed to be something definite going on."

"Penny's condition was still critical. She developed pneumonia which flooded her lungs causing her to cough painfully as she fought for every breath. Then followed encephalitis (inflammation to the brain) which caused a loss of hearing and sense of balance.

The virus also attacked the blood clotting mechanism, causing her tissues to hemorrhage. Her heart and kidneys and other vital organs were affected.

But she had survived longer than the other two who were stricken with the disease."

"Sonja Buckley prepared the material for the second run. If her first results were true, this virus was nothing to be trifled with. By the following Tuesday, March 18th, she had her answer. Again every single bottle came down with the telltale mothlike holes."

"They again called Dr. Frame with the news. There was nothing showing in the young mice. Why? Downs and Casals were stumped for an answer. Up to that time they had used only baby mice . . . what if they were to do a run using adult mice? So they repeated the test using adult mice, and the very next day when Casals picked a mouse up by the tail, he felt a slight tremor coming from the mouse. A few days later all the adult mice that were inoculated with the infected serum were found dead in their cages! Another run with adult mice was done with the same results."

"The power of the new African virus was obvious, and to find its exact strength Casals and Buckley independently began a process of tittering to see how weak a solution of the infected material it takes to kill 50 percent of the animals or destroy 50 percent of the cultures. They both used the same process."

"They used ten test tubes. Full strength went into the first tube. In the second tube the serum is diluted 10 to 1. In the third 100 to 1. The fourth 1000 to 1. By the sixth tube the diluted serum is ten million to one. By the tenth tube the dilution is 100 million to one."

"They would inoculate groups of ten mice or tissue cultures with it to see what happened. If the mice died and the cultures were destroyed, then they would go to the next diluted solution, and so on until roughly 50 percent of the animals or tissue cultures destroyed. One serum specimen taken from Penny riddled 50 % of the tissue cultures at a dilution of ten million to one, indicating a terrifying lethal virus. What's more, every specimen showed up virus positive whether the serum was taken from Penny Pinneo, Char Shaw, or Laura Wine. Obviously more safety precautions needed to be taken in the lab."

Today is September 23rd 2005 and I have not written on this chapter, it seems like for over a year. I have been busy with the things of everyday living, mostly in taking care of Marg in her three plus year battle with Multiple Myeloma cancer (for which there is no cure). I became the chief cook and bottle washer and the household shopper and many other things that were unfamiliar to me. Her struggle ended a little before midnight on July 29th as she peacefully passed away in her sleep and went home to be with the Lord. Oh God, how I miss her . . . but I would not have her back for a second to struggle on in this sin-cursed world anymore. What an awesome wonderful person she was as many of you well know. So life goes on for us who are left behind with the knowledge that we who belong to Christ will someday join her . . . what more can I say?

Much of what I have written on the Lassa Fever story was taken from John G. Fuller's book "FEVER! The Hunt for a New Killer Virus". Reader's Digest Press-New York-1974.

I wanted to give you an idea of what is really involved in the medical circles when such an episode takes place, but this chapter is becoming way too long . . . I need to get this book finished . . . so everything from here is my summary of what took place during this time.

Penny did survive. She and her sister Rose are still living in SIM's retirement village in Sebring, Florida. Jordi Casals came down with the disease and was admitted to the isolation unit on June 15th, 1969. (It is surmised that he got the disease through a hangnail on one of his fingers! . . . or possibly from his habit of always chewing on his pencil in the lab!) They took blood from Penny Pinneo and made a serum full of Lassa fever antibodies which they slowly injected into Casals and this saved his life. Through their research it was discovered that the virus was carried in the urine of the mice and, was also present in Jordi Casal's urine. Therefore, stringent measures of cleanliness had to be observed.

Casals recovered slowly but finally returned to his work in the lab. But he tired quickly and he was glad to see the day end that Wednesday before Thanksgiving. So he closed up shop and went down the hall to the elevators. On the way down he said hello to Juan Roman, a young lab technician who was working on a different research project down the hall. Roman and his wife would be going to Pennsylvania for the holiday. From this casual meeting in the hallway, Juan Roman came down with Lassa fever from which he died!

Action was swift. All research at Yale involving the live Lassa fever virus was stopped immediately, and all the live specimens were sent to the CDC hot lab in Atlanta. All remaining material and equipment at Yale was immediately incinerated or thoroughly sterilized. Any worker in any laboratory in the building was to report the first sign of any illness, no matter how small. Bulletins were sent to medical and health officials around the world . . . Yale would no longer accept any new specimens suspected of harboring the Lassa fever virus.

All the while this was happening, a yellow fever epidemic broke out on the Jos Plateau. They estimated that there were over 100,000 cases of yellow fever in which 40 percent of the people died. All SIM medical personnel were involved with this, including my wife Marg. As the rainy season came to a close, the epidemic finally faded out.

With all the diseases that attack our bodies one way or another, it seems like a miracle that the human race survives. It may be a bite from an insect. It may be a simple handshake or someone coughs nearby and you come down with a cold or the flu . . . or maybe Lassa Fever? Was that how Jordi Casals gave Lassa fever to Juan Roman? Let me sight another case for you.

I learned that Dave Epp, a SIM missionary, had Lassa fever and survived. I asked if he would do a write-up for me and this is what I got from him recently.

"Rich, It has been awhile since you asked if I would share a bit about my Lassa experience. I trust this will be something you can use.

It was either in the latter part of 1971 or early 1972 that I came down with Lassa Fever.

It was toward the end of our second term in Nigeria. Shirley and I with our two children were stationed at Sokoto. I was busy teaching Bible Knowledge Classes in about five different institutions. That meant I had up to 41 hours a week in class time. Shirley also had some classes, but her main responsibility was the family, plus caring for guests that would come through Sokoto.

I remember going to class one morning and one of the boys was missing. I was told that he was not well and had been admitted to the local hospital. That afternoon I made a visit to the hospital to see this fellow. I do not remember the details of that visit. However, the next morning in the class at school I was informed that this young man had died during the night! I was asked to take the funeral that day. Needless to say, it was a very moving experience. We never know what the Lord has in store for us. (Boy, isn't that the truth!) We do know He is faithful to provide what we need in each circumstance. He is sovereign.

It was a week or so later that I became ill. I had a sore throat and fever and didn't feel up to much. I was unable to swallow so I couldn't take any fluids. Shirley took me to the local doctor . . . He gave me an antibiotic and said to force fluids. Shirley told him that I could not swallow, but he didn't seem to hear that. But we did get the antibiotic and Shirley somehow treated me with it. I became dehydrated because of the lack of fluids.

It was exam time for my students, and I managed somehow to prepare the exams. Shirley mimeographed the exam and took them to the school. The students were monitored by other members of the school staff.

While Shirley was carrying on with her daily responsibilities, and also caring for me, Kevin and Lynette also needed care. Many times they would be in with me while I was confined to bed. We praise the Lord for His protection over them during this time. Finally Shirley decided to go to the Leprosy Hospital at Amanawa and talk to the nurse. They decided to call Jos for a plane to pick me up. Sarah Lowen came back to Sokoto with Shirley and gave me two units of intravenous solution.

Rich Schaffer, the pilot, arrived at about noon to pick me up. When we arrived in Jos I was admitted to Evangel Hospital. Dr. Hal White put me in isolation and immediately increased the antibiotic. I was told that my white blood count was extremely high at 60,000 . . . the norm is 6,000. It could have gone either way, but I guess the Lord still had more work for me to do as I began to slowly recover. Shirley called Jos as she had heard nothing from Jos for five days. All she was told was that I was at Evangel! (Good Grief!) But finally I recovered enough to be released from Evangel Hospital and flew home to Sokoto via Nigerian Airways. What a blessing to be home again with my family.

We did not hear what the diagnosis was until we returned from furlough in 1973. Dr. White then told me that I had had Lassa Fever! During the rest of my time in Nigeria I donated plasma to the Plasma Bank they were building to treat future Lassa patients."

So how did Dave Epp get it? No doubt from his visit with the sick student. Maybe just a cough or a handshake? Why didn't his kids or Shirley get it? Or why didn't I get it when I flew Dave to Jos? (Another thing in this book that is never discussed is the possibility of getting Lassa Fever from a mosquito bite. A person with Lassa is sleeping and is bitten by a mosquito and then that mosquito immediately bites others in the hut. I believe this is also a possible way that AIDs can be spread.)

But sometime in here I DID get very sick and they put me in Evangel Hospital just like they did Dave Epp. They put me in isolation and allowed no visitors . . .

I was burning up with a very high fever. They put me on Erythromycin and on constant intravenous fluids. I remember this one Nigerian nurse who was determined that I keep my arm flat on the bed.

"You must keep your arm flat on the bed or the fluid will stop flowing!"

No matter how I tried to get it across to him, "Look . . . the fluid will always flow as long as my arm is below the bag hanging on the pole! . . . look at the bag . . . you can see it dripping, can't you?"

"Ye e es! But you still must keep your arm flat on the bed!"

I gave up.

I broke out with a rash all over my body. (They said it was an allergic reaction to the antibiotic.) But eventually I did recover and was released from Evangel, and I too never ever heard what had made me sick.

Lets see . . . I need to back up in the time line a bit. Marg was pregnant with John. He was a breach baby and could not be turned around. One evening we were outside looking at one of the avocado trees when Dr. Jeanette Troup dropped by to talk to us about doing a Caesarean Section to deliver John. The date was set and John was safely delivered on April 22nd, 1969. This date is very important, for on February 18th, 1970 Dr. Jeanette died of Lassa fever! This is how it came about.

On Christmas Day the Christians in the small village of Bassa were going to have a parade. But Tamalama did not go. She felt ill and was burning up with fever. And according to standard practice her brother brought her to Evangel Hospital and registered her and her address with fictitious names. The belief is that when you get well and return home, the evil spirits which caused the disease can not find you again.

Tamalama was placed in a corner bed of Ward A where the slight breeze gave some comfort from the stifling heat where she was left coughing and gasping for every breath. Her symptoms were not similar to the yellow fever epidemic that the Plateau had just gone through. Dr. Jeannette ordered aspirin to bring the fever down, and prescribed an antibiotic to fight the unknown infection, plus Aralan as a precaution against malaria.

She recovered from her illness and returned to her village of Bassa. Three days after she returned home her two children and her mother came down with a high fever. Her mother and her little boy gradually recovered, but her little girl died in three days. All these cases remained undiagnosed and unreported to Evangel Hospital.

Shortly after Tamalama was dismissed, two other Nigerian women that were in Ward A came in with the same symptoms. One woman died within four days with all the signs of Lassa Fever.

Then four more patients came down with the same symptoms. Two ward cleaners, Adikitoi and Adung, and the chief dispenser, Raphael Adeyimi, and a male scrub nurse, Maigari . . . all were on staff at Evangel. (Maigari was trained by and worked with Marg when she was at Bauchi Leprosarium.)

Dr. Jeanette Troup was asked to say a few words at the SIM Wednesday night prayer meeting. Her reassuring words were, "Nothing can happen to a child of God, except that it pass through the heart of God. With God there can be no such thing as an accident."

The following Sunday night, January 25th, 1970, both Maigari and Adung died of Lassa fever. During the process of doing an autopsy on Maigari the scalpel slipped and

Dr. Jeanette sliced her finger. She quickly jerked her hand out of the glove. She let the nasty cut bleed profusely and then washed it thoroughly with surgical soap and flooded it with antiseptic. Then she bound it carefully with gauze, put on a new rubber glove and went back to continue the autopsy. (Question: Why didn't she remove BOTH gloves? This is what the book Fever says she did! Certainly the glove she did NOT take off would have been contaminated?)

She finished the job in about an hour and made the specimens ready to ship to the lab in Ibadan along with a letter to Dr. Carey via SIMAIR in the morning. After making his rounds, Dr. Hal White stopped by the operating room.

"Hal, I've been out here sixteen years and I have done a lot of stupid mistakes, but tonight I have done the biggest one of all!" She held up her bandaged finger. "Don't tell anyone . . . this is not the time to alarm the staff."

After reading Jeanette's letter, Dr. Carey put the specimen container in a separate fridge and immediately cabled the news to Yale requesting they air ship two units of Jordi Casal's serum as quickly as possible. (Question . . . Why didn't they have Casal's serum already on hand in Jos just in case there ever was a need for it?) He also asked if Casals would be free to come to Nigeria immediately as he was the only Lassa-immune scientist and doctor in the world.

At Evangel Hospital the cases of Lassa fever grew to nineteen . . . ten of them had already died. On January 29th, Adikitoi died.

On Tuesday February 3rd, Dr. Jeanette was not feeling up to her usual self. That afternoon she lay down and fell asleep on the sofa. When she woke up to go to bed she was shivering with a severe chill. Her muscles ached all over, especially her back.

The next morning the aching was even worse. She felt feverish. But she got up and made the rounds in the ward, only reading the charts. She avoided making any contacts with the patients and her colleagues.

On Saturday afternoon, Dr. Jeanette did not show up at Joan Potter's for her usual cup of hot chocolate. Joan checked on her Sunday morning and immediately called Dr. White.

When he checked her temperature it was over 102 degrees. So on February 10th, Jeanette was taken to Evangel Hospital where she was put in complete isolation. No-one was allowed to enter her room without full cap, gown, gloves, and mask. All the symptoms of Lassa fever manifested themselves. A former patient was allowed to visit Dr. Jeanette, and she brought her a small bottle of herbal solution from her tribal medicine man. Jeanette lifted it to her lips but she could no longer swallow.

Penny Pinneo finally got the okay to go to Nigeria, but because of the civil war, SIM was having difficulty in getting her a visa . . . they were having the same problem for Jordi Casals. Neither SIM headquarters, Yale, or Columbia had any word about Dr. Jeanette's illness.

But news of her illness spread through Jos with the speed of light. The nurses took turns caring for Jeanette and Marg was involved with this. On Tuesday night she gave her a bed bath. And on Wednesday afternoon at 4:30 PM, February 18th Dr. Jeanette passed on to her heavenly home.

She was buried behind the chapel at Miango next to the grave of Charlotte Shaw.

Only two more cases came to Evangel Hospital after Dr. Jeanette's death . . . children ages eight and six . . . their cases were relatively mild and they fully recovered in due time.

Visas for Pinneo and Casals were granted the latter part of February just before they received word that Dr. Jeanette had died of Lassa fever. Penny's first reaction was absolute shock which turned to sad remorse, but then to keen determination. She would return to the Jos plateau armed and equipped to fight the killer virus . . . she was immune to it and was also bringing her own plasma and equipment to produce it.

She flew to London via BOAC and changed planes for her flight to Kano, Nigeria where SIMAIR picked her up to fly her to Jos. She was met with a warm but subdued welcome from mission staff who were still reeling under the impact of the recent tragedies. Two days later, Jordi Casals arrived at Ibadan University. The hunt for the killer virus would now begin.

The thing to determine now was where the index case came from and what animals were carrying the disease. When the village or area was found they would try to collect blood samples from the people to see how many might have Lassa antibodies, and also trap as many animals as possible which might be acting as a reservoir for the disease.

On Monday evening, March 2nd, Don Carey, Graham Kemp, and Casals packed their equipment and prepared for their drive to Jos, They stayed overnight in Bida, and then arrived in Jos. The next morning they met with the Evangel Hospital staff. Casals was especially pleased to greet Penny.

They began to look for clues to some common experience that was shared by the first eighteen patients.

At this time no one associated the disease with Tamalama Sale. She had entered and left the hospital under a false name, and her case was buried under dozens of others, not even knowing that she had Lassa Fever.

Many of the patients lived in an area of Jos along Kazaure Street so Kemp and Stroh went there to study the dusty environment, the houses, and the people. They set traps to catch mice and rats. They caught four species of rats which they sent off to the lab at Atlanta, and they kept some that they would test when they returned to Ibadan.

By the end of the first week they had gotten nowhere. At least no more patients showed up at Evangel. So they went to the various compounds of some of the patients that they could trace, and begged the members of the family and their neighbors to let them draw blood for study. Fifty-five of them agreed. So Carey and Casals returned to Ibadan with the animals and blood specimens.

Kemp, Stroh, and Penny stayed in Jos to track down everything they could find about the twenty-three patients. When were they admitted? Who visited them and when? Who was in contact with whom? What happened before the patient got to the hospital, and what happened after they left?

It became clear that the only thing in common with the patients was they were in Evangel Hospital in Ward A. They began cataloging the flow of patients and visitors and staff in meticulous detail. They took into consideration the urinals, the laundry, the food and who prepared it. How about the locations of the patients beds and the routines of the nursing and cleaning staff? They also went through all the hospital records again.

Those of the staff who came down with Lassa . . . their routine was fairly easy to trace. Finally they studied the records of former patients who might have had symptoms of Lassa Fever, and Kemp came across Tamalama's case history. He decided to follow up on this. What contact did the staff have with her? Where was she in Ward A? What patients were there at the same time and what was their location in the Ward? Kemp began to sense a clear pattern: the first seventeen cases had been patients, workers, or visitors at the hospital when Tamalama was under treatment. Only two patients could not be pinned down ... one of them was impossible to locate, and the other claiming to have only visited the outpatient pavilion. (That is where Marg worked.)

Kemp discovered that Tamalama's bed was located in the corner of the Ward where the prevailing wind swept over her toward the other patients. She had a hacking cough that spewed out a constant aerosol of germs to be carried by the breeze to the other patients.

If that theory proved true, what about the cases that followed the first seventeen? He discovered that case 17 was the husband of case 2. Case 20 was the nephew of cases 14 and 21, and also the brother of cases 23 and 24. Case 14 was the aunt of cases 20, 23, and 24.

Also most interesting was that case 15 was the brother of Tamalama who had brought her to the hospital and had taken care of her much of the time. He too registered in under a fictitious name, so they could not trace where he had come from.

The theory had possibilities. Kemp decided that they needed to try to locate Tamalama to take her blood to see if it contained Lassa antibodies. If it did, then they would trap every animal in the area and try to get blood samples from every person in the village. But who was Tamalama and where did she live?

They ran adds in the Jos newspaper asking for help in locating her. Someone thought she might be the wife of a truck driver known as King of the Railroad, and thought that her name was Soule, and that she was living in Bauchi some seventy miles northeast of Jos. So Kemp and Don Carey went to Bauchi.

When they got there, no-one seemed to know a woman by the name of Soule who was married to a truck driver, but they were referred to a woman named Sale. Upon finding her at her compound grinding millet, she was startled to be greeted by these strangers. Yes, she had been married to a Mallam Sale of Lagos, but they were now divorced. She did not know where he lived or where he worked. But she herself had never been to Evangel Hospital in Jos, nor did she know whether he had taken another wife. And that was all the information they could get out of her.

He would go to Lagos with a population of over a half million to look for Sale, the King of the Railroad. That would be a daunting task. He was told that the Hausa term for King of the Railroad also meant King of the Motor Park which seemed more logical place to look for a truck driver. So Kemp along with Ibrahim, his Fulani helper began searching all the motor parks asking if anyone knew of a driver by the name of Sale who might also be known as King of the Motor Park. No one seemed to know anything about Sale.

That evening Ibrahim introduced Kemp to a friend who was a policeman on leave. This man knew Lagos very well and suggested there were a lot of Hausa trucking concerns in northern Lagos. When the policeman offered to help, Kemp hired him on the spot.

So they went from motor park to motor park. Finally they found a truck driver who knew a man known as King of the Motor Park. With his information they made their way to the Fawaz Trucking Company only a few minutes away.

They went to the boss ... did he have a driver who was known as King of the Motor Park? Yes, but Sale was not a truck driver, he was a mechanic.

The boss took them over to a big Mercedes diesel lorry where the King of the Motor Park's rear end was sticking out of the motor. Yes, he was from the Jos Plateau and that his wife was from Bassa, a small village near Jos.

When Kemp explained through an interpreter that he wanted to draw blood from his wife, the picture changed. A massive supply of kolanuts failed to help. Why did Kemp want his wife's blood? What was wrong with her now? She had been sick awhile back. What good could come from this?

After carefully explaining that they needed to go to her village to find the cause of the killer disease and begin to deal with it, Mallam Sale finally agreed to let Kemp see his wife and get the blood specimens they needed.

Sale's one-room house was within walking distance from the motor park. Naturally Tamalama Sale was rather fearful of these three strangers who wanted her blood. No matter how much Kemp tried to persuade her, she was not willing to let him take it. Kemp turned to Mallam Sale for his support. Surprisingly, Sale backed him up. He directed Tamalama to let him take the blood. After much arguing back and forth, finally she agreed to let him take a little blood. He wanted to get 10 cc, but he only got 8 cc when she pulled her arm away. She screamed, "Shikanan!" . . . ("finish!"). He felt lucky to get even that amount.

Kent carefully plied her with questions about her illness. Slowly the vital information came. They talked for nearly a half hour before Mallam Sale said 'finish'.

Kent and his helper hurried back to Ibadan University to get the blood tested. Tamalama's blood was full of Lassa antibodies, so that confirmed that she was the index case at Evangel Hospital.

Bringing Lassa victims blood & tissue samples to Ibadan Research Lab

Armed with a lot of syringes, animal traps, and a big bag of kolanuts to be used as bribes, Kemp and his helper headed back to the Jos Plateau. He stopped at Jos to pick up George Stroh and they drove out to the small village of Bassa.

They spent a full two days getting to know the chief and the people. They gave him a lot of kolanuts, also skin mats, a goat, calabashes full of rice, and locust bean cakes. Each night they drove back to Jos.

On the third day they left early in the morning. The chief and the villagers had agreed to let them draw blood. Being the dry season, it was very cold in the morning and it was impossible to raise the veins enough to get a needle into them. Finally they got the idea to get the villagers to do calisthenics. What a sight to see seventy five villagers in their long flowing robes jumping around. Even that failed to raise the veins. Finally they decided to lead the people on a jogging run. Everybody followed them. Soon everybody was laughing and having a good time. Kemp led them back to the village where they were finally able to successfully draw blood from the seventy five people.

They returned to Jos and shipped the specimens to the CDC hot lab in Atlanta. But the job was only beginning. They returned to Bassa and hired the local hunters to trap every kind of animal, bats, and birds. Each day they collected the dead animals, tagged them, and wrapped them, packed them in ice, and sent them off to Atlanta.

They waited patiently for weeks before the results of their work came back to them. Yes, there were antibodies found in many of the villagers which indicated a local infection, but with symptoms that were often so mild they went unnoticed. But none of the animals showed any signs of Lassa. Absolute frustration set in as to the host source of the disease.

Don Carey even went back to the village of Lassa, obtained blood samples, and animals, and came back with the same familiar results. Many of the people had Lassa antibodies, but the animals showed no presence of the virus.

Month after month went by with no more people coming down with Lassa fever, the research relaxed a bit. But not doctor John Frame . . . he checked the blood of every missionary to enter his office for Lassa antibodies. Brian Henderson at Atlanta checked doctor Frame's blood samples at the hot lab. He wrote in a medical journal that the mission station at Telekoro, Guinea appears to be a particularly favorable environment for infection of the disease with three missionaries there coming down with Lassa fever from which they had survived.

Not far from Telkoro early in March of 1972 an outbreak of Lassa fever occurred at the Curran Lutheran Hospital at Zorzor. Seven nurses were stricken with the disease. A medical alert was activated with plans to rush assistance from the United States and from Nigeria. Penny Pinneo arrived with the immune serum which was given to the stricken patients. Of the eleven, four patients died. The outbreak at Zorzor died down almost as quickly as it had arisen.

Hunters trapped 164 rodents and bats . . . blood and tissue samples were shipped to Atlanta. Again no signs of the virus were found.

Just a hundred miles from Zorzor another outbreak occurred at the Panguma Catholic Hospital with patients coming in over a nine month period with a number of them dying. Of the sixty four patients, twenty three died.

In the home of one of the victims, eight brown rats (Mastomys Natalensis) were trapped along with other animals. Again specimens were sent to Atlanta. Seven of the eight rats had the Lassa virus! At last they had found the carrier of the deadly disease. Now the problem would shift to the intelligent control of this rodent reservoir and the long involved process of developing a vaccine.

CHAPTER 35
Contributions From The Other Pilots

SIMAIR Pilot/Mechanics—Bill Tuck, Bob Swingle, Leroy Andrews, Johnny Clay,
Dave Rutt, Jim Wayner, Bob Ediger, Paul Rogalsky, Rich Schaffer

When I first started writing my book I chose for the title "The SIMAIR Story". As I progressed in my writing I realized that this was MY story, so I renamed it "Just One SIMAIR Story". Each one of the pilots should also be writing HIS story. And as I started sending out my email version of the book one chapter at a time, it inspired others to do the same. Ethelyn Abernethy wrote her memoirs and has sent it out to a number of people . . . She tells about the pioneering days in the Kagoro—Kwoi area . . . Ethelyn passed away at the age of 103!

Ruth Long has done the same . . . she tells about the beginning of Galmi Hospital in Niger. You can contact her at burulo@embarqmail.com.

Hazel and Archie Elliot have written and published their story . . . Harold and Elma Hide are also writing their story.

As I'm nearing the end of my book, I have asked the other pilots to send me of what they recall as "Their most memorable flight". A number of them have done this. Soddy passed away before he could do this, but Alice sent me copies of about thirty of their prayer letters for me to glean from. So who better can I start out with than the first SIMAIR pilot.

Clarence (Soddy) and Alice Soderberg, and little daughter Janet left for Nigeria December 10th, 1946. Their first letter from the field was a ringing challenge to the people back home to get off their rear ends and fulfill Christ's mandate to "go into all the world and preach the gospel". One thing I noticed in most of their letters, Soddy was not just a pilot, and Alice was not just a nurse; they were also busy telling the 'good news' and winning people to the Lord.

The plane (a three-place Piper Super Cruiser which they named the "Evangel" VR-NAC) was scheduled to arrive in Lagos February 18th 1947, so Soddy went down there to supervise the assembly and take care of the licensing, etc.

Jack Dreidiger and (Soddy) Clarence Soderberg with Piper Super Cruiser Evangel"

In their 1947 Easter letter they mention the need for $2500 . . . funds to build a house. While Alice was in Minna studying the Hausa Language, Soddy was busy flying out of Kano. She comments, "Since the plane arrived seven weeks ago, Soddy has only been home three times. The longest stay was for a day and a half."

Their June 1947 letter envisions, "the need for two planes and three pilots and a fulltime mechanic by another year as there is more work than I can handle. This will enable us all to go to language study and so be able to actively minister to the nationals when we aren't flying, and to keep the plane flying six days a week."

Their August 1947 letter tells about the arrival of Canadian Jack Driediger to be the fulltime mechanic. His first job was to work on the Evangel which had been grounded for some reason. After Jack got the plane going, they would be going to Minna to start language study. Soddy also hopes there will be another pilot coming soon. Also, there is the desire to have four radios to be set up at Ilorin, Minna, Sokoto, and Jos.

I learned from Penny Pinneo (remember her in chapter 34?) what the "grounded for some reason" was all about. Here is what she wrote . . . "Soddy flew a visiting eye specialist from Minna to Kano, but a severe thunderstorm caused them to return to Minna. The doctor said he had had enough of small plane flying, so refused to fly the next day.

Therefore, Soddy flew to Jos with Jane Machen, a new missionary, who was having severe headaches. She had had a brain concussion from a basketball accident shortly before leaving for Africa. I went on the flight as attending nurse. After a month, Jane did not improve, so the doctor felt that she should return to the States.

In May of 1947, Soddy, Jane, and I set out from Jos to Lagos where Jane would join five other SIM-ers on their flight to the States. Soddy got caught above the low clouds and he got lost. The gas gauges registered zero when he spotted a road and began to follow it, as the trees were too thick to land on the road.

We came to the town of Akure, about sixty miles northeast of Lagos. Soddy spotted a football field and successfully set the plane down. It was a Catholic school and the two priests invited Jane and me to their house where they fed us bacon and eggs, and offered us a bed where we could rest. I had been given a lot of money for the six who were to fly home on Pan Am that day, so I was a bit leery of sleeping.

Soddy bummed some car gas and planned to take off and fly to an airport where he could get some av-gas. He had some bushes cut at the far end of the field. He took off okay, but hit some trees and crashed, breaking the prop and damaging a wing.

An expatriate engineer offered to disassemble the plane and put it on the train to Lagos. In the late afternoon, Soddy was able to hire a Ford pickup and a driver to continue our journey. The lights on the truck did not work, but it was a beautiful moonlit night as we drove through the jungle. Jane's pulse was very weak and occasionally she became unconscious which was a great concern to us.

We arrived at Lagos airport about six in the morning. The Pan Am plane was delayed and was leaving at 10 AM, so that was an answer to prayer. Those waiting for us had heard rumors that our plane had crashed and that we had been killed!"

So this is the story as to why "the plane was grounded for some reason!" SIMAIR was able to order the wing parts and a new propeller to get the plane flying again.

The next letter is May 1948 and they announce the arrival of their second daughter, Joanne Elizabeth, 6 # 12 oz . . . Mother and baby doing well. The Evangel has been flying for one and a half months. Two medical emergency flights were made from Kano to Jos. One was for a one-year old baby, Jean Osborne, who was deathly ill with some kind of virus. Through the prayers of God's people and the flight in the Evangel she recovered to normal health. Alice says, "This is the hot season and the thermometer registers consistently 112 degrees in the shade. We are going to Miango for our holiday."

November 1948 . . . Alice Soderberg is back in the States to undergo surgery to remove a kidney stone. Soddy remains on the field because of the heavy load of flying. Soddy gives a summary of the first eleven months of flying. Total hours flown: 340 for an average of 31 hours per month. 195 flights were made carrying 263 passengers for a total of 30,875 miles. 21 medical emergencies. Soddy preaches in the Kano church and five people came forward to accept Christ into their lives.

Johnny Clay and family arrived February 18th, 1949. The Soderbergs go back to Minna to study Hausa. They return to Kano and the Clays go to language school. Another pilot, Johnny Schearer and wife are in candidate school, but they are turned down because of her poor health. SIMAIR is now averaging over a hundred hours a month and we are desperately hoping for another plane. Soddy has frequent attacks of malaria but is doing better on the new drug Aralen.

January 1950 . . . The year opens with a full week of flying for Soddy. A new engine has been installed in the Evangel. Most of the funds ($7,000) are now available to buy a new Cessna 170. Johnny Clay is in Jos supervising the building of a hangar. They also need funds to complete that project.

11 April 1950 . . . Today Soddy made his second flight into French country and gets home just before dark absolutely exhausted and goes to bed early. Holiday to Miango is postponed until the middle of May as Soddy has to fly. Johnny Clay and Jack Driediger are down in Lagos assembling the new plane. Alice tells about an old woman who is blind. She is told they can do nothing to restore her sight. Alice tells her, "We can't give you light to your eyes, but we can give you light for your soul." And she tells the woman about the way of salvation, and leads her to the Lord.

The June 1950 letter has a picture of Soddy, Johnny, and Jack standing by the new Cessna which they named the Herald . . .

"It carries three passengers comfortably where the Evangel carried two passengers tightly cramped . . . also it carries three times the baggage and goes 120 miles per hour . . . we can also put a stretcher in the plane!" In the first month Johnny flew the Cessna 72 hours, carrying 67 passengers . . . five were medical flights.

The question arises; what to do with the Piper Cruiser? In a short time the fabric will have to be replaced. We can't honestly sell it that way. Or should we fly it for another year and then completely scrap it? Or should we fly it for another year, then recover the plane, and overhaul both engines, and then sell it? It would give the customer a good airplane and that would give us the greatest profit.

Betty Greene, from Missionary Aviation Fellowship, arrived on the February 14th, 1951, and flew for SIMAIR for about ten months while the Soderbergs went on furlough. She was most noted for her service during the Second World War, working in the WASPS as a test pilot, and also ferrying bombers across the Atlantic. I met her on my first furlough when I visited MAF headquarters in California where she was working as an ordinary secretary.

Before they go, Soddy has a medical emergency flight for someone who has an appendicitis.

December 1951 . . . While home on furlough Soddy goes to school, studying toward getting an aircraft and engine license so he can also help maintain the airplanes.

The Joe and Lois Swanson family arrived in Nigeria the 11th of October, 1951. SIMAIR is now hoping to get a third plane.

Their next letter dated March 1954 says, "We just completed our first year of our second term. This past year we have flown over 1500 hours carrying some 1750 passengers. We have averaged a stretcher flight per month." One such flight is made to Kaltungo for Bob Cooke, who had spinal meningitis, in July 1956. The Soderbergs packed to go home when I arrived in April of 1957.

The next SIMAIR pilot was Johnny Clay. As mentioned before, he and Dorothy, and their kids, Larry, Lindy, and Suzie, arrived the 18th of February 1949. He was an ex-air force pilot. You can read about him in chapter 21. He was my favorite SIMAIR pilot and was like a dad to me down through the years. They had to go home in November of 1966 because of Dorothy's kidney failure. Johnny served for many years as Visitation Pastor in their church in San Diego. In his sixteen years with SIMAIR, he probably flew about 8000 hours.

Betty Greene, from Missionary Aviation Fellowship, arrived on the 14th of February 1951, and flew for SIMAIR for about ten months while the Soderbergs went home on furlough. She was most noted for her service during the Second World War working in the WASPS as a test pilot and also ferrying bombers across the Atlantic. I met her on my first furlough when I visited the MAF headquarters in California where she was working as an ordinary secretary.

As mentioned before, Joe and Lois Swanson arrived the 11th of October 1951. He was a navy pilot during the Second World War where he was credited for shooting down two Japanese planes and two probables. They are now retired in Florida. I have tried unsuccessfully to get him to write his story. Their missionary career was a hard one as they suddenly lost their dear little daughter, Barby, when she was in the first grade at Kent Academy. They went home in June of 1962 after serving the Lord with SIMAIR for about ten and a half years.

Paul and Bea Rogalsky arrived in Nigeria on the 11th of October 1952 and served the Lord for 22 1/2 years with SIMAIR. You see him mentioned in other chapters of my book. He is the most non-communicative person I have ever known. Not once has he ever replied to any letters that I have written to him, so needles to say, I have no memorable story from him.

I remember him most for efficiently running the parts department . . . a job I unhappily inherited when they stayed home.

Rich Schaffer, Paul Rogalsky, Bill Tuck, Joe Swanson   *Checking a parts order from the USA*

They retired from the field because of Bea's health problems. She passed away and years later Paul married Birdie. They now live somewhere in New Mexico. Paul now has Parkinson's disease that is making life hard for him. He was a fantastic guy.

(Just got word from Johnny, his son, saying that his dad had a stroke and passed away.)

SIMAIR Pilots Paul Rogalsky, John Clay, Joe Swanson

Dick and Joanne Vossler arrived the 27th of November 1953 and had a wild missionary career of about three and one half years. You can read a bit about him in a couple of other chapters. He was a guy who could never say no to anyone and as a result he went home a burned out man. Sad to say, this happens to a number of missionaries. I got a letter from Dick one time telling about an airline flight from Connecticut to Florida. They were encountering a number of thunderstorms . . . and then he said, "You will not believe how scared I was of those storms in Nigeria!" You would have never known that about Dick Vossler. Joanne is living in Florida and I communicate with her often by email.

I received a letter from Dick dated the 14th of December of 1962 in which he tells about some of his memorable flights.

"July 26, 1956 . . . A call came in that Mrs. E. Jones was suffering from an ectopic pregnancy and needed to be flown to the mission hospital. The flight went from Jos to Wukari to drop off two SUM missionaries to their station. From Wukari we flew over to Makurdi to pick up another SUM missionary and to take on fuel. Then we flew west to Ilorin to pick up Mrs. Jones. It was now late in the day and heavy rain squalls could be expected on the Jos Plateau.

As we approached the escarpment, heavy dark cloud masses covered the plateau right down to the ground. I couldn't find a way into Jos so I decided to fly back to Keffi where there was a Baptist mission hospital and a doctor.

After we landed, we learned that the doctor was out visiting in the villages, taking care of any medical needs, and was not expected back for several days. There were competent nurses at the hospital. However, there were no tie-downs and it would not be very wise to leave the plane unsecured overnight at the airstrip, so I decided to make another try for Jos. If unsuccessful, I would fly on to Kaduna and stay there overnight.

There were openings on the edge of the plateau. By hugging the ground and weaving my way through the weather, I reached the main road at Bukuru. By now it was dark so I followed the car-lights northward until I came to the road leading to the airport, landed okay on runway 08, and took Mrs. Jones to the hospital. (My comments here: Flying at night in Nigeria is definitely not recommended. You can go back to chapter 26 and read of my experience when Lynn and I were flying the Aztec at night into Kano.)

"I'll tell you of another incident. SIMRAD received a call during the noon watch that Bob Cooke was suspected to have spinal meningitis. I picked up Dr. Roger Troup and we rushed out to the airport. I filed my flight plan with the tower by radio as we taxied out for takeoff on runway 08. The weather was clear and we reached Kaltungo in one and a half hours.

Roger went to the house and examined Bob and confirmed that he definitely had meningitis. They brought Bob to the plane and we loaded him onto the stretcher.

Later, Bob's wife confided to me that when she saw that plane take off, she felt that she would never see her husband alive again. But thanks to the use of the radio, the airplane, modern medicine, and well trained missionary personnel, God worked in Bob's life to heal and return him to his ministry at Kaltungo."

"I'll throw in another story to show people that not everything we did was of a catastrophic nature and that there was fun and humor in our work at times.

On one of my flights to take missionary kids to school at Kent Academy, I picked up three boys at Ilorin, and then flew up to Minna to pick up Dr. Cummins' two girls. It was getting too late and with the bad weather, we decided to stay overnight.

The three boys had a room to themselves while I was to sleep in a cottage a short distance away. Without a chaperon, the boys were having a ball fooling around. I finally went over and told them to shut up and get some sleep . . . we would be leaving at the crack of dawn. But they kept on, and I gave them my third and final warning.

One of the boys became the pastor of the church where my son, Greg, attended in Connecticut. He still remembered the event 30 years later. I growled at them, "The next one who makes a sound will have to come over to my room and spend the night with me!" Donny was so sure that his squeaky bed would make a noise that he was afraid to move a muscle and he awoke the next morning feeling very stiff."

"I hope these incidents will be what you want. There were others, but these are representative both of our flying and types of events that made our flying worthwhile. So much of our flying was the day to day ho-hum routine, but people need to hear about these events in order to appreciate the value of the technical missionaries . . . and people who have these skills need to come and join us."

"My totals for the four years with SIMAIR were 1867 hours, flying 208,560 accident free miles, and 443,820 passenger miles."

Bill and Gladys Tuck and their two girls, Becky and Debbie, arrived the 24th of January 1956. Bill was our fulltime mechanic. I pay tribute to him in my book dedication. He is mentioned a number of places in my book. We owed our lives to this guy. Gladys was a nurse and worked in X-ray at Evangel Hospital. They went home in June of 1983 after 26 1/2 years of faithful service to the Lord. A number of years ago Bill died of a brain tumor. Gladys is still retired in the Toronto area.

I also want to add Ray Browneye here. Although he wasn't a SIMAIR pilot, we considered him as one of us. Here are his words.

"The Sudan United Mission (Christian Reformed Church . . . or CRC branch) began an aviation program under the guidance of SIMAIR. I, Ray Browneye, was their pilot/ mechanic. Due to my lack of experience, SIMAIR was requested to pilot ride with me until I had 350 hours of pilot time.

The SIMAIR pilots were most helpful. They had more than enough to do without this added burden, but they willingly gave of their time and expertise to this novice pilot and the new program.

Rich Schaffer was the monitoring pilot one day on a trip from Jos to Kaduna. The weather was marginal. We slipped off the northwest edge of the plateau just under the overcast in moderate rain. Rich gave guidance and we avoided the heaviest of what became heavy rainfall. I was unfamiliar with this kind of hedge-hopping, but I was getting a real initiation to the type of flying that had to be done and could be done safely in the tropics if there were definite limits. I didn't know the limits . . . Rich did. The 120 mile trip was loaded with instruction. Just as things really got dark and turning back became a real option in the decision making process, a path to lighter rain opened and then we suddenly burst out of the front end of the westerly moving line squall. I breathed a lot easier and Rich had the look of a satisfied instructor.

Had there been lightning, heavy turbulence, or other factors that elevated the dangers of the operation, it would have necessitated a 180 degree turn, but that day everything worked out and we were able to complete the flight safely, but under different conditions than I had ever flown through.

The CRC Mission, their aviation department, and I personally, owe a huge debt of thanks to SIMAIR for the patient and skillful orientation given to me at the beginning of our flight program. The SUM flight service continued for years and thousands of hours. It had its humble beginning under the guidance of SIMAIR. A cordial cooperation developed from that beginning, but it always seemed as though SIMAIR gave far more than it received."

Graduate of Moody Aviation, Dave and Lyda Rutt and family arrived October 23rd, 1959 and flew for SIMAIR until 1974 when he took himself off flying for medical reasons, but then continued on until September 1981 teaching Bible at various places. Lyda passed away and later Dave married Carol Edger. They now live at the Sebring Village in Florida. Here is his story.

Did you ever hear the statement, "don't trust your fuel gage?" Well, I have often given that advice and thought I believed it. But my day came on March 7th 1973 while on an instrument flight from Maradi, Niger to Kano, Nigeria. I was cleared down to 4,000 feet to report beacon outbound for an instrument approach to Runway 07 at the Kano International Airport. I was estimating the beacon at 33 past the hour. It was now 32 and the unbelievable happened! The fuel pressure gage dropped to zero followed by that deathly silence from a loss of power. Latest visibility report was 200 meters in Kano, the sky was obscured in thick dust haze. I was on solid instruments and going down in a power off glide to that dusty earth below. How did I ever get into this predicament?

I had been flying for over twelve years with SIM and had recently passed the one million mile mark in West Africa. This Harmattan was nothing new to me but it seldom gets this thick. My logbook boasts of 7299 hours of which 506 is instrument time. Ninety percent of this was in Africa. I knew the terrain over which I was flying even though it was now invisible.

I had been up in Niger for the past eight days. Half that time I had been flying in thick Harmattan conditions. One day I was flying up to Tahoua and only minutes away when I ran into a sandstorm and the visibility suddenly went down to 300 meters. I squeaked into Tahoua and there I sat all day as the visibility dropped below 200 meters. My next destination was reporting visibility down to 80 meters!

But now I was on my way home. I had topped the fuel tanks at Niamey, giving me a 900 mile range for a 585 mile flight to Kano with four stops along the way. I was flying George Learned on one of his TEE trips (Theological Education by Extension) where we would fly him in a circuit around Niger so he could teach the national pastors. We would go into a station where the class was held. At each stop I would pre-flight the plane before taking off which included opening the fuel cover lid, removing the fuel cap, and taking a satisfying look at the fuel in each tank.

(Rich's comments: Evidently Dave did not have a dip stick along on this trip with which to measure the fuel in each tank. The dip stick is a half inch square piece of mahogany which was made for each plane. We put in five gallons of fuel, dipped the tank, and marked the stick, and did it again and again until the tank was full. So when you dipped the tanks you would know exactly how much fuel you have in each tank. The Comanche 180 burns about 8 gallons per hour at a 65% power setting so 50 gallons or full tanks would give you approximately 6 hours and 25 minute of flying time. At one of those stops with the planes unguarded, someone could have stolen fuel from the plane. Also, if you didn't fasten the fuel cap properly (they are adjustable) fuel will siphon from the tank. So just looking in the tank, you don't really have a clue how much fuel is in there).

Our last stop in Niger was at Maradi where we checked out of the country. I filed an IFR flight plan for 7,000 feet for Kano just one hour away. At 5,000 feet we topped the Harmattan dust and were flying smoothly in bright blue skies. I was flying with the fuel selector switched to the left tank. About 20 minutes into the flight the engine faltered and I switched to the right tank.

As we were coming closer to Kano, we began picking up the clear crisp English voice of Kano center.

I contacted Kano Center and he replied, "Five November Alfa Charlie Charlie . . . You are cleared IFR into Kano . . . flight level seven zero . . . no delay expected for your approach to runway zero seven . . . visibility 300 meters and deteriorating rapidly.

"Roger Kano Center . . . Charlie Charlie copied that."

"Okay Charlie Charlie . . . change now to Kano tower . . . 118.1 for descent and landing instructions."

"Roger Charlie Charlie."

I switched over to the 118.1 . . . "Hello Kano tower . . . Five November Alpha Charlie Charlie . . . requesting descent from seven zero . . . estimating Kilo Alpha Beacon at 36."

"Roger Charlie Charlie . . . you are cleared down to 4000 feet to the beacon . . . QNH 29.87 inches . . . report Kilo Alpha outbound at four zero . . . visibility now 200 meters."

"Roger Kano tower . . . Charlie Charlie leaving seven zero for four zero. QNH 29.87 200 meters . . . report over the beacon outbound for approach to runway zero seven."

At that point George nudges me and points to the fuel gage which is now showing empty, "Aren't you concerned about that?"

I sorta laughed, "Aww . . . you can't trust those gages . . . we have plenty of fuel."

We were now at 4000 feet approaching the beacon. I reduced power and slowed the plane down to 120 MPH. And then it happened . . . the engine began sputtering and quit completely. It was deathy quiet. George looks at me and I look at George.

George gasps, "What do we do now?"

"You pray and I'll see what we can do to get her down safely!"

So George removes his hat and that cockpit became a sacred sanctuary. I, the optimist, expected within sixty seconds to arrive over the beacon, turn left to the runway and make a smooth landing on 07.

"Kano tower . . . Five Charlie Charlie declaring an emergency . . . we just lost our power and are descending for an emergency landing!"

"Five Charlie Charlie . . . confirm that you are making an emergency landing short of the airfield?"

Looking straight down I could see some fields and trees below. We were barely 200 feet above the ground.

"George . . . Do you see the road?"

"Yeah . . . I see it . . . a paved road!"

"Which way is it going?"

"It's coming over to your side!"

I dropped the gear. The Katsina road appears. Plenty of room between the trees.

"Roger Kano . . . we are landing on the Katsina road!"

"Confirm you are landing on the Katsina road?"

We flare out and touch down smoothly on the road.

"Okay Kano . . . we are now on the road!"

"Charlie Charlie . . . we are barely reading you . . . Confirm you are now on the road?"

"Affirmative . . . affirmative . . . Charlie is safe on the ground!"

Roger Charlie Charlie . . . come to the control tower as soon as possible!"

We rolled to a stop just behind a lorry traveling in the same direction. "Thank You Lord . . . for Your protection!"

We hopped out and I grabbed the tow bar and parked the plane far enough off the road so it wouldn't get hit by any road traffic. I made my way to the airport while George stayed with the plane. We were two miles from the beacon . . . just one minute out!

Some of you would call this just plain dumb luck. Well . . . we call it a miracle . . . a miracle of our wonderful God who looks out for His own.

When they heard my story . . . one of the guys in the tower said, "Your God is very great . . . He has done something wonderful for you today . . . now you must go and make a sacrifice to Him!"

I quickly responded, "My God provided Himself a sacrifice for me in the person of Jesus Christ, and now all that I owe Him is a living sacrifice of my life to be lived for His glory!"

In 4 hours and 45 minutes I did away with 6 hours of fuel. I'm sure that ol' Charlie Charlie didn't burn all that. I could find no leaks and the gas caps were on tight. But one thing for sure . . . I now always carry a fuel stick to dip the tanks to confirm exactly how much fuel is in those tanks. Lesson learned.

Bob Ediger, Dave Rutt, Bill Tuck, John Clay, Joe Swanson

Bob and Yvonne Ediger, 3 year old David, 18 month old Suzanne, and one in the saddle yet to be born, Danny, arrived in Nigeria 28th of March 1959. And they left the field in June of 1983 after about eight years with SIMAIR.

Several weeks ago I phoned Bob to see if I could get him to contribute to this chapter. In about four tries, all I ever got was their answering machine. Then I got a surprise call from their son David, saying that he was at Bob's place to begin clearing out the place as Bob had just passed away about a month ago. Yvonne had passed away about a year before. When I told David my reason for calling, he said he would send me some stories written by his Mom about some of the events that took place over the years. So here are some of those stories.

CAN A MUD PUDDLE GUIDE AN AIRPLANE TO A REMOTE AIRSTRIP?

"I had flown some missionaries back to their station in Upper Volta from their holiday at Miango and needed to pick up another missionary at Mahadaga who was flying out of Kano the next day for her furlough. It was getting late when I took off. In fact, it got dark before I reached my destination! It would be like "hunting for a needle in a haystack" to find this grass strip in the middle of nowhere. There is no tower, no lights, and no navigational helps. But God (Ahh . . . I like that . . . BUT GOD!) provided a moonlit night which reflected in a puddle of water at the low end of the airstrip, left there from the thunderstorm that had passed through there that afternoon! I lowered my gear and landed, stopping at the edge of that puddle! The next morning I flew the missionary on to Kano just on time to catch her flight. Is God faithful or what?"

VISITED BY AN ANGEL?

We were home on furlough and living in Santa Cruz, California. As many of you know, missionaries have a low income. Sometime earlier I had signed up to provide a meal for the

318

assistant pastor who just had surgery. Usually that is not a problem, but on that particular day I had nothing in the house with which to make the meal, nor the money to buy it. So we did what we always do when we have a need . . . we prayed.

Bob was away at the time. Around 0900 in the morning there was a knock on the door. I opened the door to find a young teenager who asked, "Are you Mrs. Ediger?"

"Yes, I am?"

With that he handed me a check for $30.00 and disappeared. We have no idea who he was or where he went.

It didn't take me long to cash the check and buy the groceries we needed. And we delivered the meal on time.

(My comment: "Who wrote the check ?")

CAN THE AZTEC TAKE OFF ON ONE ENGINE?

I had just flown a load of missionaries from Sokoto to Jos. Hopped down to Oyi for another load in the Aztec. The baggage and passengers were loaded, but one of the engines would not turn over . . . the solenoid would not engage the starter. I had the passengers get out and unload the baggage to make the plane as light as possible. I restarted the one engine, roared down the runway and took off. The bad engine was wind-milling so I feathered it. When I got to a sufficient altitude, I re-feathered it and it started right up. Then I returned and landed and kept both engines running while the baggage and passengers were reloaded. I flew home to Jos as if nothing had ever happened. When Paul Rogalsky heard about it he really gave me a good chewing out. This happened to me again in Maradi, but this time I didn't tell anybody. So yes, the Aztec will take off on one engine! And all the missionaries met their schedules safely.

(My comment: "How dumb can you get?")

EVACUATING KALTUNGO

At the start of the Nigerian—Biafran civil war the northern Hausas started killing all the Ibos in the North. This also took place in Kaltungo at the schools and the hospital. Jos alerted Kaltungo that they were sending a plane to evacuate all the women and children. I took off in the Aztec and headed to Kaltungo 160 miles away. As I neared Kaltungo I dropped down to treetop level to alert as few as possible, and landed from the South. We had radioed the missionaries to have the evacuees waiting near the North end. Without stopping the engines the women and children (11 in all) were quickly loaded into the six passenger Aztec. As I swung the plane around, half way down the airstrip came a murderous mob running onto the runway brandishing sticks and machetes and rocks. I poured the coal to the engines and accelerated toward them. Fortunately, they scattered enough so that we took off safely. Many of the Ibos in the schools and in the hospital were killed that day.

Leroy and Charlotte Andrews were the next SIMAIR pilot. Andy graduated from the Moody Aviation Course and Char was a Missions major. They arrived in Nigeria in April of 1963 and retired about seven years later in June of 1970. Andy was a quiet guy who didn't say much and he was a nice addition to the aviation department. I couldn't get him to contribute to this chapter, so I'll give you the email that he wrote to me on the 28th of November 2003.

"Thank you. I feel like I know you better than I did in Nigeria. You can send me more than four chapters at a time. We both grew up poor. When I was one year old, we lived in a cave in the desert west of Glendale, Arizona. It was dug into the side of a hill. The roof was Saguaro cactus ribs with canvas and dirt over them. My dad was responsible for keeping the water trough for someone's sheep.

After that we moved into a migrant labor camp in a grapefruit orchard. My dad worked in the orchard. When I was about four or five we moved to Marion, Ohio and lived with one of our uncles until we rented a four-bedroom house from the local junk yard. It cost us $15.00 a month, and the outhouse was about a hundred feet behind it. Another hundred feet beyond that were the railroad tracks that were pretty busy most of the time.

After the 6th grade, we moved back to Arizona again and lived in the same migrant labor camp. We went this time to conduct Sunday School services in several of the migrant camps in the area. We picked, chopped, and hoed cotton for our spending money, or picked grapefruit. I have picked beans, tomatoes, grapefruit, cotton, peaches, plums, grapes, and watermelons from Arizona to California. One summer we lived in an old bus and worked different places around Visalia, California, picking different crops.

Anyway, I have really enjoyed reading the chapters you have sent.

Thanks, Leroy"

(My comments: Wow! Now I know more than ever before why I changed the title of my book to "Just One SIMAIR Story." Indeed, each one of us has a story to tell of how our wondrous God led and worked and cared for us and made us what He wanted us to be. I wish we knew more of Andy's story. Maybe how he came to know the Lord and how he was led to apply for the Aviation Course at Moody).

Jim and Julie Wayner, another Moody Aviation grad, arrived in Nigeria the 1st of March 1964 and was in the Aviation Department off and on for about eight years until June of 1972. He flew a total of 2989 hours.

"On one of my overnight trips into Chad during the Harmattan season, the next morning visibility was between 50 and 100 yards with Jos reporting about 400 yards. While waiting another day for better visibility, one of the French Embassy wives became deathly ill with kidney or liver problems. The next morning was no better and they feared for her life if I couldn't get her to Evangel Hospital in Jos. Weather at Enugu and Port Harcourt near the ocean was reported to be 1000 to 1500 yards where I could do an ADF Approach if necessary. With only 50 yards visibility at N'Goure and full tanks, I taxied twice down the gravel strip only seeing the edges. By setting the DG compass at 60 degrees the plane seemed to stay in the middle of the strip.

Jim Wayner

After much prayer, we took off flying the DG and not seeing the strip. Flying instruments all the way to Jos, I was able to pick up the local radio station (the antenna is just west of the airport). On the second try I found the west end of runway 28. The next day one of the nurses commented that she would have probably died if we hadn't gotten her in that day. Praise the Lord she recovered and she also accepted the Lord while at Evangel."

"Another miracle experience was when I lost eight inches off one propeller blade on the right engine of the Aztec. I had been in and out of small airstrips like Kwoi all day. My last leg of the day's flights was into Kano International Airport to pick up a family who had just arrived from the USA and take them to Jos. On takeoff we were about fifty feet in the air when the tip of the blade broke off. The plane began to shudder violently. I immediately pulled back on the power and glided to a safe landing. As I touched the ground, I pulled the fuel mixture and killed the engine. A replacement prop was flown up from Jos. If this had happened earlier in the day at one of our short strips, it would have meant loss of the airplane and possibly loss of life as well. Thank you, Lord!"

Bob Swingle arrived 19 May 1964 and served with SIMAIR until June 1977. They had two boys out there, Tim and Steve. Tim is presently on deputation to raise his support, getting ready to work in the hills of West Virginia. The Swingles came home on the charter flight at the same time as we did to retire from SIM. They were detained for three days by the health officials as Steve had a fever. (This was the height of the Lassa Fever scare). I asked Bob if he would do a write-up of that incident, so hopefully he will do that for us. The following is one of Swingle's stories.

OF AIRPLANES AND LIONS

It was a beautiful day with no haze and no thunderstorms . . . the kind of day pilots dream of. The kind of day that pessimists have time to imagine the engine is running rough but not even that could be felt. I left Jos solo and flew the 150 miles to Kano to check out of the country and then headed west 550 miles to Upper Volta (now called Burkino Faso). After checking in at Diapaga, I flew on to Fada-Ngourma for a night stop. I buzzed the mission station and then landed at the airstrip. It was early afternoon and I was looking forward to a great time with our missionaries and the students at the Bible School. I had bought about 20 bicycle tires for the students and was always interested in their progress.

Today, however, I was met by two pickup trucks and several French expatriates. Since my French consisted of three days in high school, we had a problem. The missionaries were about ten minutes from the airstrip, so the men took me over to one of the pickups where a man lay bandaged from head to toe. He had been hunting lions and after wounding one, his gun jammed, and the lion attacked him. He managed to pull out his pistol and finished off the lion, but not before he received an extensive mauling.

His guide dragged him to a dirt road where "two cars a day was heavy traffic", but within twenty minutes a doctor came along. The doctor brought him to the village, but all that was available was aspirin and bandages. (comment: I'm surprised that the good doctor didn't have his black bag with him.) They had called the Capitol on short wave radio, but the only airplane available was "on tour" and couldn't be contacted. While they were deciding what to do, I arrived on the scene. Thinking that I was the rescue airplane, they couldn't understand why I knew nothing of their situation. Our missionaries arrived about that time and all was cleared up. Our missionaries went back to their station for the stretcher that SIMAIR had placed at a number of our stations. I removed the rear seat and installed the stretcher, and I checked the map for the route to Ouagadougou as I had never flown there before. Many times during that one-hour flight I heard him say, perhaps the only two English words he knew, "Thank you, Thank you!"

The flight saved many hours of hot, rough road travel over a dirt road. We called ahead and had an ambulance waiting at the airport. The tower accepted my flight plan via radio and I returned back to Fada just before dark.

The next morning I was on my way back to Jos with the missionaries I had gone for. I heard later that the lion hunter would have lost both his legs if he had gone by road to the hospital, but as it was, they removed over four pounds of gangrenous flesh. Yes, he survived to hunt lions again.

We wish we could tell of great spiritual victories from this incident, but I was told he was not responsive to contacts made by the missionaries. We trust that the seeds of kindness will some day win this guy to the Lord.

Bob Swingle

Bob and Anita Swingle Visiting

Gary and Pat Sheppard arrived in December of 1967 and were with SIMAIR until June 1979 . . . almost 12 years. Gary flew a little over 9500 hours. Even though he was black-balled by Moody Aviation, SIM accepted him and he proved to be a valuable asset to the Mission. In fact, he and Pat are still faithfully serving the Lord here on the home front wearing many hats around SIM Headquarters and Sebring Retirement Village. SIMAIR had four Comanche 180's, and later got two Comanche 260's. Here is Gary's most memorable flight in 5N-AHS.

On December 13th, 1976, I was flying VFR on top of a thick layer of heavy Harmattan dust from Jos to Lagos to pick up Derek Frost, our mission photographer. Suddenly, the engine coughed and sputtered and then began running smoothly again. I checked all the settings. Everything looked normal. I thought that probably some water had gone through the fuel system . . . no big deal.

Gary Sheppard

323

Upon landing at Lagos, I drained the gascolators, and then ran and checked the engine. All seemed well, so Derek and I took off for Igbaja where we picked up four young seminary students who had never been in a plane before. After takeoff, I again climbed up to cruising altitude above the dust and set course for Jos. About an hour into the flight I poured myself a cup of coffee and settled back to enjoy it. I was thinking about all the things I wanted to do at home that evening. Suddenly, the engine began to speed up! I set the cup of coffee on the floor and scanned the gauges on the instrument panel. All were okay until I got to the oil pressure gage that read ZERO!

I immediately throttled back the engine and turned the plane toward Bida airport. As I had not seen the ground for an hour, I had to make an educated guess as to the location. I prayed and asked the Lord for protection and wisdom. Then I picked up the mike and began calling, "Mayday! Mayday! Mayday! This is Five November Hotel Sierra . . . Six souls on board . . . Engine failure in the vicinity of Bida!" I called and called, but received no answer. At a time like that, silence is not golden!

I knew we were paralleling a road to the north of us. It was the only place where I could possibly land the plane. If we could only find that road! As we descended into the dust, I could see nothing ahead or even straight down until we were about five hundred feet above the ground.

Sometime during the descent, I looked down and saw that cup of coffee on the floor. I thought, "That may be the last cup of coffee I ever have. I might as well enjoy it!" I picked up that cup and began drinking. The passengers, seeing this, thought, "Everything must be okay." And no-one panicked.

Suddenly, the road appeared out of nowhere and I turned the plane to line up for landing. No way! . . . Mounds of gravel had been placed down the center of the road in preparation for repairing it! "Lord, PLEASE give me a place to land this airplane!"

By this time, we were very low to the ground. And just ahead a tiny village came into view. We barely skimmed over the tops of the huts! And just ahead was an open field. I kept the wheels up. Just before touching down, the engines went to pieces and the plane shook like a dog shaking a rag doll. I shut down the engine and we skidded to a safe landing in the tall elephant grass.

"Get out . . . Get out!", I yelled to my passengers as there would be a danger of fire. But there was no fire. We bowed our heads and thanked the Lord for a safe landing. The time was about 1500.

Just as we lifted our heads, a young man came pedaling down the path that we had just skidded across. He stopped and exclaimed, "Sorry", which is their culturally normal response. I asked, "Can you take me to the village we just passed over?"

In the village there was a small police post where I spoke to the Sergeant in charge. I told him that I had crash-landed an airplane in a nearby field and my passengers were walking to the village. Since there were no phones in the village, I asked if there was a vehicle that could take us to Bida so I could contact our people in Jos. After some time had passed, the chief of that area with his retinue arrived. They wanted to have feasting and dancing to celebrate our safe "arrival". I finally persuaded them that we needed transportation to a telephone. Upon arriving at the police post at Bida, a message was sent to Jos via Kano informing the SIM of our location. I asked for the Aztec to be flown down to pick us up.

Meanwhile back in Jos, Pat had been busy cutting some of our missionaries' hair. When she finished, she realized that I hadn't buzzed the house as I usually did when returning from a flight. Darkness had fallen and I hadn't arrived home, so she walked across the compound to Rich Schaffer's house and asked if he knew where I might be. He said that he had seen me in Lagos earlier that day but not since then. He ran over to the High School Hostel that had the only phone on our compound. Then Bob Swingle, the department head arrived, looking for me as he realized that I had not returned from my flight. Pat walked home to feed our five-month old son, Paul, and to wait for further word. This had happened before, so she was content to wait until morning. A couple of hours later, Harold Fuller knocked on our door. He exclaimed, "Good news! Gary crash landed down near Bida, but no-one was hurt!"

The next day, Rich Schaffer flew down to Bida and picked us up. Some of the passengers exclaimed that they were afraid when the engine quit and I abruptly turned the plane in another direction. But they relaxed when I picked up my coffee cup and started drinking it. We all rejoiced in our Lord's goodness and protection.

Several weeks later 5N-AHS was dismantled, placed on a truck, and brought back to Jos where we repaired it. The engine failed because the oil pump shaft had sheared. It took about two years for all the repairs to be completed.

My last flight in Nigeria before retiring from SIMAIR was the first flight of 5N-AHS after the accident. I felt privileged to be able to fly it again.

I continued serving the Lord in SIM at home. Three years later, I was speaking in a church where I used this illustration of how God protects us. I did not mention the date of the accident. After the service, a lady came up to me and asked if the accident happened on December 13th, 1976. When I told her that was when it happened, she said, "Now I know why God woke me up that morning and told me to pray for you. I spent the whole day praying for you and your safety, and made a note to ask you what happened that day!"

So if God ever brings someone to your mind, don't neglect to pray for that person. Prayer is the most important thing you can do.

And the next is from Jim Rendel.

This was written the 22nd of September 2003. We are still enjoying being with SIMAIR here in Niger, but I often think about the days in Nigeria and miss the "old SIMAIR gang!" You guys had some great years in Jos and I was privileged to be able to get in on the tail of them. Thanks for the great memories!

To answer some of your questions, I guess I would have to say I started flying with SIMAIR in 1951 when mom flew to Jos to deliver my twin sister and me. Then I was one of the SIM kids who got to fly to school and then home for the holidays with SIMAIR, so from the second grade through the ninth I was one happy passenger. The most memorable time was when Bob Ediger showed up with the Aztec in Sokoto to pick us up to began ninth grade. We might have all fit in a Comanche, but I had 5 or 6 model airplanes to bring to school and Bob was in charge of the model airplane club at school!

It was the 13th of September 1973 that I got to come back to fly for SIMAIR. Those years have all been here in Niger except the two years I flew in Nigeria. Total hours are approaching 10,000 hours for a bit over one and a half million miles. And now for my most memorable flight.

We wonder if someone was praying specifically for me one dry and dusty February afternoon? Sandy and I were enjoying a quiet evening with the family, glad to have a weekend break from all the flying. The Harmattan dust was blowing, although this particular day it wasn't too bad with a visibility of about one mile. At about 0800 that evening a call came from the control tower saying that someone in Mali was trying to call Jim on the HF radio. Ken Singleton, a good friend and director of World Vision, had traveled with his family to a remote village in Mali for the weekend to visit one of their projects. I had a good idea it would be Ken calling since he had worked up there for a few years before becoming the World Vision area director. During his time in Meneka, there had been some rebel activity in the area, so Ken and I had set up procedures for contacting SIMAIR, and indeed, on a couple of flights, Ken had called, warning Jim to turn back because of gun shots being fired in town as SIMAIR was approaching.

The radio contact was poor and the tower did not have any idea what was happening so I drove out as quickly as possible and called Ken from the control tower. I could barely hear Ken answer to tell me there was an emergency, and then the reception just faded out. I called back and told Ken to switch to the mission frequency and to call me in a few minutes. I went to our hangar and listened for Ken's call on the radio in our plane. Ken's call came in loud and clear saying their three year old son had fallen down a thirty foot well and was unconscious and needed to be evacuated immediately to Niamey!

SIMAIR does not normally fly at night because of the risks involved. This remote airstrip did not have any landing lights, so Jim told Ken to have three cars to guide him in for landing with two cars at the approach and a single car at the other end. With no moon it was a dark night and the Harmattan could make it a real challenge. I took off at about 10 PM while Jim Knowlton went to the SIM office to maintain contact with me as I flew. With the new GPS navigation system it was no problem flying directly to Meneka.

The Harmattan was much less, so I had no problem spotting a lone light as I approached the airstrip. I circled around and came over the two cars and made a safe landing. Little Peter had regained consciousness and recognized me, as he had been out to the hangar a number of times. "Hi Peter . . . How would you like to go on an airplane ride with Uncle Jim?"

We lifted off a little before midnight and by one PM we were safely back to Niamey with the whole family. Peter was rushed to the French clinic where he was cared for until the following day when he was evacuated to England for further tests and treatment. The swelling on the side of his head was the biggest concern. Good reports came back from England and six weeks later the family returned to Niamey.

We were so thankful that God answered the prayers of so many people by healing Peter and protecting him from serious harm. And we are thankful too for all your prayers when we fly out here. When we are in the States and Canada on furlough, we challenge people to pray for us anytime they see a tiny plane flying overhead.

Here is a poem that a friend gave me when we first went out to the mission field.

PRAY FOR ONE ANOTHER

I cannot tell why there should come to me
A thought of someone miles and miles away,
In swift insistence on the memory . . .
Unless there be a need that I should pray

Too hurried oft we are to spare the thought,
For days together, of some friend far away,
Perhaps God does it for us, and we ought
To read His signal as a call to pray.

Perhaps, just then, my friend has fiercer fight,
Some overwhelming sorrow or some danger
Maybe the need for courage to brave the storm,
or try to find the way. And so I pray.

Friend . . . Do the same for me! If thought of me
Should intrude upon you on your crowded day.
Give me a moment's prayer, in passing thought,
Be very sure I need it just for this day.

By Marianne Farmingham

And changed a bit by rich schaffer

Bill Tuck giving aircraft keys to Jim Rendel

Jim Rendel drawing of a SIMAIR Niger plane

Ian and Beka Rideout started with Niger SIMAIR in October 2001 and are still there. This is a flight that he recalls

A film crew had contacted SIMAIR several times about wanting us to assist them in doing a documentary film about the sand dunes in the Sahara Desert. In that we were a private organization, Civil Aviation officials did not allow us to do any commercial flying except for emergency situations. We explained that to them and suggested they contact a company that could fly them, which they did.

They were flown out into the desert to a place called Bilma. Several days before they were to be picked up, they were told that the plane was down for maintenance, so they were stuck out in the Sahara Desert, and they needed to be back in Niamey by Friday to catch their flight on Air France. So they contacted us about their problem.

We contacted Civil Aviation and they gave us the okay to go out and get them. The group consisted of eight people and all their camera gear which would take two planes, the Piper Cheyenne and the Saratoga. The airport at Agadez, where we would need to refuel, was closed to repave the runway, so we contacted missionary Dave Evans to see if he could get us permission to land at the old dirt runway. Permission was granted which was fine for the Saratoga, but it was too short for the Cheyenne, so Jim Rendel would spend the night at Maradi and leave from there.

I fueled up the Saratoga to the top and headed for Agadez Thursday afternoon. A large thunderstorm was blocking the path over Tahoua about halfway there. I was forced to circumnavigate the storm to the south for about a half-hour. Jim, flying further to the south, was able to see the storms and help me figure out how extensive they were. We communicated via the VHF radio. A small instrument in the plane called a strike finder also helps us locate where the storms are. After Tahoua, I headed back on track for Agadez only to find I was headed into another storm and needed to deviate around to the north. The rain cleared up before I reached Agadez and it was fairly easy to find the airport. I called the tower to report my arrival.

"Roger . . . November Nine Five Tango . . . You are cleared for landing on the dirt runway."

I replied, "Thank you for the clearance." Having never used the dirt runway before, I gave it a buzz job to check it out. It looked okay and I came around and landed.

In Africa, one never leaves important jobs for tomorrow when they can be done today. So I called Mobile to fuel the plane when I arrived.

After a half-hour of waiting, I realized they were taking an awfully long time because the tractor that pulls the fuel cart was broken, and they were pushing the cart by hand. Then they had to pump the fuel by hand because the tractor also runs the electric pump. Dave Evans drove me to a nearby hotel with the arrangement that he would pick me up again at 0530 in the morning.

The hotel looked very nice by African standards. A French pilot owned it. I checked into my room and dropped off my belongings and went to dinner.

It was an interesting dinner, sitting at a table with another French pilot who was volunteering for a few months at Agadez, a camera man from South Africa, and an American lady directing a project to give people radios for guns. These are the times we have to share why we are there, which sometimes leads to an opportunity of sharing the 'good news' of Jesus Christ with these kinds of people.

After dinner I went to my room. On the whitewashed walls I could easily see all the mosquitoes just sitting there waiting for their dinner. "Oh Lord," I prayed, "You know I can't sleep with mosquitoes like this."

I spent the next half-hour killing at least 30 mosquitoes. Then I got ready for bed and chased a few more before tucking in.

Then I prayed, "Lord, Daniel spent the night in the lions' den and not one lion touched him. Lord these are just little mosquitoes. You know that tomorrow is going to be a very hard day for me if I don't get some sleep. Please keep those mosquitoes away from me." That was it. I slept as well as anyone could in that lumpy bed. In the morning I turned on the light and immediately saw several mosquitoes flying around the lamp a few feet from my head. The amazing part is that I did not hear a single mosquito all night long, and I didn't have a single bite. God is good! Lions or mosquitoes . . . It's all in a day's work for Him.

It was a beautiful cool morning takeoff out of Agadez. The sun was just coming up. I raised the gear and started a slow climb as I left Agadez behind. The sand soon turned into hills of solid rock below. What a rugged country. I would not want to have engine trouble here. But the engine was purring like a kitten as I headed out over the heart of the desert for the next several hours. The view vanished below as the Harmattan blended with the sand below. Thank you Lord for the GPS to show the way. It's a lot better than back in Rich Schaffer's day when you had to navigate by sight. I began a slow descent about 20 minutes out and began looking for the ground. Only a few thousand feet left and five miles out I still could not see the ground. "Lord please show me the runway!" I descended from 1000 feet to 500 feet . . . It was a safe altitude for that area . . . And suddenly there it was . . . There was the black pavement. "Thank you, Lord!" That runway was the only part of the desert I saw that day.

I did a tight circle to the left, keeping sight of the runway, and managed to bring it in for a safe landing. The wind was blowing hard.

Bilma is a military outpost, and a few soldiers came out to the plane to greet me. I heard Jim on the radio, so I jumped back into the plane.

Jim said. "I'm 20 miles out."

"Roger, Jim . . . The visibility is not very good here."

"Okay . . . Let me know when you hear me overhead."

"Okay . . . Will do."

"How far is the runway from the VOR? . . . I'm picking it up and the GPS is telling me the distance."

"I'll ask the soldiers."

The commander told a soldier to drive out to the VOR to measure the distance. "C'est Afrique!" (That's Africa!) He never did make it back in time.

Landing was difficult in the Saratoga, but the Cheyenne is bigger and faster and harder to see out of with the two engines on the wings. Jim passed right over the runway and didn't see it.

"I saw you overhead, Jim."

"I didn't see a thing. Wait! I see the VOR below. I'll circle around."

He came back over and managed to see the runway. At the last second, he picked up the tires marking the area leading up to the runway and was able to maneuver to land. God is good! All the time!

I greeted him at the door. As he was trying to fill out the time sheet he was shaking like a leaf.

The camera group was almost an hour late as they filled out all the paperwork at the office in town. Apparently, they had called my wife to see if we were still coming. In the morning when they woke up, they saw all the dust and were sure that we would not be coming that day. Needless to say, they were ecstatic when they saw the planes. We managed to fit all the people and baggage in the planes and headed for home.

We took off and the ground faded into oblivion. Jim headed back to Maradi to refuel on the way home. I took one passenger and flew straight to Niamey. Five and a half hours later, we landed only five minutes apart. They made it back in time for their Air France flight.

Typical flight? Not entirely, but we had one more opportunity to share the good news of Jesus Christ that had brought us to this distant land and arid country. After all, that's what this is all about.

Then Ian adds this note. I just got home from three days in Galmi. I diverted there from Maradi because of engine trouble that turned out to be a bad magneto. I found several teeth missing on the gear inside it. Had to wait for parts from Niamey which came by bush-taxi. But all is well and God is good.

And later he wrote.

"Sorry for the delay. There is another story I want to write up and send you, but I figured I better send this one in case I get too busy. We are really enjoying your story. My wife commented, "This guy had all kinds of crazy things happen to him . . . Almost electrocuted . . . Hit by a bird that broke the windshield . . ." Thanks much, Ian."

The whole SIMAIR Family

CHAPTER 36
THE LEN DYCK STORY

Len Dyck

Canadians Len and Lu Dyck and their two daughters, Kim and Kendra arrived in Jos sometime in June, 1969 and were with SIMAIR for almost five years.

Len Dyck with Chuck Forster

Les Williams, unknown lady, George Learned and Len Dyck

This is going to be a hard chapter to write for he was the only pilot to be killed flying with SIMAIR. Other than this, no person flying on SIMAIR has ever been injured or even scratched in the whole history of the Aviation Department up to this date 27 February 2007.

When we were not flying we are busy maintaining the airplanes. We did a 50 hour inspection, a 100 hour inspection, and then at 2000 hours we did a complete rebuild of the airplane where we remove and overhaul the engine, and did a meticulous inspection and repair of the airframe. On 5N-ACB this included a new paint job, installing new radios including HF radios, and the installation of an auto pilot.

On February 5th 1978, we completed that 2000 hour rebuild, and Len was to go up and do an hour of slow time on the engine, all the while circling the airport in case any problems developed. The rest of us guys were busy working in the hangar and paid no heed to him. When noontime came, and we were ready to go home for lunch, Len still had not returned. We went out and heard no plane circling the airport, so we got on one of the radios and gave Charlie Bravo a call. We got no answer, so we asked the radio tower to give him a call. Likewise, he got no response. We looked at each other wondering where he had gone. He was supposed to be staying over the airport. So we went up to the tower and questioned the tower operator. He replied that Charlie Bravo had circled the airport once and then left. With nothing more to do, we went into town for lunch.

When we returned to the hangar at 1 PM, Len had still not returned. The tower had no contact with him. Where had he gone? We contacted SIMRAD and asked them to contact Kagoro and Kwoi to see if he was there, or if they had heard a plane flying in the vicinity. We discussed among ourselves as to where he had possibly gone sightseeing. Someone said he used to go just north of the road to Bauchi to look for giraffe. Maybe he went out to the Yankari Game Reserve, or maybe the Horsetail Falls on the south end of the Plateau? It was decided that we would go looking for him. We called into the office and asked them to send out some people to ride with us so we could be looking out both sides of the airplane. It would be like looking for a needle in a haystack. So I said I would go out and search the game reserve. Another would search the Sheri Hills and north of the Bauchi road. Another would search the south end of the Plateau and around by Kagoro and the western edge of the Plateau. I took off in Charlie Delta flying out on the route to Kaltungo. When I got out to the Little Grand Canyon, I flew down this beautiful area and then back up to the Kaltungo route. When we got out to the Wikki Warm Springs, we flew up and down the whole swamp area. We spotted all kinds of game but we did not find Charlie Bravo. We flew north of the Kaltungo route and then swung up over Bauchi Airport to see if he had landed there, and then we did a swing around all of the Sheri Hills and landed at Jos Airport as the sun was setting. I had spent 4 hours and 10 minutes in fruitless search. We never ever got a signal from the emergency locator beacon that every one of our planes carry.

At the 5 PM SIMRAD broadcast, all the stations were alerted that Len Dyck was missing. Lu and the girls went to bed wondering where he was.

On February 8th, I flew out to Miango and picked up three people for more eyes, and for four hours and fifteen minutes we thoroughly searched every canyon and gully of the western and northern edge of the Jos Plateau. Then in the afternoon, I flew down to Kagoro and picked up three more people, and we spent three hours and twenty five minutes searching the rugged Kagoro Hills and around the southern edge of the plateau, as the people at Kagoro had heard a low flying plane, but did not actually see it. (I'm guessing it was probably one of our search planes.)

SIM had the local radio station alert the local people of our missing plane and we offered a reward to anyone who could lead us to the missing plane. One person said he saw the plane flying low along the western edge of the Sheri Hills and that the plane was on fire with smoke trailing out behind. So a couple of our guys searched all of the Sheri Hills and the eastern edge of the plateau. It was a fruitless day.

We had every Tom, Dick, and Harry coming with every cock and bull story you can imagine, claiming that they had seen the plane, in hopes that they might lay claim to the reward if they happened to guess right.

The next day I had to fly some people out to Kaltungo, and we spent three hours and ten minutes searching all the way. I flew back empty in 1:10 hours. Then I went up with another load of people searching, (I don't remember where), for another 3:25 hours, making it another long, fruitless, frustrating day.

My logbook doesn't record my doing any more search flights. I think maybe we may have been grounded for a couple of days because of heavy Harmattan.

On about the seventh day, a couple of guys showed up at the hangar about quitting time. From their description we got a pretty good idea that they had actually seen the plane. One was a farmer who had a farm on a little flat area in the Sheri Hills. He said the plane was down in the canyon just off the west end of his farm. We asked if they would be willing to stay in the Jos Guest House overnight, and lead us to the plane next morning. They said they would. They said it was over a three hour hike through the rugged hills, starting from the east side of the mountains.

We got them to the guest house in time for supper where they were fed royally, and had them put in one of the best rooms. Then we alerted everyone in the Jos family, and picked a party of those who would hike in to retrieve Len's body, including a number of nationals to help carry the body. We planned to leave at 3 AM in the morning.

We made up a party of about fifteen individuals, but the only ones I remember were Dr. Hal White, Jim Plueddemann, Gary Shepherd, Bill Tuck, and myself. I believe there was also another doctor from another Mission. Jim believes there were a couple of guys from Hillcrest school, including Steve Dowdell.

We arrived on the east side of the mountains and started our climb in the dark. The higher we climbed the harder it got, as we wound our way among the granite boulders, some of them as big as twenty or thirty feet in diameter . . . Some places we could barely squeeze through on the narrow trail winding back and forth. When it became light, we marveled at the beauty of the place, wondering about the earthquake that must have taken place that broke up some of the mountain into these gigantic boulders.

In about two hours we topped the ridge and found that we would lose much of what we gained as we had to descend into another canyon.

What was interesting here was the small black fat cattle that looked exactly like a black Angus, only they were about one-third the size. We never saw any on the rest of the Jos Plateau. They did not look anything like the Fulani cattle.

We topped the next ridge and then followed it around over to a small flat area which was the man's farm. He lived in a small, round, mud hut that was thatched with a grass roof. In the middle of the farm was a bunch of neatly stacked stones, which the man indicated was the grave of his wife who had passed away not too long ago.

We took a good break here and then followed the man westward across his farm where the land dropped suddenly into a deep canyon. He said the plane was down there at the bottom of the canyon.

We followed him down into the canyon, sliding a lot of the way until we got into the boulders and trees. We came around a huge boulder and there was the plane. It had crashed and burned . . . all that remained was part of the tail and part of one wing. The position of the wing and tail indicated that the plane had struck the ground nose down at about a forty-five degree bank. You could see where the plane sliced down between the trees.

Later on when I circled over the area, I could just catch a glimpse of the wing panel when you knew where to look. No wonder we never saw the plane when we flew over this canyon. Len was flying up this deep canyon toward the high mountain when he came to this place where a smaller canyon branched off to the left. This was where he decided to make his turn-around. It looked like he made a steep turn to the left, lost speed, and stalled out. Maybe there was also a downdraft off the farmer's plateau? Who really knows, but the end result was a destroyed Piper Comanche and the death of a pilot whom we all loved very much.

Somewhere in the that burned debris were the charred remains of Len Dyck. Gary jumped into that mess, and several of the guys as well, and started pulling away whatever, digging for Len's body. I documented the whole affair with my eight millimeter camera as I did the whole trip. It took them about a half hour to find Len's body. He was charred beyond recognition. They recovered Len's watch and his diamond ring. The doctors did an autopsy right on the spot. There was no smoke in his lungs which proved that he had died on impact. I later destroyed this part of the film.

And how did this happen? SIM Ethiopia had asked us if we could send a couple of pilots over to help them set up a SIMAIR program there, as they were very unhappy with the service that MAF was providing. They were unreliable and very expensive. So Len was hoping to be one of the pilots to do this. I mentioned that if he wanted to go, it would be a good idea if he went to MAF in California to take their 40 hour mountain flying course because Ethiopia was all mountains . . . High altitude mountains, and you really needed to know what you were doing. I told him about the time at Moody when we went out to California and they had one of their pilots take us up into the mountains to give us a taste of what it was like to fly in the mountains. One thing was to fly up a box canyon and learn how to get out.

And so that was what happened on that fateful day when he was supposed to give some run-in time on the newly overhauled engine in 5N-ACB. Instead he went over the Sheri Hills to do some mountain flying and dies in the attempt. He is the only person in all the history of SIMAIR from the beginning to this date 3 June, 2007 to have ever been killed. We had accidents, yes, but no one was ever killed or even injured or scratched for that matter. No other aviation program can claim that. We give God and our meticulous maintenance program the credit for our wonderful safety record.

Jim Plueddemann, and a small African boy, and I started the climb out of the deep canyon. About halfway up we stopped and had a drink. I shared my last cup of water with the boy. When we got to the top we stopped again. That was when Jim told me he was supposed to go with Len on that flight.

I sent Jim an email, asking if he would tell me about that day. I received this reply from Carol, as Jim was prepping for a Board of Governors meeting, and then they were going to Paraguay.

Carol wrote, "Yes, Jim and Len had been making plans to go together on that test flight. The Dycks were at our house for pizza, and Len said, "Jim, do you want to go up with me for a test flight?" Jim had done test flights with Len before and enjoyed taking aerial photos of the area. He said he'd like to go.

The next day, just as they were about to leave, some national pastors showed up to talk to Jim. So Len went on the flight alone. We have often pondered what might have been.

Jim took Len's death very hard. Living right next door, they had become great buddies. They often played squash together or spent time in the darkroom together developing photos. Our families were back and forth every day.

You might remember that when the Harmattan dust became too thick to continue searching by air, Jim went from town to town, leaving messages with every village chief. He gave out copies of our picture prayer card and said, "If anyone hears of a plane that has fallen from the sky, bring this card to the Challenge Bookshop in Jos to tell us." What a sad day it was when a farmer arrived at the bookshop with our well-worn card in his hand to say that he knew where the plane was.

Jim well remembers the day when we hiked into the Shere Hills to retrieve Len's body. It was a harder trip than any had expected. I remember Jim and Dr. Hal White going to Lou's house that night to give her Len's ring. A number of us had been there all day waiting for the group to return.

Len's death was a life marker for us. It was the first personal tragedy we had experienced as 30 year old missionaries and it changed us in many ways. We continued to live side by side with Lou, Kim and Kendra. A few months later little Kerry was born, and today he flies planes like his daddy did."

Len was buried out at Kent Academy behind the Chapel in the missionary graveyard. Lou came out to the hanger office to do the billing and various other office tasks. Then later she moved out to KA where she could be closer to her kids and became a dorm mother.

As I write this chapter of SIMAIR's history it brings tears to my eyes to realize that this should never have happened

I sent this chapter to Gary Sheppard to critique and I need to add his response to this chapter.

Gary replied, "The story about Len is good. One thing I can add is that 5N-ACB was to be the plane to be used in the new Francophone program. I had come back from Niamey with a medical emergency. That afternoon the final paperwork arrived from the Federal Air Administration changing the plane back to US registration so it could be permanently based in Niger. I wanted to fly the plane back to Niamey. Since I had to go to Lagos to do some of the paperwork in one of the government ministries, I asked Len if he would slow fly the plane for me in preparation for my taking it to Niger. He agreed and I flew to Lagos with Bob Cowley who was flying for the Evangelical Bretheran Mission in Niger as he also had to go to Lagos. We heard news of Len's disappearance, so Bob and I came back to Jos immediately to help in the search.

Later, I flew Lu and the girls to Miango for the funeral. I sat with Lu during the funeral as Pat was still in Niamey. I was amazed that she sang so well during the funeral as Len's casket was directly in front of us. Len's death hit me so hard that I actually went outside after the service and cried. He took my place!

On the flight back to Jos, I asked Lu how she could sing at a time like that. She said, "Gary, I don't know. The Lord just gave me the strength to sing." I didn't understand at that time, but several years later on a furlough, Pat and I stood by the casket of our little boy Paul who had drowned in the swimming pool of some friends that we were visiting. God gave us such strength at that time, we ended up comforting the people who came to comfort us!

By the way, a couple of years ago, Pat and I spent the day with Lu and her new husband when they were visiting the Retirement Village in Florida and we were working there. It was a great time to renew our friendship and meet Lu's new husband."

CHAPTER 37
HOW TO PRAY FOR YOUR MISSIONARIES

One thing I think I need to mention about missionaries is the medical problems they have so you can better pray for them. Most missionaries never let you know about this. They are supposed to be upbeat, on top of the world type of people, never complaining about anything.

My problems were that all through my missionary career I was plagued with back problems. I was always having some person working on my back to get the kinks out. On furloughs I was always going to a chiropractor. This eventually worked out to be one of the reasons why we came home after only twenty years of service. Another problem I had out there was allergies all year round which gave me that worn-out, run-down feeling, just not at the top of my game. I'll have to tell you about something that happened one furlough that changed all that.

We were on our second furlough and living again in Seattle in the Carlson's house. It was time to travel down to California to visit all our friends and supporters. In northern California, we stayed a couple of days with Doctor Bob and Nancy King in a little place called Happy Camp. They had a couple of small dogs in the house and after a day my hay fever was driving me nuts.

Bob commented, "You know, you ought to visit a friend of mine in Riverside, California."

"And why is that?"

"I think he could cure you of your allergies!"

What follows here is the whole story of how I was cured of all my allergies.

MY TESTIMONY

I was cured of my allergies . . . and the good news is that you can be cured of your allergies too! I'm not just talking about relief . . . I'm talking about a complete cure . . . finish! In just eight weeks . . . no more allergies! Have I got your attention? . . . then listen to my story.

My allergies started when I was a sophomore in high school. You know . . . the sneezing, the runny nose, the itching eyes. A doctor gave me some pills which gave some relief, but mostly, they just put me to sleep. I couldn't stay awake in class! Every summer, the same old thing.

When I was at Oregon State College, someone suggested that I go to the dispensary and have some allergy shots. They did a bunch of scratch tests on my arms to see what I was allergic to, and then they made up a personalized serum just for me. Twice a week for TWO YEARS I took those shots. I really hate shots, but they helped some. But a year later, after leaving Oregon State, I started developing those familiar symptoms again and was soon popping the allergy pills. I was absolutely miserable. People who do not have allergies fail to realize what a miserable life it is . . . they think it is a joke.

After four years at Moody Bible Institute, I went to Africa as a missionary pilot/ mechanic where I was privileged to serve the Lord for twenty years under the Sudan Interior Mission. I took my allergies with me, plus I developed some new ones. I was not only allergic in the summer, but I had allergic reactions throughout the whole year.

I had the sneezing fits . . . my runny nose was like a fountain . . . I would rub my itching eyes and couldn't quit. I ate allergy pills like they were candy . . . not much relief . . . and they destroyed my sense of smell.

I began having asthmatic reactions in my lungs.

When I came home on my first furlough the mission doctor gave me a hundred scratch tests. "Schaffer . . . you're allergic to every blade of grass and tree that you ever came in contact with!" He made up a serum of universal grasses, but he wasn't kidding me.. He doubted that the shots would do me any good. He was dead right.

Then on another furlough, as we were traveling around visiting our friends and supporters, we were staying with Dr. Bob and Nancy King for a couple of days. They had a couple of dogs in the house. Soon I was sneezing up a storm. After a day of this, Dr. King said, "You should visit a friend of mine in Riverside." "Why?" "Well, I think he could cure you of your hay fever!"

And so he told me about his friend, Dr. Carl Eckhardt, who had an unusual way of treating allergies of all kinds with a complete cure rate of 80% for his patients. (He treated some 19,000 patients before he was killed in an automobile accident in 1973). It is called AUTO-URINE Therapy, and it is an often used method of treating allergies in some European countries.

You know how doctors who use the scratch tests to find what you are allergic to, and then make up a special serum just for you. Then by giving you injections of this concoction once or twice a week, your body builds up a resistance to these allergens which is supposed to give you some relief from your allergies. Relief is usually the sum of it. After you discontinue the shots, usually your allergic reactions return, as they did in my case.

Here is the theory behind AUTO-URINE Therapy. Your body rids itself of all the allergens through the urine . . . a specialized serum, if you please, of EVERYTHING that you are allergic to. The wonderful beauty of this method is that the doctor, and you, don't even need to know what causes your allergic reactions! All he has to do is give you a 5 CC injection of your OWN urine once a week for eight weeks, and your body goes to work on your allergies. every one of them!

The awesome beauty of this treatment is that instead of only getting temporary relief for awhile, often, you get a complete cure!

No more allergies! YIPPEEE!

As it turned out, our deputation schedule was so tight that we had no chance of dropping in at Dr. Eckhardt's clinic in Riverside, California. Back home in Seattle, I was down in the basement packing our loads, ready for shipment to Africa. It was damp and musty smelling down there, and my allergies were kicking up a storm. My wife said, "I wonder if you wrote to Dr. Eckhardt and told him who you are . . . maybe he could give you some instructions on how to take the shots . . . then one of the doctors out there could give them to you?" The enclosed information, rather technical, is what I received from Dr. Eckhardt.

When we got out to Nigeria, West Africa, I presented these papers to Dr. Janet Troup. She read them, raised her eyebrows, "Well, if you want to be a guinea pig . . . I'll give you the shots!" So I had a course of eight shots of my own urine one week apart. My response to the treatment was like that described in category three in the doctor's report . . . by the end of the eight weeks, I had no more allergic reactions of any kind! I remained symptom free for about three years! Then I began developing some mild allergic symptoms again, so I had another eight week course and was symptom free for another three years. I'm one of the 20% that has to take a repeat course periodically. When we came home to stay my wife used to give me a shot or two during the summer when something gave me a problem, and that took care of it for the whole year. But can you imagine . . . going from constant year-round allergic misery to absolutely none in just eight weeks! Praise the Lord!

The next person they treated was a small missionary kid in the first grade at Hillcrest who was allergic to almost every food that we humans normally eat. He had never slept a normal night's sleep in his whole life. His parents had to prop him up with pillows to keep him in a sitting position at night when he slept. A few weeks later, in church, I saw the father and asked, "How's your little boy doing?"

He gave me a crushing bear hug and burst into tears, "My little boy is sleeping normally for the first time in his life!"

The next person they treated was the anesthesiologist at Evangel Hospital who was allergic to rubber, including the elastic in her panties, her bra, or when she put on rubber gloves during surgery. She took the shots of her own urine . . . no more allergy!

Today, Auto-urine Therapy is the prescribed method of treatment for all kinds of allergies for patients who come to Evangel Hospital.

Hey, this all sounds too good to be true . . . and it can work for you! BUT.. and there is a but to it. Let me explain . . .

One furlough we were going the rounds visiting our people. When we visited my niece, one of the daughters was having a severe allergic reaction to some food, just as we arrived, and they were on their way to their allergist for treatment. I told them my story with

Auto-Urine Therapy, which they passed on to the doctor. This doctor phoned and asked if we would drop by his clinic and talk to him about this . . . "uhh treatment!" This we did for over an hour. His final comments were, "If I could actually CURE people of their allergies . . . why, I would have people lined up for six blocks trying to get in my door . . . BUT if I tried this . . . "uhh treatment", the American Medical Association would jerk my license for being some kind of a quack!" And that is about it. To find a doctor who will administer this kind of therapy here in the States is nearly impossible, especially with all the sue-happy people we have running around these days.

Not many doctors know about this Auto-Urine Therapy, especially here in the States. You could try your doctor. He may be willing, if you are willing. Most likely, he will be rather skeptical. I told my regular doctor here in Salem about it, and he just shrugged his shoulders . . .

His comment was, "What the heck . . . it wouldn't hurt you!"

Now for the doctor's report

AUTO-URINE THERAPY

A tremendous amount of work on this subject has been done by a Dr. Pleash of London, England. Work along this line has been done by Frenchmen and also Hungarians. The technique herein described is original and worked out in this office.

Out of more than 40,000 injections there have been 21 abscesses at the sight of injection . . . 17 were in women and 4 in men. The average duration of the abscess was six days. Fluctuation is present on the third day. Then drainage is established by a small incision with a no. 11 blade. In all cases the culture was B. Coli. Of the 21 patients that had this complication, when the abscess was over in 13, so was their allergy. The remaining 9 did not think it was so bad, and finished the treatment.

So far the bonifide uses for this treatment are: hay fever, asthma, urticaria, migraine, infectious mononucleosis, eczema, pertussis, some types of arthritis (both rheumatoid and osteo-arthritic types). Work is also being done with endocrine therapy. If a urine injection is given simultaneously, the effects of the hormone will last for a much longer period of time.

I also have a missionary friend who has Lou Gehrig's Disease and has been alive for 20 to 30 years with injections of his own urine. He went from a weight of 98 pounds to his normal weight of 140 pounds. He went back to a normal life full of energy doing all the things necessary on his hobby farm. When he began improving, his doctor commented, "What's going on? . . . You're supposed to be dieing instead of getting better!" When Don Williams finally told him what he was doing, the doctor could hardly believe it. He was also treating another person who had ALS. He started giving this patient shots of his own urine, and he also got better.

ADMINISTRATION: Many modifications have been made in this office since the work was begun.

At this time, I will describe the method now being used. If the patient is a male, he is given a sterile glass urinal. The top or mouth of the urinal is covered with a square of aluminum foil which is crimped on the sides. The patient is instructed to refrain from touching any part of the upper quarter of the urinal with any part of his body. He is instructed to void and allow the first ounce to go into the toilet and the remainder to go into the urinal.

The equipment for injecting is a 5 CC plastic throw away syringe, Leur Lok, fitted with a 3/4" 25 gauge needle. At first aspirate 1.0 CC of 2% Procaine Hydrochloride containing 1/2% Chlorobutanol. Next aspirate the urine direct from the urinal to the 5 CC mark on the syringe. Now invert the syringe and aspirate 0.5 CC of air into the syringe. At this time invert the syringe about 10 times and in this way the bubble of air will mix the urine and Procaine solution. Leave the air in the syringe. Lay the loaded syringe to one side after placing one drop of the urine onto a glass slide and then examine directly under the low power microscope for bacteria using subdued light. By allowing a few minutes to go by before the injection is made, the Chlorobutinol in the Procaine solution will mix sufficiently with the urine to act as a bacteriostatic. The upper outer quadrant of the gluteal region (buttocks) is selected for the sight for the injection. Alcohol is wiped on the skin, the needle injected, then aspirate the 5 CC plus the 0.5 cc of air. By injecting the air, very little urine will ooze back through the needle puncture.

With women, the technique for collecting the urine is a bit different.

The container is a 500 ml. stainless steel "pitcher". She is given a 3"

Johnson and Johnson STERI-PAD and a plastic container of Phisohex. If anyone is sensitive to Phisohex, use Ether. Before voiding into the steel container, the woman is instructed to place a half teaspoon of

Phisohex on the gauze, to cleanse the urethra well, and then the adjacent tissue for a radius of about 2 inches except for the rectum. She is instructed to void directly into the container without the body touching it. Do NOT use a catheter for obtaining the specimen as there would be more danger of infection when subsequent injections are due. Examine microscopically, the same as with a male specimen.

With babies, the technique is different for collection of the specimen.

In order to save time waiting for a specimen, the mother is given an autoclaved glass baby food jar to take home with her. If the infant is a girl, the genitals are washed with soap and water. Disrobe the child as it is more prone to void when naked. Have the child lying on its back, and when it voids, the mother is to quickly remove the cover from the jar and catch the stream. The same procedure is used for the infant male.

Immediately after the collection, the mother brings the child and the specimen to the clinic. The same amount (5 CC) is used for infants as well.

For hay fever, the patient is instructed to be in the environment that aggravates the condition the day before and also the day of the treatment. In that way there will be a good concentration of allergens within the system. ALSO, IT IS RECOMMENDED THAT THE PATIENT RESTRICT FLUIDS THE DAY OF THE TREATMENT. THEN THE SPECIMEN WILL BE MORE CONCENTRATED.

The treatments are given once per week with the average number being eight. Some require more, others less. There have been 11 patients who were rendered completely free from symptoms after the first shot, and have continued that way for the past 15 years!

If food allergy is present, instructions are given for the patient to eat all the foods known to bother them (10 foods may be eaten at a time) on the day of treatment and then continue eating them. If the individual is ultra sensitive to certain foods and will break out minutes after ingestion, the patient eats the food at the clinic and is given the treatment within 30 minutes. The results in food allergy cases are very gratifying. This is very useful with infants that have an allergy to milk, wheat, or any other foods.

So far with the 40,000 urine injections given since 1950, no side reactions have been noted as sometimes occurs with prepared antigens.

Three patients felt a bit light headed for a few minutes, but that was all. Always inquire beforehand if there is a sensitivity to Procaine, and if so, then give the urine straight. With asthma patients, the results are good, but may require more than 8 treatments.

It is good plan to give a series of eight shots, wait 6 weeks, and try again with the few that do not respond. There are some patients that are completely free, but are so afraid that the condition may come back that they insist on coming back about once per month for a booster shot. This seems to have virtue.

Another item worth mentioning . . . some children with a chronic cough, not related to allergy, show a marked improvement from one to three injections given at weekly intervals.

When the treatment is used for virus infections such as Herpes Zoster, Infectious Mononucleosis, Infectious Hepatitis, Pertussis, etc., allow the infection to run more than a week before giving the treatment. The rational behind this is to allow antibodies to be formed in sufficient concentration to be of value. (My thoughts . . . could this possibly be a cure for AIDS? . . . how about Lassa Fever?)

The youngest patient treated was an infant 7 days old. The baby had a severe nasal allery and had trouble nursing. After one injection the child was able to nurse the next day and continued that way. In all, it required 3 injections. The oldest patient was a woman 78 years old with migraine headaches.

Dr. Carl Eckhardt, M.D.
4445 Tyler Street
Riverside, CA 92503

NOTE: Dr. Eckhardt was killed in an automobile accident about 35 years ago and his clinic is now closed.

Response to treatment falls into seven categories:

1. This exceedingly small group became free from symptoms after the very first injection.

2. With this type, the symptoms are aggravated for about two days following, and then will level off until the next treatment, only to have the aggravation for another two days.

3. There is marked improvement for about three days after each injection, only to have the symptoms re-occur by the end of the week.
    The recurrence of the symptoms becomes a little less in intensity with each treatment.

4. Improvement is very slow from one treatment to the next. They have fewer paroxysms, the intensity of each attack may be a little less, or the duration shorter.

5. No change from one treatment to the next, then somewhere along the line a striking improvement will occur. So don't give up on giving the treatments when you don't see any results right away.

6. No change at all during the entire treatment. Wait six weeks.
   Many will get better during this interval. This is a delayed reaction.
   If there is no improvement after this time interval, repeat the series.

7. Complete failure. This amounts to about 20%.

   With some very severe cases, small amounts of steroids have been used. Dexamethasone .75 mg is given qid the first day, tid the next, bid the next, and then maintained on .75 mg daily until subjective symptoms warrant discontinuance.

   Patients that have had previous desensitization treatment without success often have marked improvement from this treatment.

   If there are signs of an impending abscess, inject Penicillin or Terromycin, or Lincocin directly into the indurated area, and this will subdue the infection without the need for drainage.
   end of report

   As you can see, this report is quite technical. But you can keep it simple. Marg used to give me the shots like this. If you do not have a bladder infection, then most likely, your urine is free from bacteria.
   Sterilize the collection container by boiling for five minutes.
   Clean your body parts thoroughly. Urinate the first part of your urine in the toilet, and collect some of your mid-stream urine in the container. Use a new sterile throw away 5 CC syringe and suggested size needle. Use alcohol to sterilize the injection area.
   Give a 4 CC shot without the procaine and no air bubble once a week for 8 weeks. Continue the shots if you are still having problems. Sure it stings, but it is worth it! One to three shots would fix me up for the summer.
   Can't do the shots? Well, you can also drink it! . . . YUK you say?
   Actually, most urine therapy is done this way. (To do a search on the internet, type auto-urine therapy). Here's the easy way you do it.
   Collect about 1 inch of mid-stream urine in a tall clean glass. Mix in three tablespoons of a chocolate drink powder, fill it up with milk, mix it, and drink'er down! . . . you wont even taste the urine. Do this three times a day when you are showing allergy symptoms. No way you say? All I can say is that I know from experience that having allergies is one miserable experience . . . why keep living with all that when you can get rid of it . . . and hopefully in your case, once and for all.

I would appreciate knowing what you do with this info, and if you have any questions, I'll try to answer them the best that I can.

That's it folks

PS: I just thought of another thing that is really hard on missionaries especially in the desert and tropical regions of the world, and that is the intense heat that drains your energy like a sponge. Up on the Jos Plateau where it was cooler and healthier to live than in the lowlands. About the highest it would get was 90 degrees, but many a night I can remember crawling into bed and the sheets felt like they had just come off the ironing board. In the lowlands in Nigeria and Niger, the temperature could get up to 120 to 130 degrees, and somehow the missionaries seemed to adapt to the heat and get on with their work. But when I had to spend an overnight off the plateau, I was not used to that heat and I really suffered. And I could never adapt to the heat because I was only there for a night or two. When we started doing the 10 day tours in Niger, to me, it was like going to purgatory. I kept a diary on one of these trips and this is how it went.

5 October 1972. The beginning of my turn up in Niger . . . 10 days this time. Today I flew Jos to Kano to Maradi to Malbaza and night-stopping at Niamey. Just like I used to pray before a tough exam . . . "Even now Lord come quickly!"

I have a 310 pound drug order for Mahadaga. My passenger wants to take a drill press, a jointer, plus another 100 pounds of stuff, so I repack my overnight bag with 3 pair of shorts, 3 pair of socks, 3 shirts, flashlight, bug bomb, medicine, and letters to write . . . 10 days . . . I will wash clothes along the way.

I also have 175 pounds of stuff to set up house at Maradi. There is only room for my passenger plus his 100 pounds of stuff, the drug order, the mailbag, and my bag. We leave the drill press, jointer, and the household stuff. My passenger, R. French, who is going to Galmi Hospital to do some building work is very unhappy, but he got the message when he saw how we barely staggered off at Jos. We were really loaded.

At Kano, we have to go through Customs, Immigration, and Health. Our SIMAIR baggage cart has a flat tire. We almost died carrying all this junk into Customs . . . My aching back. I'm dripping wet with sweat . . . It is really hot . . . The flies drive me crazy.

At Maradi, they invited us in for lunch . . . really good food. Here, Mrs. VanLerop, and A. Galadi want to go to Niamey. So we leave the 310 pound drug order and off we go to Malbaza. It's so hot and we are so loaded that the plane only climbs 100 feet per minute on thermals, so we stay at 4500 feet . . . Real bumpy flight. We buzz Galmi Hospital and then go out and land at the airstrip. Al TerMeer shows up in about a half hour to pick up R. French.

We take off and climb up to 10.5 for Niamey. I call Niamey on the HF radio and give them my ETA. It's cool at 10.5, but we are still below the cloud level so it is still bumpy. Good tailwind and we arrive ten minutes ahead of schedule. Howard Dowdell shows up with his two kids in his VW bug. We are a really loaded going into town.

Niamey is 110 degrees in the shade and there's not a breath of air. I slept in the new place and the room is like a bake oven. I have the fan going full blast, but it makes no difference. At one in the morning, I wake up lying in a pool of sweat. I'm crazy and like Paul and Silas, I began singing songs of praise to the Lord! I keep washing myself off with a wet towel and finally dropped off again at three. 4:40 hours flight time for 635 miles . . . Dip stick loose and there's oil all over the place!

6 October 72 Today I flew Niamey to Maradi to Kano to Maradi . . . 5:05 hours for 630 miles. Mr. and Mrs. Gordon Bishop arrived on Sabena Airlines at 0600 in the morning and they were ready to go on to Maradi. We took off and climbed up to 7.5 where it was cool and smooth. There was a strong headwind, so the flight took 2 hours and 50 minutes. I have the visas for Mr. and Mrs. Williams + 2 kids, and also for M. Lowry, so they came out to the airport and I flew them down to Kano. The kids are real prone to airsickness so we went up to 9.5 where it is smooth and they did okay. SIM Kano didn't know we were coming, so Customs plus waiting took over two hours. It's so hot the kids are crying. I give them all my water and cookies to eat. My sandwiches are spoiled. Kano has 548 pounds of paint, wire, and glass for Galmi Hospital. The tire on the pushcart was repaired . . . "Thank you, Lord!" I arrive back at Maradi at 04:50 and stay overnight.

I'm up until 0930 doing all the bookwork, sitting in a pool of sweat even though the ceiling fan is going full tilt. It cools off a bit during the night and I have a pretty good sleep.

7 October 72 Woke up with a splitting headache. Flew from Maradi to Malbaza to Mahadaga to Niamey to Diapaga to Parakou. Flight time was 4 hours and 50 minutes and 640 miles. Took the 368 # of paint, wire and glass to Malbaza and the 310 # of drugs to Mahadaga. Al TerMeer is real happy about all the stuff for the hospital.

At Niamey, Mrs. McDougall gets on for the Upper Volta and Dahomey tour. Howard Dowdell has ulcers so he is trying to take it easy by sending her. The Niamey commadant chews me out for not reporting on HF radio. Turns out that Len Dyck is the guy he is after, for not reporting when he had to stay in the plane overnight at Dosso after getting caught in a sandstorm when he was going to Gucheme.

The Rutens at Diapaga have a nice fish dinner waiting for us. The big lake there is full of Nile Perch . . . They got one that weighed 160 pounds!

We arrive at Parakou ten minutes ahead of schedule. No one knew that we were coming. The Customs official is really mad. They are having a youth retreat at Parakou so the place is crawling with people. It's cooler here and I have a good sleep.

8 October 72 It's Sunday. I wake up with a headache and feel sick to the stomach . . . Probably coming down with a bug of some kind. I usually catch something every time I go to French country. Washed clothes this morning and wrote this up . . . I need to lie down.

9 October 72 Flew from Parakou to Cotonou . . . 1 hour and 35 minutes for 205 miles. Real nice flight. Mrs. McDougall and John Isch for passengers. I feel a little better today. Charles Carpenter was waiting for us.

I did a lot of running around with Chuck . . . Embassies, and shipside checking on loads for SIM. I hear about a 1967 Cheve Six for sale for 100,000 francs . . . New tires and shocks . . . Lots of spare parts. Sounds like a possibility so we go to see it. Looks fair, sounds good, and drives okay. Chuck to check at the border tomorrow about customs for importing into Nigeria. He will let me know. I went fishing for about an hour on the beach. Then Chuck came and picked me up. I stayed overnight at the Isch's.

10 October 72 Tuesday . . . Today I flew from Cotonou to Parakou to Diapaga to Mahadaga, back to Diapaga, back to Mahadaga, and night stopping at Fadngourma. 4 hours and 45 minutes for 640 miles. At Parakou. I picked up Mary Carney, plus 233 pounds of food for the French council meetings. I check into Customs and they want me to dump all the food. Okay, there's a 180# bag of sugar there for Fada so we take that. I

buzzed Mahadaga and landed. The grass is only cut 15 feet wide and 1200 feet long. Just about pulls me off the runway. They will have to cut more grass before we can take off. We go in and have lunch. The heat is murder and there is not a whisper of a breeze. I decide to do a shuttle back to Diapaga first with Mary Carney and the sugar. We barely squeak off with inches to spare. I surprise Diapaga. Then I went back and got Mrs. McDougall, stopped at Diapaga for Carney, and then on to Fada. We land at Fada at 0605 PM, and I'm surprised to see Ed Lochstampfor is waiting at the airport for us. He said they were following us on the radio on 8826 ever since the 6th as we reported into Niamey Control. Others could do that and know when we are coming too. It's really hot and I'm dead tired. Eleanor Beckett gives me a big lime drink . . . Boy, is it ever good.

11 October 72 Thursday Flew Fada to Piela to Fada to Diapaga to Niamey. Lockstampfor wants to go to Piela with 200 pounds of medicine and other supplies. I followed the road and what a road it was.

Florene Guess really looks shot. She had one of her dizzy spells while we are there and breaks down crying. We'll have to haul her out of there before she goes over the bend. Telford Ruten is to go there the end of the month. Maybe that will help? We fly back to Fada where I add 60 liters of gas to my tanks. We check out of the country at Diapaga where we picked up the groceries. Howard Dowdell is at the airport to take us into Niamey.

12 October 72 Thursday I spent the day drawing up the plans for the office complex that Howard wants to install at the new place. Not much room but may be feasible if they use air conditioners. What a hot day! Nobody lives in this country . . . You just exist. Three days in Hell . . . Then O happy resurrection!

13 October 72 Worked some more on the plans, putting in more details. Howard thinks they are great but a little tight, and he is right. There just isn't that much room on that property.

I must be drinking about three gallons of water a day and I salt my food like I was using sugar. I even put salt in my water.

I bought and put some plastic on the window and the door of my room to form a barrier in an attempt to keep the heat out. Every little job is a big undertaking in the heat. The food is good at Mrs. McDougall's so eat there if you can!

14 October 72 Niamey to Parakou to Kandi to Kano to Jos. 7 hours and 20 minutes. Yippee! I'm heading for the barn and my foot is in the carburetor. Now I know what purgatory is like . . . I repent and I never want to go back

So this gives you an idea what it's like here, and now you know how to better pray for your missionaries.

CHAPTER 38
THE LAST CHAPTER

I need to wind this book down to a close, as it is getting way longer than I ever intended, so this is it, the last hurrah, or whatever you want to call it.

When Len Dyck passed away, it profoundly affected all of us flyboys in SIMAIR. From then on, as I was flying, and as I looked down at our beautiful world, there was always the thought tucked way back in my mind, "Hey, I could get killed doing this!" Yet we kept on flying. Not a one of us quit.

At the time this happened, I had 8,168 hours logged on my rear end. I still had a couple thousand hours to go before I would take down the shingle and call it a day to my missionary aviation career at 10,099:55 hours on June 7th, 1977, never to fly again in a small plane when we came home to stay after 20 wonderful exciting years of serving the Lord with SIM.

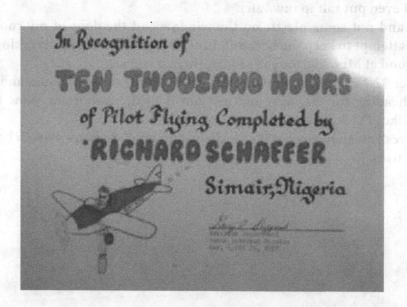

All down through the years, even when I was just a little boy, the Lord put in my heart that someday I was going to be a pilot. And as I was growing up He kept that desire alive to the point where someday I said, "I'm going to be a 'missionary' pilot to live and serve

Him wherever He wants me to go." Now you have read my story, "Just One SIMAIR Story". And this life was lived by every SIMAIR pilot.

I would challenge you to follow in our steps. Not necessarily to be a missionary pilot, but to use your talents to be a missionary of some kind. If you are a born-again Christian, Jesus' call to go out into the world and preach the Gospel to every creature is as valid today as it was to his disciples in that day. It is the obligation of every Christian to obey that mandate. That is to be your marching orders until the Lord says, "No, I want you to serve Me here at home." But whether overseas or here at home, we are to serve Him, to live for Him, to be a witness for Him, so that those who do not know Him, will come to know the salvation that comes by believing in the Gospel that He forgives people of their sins, and sets them free from the power of satan for all eternity. For if they do not hear this 'good news', they will die in their sins and will go to Hell. Do you believe that? Do you REALLY believe that? Then I challenge you again to be a witness for Him. That is your obligation. You might be the only one who will ever get through to them. You might be the only one they will ever listen to. Sorry to get so preachy, but it was something that needed to be said!

From the 9th of February, when I did the last search for Len, I did not fly again until the 27th, when I did a test flight on the Aztec and then I flew Jos to Egbe to Ilorin to Jos with five passengers. Then I never flew again until the 18th of March. Was I so rattled from the whole affair? Did we take our annual holiday? I don't know.

Anyway, from then on I was back in the saddle again. On the 18th, I flew local for a half hour, evidently working out the cobwebs, and honing my skills. On the 19th, I flew Jos to Miango to Kano to Miango to Jos, doing an ADF instrument approach at Kano because of the heavy Harmattan dust taking the visibility down below 200 yards. My passengers to Kano were Mrs. Spady plus 1 child, and taking Bonnie Husband from Kano to Miango. On the 19th, I did another instrument flight up to Kano, to pick up Dr. and Mrs. Hewitt and take them to Miango.

I was flying almost every day hauling a lot of people. In looking through my logbook, nothing notable catches my eye, except on the ninth and tenth of July we did Search and Rescue Practice. A couple of the guys went out somewhere with the VW bus carrying one of the Crash Locator Beacons. Then at a designated time, they would turn on the beacon and we would go up in the plane and hunt for them. Each plane was equipped with an instrument that would pick up the signal and we would home in on it. I forget how many miles out you could pick up the signal . . . I'm guessing about 30 or 40 miles and if you didn't have a clue where the plane went, it would still be like hunting for a needle in a haystack.

On 5 June 1975, I flew Jos-Kano-Miango-Jos-Miango-Kwoi-Kano-Jos-Kano delivering 14 people, including my family, to catch the charter flight home for furlough for three months. SIM was giving their missionaries the option of serving for 4 years with a one year furlough, or serving for 21 months with a 3 month leave. They were hoping to lessen the burnout rate of a 4 year term. It also ended the problem of having to find and set up house for a year and getting your kids into a school environment that was often hostile to them. But with only three months, it required the missionary to be constantly on the road visiting their supporters, friends, and relatives. It also ended my opportunity to work for 6 months to save money for our outfit and build up a nest-egg for the rainy day. Anyway, we switched to the 3 months leave program. So during my 20 years I had three 4 year

terms, and three 21 month terms, finally coming home to stay on the 7th of June 1977. We spent three months traveling all across Canada and the States and finally settled down in Salem, Oregon where I have lived in the same house that we bought on the GI Bill for $37,500.

Marg and the boys hiking and fishing at Jos Reservoir

Marg and the boys near Gog & Magog

Potluck at the Jos Reservoir

Working on our 1964 Opel Kadet

Why end our missionary career after only 20 years? Because SIMAIR was starting to shut down in Nigeria (which they actually did 2 or 3 years later, moving everything to Niger). Also because of my constant back problems.

And our number 3 son John was having problems in school. He just wasn't getting the phonics and the teachers were at a loss as to what to do. They thought he may have some kind of dyslexia, and we should get him checked for that. You can't imagine what we went through to get this figured out . . . All the dumb things various doctors told us to do to cure him of his dyslexia.

We even took him to a teacher's college where they gave John a bunch of aptitude tests which showed that he was a borderline genius. Finally we got a doctor who said the reason he wasn't getting the phonics was because he couldn't hear because of all the earaches and infections he had when he was small.

John Schaffer in Nigeria

John Schaffer all growed up   *One of John's remote control catarpillars*

So John always had trouble with school and he became our high school dropout in his Sophomore year. He went to Chemekata Community College and got his GED in three weeks and went into the work-a-day world. Today he has his own corporation where he earns 40 to 75 thousand each month. Pretty good, I'd say, for a high school dropout.

Our son, Mark, works for the Sandy School District as head of their accounting department.

Rich Schaffer

Mark at Kent Academy

Mark, Jim and John in Nigeria

And our son Jim went back to school to become a teacher in Rhode Island where he is doing substitute teaching in their lousy school system for only 75 dollars a day hoping to work into a fulltime job. And our Son John is working in the oil fields of North Dakota where he is making a lot of money.

Jim Schaffer & Todd Sheppard at KA

Jim and Bonnie Schaffer at Kent Academy

We also got into the work-a-day world . . . I, as a heating and cooling serviceman, and Marg as a nurse. We retired at 62 and went back to SIM headquarters in Charlotte, North Carolina and worked as volunteers for free for a year. It's a fun thing to do and SIM could also use your talents. About 25% of my income goes to supporting missionaries, and that is something you should be doing.

352

Marg at one of our Bible Studies   *Marg and I at our 40th Anniversary*

So we are pro-missionary, and especially SIM who now works in about 44 countries all over the world. I challenge you to answer Christ's mandate to take the Gospel into all the world, and there is no better place than to do it through SIM. So for the close of my book I am giving you a Preliminary Application form to SIM. They would like to hear from you.

THE END of "Just One SIMAIR STORY"